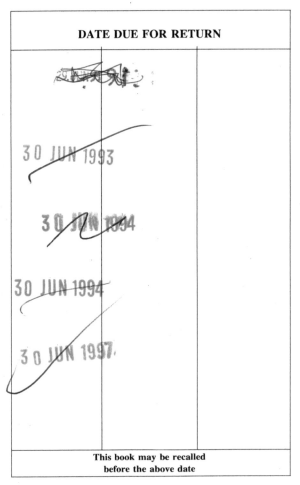

Geology of the country around Chipping Norton

The district described in this memoir includes the Oxford-shire Downs and lies at the north-eastern limit of the Cotswold Hills. It lies to the north-west of Oxford and except for Chipping Norton is entirely agricultural. Most of the district comprises an upland plateau produced by the outcrop of limestones in the Middle Jurassic. This upland is dissected by deep valleys which expose the underlying softer Liassic strata. In the west and the north the Lias outcrop is marked by low ground with rounded hills capped by harder strata.

The area was extensively quarried but most sections have been obscured and much of the new information has been obtained from boreholes. Cored sequences in the Middle Jurassic have given a picture of the pattern of sedimentation at that time. A large number of boreholes were drilled as part of an investigation into the feasibility of storing natural gas in deeply buried anticlinal structures in the Bromsgrove Sandstone Formation. The idea was abandoned with the discovery of North Sea gas but the data has elucidated the subsurface structure of the Triassic and Lower Jurassic strata. It proved the presence and persistence of geophysical marker horizons and confirmed the onlap of successive Lower Lias beds onto the London Platform. The BGS cored borehole at Steeple Aston, and others in adjacent areas have indicated the presence of Coal Measures with coal seams beneath much of the district.

Glacial deposits are restricted to the western parts of the district. Fluvial gravels, together with alluvium, solifluction deposits, and calcareous tufa complete the geological record.

Other sections of the memoir deal with the mineral products and hydrogeology of the district, the stratigraphic palaeontology of the Jurassic strata, the palynology of the Triassic sediments and the petrology of the Marlstone Rock Bed.

IN MEMORY
OF
WILLIAM SMITH
"THE FATHER OF
BRITISH GEOLOGY"

BORN AT CHURCHILL
MARCH 23 1769
DIED AT NORTHAMPTON
AUGUST 28 1839

ERECTED BY THE EARL OF DUCIE
1891

Plate 1   Monument to William Smith near his birthplace, Churchill, Oxfordshire (A 9911)

BRITISH GEOLOGICAL SURVEY

A. HORTON,
E. G. POOLE,
B. J. WILLIAMS,
V. C. ILLING and
G. D. HOBSON

CONTRIBUTORS

E. A. Edmonds, V. Wilson

Geophysics
J. D. Cornwell

Palaeontology
H. C. Ivimey-Cook, G. Warrington
I. E. Penn

Petrology
J. R. Hawkes, G. E. Strong

Water supply
J. W. Lloyd

Geology of the country around Chipping Norton

Memoir for 1:50 000 geological sheet 218, New Series
(England and Wales)

BRITISH GEOLOGICAL SURVEY
Natural Environment Research Council
LONDON: HER MAJESTY'S STATIONERY OFFICE   1987

© *Crown copyright 1987*

First published 1987

ISBN 0 11 884397 4

Bibliographical reference

HORTON, A., POOLE, E. G., WILLIAMS, B. J., ILLING, V. C., and HOBSON, G. D. 1987. Geology of the country around Chipping Norton. *Mem. Br. Geol. Surv.*, Sheet 218 (England and Wales).

Authors

A. HORTON, BSc
British Geological Survey, Keyworth

B. J. WILLIAMS, BSc
British Geological Survey, St Just, 30 Pennsylvania Road, Exeter EX4 6BX

E. G. POOLE, BSc
Formerly British Geological Survey, 20 Fountains Avenue, Boston Spa, Yorks

the late V. C. ILLING AND G. D. HOBSON
V. C. ILLING & PARTNERS
Cuddington Croft, Ewell Road, Cheam, Surrey SM2 7NJ

Contributors

J. D. Cornwell, MSc, PhD, J. R. Hawkes, BSc, PhD, G. E. Strong, BSc, H. C. Ivimey-Cook, BSc, PhD, I. E. Penn, BSc, PhD, and G. Warrington, BSc, PhD
British Geological Survey, Keyworth

E. A. Edmonds, BSc, J. W. Lloyd, BSc, PhD, and *the late* V. Wilson, MSc, PhD, DIC
Formerly British Geological Survey

C

Other publications of the Survey dealing with this district and adjoining districts

BOOKS

British Regional Geology
Central England, 1969
London and Thames Valley, 1960

MAPS

1:625 000
Solid geology (South sheet), 1979
Quaternary geology (South sheet), 1977
Aeromagnetic map of Great Britain (South sheet), 1965

1:250 000
Solid geology
East Midlands Sheet (52°NW 02°W), 1983

Bouguer Gravity Anomaly
Chiltern Sheet (51°N 02°W), Provisional Edition 1980
East Midlands Sheet (52°N 02°W) Provisional Edition 1982

Aeromagnetic Anomaly
Chiltern Sheet (51°N 02°W), 1980
East Midlands Sheet (52°N 02°W), 1980

1:63 600
Sheet 202 (Towcester), Solid and Drift, 1969

1:50 000
Sheet 200 (Stratford on Avon), Solid and Drift, 1975
Sheet 201 (Banbury), Solid and Drift, 1962
Sheet 217 (Moreton-in-Marsh), Solid and Drift
Sheet 236 (Witney), Solid and Drift, 1983

Printed in the UK for HMSO.Dd.0240403.2M.52819

CONTENTS

PLATES

FIGURES

LIST OF SIX-INCH MAPS

Geological six-inch maps included wholly or in part in the one-inch map Sheet 218 (Chipping Norton) are listed below together with the initials of the surveyors and the dates of survey. The surveyors were E. A. Edmonds, A. Horton, E. G. Poole, B. J. Williams and V. Wilson. Manuscript copies of these maps are available for public reference in the libraries of the British Geological Survey in Keyworth, and Edinburgh.

National Grid Maps: all within the 100 kilometre square SP

21 NW	Fifield	A.H.		1960
NE	Shipton-under-Wychwood	A.H.		1960
22 NW	Adlestrop	E.G.P.		1959
NE	Salford	E.G.P., A.H.		1959 – 1960
SW	Bledington	A.H.		1960
SE	Kingham	A.H.		1960 – 1961
23 NW	Stretton on Fosse	E.G.P., E.A.E.		1957 – 1959
NE	Burmington	E.G.P., E.A.E.		1957 – 1959
SW	Moreton-in-Marsh	E.G.P.		1959
SE	Long Compton	E.G.P.		1959
31 NW	Leafield	B.J.W.		1961
NE	Fawler	B.J.W., E.G.P.		1960 – 61
32 NW	Chipping Norton	A.H.		1959
NE	Little Tew	A.H.		1959
SW	Chadlington	B.J.W.		1961
SE	Spelsbury	E.G.P.		1960
33 NW	Lower Brailes	E.G.P., E.A.E.		1955 – 1959
NE	Swalcliffe	B.J.W., E.A.E.		1955 – 1960
SW	Rollright	A.H.		1960
SE	Swerford	B.J.W.		1958
41 NW	Woodstock	E.G.P.		1960
NE	Shipton-on-Cherwell	B.J.W.		1961
42 NW	Sandford St. Martin	B.J.W.		1959 – 1960
NE	Steeple Aston	B.J.W.		1959 – 1960
SW	Kiddington	E.G.P.		1960
SE	Tackley	B.J.W.		1960 – 1961
43 NW	Bloxham	B.J.W., E.A.E.		1955 – 1960
NE	Bodicote	B.J.W., V.W., E.A.E.		1955 – 1959
SW	South Newington	B.J.W.		1958 – 1959
SE	Deddington	B.J.W., V.W.		1959
51 NW	Bletchingdon	B.J.W.		1961
52 NW	Fritwell	V.W.		1960
SW	Middleton Stoney	B.J.W.		1961
53 NW	Great Purston	V.W., E.A.E.		1956 – 1958
SW	Aynho	V.W.		1959

PREFACE

The district represented on Sheet 218 (Chipping Norton) of the New Series One-inch geological map was originally geologically surveyed on the one-inch-to-one-mile scale by H. Bauerman, A. H. Green, E. Hull, T. R. Polwhele and W. Whitaker, and included in the Old Series hand-coloured geological sheets 44 NE, 44 SE, 45 NW, 45 NE, 45 SW and 45 SE which were published in 1859 and 1863. Revised maps of these areas were published in 1871, and included amendments to the Northampton Sand boundaries by J. W. Judd. A six-inch survey of the Marlstone Rock Bed ironstone, together with the rocks immediately above and below it, was carried out by T. H. Whitehead between 1939–43; the results were incorporated in The Liassic Ironstones, Memoir of the Geological Survey, 1952. The present six-inch primary survey was made in 1955–61 by Mr B. J. Williams, Mr E. G. Poole and Mr A. Horton, with smaller areas completed by V. Wilson and Mr E. A. Edmonds. The one-inch map (Solid and Drift) was published in 1968.

In 1961, the district was chosen by the late Professor V. C. Illing, then consultant to the British Gas Corporation (Gas Council), as one in which suitable structures for gas storage could be expected to occur in the 'Keuper Sandstone'. Some 432 boreholes and 17 permanent wells were put down to prove the structure. The Survey worked in close collaboration with V. C. Illing & Partners, the British Gas Corporation and British Petroleum during these investigations, and is most grateful to the British Gas Corporation (Gas Council) for allowing us to publish the results obtained from them. Dr G. D. Hobson of the Imperial College of Science and Technology and V. C. Illing & Partners has prepared a short account of these results which is incorporated in Chapter II and in several figures.

Microfossils from the Devonian in the Steeple Aston Borehole have been named by Dr B. Owens and Mr M. J. Reynolds, and by Professor C. Downie (University of Sheffield). The remaining Devonian fauna has been identified by Dr D. E. Butler. Carboniferous plant remains and spores have been identified by Professor W. G. Chaloner (University of London) and Dr A. H. V. Smith (National Coal Board); the fauna has been named by Dr M. A. Calver. In the Mesozoic, Triassic palynomorphs have been identified by Dr G. Warrington and Liassic ammonites by Professor D. T. Donovan (University of London) and Dr M. K. Howarth (British Museum, Natural History); the remaining macrofossils were identified by Dr H. C. Ivimey-Cook and Mr R. V. Melville. The water supply of the district is described by Dr J. W. Lloyd, and the petrography of the Marlstone Rock Bed by Dr J. R. Hawkes. The photographs (Appendix III) were taken by Mr J. M. Pulsford. The memoir was edited by Mr W. B. Evans.

Thanks are given to the ironstone companies for supplying records of trial boreholes and analyses, to various public authorities and water undertakings for information given and help received, and to the many landowners and tenant farmers who allowed us access to their properties.

G. Innes Lumsden, FRSE
Director

British Geological Survey
Keyworth
Nottinghamshire

13 June 1986

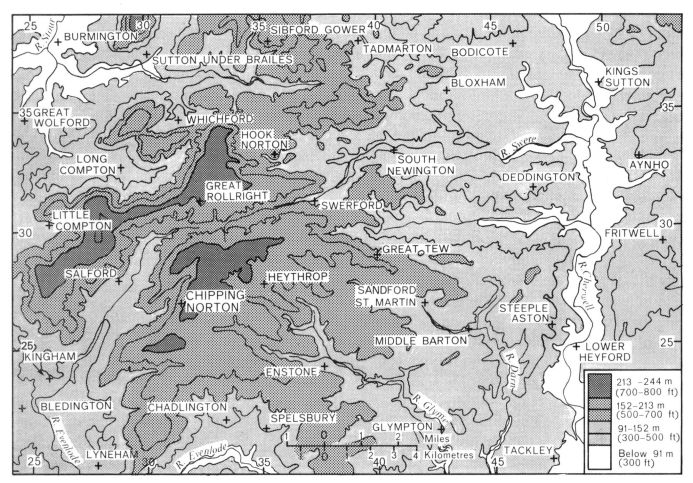

Figure 1 Topography of the Chipping Norton District

CHAPTER 1

Introduction

AREAS AND INDUSTRIES

The geology of the district* described in this memoir is represented on One-Inch New Series Geological Survey Sheet 218 (Chipping Norton); the district lies mainly in north Oxfordshire but also includes parts of the counties of Gloucestershire, Northamptonshire and Warwickshire. Chipping Norton is the only town of any size within the district, most of which is an upland plateau dissected by broad valleys (Figure 1).

Agriculture remains the chief industry of the district; its character has changed over the centuries with arable farming now occupying prime place of importance over sheep-rearing which, in the Middle Ages, provided the main source of wealth. Limestone and ironstone have been quarried in many places in the past, but limestone quarrying is now concentrated in a few large quarries, whilst the ironstone workings ceased during the 1960's. Similarly, the extraction of sand from the Middle Jurassic, and of sand and gravel from the Pleistocene drifts, formerly carried out in many small pits, was confined to one or two larger ones at the time of survey.

The natural water supply of the district is almost entirely derived from small wells and springs in the Middle Lias and Middle Jurassic formations. It is generally inadequate, and substantial areas, including Chipping Norton itself, now derive their supply from outside the district. Banbury and part of the surrounding area are supplied from the River Cherwell. In some areas, strong dependable springs occur, as at Hook Norton where small-scale brewing is still carried out using iron-rich water directly issuing from the Marlstone Rock Bed.

HUMAN SETTLEMENT

The district abounds with evidence of settlement. Neolithic farmers cultivated the drier limestone uplands, and erected a well-known stone circle (the King's Men) on the summit of a hill [296 309] west of Rollright village; it is composed of massive, locally-quarried, oolitic limestone blocks. The Hoar Stone [3778 2374] near Enstone marks a Neolithic burial chamber, and has been wrought from a massive block of local, coarse, shelly, oolitic limestone. Numerous barrows and tumuli of Neolithic and Bronze Age dates occur in the southern part of the district.

Later invaders of Celtic origin built several Iron Age hill forts, and the Ash Bank and Grim's Ditch in the southern part of the district may mark tribal boundaries of similar date. The district was well settled and peaceful during Roman times, and the abundance of place names which end

in 'ford', 'ham' and 'ton' testify to the widespread Anglo-Saxon occupation. In the Middle Ages the region thrived on the woollen trade, while the many large country houses date from Elizabethan times or from the 18th century. The birthplace of the 'Father of British Geology', William Smith (1769–1839) was at Churchill, where a monument of local limestone has been erected (Plate 1).

PHYSICAL GEOGRAPHY

The Chipping Norton (218) district is situated at the north-eastern end of the Cotswolds, which locally attain a height of 246 m above OD to the east of Little Compton [265 302]. In general these hills consist of faulted cuesta blocks which dip gently towards the south-east and present steep-sided north-westerly-facing scarps, as for example the scarps between Harrow Hill [285 338] and Whichford Mill [316 365], and between Chastleton [248 291] and Long Compton [288 325]. The margins of these blocks are generally cambered and are separated by deeply-incised valleys.

The principal watershed between the Thames and Avon river systems passes from near Kitebrook House [245 313] through Barton Hill, Great Rollright, Oatleyhill and Tadmarton Heath to the Swalcliffe area (Figure 1). The streams in the north-west drain into the River Stour and thence into the River Avon. The south-west of the district is drained by the River Evenlode, a tributary of the Thames, which flows through a steep-sided valley south-east of Chadlington (the 'Evenlode Gorge'). In the south the rivers Dorn and Glyme also flow in deeply-incised valleys and join at Wootton [439 196]. Most of the east of the district is drained by the River Cherwell, a major tributary of the Thames, which flows southwards through a broad steeply-incised valley. In its northern reaches it receives the waters from a large number of streams draining the ironstone plateau areas, but farther south its waters mainly derive from the Inferior Oolite and Great Oolite Groups. Its valley narrows as it flows through these limestones south of Northbrook. A small area in the extreme north-east lies within the River Ouse catchment and drains to the north-east.   EGP,VW

SUMMARY OF STRATIGRAPHY

The formations cropping out in the district are shown on the New Series geological map and tabulated in the vertical section. Although the oldest rocks at outcrop fall within the uppermost part of the Lower Lias, older formations have been proved in Gas Council boreholes, in the BGS Steeple Aston Borehole (Poole, 1971; 1977) and in the Withycombe Farm Borehole (Poole, 1978) immediately to the north of the present district (Figure 2). Silurian (Upper Llandovery) rocks were proved in the Batsford Borehole (Strahan, 1913;

---

* Throughout this memoir, the word 'district' refers to the area represented on New Series Geological Sheet 218 (Chipping Norton).

Williams and Whittaker, 1974) just beyond the western margin of the district. It is thought likely that some part at least of the Lower Devonian sequences proved in the Apley Barn Borehole in the Witney (236) district (Poole, 1969, pp. 25–26; Richardson, 1967) extends into the Chipping Norton district, and Upper Devonian rocks were proved in the Steeple Aston Borehole. It would appear that Upper Coal Measures strata underlie the whole of the district (Wills, 1973; Dunham and Poole, 1974, fig.1); they contain a few coals of workable thickness and quality, and link at depth with the exposed Upper Coal Measures of the Warwickshire Coalfield. The youngest Carboniferous rocks proved to date are conglomerates and breccias similar to those classified as Enville Beds (Permian) in the nearby Stratford-upon-Avon (200) district (Richardson and Fleet, 1926; Williams and Whittaker, 1974).

These Carboniferous (and possibly Permian) rocks are overlain unconformably by Triassic conglomeratic sandstones, the Bromsgrove Sandstone Formation, belonging to the Sherwood Sandstone Group. This Triassic unconformity

is an important feature of the English Midlands. The Bromsgrove Sandstone (formerly 'Keuper' Sandstone) was laid down by a river system flowing across a low-lying peneplain. Occasional floods formed widespread temporary lakes in which *Euestheria minuta* (Zeiten) flourished and there was at least one marine incursion, indicated by the presence of *Lingula keuperea* Zenker, *Modiolus?* and ostracods (Poole, 1978, p.13). The overlying Mercia Mudstone Group (formerly Keuper Marl) is mainly made up of red mudstone and siltstone. It contains a little coarse material, in the form of medium-grained sandstone bands and scattered, millet-seed, wind-blown sand grains in the mudstones. Silt-filled mud cracks, penecontemporaneous brecciation due to secondary gypsum formation from anhydrite, and salt pseudomorphs, are common. The palaeogeographical setting of the Mercia Mudstone has been presented by Wills (1970), who favoured cyclically-changing controls over sedimentation, involving phases of flooding of the land areas either by the sea or rivers, with periodic complete or partial drying out of the flooded areas. In the western part of the

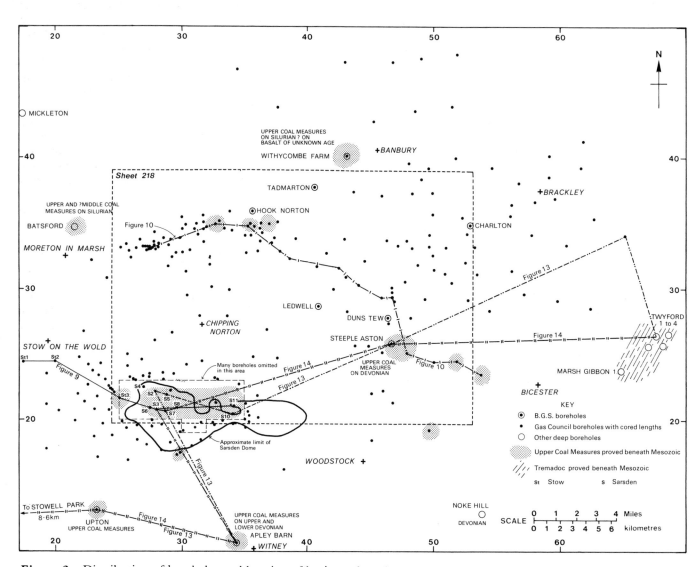

Figure 2 Distribution of boreholes and location of horizontal sections

district the Blue Anchor Formation succeeds the red mudstones and is probably a primary deposit of pale greenish grey mudstones and thin sandstones with a sparse fauna of fish debris and *Euestheria sp.* Farther east, however, the distinctive colour may result from secondary alteration of the red mudstones by the reducing action of the sea during the subsequent Rhaetian transgression.

The Gas Council boreholes have produced clear evidence of slight but widespread erosion at the base of the Penarth Group (p.14) similar to that noted in the Banbury district (Edmonds and others, 1965, p.6). The marine black shales of the Westbury Formation at the base of the Penarth Group pass upwards into the lagoonal, pale green, silty mudstones of the Cotham Member of the Lilstock Formation. The Cotham Member contains *Euestheria sp.* and locally resembles the Blue Anchor Formation. These boreholes prove that all or most of the Cotham Member and Westbury Formation pass into white sands and conglomerates (Twyford Beds) along the eastern extremity of the district adjacent to the former land mass of the London Platform (p.14).

In late Triassic and Jurassic times the district lay between the steadily subsiding Worcester Basin and the relatively stable London Platform. The sediments of this intermediate district exhibit non-sequences, overlaps, facies changes and minor unconformities. For example, the Westbury Formation of the Penarth Group unconformably overlies the Mercia Mudstone Group. The Langport Member rests nonsequentially upon the Cotham Member of the Lilstock Formation (see p.17). In this region the Langport Member, is a very pure, fine-grained, shallow-water limestone containing only a few marine shells and scattered burrows; only in the shoreline area near the London Platform does the latter become sandy due to incorporation of terrigenous deposits. In the east it may pass laterally into the Twyford Beds or may be entirely removed by erosion. The lowermost zones of the Lower Lias are missing due to non-deposition and progressive onlap of younger sediments. The local conglomeratic base of the formation includes pebbles of Langport Member limestone and worn fossils derived from pre-existing Liassic rocks. Further minor disconformities occur within the Lower Lias. The Middle Lias and Marlstone Rock Bed generally thin southwards, possibly due to erosion before the deposition of the Upper Lias as well as to original variations; the Upper Lias thins in the same direction.

Great variations in lithology and thickness occur in the Middle Jurassic rocks. At the base, the Northampton Sand (including the Scissum Beds) and the 'Lower Estuarine Series' were laid down in the north-eastern part of the district. South of Traitor's Ford [337 365], the Scissum Beds are overlain by the much younger oolite and pisolitic, highly fossiliferous Clypeus Grit, which thickens southwards and westwards and cuts into the underlying formations so that in the southern part of the district it rests directly upon the Upper Lias. The Clypeus Grit is succeeded by the sandy, oolitic Chipping Norton Limestone. Around Swerford and Great Tew these sandy limestones pass into rocks that weather into yellow sand, and appear to rest upon fine uncemented sands of 'Inferior Oolite age', the junction being difficult to distinguish in the field. Elsewhere the Chipping Norton Limestone in its type area contains the *Trigonia signata* Bed which has been taken previously as the junction between the Inferior and Great Oolite Groups[1]. In the present memoir, the base of the Great Oolite Group is lowered to the base of the Chipping Norton Limestone and this Group thus includes both the Swerford and Hook Norton Beds of previous authors. Highly fossiliferous clays and shelly limestones of the Sharp's Hill Beds and Great Oolite Limestone conformably succeed the Chipping Norton Limestone. A minor nonsequence occurs in places between the Great Oolite Limestone and the Forest Marble clays and limestones. These latter are succeeded by the highly fossiliferous Cornbrash limestones, which may contain a significant disconformity but are apparently conformably overlain by the Kellaways Beds and Oxford Clay.

Early in the Pleistocene the whole region was overwhelmed by ice from the north-west which surmounted the highest parts of the Cotswolds. Triassic pebbles are almost universally present, and Welsh slates and Old Red Sandstone fragments are common. This drift (the Northern Drift of Hull, 1855; Arkell, 1947a; Kellaway and others, 1971) predates the Fourth or Hanborough Terrace of the River Thames. Later in the Pleistocene, Eastern (Chalky Boulder Clay) ice probably entered the Vale of Moreton and reached its maximum advance in the western part of the district (Shotton, 1953, pp.242-245). Melt-waters from this ice sheet flowed down the Evenlode Gorge and Cherwell Valley, thus providing a direct correlation with the Third or Wolvercote Terrace of the River Thames (Shotton, 1953; Bishop, 1958). With the retreat of this Chalky Boulder Clay ice sheet, the modern river system was initiated.   EGP

---

1 The term 'Series' which was used on the 1:50 000 Sheet is replaced in this memoir by 'Group', where it refers to Inferior Oolite and Great Oolite strata.

CHAPTER 2

Structure

The main structures affecting the Mesozoic rocks are a number of small subsurface domes aligned in a roughly east–west direction, which are crossed by somewhat later east-north-easterly trough faults (Figure 3). These structures are additional to the gentle regional dip to the south-east. Their precise age is unknown. They may have been produced during either of the two widespread post-Jurassic periods of earth movement that have affected the rocks of southern England, i.e. early Cretaceous or mid-Tertiary. However, thickness variation within the Lias has led two of the authors (VCI, GDH) to suggest that the trough faults may be in part syn-sedimentary. In southern England generally, the main effect of the mid-Tertiary earth movements has been to produce the broad folds of the London Basin, Wealden Anticline and Hampshire Basin; perhaps some part of the south-easterly regional dip demonstrated in the Chipping Norton district derives from this broad folding and the remainder from epeirogenic tilting deduced by Arkell (1939, 1941).

STRUCTURE AND SEDIMENTATION

During the greater part of Mesozoic times, the district lay between a subsiding sedimentary basin (the Worcester Basin) to the west, and a relatively stable non-subsiding block of Palaeozoic rocks (the London Platform) to the east and south-east. In spite of many variations in the thicknesses and lithology of the Mesozoic rocks, the overall structural pattern demonstrated in different formations is closely comparable (Figures 4, 5 and 6) and seems to have been produced by one main episode of earth movements acting upon a consolidated sequence; some of the minor differences may be attributed to differences in competence of the included formations.

During late Permian and early Triassic times, the Worcester Basin was the site of a deep depression cut through highlands raised by the Hercynian orogeny (Audley-Charles, 1970b, pl. 7). This depression gradually filled up during Triassic times with continental sediments,

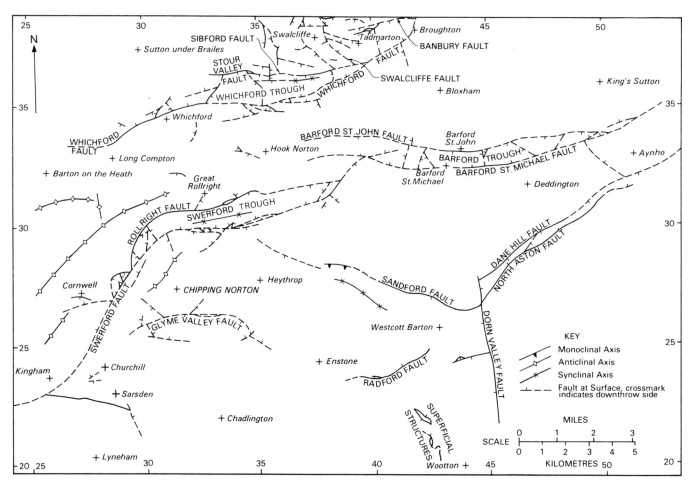

Figure 3 Main surface structures of the Chipping Norton district

and continued downward movement probably led to the accumulation of a thick Jurassic sedimentary sequence; in contrast Jurassic rocks are thin or absent over the London Platform (Kent, 1949). The Mesozoic rocks of the Chipping Norton district reflect their intermediate geographical position, and show a general south-eastwards thinning of most formations with many non-sequences, erosion surfaces, overlaps and facies changes.

In the Worcester Basin, Buckman (1901) demonstrated the presence of penecontemporaneous north- and north-west-trending anticlinal axes during Lower Bajocian times, which were eroded in Upper Bajocian times so that the Upper Trigonia Grit now rests unconformably upon the earlier formations. The easternmost of these anticlinal structures—the 'Vale of Moreton Axis'—lies close to the western margin of the Chipping Norton district. Arkell (1947b) coined the term 'Oxfordshire Shallows' to describe a wide 'shelf' area to the east of the Moreton Axis, characterised by sedimentary breaks and reduced sedimentation in Jurassic times. Hallam (1958) further developed this idea and put forward the concept of basins and swells as used on the Con-

tinent, basins being areas of relative downwarping and comparatively rapid sedimentation which persisted for long periods, and swells—such as the London Platform—being areas of relative uplift, occupied by shallow water or land, towards which the sediments wedged out.

The Gas Council boreholes (see below) have elucidated much detailed structure and stratigraphy in the area. In the south-west of the district they proved substantial complex domes trending east–west and lying south and south–east of Stow-on-the-Wold, in the Church Icomb–Sarsden–Charlbury area. The critical Stow-on-the-Wold–Moreton area to the north was not drilled in detail. A major dome between Stow-on-the-Wold and Chipping Norton has been inferred from outcrop data (see p.106). Its apparent amplitude may owe something to local cambering.

Geophysical maps of this region (Institute of Geological Sciences 1980a, 1980b, 1982, 1983) show a pronounced north–south contour alignment (see p.8), which sugggests the presence of a fundamental pre-Triassic basement fault passing through the Stow-on-the-Wold area. This buried structure may mark the eastern side of the Worcester Graben

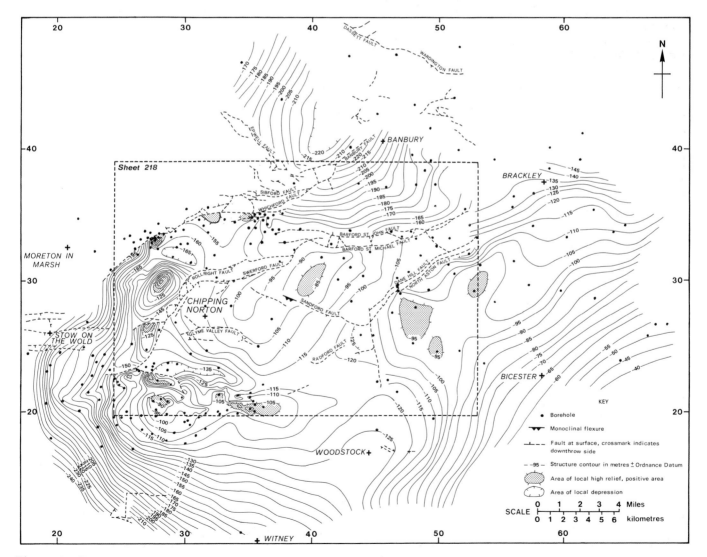

Figure 4   Contours on the surface of the Palaeozoic

(Wills, 1956) although there is no positive evidence of intra-Triassic faulting directly affecting sedimentation in this area (Poole *in* Audley-Charles, 1970b, p.178). This postulated north–south basement structure appears to have acted as a hinge line (the Moreton Axis) during much of the earlier part of Mesozoic times.

The same broad sedimentary pattern seems to have continued intermittently until at least the beginning of the deposition of the Inferior Oolite. The Westbury Formation, Cotham Member and Langport Member (White Lias) show only slight thickening into the Worcester Basin although they wedge out against the London Platform. The Lias thins substantially eastwards from the basin. Variations in the Inferior Oolite both within the Worcester Basin (Buckman, 1901) and within the Chipping Norton district (p.48) may be related to deep-seated movements producing areas of broad downwarping and uplift, facies change, and contemporaneous erosion. Sedimentation appears to have been more constant over both areas during Bathonian times, though with some facies changes and non-sequences.

Major uplift above sea level of the London Platform and English Midlands occurred towards the end of the Jurassic, with consequent erosion of the Jurassic rocks, and culminated in the early Cretaceous earth movements which may have produced the folding and faulting of the Chipping Norton district. The Lower Greensand is local in its deposition, but the Chipping Norton district was probably completely submerged during the Cenomanian transgression and covered with a thick blanket of Chalk, though subsequent erosion has removed all these Cretaceous and any later Tertiary deposits.

CONCEALED STRUCTURES

In the late 1950's Professor V. C. Illing was asked by The Gas Council to look into the possibilities of gas storage in British aquifers. After a comprehensive study of the geological possibilities, he focused his attention on the Triassic as one of the few widespread and suitably located units that contains thick continuous bodies of highly porous and permeable sandstone. The pressure requirements envisaged at that time called for storage at a depth of between about 250 and 300 m. The Sherwood Sandstone of parts of the Cotswold region was known to satisfy these conditions. Furthermore, it was expected that the water in the sandstones near their pinch-out against the London Platform would be decidedly sulphate-rich: hence displacing this water to store gas would not interfere with supplies potentially suitable for domestic and industrial purposes.

Investigations began in the Stow-on-the-Wold—Chipping Norton area where the outcrops of Middle Jurassic beds showed evidence of gentle doming. The following account of the subsurface geology of the Chipping Norton and adjacent districts derives from the ensuing exploration campaign carried out on behalf of The Gas Council, in the course of which some 459 boreholes were drilled; of these, 36 reached the Palaeozoic Basement.

Officers of the Geological Survey were resurveying this district at the same time, thereby affording a good opportunity for surface and subsurface work to become associated in an area of considerable geological interest. Arrangements were made with The Gas Council for Professor Illing to prepare a contribution of the subsurface geology for publication in the BGS Memoir on the Chipping Norton district. At his death in 1969 he left a number of memoranda, notes, maps and sections prepared for this purpose. These have been collated by his co-authors. The planning, control and supervision of the exploration were carried out by Professor Illing on behalf of The Gas Council. In the initial phase he had the help of Mr L. O. Gay of British Petroleum together with one or more of its field geologists to conduct the drilling campaign. Subsequently these responsibilities were taken over by Dr D. Biggins and Mr M. C. Smith of V. C. Illing & Partners. The surveying and site agreements remained in the hands of Mr C. D. Adams, formerly of British Petroleum. Dr C. J. May of V. C. Illing & Partners was concerned with the analysis of water-injection data which were obtained at a late stage in the project.

An initial review of published information, based in part on a few scattered deep holes, indicated thinning of the Lias from Chipping Norton and Banbury in the north-west towards Bicester to the south-east where the Palaeozoic is close to the surface. It was inferred that the underlying Mercia Mudstone would also thin in this same direction towards the margin of the London Platform. The Sherwood Sandstone was known to be present at depth both to the north and south of Stow-on-the-Wold.

Very gentle dips, together with some faults and unconformities, were expected in the subsurface, and it seemed unlikely that seismic techniques available at that time would yield a sufficiently accurate picture of the strata relevant to the study. There were certain features which precluded reliable downward projection of the results of surface mapping; cambering, in particular, is known to hinder surface structural analyses in this part of England. It was, therefore, decided to drill and log a number of shallow boreholes with a light mobile rig, to identify and determine the attitude of a marker nearer to the objective beds. In combination with the isopachytes of the interval from such a marker to the Sherwood Sandstone (derived from the results of a small number of deeper holes) this would determine the form of the top of the Sherwood Sandstone.

The limestones of the Langport Member (p.17) proved to be an excellent marker horizon for this purpose; their purity and hardness led to a characteristic signature on the Schlumberger Gamma-ray and Electric logs, and to its easy recognition in drill cuttings. Moreover, this limestone, or an equivalent facies, occurs beneath the entire district. As drilling progressed it became clear that there were also numerous limestone marker beds within the Lower Lias which could be traced over considerable distances. Two of these, here labelled the '70' and '85' markers, proved to be useful for the whole of the area examined. Gamma-ray logs were satisfactory for correlation in the Lias and were used extensively in the interests of economy. Electric micro-logs were particularly helpful in the Mercia Mudstone and Sherwood Sandstone Groups.

The shallow boreholes made it possible to determine the general subsurface structure quickly and economically. Surface mapping having located the positions of the major faults and the drilling having indicated the main subsurface highs, deeper boreholes were drilled at critical points to obtain information on the characteristics of the Sherwood Sandstone reservoir rock and to ascertain its relationship to the shallower markers. The deep holes entered the underlying Palaeozoic beds. Cores were taken at various depths to obtain detailed information on the nature of the various geological units, including the lithology, minor structures, porosity, permeability and cap-rock properties. The many stratum contour maps constructed from the borehole data are exemplified in Figures 5 and 6.

Structural features

Surface mapping by geologists working for The Gas Council located a gentle dome in the Lias centred on Icomb Hill, some two miles south-east of Stow-on-the-Wold. Drilling began in this area and spread mainly eastwards.

One of the early conclusions from the drilling was that in the Stow-on-the-Wold area the domal condition shown by the near-surface beds becomes weaker downwards, although it is still evident in the Langport Member. The deep

boreholes, Stow No. 1 [1925 2346] and No. 2[2020 2074], proved up to 35 m of Bromsgrove Sandstone Formation below the Mercia Mudstone Group; Stow No. 3 [2508 3475] had some 20 m of these sandstones. Stow No. 4 [2932 2351] showed a marked drop in the level of the Langport Member relative to Stow No. 3. This drop was ascribed to faulting, although at that time surface mapping had not indicated any considerable faulting in this neighbourhood. Further drilling south of Chipping Norton proved a major, complex, east to west-trending structure, the Sarsden Dome, situated in the Bledington–Sarsden–Charlbury area and extending beyond the south-western margins of the district. Immediately to the north a narrow broad structural depression separates this dome from another broad high to the east of Chipping Norton (Figure 5). Southwards from this east–west depression the interval from the base of the Lias to the '70 marker' thins significantly (see p.21); so does the Langport Member limestone; both are thinner on the uplift than immediately to the north in the structural depression. One interpretation of this is that an east–west feature influenced the thickness of sediment accumulated, and led to a

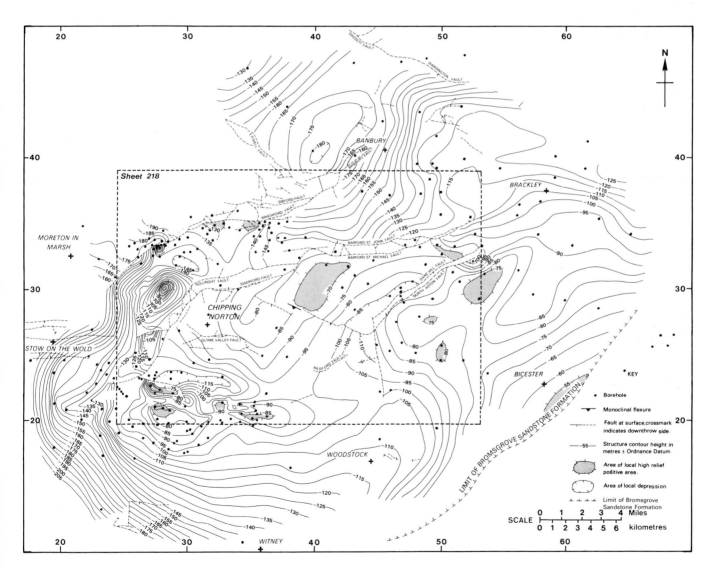

Figure 5   Structure contours on the surface of the Bromsgrove Sandstone Formation

modification of the regional thickening which is broadly towards the north-west. However, there are other variations of thickness within units of the Lower Lias which are not clearly related to structural features and their origin requires further explanation.

In the Lias the Chipping Norton dome has its crest some 5 km east-north-east of Chipping Norton (Figure 6). Drilling showed that the main structure between Deddington and Chipping Norton is an approximately east–west anticline, faulted on the northern side, and with an extensive southern flank. Faulting occurs south of Deddington.

Drilling in the Hook Norton area revealed the presence of a faulted uplift centred on Whichford, and extending westwards to Long Compton. Its characteristics are similar to those of the Chipping Norton uplift, with faulting on the northern and north-western margins and a broad southern flank. As in the case of Sarsden there is evidence that both the interval from the base of the Lias to the '70 marker' and the Langport Member are thinner on the high than directly to the north on the downthrown segment.

Undoubtedly the more complex form of the structure contours and the isopachytes near Sarsden reflects the greater density of drilling information in that area. Some of the complexities may be caused by undetected minor faulting. It is possible that the main faults are linked with faults in the basement which have moved intermittently, and some movement may have occurred during the course of deposition of the overlying beds. Other faults may be entirely of post-Jurassic age. The faults are commonly multiple, with a net drop to the north. Usually there is a fault trough north of the main fault, as exemplified by the North Aston Fault near Deddington.

Inspection of the various maps and cross-sections shows extremely gentle dips everywhere in the Mesozoic strata, 1° being about the maximum beneath most of the area. The sparseness of the observations at the deeper levels means that the inclinations shown tend to be generalised, and locally there could be steeper dips than are indicated by the contouring. The overall picture, however, is one of very gentle undulations with more rapid drops resulting from faulting.

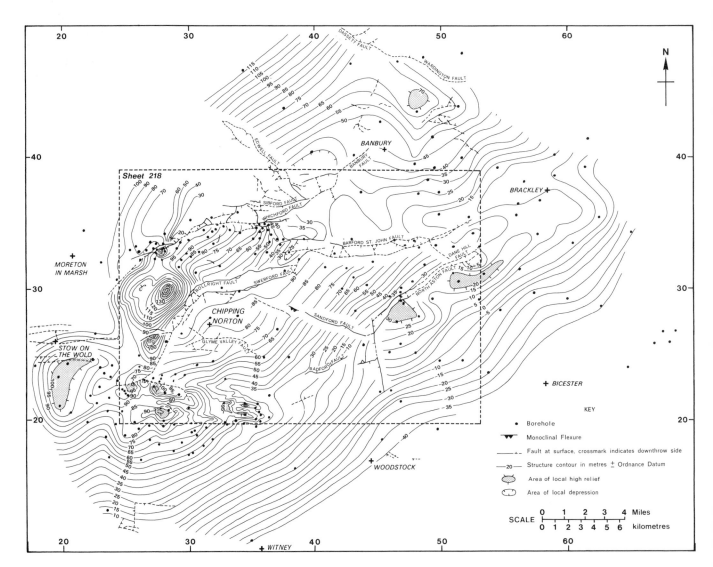

Figure 6 Structure contours on the Lower Lias '70 marker'

Some of the faulting inferred from surface mapping has not been confirmed by the boreholes. On the other hand a substantial east–west fault indicated by the subsurface information north of Sarsden was not suspected from the original surface surveys, although some evidence of its presence has since been noted. Confirmation of its existence at depth was obtained during investigations into the continuity of the Sherwood Sandstone: these involved water injection through one borehole and prolonged pressure observations on surrounding deep boreholes on both sides of the fault.

Figure 5 shows the position of the top of the Bromsgrove Sandstone Formation, inferred from boreholes entering it and from the combination of the isopachytes and the stratum contours on the top of the Langport Member. Figure 4 illustrates the form of the Palaeozoic surface, derived similarly from limited direct borehole information, isopachyte data, and faults taken from published maps of the surface geology.

EGP,GDH

STRUCTURES AT OUTCROP

The area is traversed by several major, high-angle, east-north-east-trending normal faults, which are readily determined by surface mapping except where they occur entirely within the Lower Lias clays.

At surface the broad folds are hard to recognise with certainty due to extensive cambering, particularly of the Inferior Oolite and Marlstone Rock Bed, which produces superficial anticlinal structures and masks those of more deep-seated origin. Thus, between Chipping Norton, Swerford [372 310] and Wootton [440 196], Middle Jurassic limestones cap the hills and apparently dip gently to the south-east; the pronounced cambering of these beds along the valleys of streams tributary to the River Glyme obscures the general structure of this area. However, there appears to be a large broad (tectonic) dome in the Little Compton–Salford area trending north-eastwards from Chastleton Hill though the interpretation is complicated by cambering. A parallel subsidiary anticline trends north-eastwards through Little Compton, and is indicated by the base of the Middle Lias, although the southward camber of Marlstone Rock Bed on the hill to the north of Little Compton has disguised the northward-trending regional dip. Rivers and streams have commonly developed along lines of structural weakness, as for example the River Swere in the Great Rollright area, which follows an easterly-trending syncline trough-faulted between the Rollright Fault and the Swerford Fault. A few of the faults, e.g. at Cornwell Manor, appear to be related to a compressional phase of movement, but the majority, such as those of the Barford Fault trough, appear to be related to a phase of tension as shown by the sagging of the strata in tectonically associated synclines.

EGP

CHAPTER 3

Pre-Jurassic rocks

PRE-COAL MEASURES STRATA

In this broad region the Palaeozoic rocks of the London Platform occur at relatively shallow depth (Figure 4). The Noke
Hill Borehole (Falcon and Kent, 1960, pp.46–7) proved
Mesozoic rocks resting directly upon Old Red Sandstone at a
depth of only 121.0 m and boreholes at Calvert proved
115.8 m and 135.2 m of Jurassic rocks resting directly upon
steeply-dipping Tremadoc mudstones. In the same general
area, British Petroleum boreholes at Twyford (Appendix 5)
proved Jurassic rocks directly overlying steeply dipping
Tremadoc mudstones at an average depth of about 137 m.
Just beyond the western boundary of the district (Figure 2),
Silurian (upper Llandovery) rocks were proved beneath Coal
Measures in the Batsford (Lower Lemington) Borehole
(Strahan, 1913; Williams and Whittaker, 1974).

The oldest rocks yet proved within the district are Upper
Devonian rocks found in the Steeple Aston Borehole [4687
2586]. This hole (sunk in 1970–71) was situated in the
south-eastern part of the district (Figure 2) between Bicester
and Chipping Norton; it proved Jurassic and Permo-
Triassic rocks resting upon Upper Coal Measures with
basaltic intrusive igneous rocks which overlie Upper Devonian rocks, then further basaltic intrusives from 966.9 m to a
final depth of 975.1 m (see Poole, 1971, pp.394–395; Poole,
1977). Determinations on the miospores by Dr B. Owens
and on the acritarchs and chitinozoa by Dr C. Downie, and
the macrofauna by Dr D. E. Butler show that the greater
part of the Devonian sequence is of Frasnian age, with the
probability of a Lower Famennian age for the highest beds
between 775.8 and 790.9 m. The proved sequence probably
terminated above the Upper Devonian conglomerates found
in the Apley Barn Borehole near Witney (Poole, 1969, p.
25); in the latter borehole these beds rest unconformably
upon Lower Devonian (Old Red Sandstone facies), which
includes the Breconian, Upper Dittonian and upper part of
the Lower Dittonian (Richardson, 1967).

Just to the north of the present district, the Withycombe
Farm Borehole, near Banbury, proved Upper Coal
Measures resting unconformably upon mudstones of possible Silurian age, which in turn, rest upon basaltic igneous
rocks of presumed Ordovician age (Poole, 1978). Thus, in
the north of the district, the Coal Measures probably rest on
Silurian rocks, and in the south on Devonian rocks. The
present state of knowledge of the sub-Mesozoic floor of
Southern Britain is shown by Wills (1973; 1978) and Smith
and others (1985).

COAL MEASURES

?Middle Coal Measures

The Batsford (Lower Lemington) Borehole proved 12.8 m of
?Middle Coal Measures seat earths and mudstones beneath
their contact with the Upper Coal Measures at a depth of
452.9 m. These beds, which contain representatives of the
miospore genus *Lycospora* and accessory spores typical of
Westphalian B to Lower Westphalian C strata (Owens *in*
Williams and Whittaker, 1974, p.9), are apparently the
oldest Coal Measures rocks yet recognised in this part of the
Palaeozoic Platform.

Upper Coal Measures

Upper Coal Measures probably underlie the whole of the
district at depth (Dunham and Poole, 1974, fig. 3). Poole
(1975, 1977 and 1978) considers that all these Upper Carboniferous strata are of Stephanian age; however Chaloner
and Calver (in Poole, 1977, p.15 and 1978, p.16) consider
that these beds in the Steeple Aston and Withycombe Farm
boreholes are of Westphalian age. Measures with *Anthraconauta tenuis* (Davies and Trueman) were proved in the
Batsford Borehole between 311.3 m and 452.9 m. They
probably correlate with the Halesowen Formation of south
Staffordshire and Warwickshire, and with the uppermost
part of the Arenaceous Coal Formation (Pennant Formation) in the Apley Barn Borehole [3438 1066] at Witney,
(Poole, 1969, pp.23–24). This borehole proved 959.41 m of
Upper Coal Measures strata above the base of the Zone of
Anthraconauta tenuis; these were classified (originally as
Groups, in ascending order) into the Arenaceous Coal Formation, the Witney Coal Formation, the Crawley Formation, the Burford Coal Formation and the Windrush Formation (Poole 1969, pp.17–34). Previously the Upton
Borehole, near Burford (Worssam, 1963), had proved the
uppermost part of this succession commencing near the top
of the Crawley Formation. In the Steeple Aston Borehole the
succession, although much thinner than at Apley Barn, continued from almost the top of the Burford Coal Formation to
the Arenaceous Coal Formation. The Steeple Aston succession contained seven coal seams of workable quality more
than 0.60 m thick, totalling in all 7.85 m of coal; these gently
dipping seams are thought to underlie the greater part of the
district. Northwards from Steeple Aston, the Upper Coal
Measures continue to thin, and the Arenaceous Coal Formation, the Witney Coal Formation, the Crawley Formation
and the Burford Coal Formation probably coalesce to form
the Halesowen Group of the Warwickshire Coalfield, the
predominantly red Windrush Formation presumably being
equivalent to the Keele Formation of part of the Midlands

(Dunham and Poole, 1974, fig. 2; Poole, 1975, fig. 2)[1].

Good fossil sequences were obtained from the Steeple Aston and Apley Barn boreholes. *Anthraconauta tenuis* with *A. phillipsii* (Williamson) occur at various horizons in the Arenaceous and Witney Coal formations, and *Anthraconaia pruvosti* (Chernyshev) was recorded at several horizons in silty mudstones. *A. tenuis* was also found in the lower part of the Crawley Formation in Steeple Aston, while *A. pruvosti* ranges upwards into the base of the Burford Coal Formation in the Upton Borehole (Worssam, 1963, p.124). *A.* aff. *pruvosti* was recorded towards the top of the Burford Coal Formation in this borehole, and *Anthraconaia calcifera* (Pruvost *non* Hind) was found at a similar horizon in the Apley Barn Borehole. In the Steeple Aston Borehole *Anthraconaia sp.* was found in about the middle of the Burford Coal Formation. The only non-marine bivalves known from the Windrush Formation to date occur between 397.7 m and 399.4 m in the Upton Borehole where *Anthraconaia prolifera* (Waterlot) and *A. saravana* (Schmidt) have been recorded (Calver *in* Worssam, 1963, p.121). The arthropods *Leaia* cf. *boltoni* Raymond, *L.* cf. *bristolensis* Raymond and *L.* cf. *paralella* Raymond occur in the Arenaceous and Witney Coal formations of Apley Barn with *L.* cf. *baentschiana* Geinitz in the Burford Coal Formation. *L. bristolensis* was also recorded at two horizons in the Burford Coal Formation of the Upton Borehole. *Euestheria limbata* (Goldenberg) was recorded from Apley Barn in the highest beds of the Windrush Formation. Other significant fossils include the pulmonate gastropod *Anthracopupa* cf. *britannica* Cox which occurs at various horizons in the Windrush Formation, whilst *E. limbata* ranges upwards from the upper part of the Burford Coal Formation.

The flora in the boreholes is well preserved, abundant and diverse. It is typical of floral Zone H (Dix, 1934), with elements of floral Zone I occurring in the Burford Coal Formation and the Windrush Formation, for example *Acitheca polymorpha* (Brongniart) and cf. *Dicksonites pluckeneti* (Schlotheim). The form cf. *Walchia sp.*, which typically occurs in the Middle and Upper Stephanian of the Continent, was also recorded in the Windrush Formation at the Apley Barn Borehole. The Windrush Formation, which includes thick suites of primary red beds (Krynine, 1949), was not encountered in Steeple Aston, but red beds of Upper Coal Measures age were proved in the following Gas Council boreholes and wells: GCN 1, 2, 4, 5, 46, 62, 111, 116, 158, 160, 163, 168; GS 12; Sarsden 2, 3, 4, 5, 6, 7, 8, 9, 10, 11; Stow 1, 2, 3, 4; and Whichford 1, 2 and 3 (Appendix 5). Whilst many of these rocks are obviously normal grey facies which have been secondarily reddened beneath the Triassic

unconformity (Trotter, 1953, 1954, Horton and Hains, 1972), some of the sequences proved in the Stow and Sarsden wells include conglomeratic beds, similar to the Permian Enville Beds (Heune, 1908; Haubold and Sarjeant, 1973) recorded in the Knight's Lane Borehole (Williams and Whittaker, 1974, pp. 106–109) and primary red beds similar to the Windrush Formation of Apley Barn (Poole, 1969, pp.17–21) and the Keele Formation of the Midlands. It would appear, therefore, that Permian and the youngest Upper Coal Measures occur in the south-western part of the district, with older Upper Coal Measures forming the pre-Triassic land surface northwards towards the Batsford area. Enville Beds also occur, however, in the north-western part of the Banbury district (Poole *in* Edmonds and others, 1965, p.8) and in the adjacent Stratford-upon-Avon district (Williams and Whittaker, 1974, pp.8–9); it would thus appear possible that the general structure of the concealed Upper Coal Measures between Chipping Norton and Stratford-upon-Avon is broadly anticlinal.

The gravity anomaly maps of the district (1:250 000 Chiltern and East Midlands Sheets) show a shallow negative gravity anomaly centred around Steeple Aston, and a region of high gravity anomalies centred around Banbury and extending westwards to Shipston on Stour. The BGS boreholes at Steeple Aston and Withycombe Farm, sunk near the centres of these two anomalous areas, proved that the anomalies are caused by variations in thickness and lithology in the pre-Carboniferous basement (Dunham and Poole, 1974, p.390; see also pp.111–114). The aeromagnetic maps (1:250 000 Chiltern and East Midlands sheets) shows a somewhat confused pattern for most of the district, except in its northern part where a number of strongly positive aeromagnetic values occur and continue north-eastwards into the Banbury district. Bullerwell (*in* Edmonds and others, 1965, pp.101–104) suggested that these anomalies are due to the presence of a large basic igneous intrusion with its top at about 640 m below OD: the Withycombe Farm Borehole proved the base of the Upper Coal Measures to lie at 84 m above OD. It is notable that a very thick sequence of very late Carboniferous or early Permian basic igneous intrusions (dated at 298 ± 6 Ma) was encountered in the Steeple Aston Borehole between 610.17 m and 775.81 m, and that thin olivine basalt sills, probably of the same age, were intruded into Tremadoc mudstones proved in the easternmost of two wells drilled near Calvert Station (Davies and Pringle, 1913, pp. 325–326); these wells are over 22 km to the east of the Steeple Aston Borehole and suggest that concealed late Carboniferous igneous intrusives occur within a large area of the south-east Midlands.   EGP

---

1 Mr A. Jones (personal communication) reports that seismic reflection surveys undertaken by the National Coal Board, since the Sheet was surveyed, and memoir written, confirm that the Upper Carboniferous rocks dip gently to the west and south-west. Along the eastern edge of the Chipping Norton district the older formations are progressively truncated by the unconformable Triassic cover. The western limit has not been proven but must lie close to the western margins of the district and may be defined by continuation of the Western Boundary Fault of the Warwickshire Coalfield. National Coal Board exploratory boreholes in the region have confirmed the correlation with the Coventry area. Some of the seams in the Burford Coal Formation can be traced to the vicinity of Coventry.

TRIASSIC ROCKS

Sherwood Sandstone Group

Within much of the district this Group, represented by the Bromsgrove Sandstone Formation, varies between 12.5 m and 25 m in thickness (Figure 7), these variations probably reflecting infillings of the uneven pre-Triassic floor. To the south-east, the formation pinches out against the London Platform whilst to the west it thickens to 35.4 m in The Gas

Council Stow No. 2 Well [2020 2074]. The formation generally consists of poorly cemented, current-bedded, pebbly, red and brown, gritty sandstones with finer-grained sandstone and silty mudstone beds (fining-upwards sequences). Hard, calcareous-cemented patches and beds occur locally in these sandstones, together with uncemented and decalcified beds of sand and conglomerate which tend to result in poor core recovery and difficult drilling conditions. Audley-Charles (1970a, fig. 4) has wrongly interpreted the Sherwood Sandstone of the Apley Barn Borehole as 'Keuper Waterstones' facies, a facies absent from the Upton and Apley Barn boreholes (Poole, 1978, fig. 6).

The mudstone beds form distinct marker horizons on the Schlumberger logs and can be correlated over considerable distances. Towards the top of the formation a red and green mudstone bed with the conchostracan *Euestheria minuta* was found in both the Upton and Apley Barn boreholes which are separated by a distance of some 11 km. This bed appears to correlate with the *Lingula-Euestheria* bed found in the Sherwood Sandstone of the Withycombe Farm Borehole and represents a major marine incursion (Wills, 1970, p.264; Poole, 1978, fig. 6 and p.13).

Mercia Mudstone Group, below the Blue Anchor Formation

The Mercia Mudstone of the district apparently succeeds the Bromsgrove Sandstone Formation conformably. The isopachyte map of the Group (Figure 8) shows a steady increase in thickness from 1 or 2 m in the south-eastern extremity of the district to 146.3 m just beyond its north-west limit. This westward thickening continues steadily into the Worcester Basin, where Green and Melville (1956, fig. 1) estimate the maximum thickness to be in excess of 533 m.

The dominant lithology of the Mercia Mudstone Group consists of bright reddish brown, silty, blocky, poorly bedded or unbedded mudstones with subconchoidal fracture; these can contain much sand as separate wind-blown grains. Finely laminated beds of silt and mudstone occur at intervals together with thin beds, especially towards the base, of wind-blown sand and well bedded micaceous sandstone. Evaporites are represented by nodules and veins of gypsum and/or anhydrite. Green 'fish-eyes' with black radioactive centres are common at some levels (Ponsford *in* Green and Melville, 1956, p.64 and pl. 1), and the presence of pronounced radioactive horizons has helped inter-borehole cor-

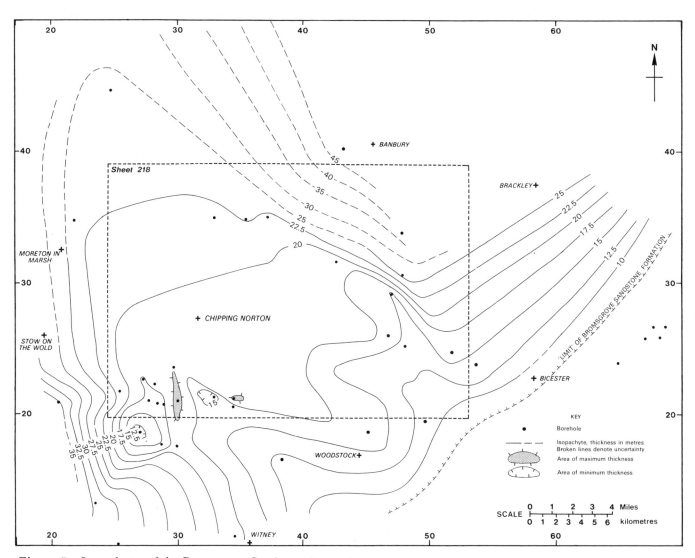

Figure 7   Isopachytes of the Bromsgrove Sandstone Formation

relation within the district (Figure 9) which demonstrates that there was deep erosion (?60 m +) of the Mercia Mudstone towards the London Platform.

BLUE ANCHOR FORMATION

Whilst the position of the above-mentioned horizons demonstrates a steady easterly thinning of the individual beds comprising the Group it also demonstrates a progressive eastward erosion of the Mercia Mudstone at the base of the Penarth Group (Figure 9 and 10). The presence of reworked middle Triassic miospores in late Triassic palynomorph assemblages from the Cotham Member provides strong presumptive evidence that the Sherwood Sandstone in the marginal area of the London Platform was also undergoing erosion during late Triassic times (Appendix 2). This suggests that the London Platform and Oxfordshire Shallows were being uplifted, and that the Mercia Mudstone and Sherwood Sandstone Groups originally occupied larger areas than at present. In south-west England, the Worcester Basin, and possibly in the western extremities of the Chipping Norton district, the Blue Anchor Formation (including the Tea Green Marl) is a primary deposit, probably of lacustrine origin, since scarce fish scales and trace fossils occur in fine-grained, thinly bedded mudstones within it. Eastwards, this formation apparently becomes more sandy, but log correlations indicate that the Tea Green Marl here was originally red Mercia Mudstone which has been secondarily reduced and dolomitised during pre- or early-Rhaetian uplift and erosion (Figure 9). Erosion and channelling of the highest Mercia Mudstone deposits, with inclusion of angular fragments of these mudstones in the basal Penarth Group, have been recorded in several boreholes in the Sarsden area. Elsewhere the surface of the Mercia Mudstone has been bored, and in Sarsden No. 4 Borehole [2695 2258] the Penarth Group and Mercia Mudstone lithologies are so intermingled as to suggest that the earlier mudstones were either softened or still not compacted when burrowed by Penarth Group organisms.

The wider geographical setting and mode of formation of the Mercia Mudstone have been summarised by Wills (1970) who put forward evidence of cyclical control of sedimentation in an attempt to reconcile the association of obvious shallow-water structures in the mudstones with thick deposits of rock salt which could have been precipitated only

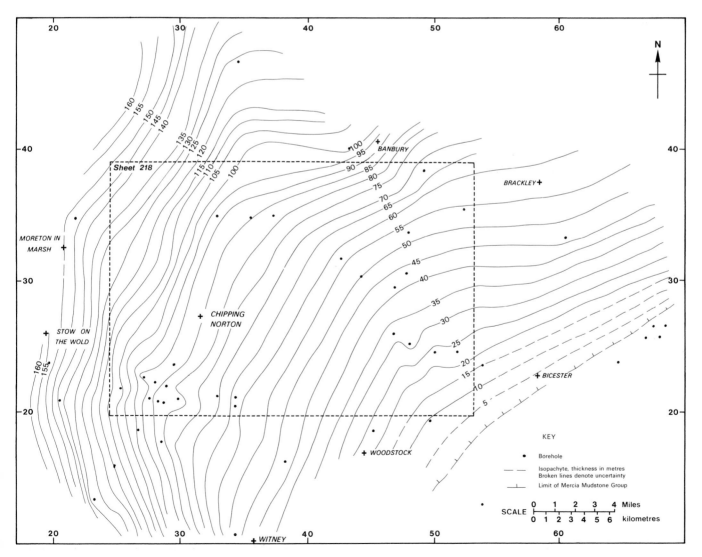

Figure 8 Isopachytes of the Mercia Mudstone Group

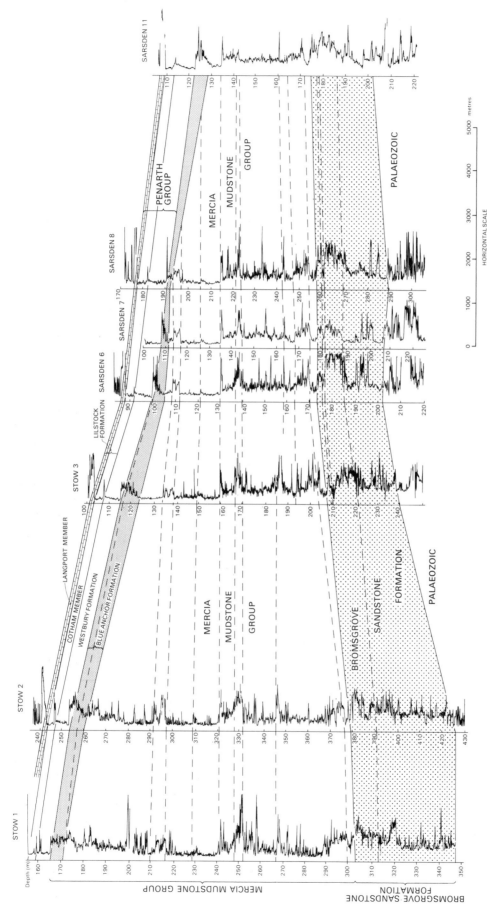

Figure 9   Correlation of the Triassic to show overstep of the Penarth Group and the development of the altered sediments at the top of the Mercia Mudstone Group

The Blue Anchor Formation may be present in the vicinity of Stow 1 as primary green beds. Traced eastwards the upper part of the underlying Mercia Mudstone Group is secondarily reduced, the beds resembling in lithology parts of the Blue Anchor Formation

from constantly replenished oceanic waters in the hollows of the main subsiding basins.   EGP

Penarth Group

These rocks are known only from boreholes and wells. The nearest outcrops lie to the north-west and north in the Stratford-upon-Avon (Williams and Whittaker, 1974) and Banbury (Edmonds and others, 1965) districts. In the Deddington–Brackley–Bicester area, parts, and possibly the whole, of the Penarth Group pass into a marginal arenaceous facies here named the Twyford Beds.

Isopachytes of the Penarth Group and the Twyford Beds show a progressive south-eastward thinning, the sequence pinching out beyond Bicester. The thicknesses are variable and the area of maximum deposition lies to the south-east of Banbury. Although this area is peripheral to the littoral area in which the Twyford Beds accumulated, its north to south elongation is apparently unrelated to the NE–SW trend of the shoreline of the London Platform. Changes in thickness of the combined Westbury Formation and Cotham Member show comparable trends (Figure 11), but those of the Langport Member (Figure 12) are much more complex (p. 18). The succession is summarised in Figure 13.

WESTBURY FORMATION

The Westbury Formation ranges from 6 to 11 m in thickness at outcrop in Warwickshire, though possibly only 4.9 m were proved in the Armscote Manor Borehole [244 448] near Shipston on Stour (Edmonds and others, 1965, p.11). Within the present district the thickest cored sequence (6.3 m) was proved in Sarsden No. 10 Borehole [3414 2043], whilst 5.85 and 4.7 m were proved at Withycombe Farm and Steeple Aston, respectively. In the Worcester Basin the medium to very dark grey micaceous mudstones and black 'shales' of the Westbury Formation rest disconformably upon the non-marine mudstones of the Blue Anchor Formation. In the Chipping Norton district, however, they overstep various horizons of the Mercia Mudstone Group towards the London Platform (Figure 9 and 10), indicating uplift and erosion of this marginal area before the Rhaetian submergence. The thin 'Rhaetic Bone Bed' sandstone, which sporadically defines the base of the Westbury Formation in southern Britain, is locally absent. The geophysical logs of several of The Gas Council boreholes indicate the presence of a thin basal sandstone which may represent it. Generally the basal beds of the Penarth Group in the district comprise dark grey, gritty-textured, pyritic shales or mudstones, containing coarse sand grains and sand wisps with abundant fish debris.

Thin partings, lenses and, rarely, beds of pale grey fine-grained sand and coarse silt occur throughout the Westbury Formation. Some are lime-cemented and locally pyritic. They are commonly gently cross-stratified and a few have ripple-marked upper surfaces. Shallow-water slump and load-cast structures with associated micro-faults occur in the upper part of the sequence. There is a tendency for the formation to become less fissile and pyritic, but more calcareous and paler grey, upward. The pyrite occurs as idiomorphic grains, as cement, as a coating on shells, and as the lining and infill of burrows. Plant fragments and sporadic ostracods are also present locally.

The Westbury Formation fauna is dominated by bivalves – often present in thin bands with large numbers of one or a few species. Small gastropods, echinoderms and fish remains occur, the latter are especially common in the coarser beds near the base (see Appendix 1, p.120).

LILSTOCK FORMATION, COTHAM MEMBER

The maximum thickness of the Cotham Member proved in the district was 12.03 m at Withycombe Farm (Poole, 1978). In the Sarsden area the thickness varied from 8.4 to 8.9 m, but this decreased to 7.16 m at Steeple Aston, 5.8 m* at Upton, Burford, and 3.35 m, at Apley Barn; in the latter borehole the beds have been subjected to intra-Liassic erosion. At outcrop in the Banbury district the Cotham Member is about 6 m thick, whilst in the Armscote Manor Borehole it is reduced to 2.4 m.

The Cotham Member comprises pale greenish grey mudstones with minor pale grey and pale chocolate to olive-brown beds. Throughout most of the Midlands and North Cotswolds there appears to be an upward passage from the Westbury Formation. This was seen in many of The Gas Council boreholes where fissile mudstones of the Westbury Formation were followed upwards by more blocky paler mudstones, which in turn give way to the pale green mudstones with subconchoidal fracture that are typical of the Cotham Member. In a few places the boundary is abrupt; for example, in the Apley Barn Borehole (Poole, 1969, p.16), the uppermost Westbury Formation mudstones have an imbricate appearance with thin, steeply inclined calcite veins extending down for about 0.15 m from the sharply defined base of the slumped Cotham Member mudstone.

The Cotham Member is often very thinly and regularly laminated with partings of very fine sand and silt. As in the Westbury Formation, some of the coarser units have erosional channel bases and show gentle cross-stratification, weak load casts, micro-faulting and ripple-marked surfaces. Generally the coarser beds are less than 5 mm thick, but exceptionally some siltstones may be 0.3 m thick. The thicker beds are commonly lime-cemented, whilst thin porcellanous limestones are also present. Evidence of desiccation is provided by the common silt- and sand-filled mud cracks. Mudstones with a pseudo-breccia structure, similar to beds in the Mercia Mudstone, have been noted, and a mass of ramifying veins of anhydrite at one locality may denote arid conditions. The pale chocolate to olive-brown mudstones are similar in lithology to the pale greenish grey mudstones which characterise the Cotham Member. Kent (1970, p.365) suggested that similar brighter coloured mudstones in Lincolnshire and the North Sea may be due either to the temporary development of oxidising conditions or to the introduction of sediment produced by contemporary erosion of red Mercia Mudstone over rising salt structures in the North Sea. They could also have originated by the trapping of oxidised wind-blown dust or result from the oxidation of primary greenish grey sediments. Disturbed bedding with slump-like structures is a widespread feature of the Cotham Member (Figure 13; Poole, 1978, fig. 5). This may result

---

* Ivimey-Cook (*in* Orbell, 1973) suggested that, of this thickness, the lowest 1.5 m have a Westbury Formation fauna, and that the true Cotham Member thickness at Upton may be 4.21 m; these beds are slumped and may incorporate some underlying Westbury Formation.

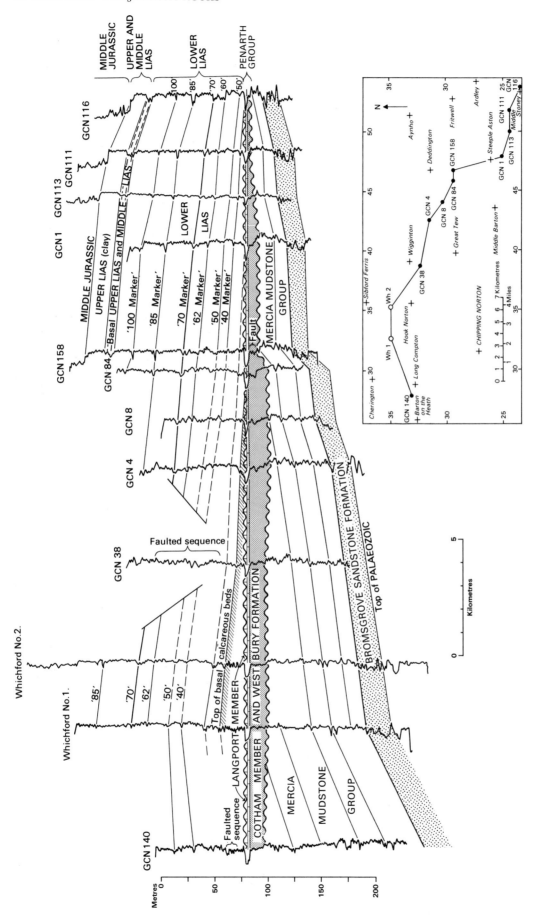

Figure 10 Correlation of the Jurassic and Triassic between Long Compton and Middleton Stoney based on geophysical logs with base of Langport Member as datum

from dewatering of the sediment but may have been produced by earthquake shock waves disturbing unconsolidated sediment (Poole, 1969, p.14).

The Cotham Member is poorly fossiliferous, the most common macrofossil being the conchostracan *Euestheria minuta*. This is associated with plant debris, which at Witney includes the bryophyte *Naiadita lanceolata* Buckman emend. Harris, 1938, a species which is thought to colonise fresh- to brackish-water lakes. An algal limestone has been recorded from the calcareous beds of the Cotham Member in the Banbury district (Poole *in* Edmonds and others, 1965, p.11). Foraminifera and ostracods, including *Darwinula sp.*, and fish fragments are also found as are, locally, poorly-preserved bivalves including *Modiolus sp.*

A thin bed of medium to pale grey silty micaceous mudstone with silty shell-debris partings, diminutive bivalves and fish debris underlies the Langport Member in Sarsden No. 2 Well [2769 2220]. The lithology is transitional to the typical Cotham Member mudstones. It becomes more greenish grey and blocky downward with gently cross-stratified thin silt lenses and indefinitely mottled layers. It is overlain non-sequentially by the Langport Member and

rests abruptly on greenish grey silty mudstones. The bed yielded bivalves (see Appendix 1. p.120) reminiscent of those of the Langport Member. A similar but slightly greenish grey bed occurred in Sarsden No. 8 Well [2970 2097]. A comparable bed of dark grey mudstone has been recorded in the Banbury district (Edmonds and others, 1965, p.11), in the Upton Borehole (Worssam, 1963, p.116) and the Stowell Park Borehole (Green and Melville, 1956, p.47), and on faunal grounds was grouped with the Langport Member. In this account the latter term is restricted to the main limestone development.

At times this horizon, or the base of the overlying Langport Member, has been used locally to define the base of the Jurassic. Current practice is to separate biostratigraphic and lithostratigraphic units and the base of the Jurassic System is now taken at the first appearance of the ammonite *Psiloceras* (Coope and others, 1980, Ivimey-Cook and others, 1980). However, one of the authors (Poole, 1979 and 1980) believes that the base of the Lias Group should be drawn at the base of the Langport Member, i.e. at the top of the Cotham Member, and that this horizon should also define the base of the Jurassic System.

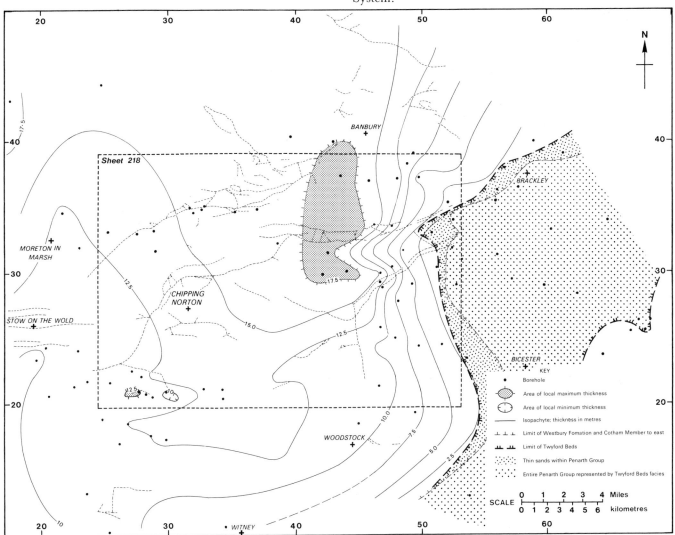

Figure 11 Isopachytes of the combined Westbury Formation and Cotham Member

LILSTOCK FORMATION, LANGPORT MEMBER

In southern Britain the Langport Member (White Lias), or locally the underlying thin grey mudstones, marks the return of widespread fully marine conditions which then continued throughout early Jurassic times. The thickness varies from 0 to 5.2 m. Locally the member comprises pale grey to white fine-grained porcellanous limestone with thin wispy marl and clay partings, and beds showing pseudo-nodular or pseudo-brecciated texture. It is extremely hard and massive, and commonly possesses a subconchoidal splintery fracture. The limestone is very pure and is generally thought to have been formed by recrystallisation of chemically-precipitated calcareous mud. Less common features that indicate shallow-water deposition include shallow channel structures, ripple-marks, gentle cross-stratification and load casts. Partings and lenses of marine shells and shell debris occur at some levels but the fauna is sparse and poorly preserved. Determinable macrofossils are uncommon but include bivalves, some fish remains, diademopsid spines and ostracods. Evidence of bioturbation is rare but cylindrical burrows occur, particularly in the argillaceous bands, and *Chondrites*-type mottling has been noted.

The base of the Langport Member in the district is generally sharp and probably non-sequential in places; some reworking of the underlying unconsolidated sediments may have occurred. In the Sarsden No. 3 Well a dyke filled with greenish grey mudstone flakes set in a silty matrix extended down 0.18 m into the underlying Cotham Member. In the Banbury district, however, the Langport Member appears to succeed the marine mudstones of the Cotham Member conformably (Edmonds and others, 1965, p.19). The upper surface of the Langport Member is locally eroded and a few pebbles of Langport Member-type limestone occur in the overlying basal Lias Group strata. Elsewhere the surface is pitted or cavernous, and borings and encrusting oysters have been noted in Warwickshire. In places the top surface is encrusted with pyrite, and euhedral crystals of pyrite line some of the stylolitic closed joints and bedding surfaces which occur throughout the rock.

The Langport Member is thickest in the Hook Norton–Duns Tew—Banbury area, the recorded maximum being 5.18 m. The isopachytes show no obvious regional trend though the member dies out to the south and east (Figure 12). Its absence at Witney, and part of its variation in

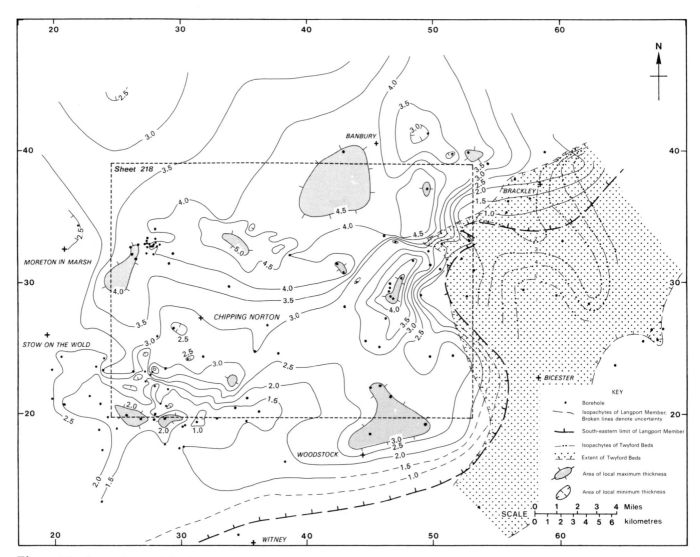

Figure 12 Isopachytes of the Langport Member and Twyford Beds

thickness elsewhere, may be due to pre-Liassic erosion. Part of the thickness variations may be related to irregularities on the sea floor consequent upon erosion of the Cotham Member, and part may result from differential subsidence.

AH, EGP

Twyford Beds

In the eastern parts of the district a marginal arenaceous facies, the Twyford Beds*, appears at the position of the Penarth Group (Figure 13). The lithologies comprise coarse sandstone, conglomeratic sandstone, dolomitic and calcitic sandstones and siltstones, and a few dolomitic siltstones. The rocks are generally poorly bedded and of low to moderate sorting. Clay partings are rare. Strong (1972) reported the

* The term Twyford Beds has been used (Donovan and others, 1979) for the arenaceous and rudaceous strata developed between the Mercia Mudstone Group and the Lower Lias in the Twyford area, Buckinghamshire. It is presumed to represent a marginal facies of the Penarth Group. A cored borehole (Twyford No. 1 Well) is proposed as the type section, with supplementary information provided by Twyford No. 2 Well.

occurrence of large clasts of greenish and pale olive-grey mudstones and dolomitic mudstones. These are poorly indurated and may have been derived from the underlying Mercia Mudstone. They are associated with more exotic fragments which include micrite intraclasts (possibly of penecontemporaneous origin or derived from the Cotham Member or the Langport Member), mudstone pellets, iron-stained and millet-seed quartz grains, glauconitic pellets, and pieces of pyritic and calcareous sandstones, dolomicrite, chert, metaquartzite and siltstones (some of which are schistose), quartz-mica-chlorite metasiltstones, metagrey-wackes, quartz-chlorite pelites, quartz-microcline aggregates of granitic origin, granophyres, perthites and micro-perthites, intermediate plagioclase grains, spilites and microspilites, rhyolites and microrhyolites, and tuffs of vitroclastic, spilitic and chloritized types. The fragments of igneous and metamorphic rocks are generally well rounded and are probably polycyclic, some perhaps having been derived from Devonian and older sediments. The millet-seed quartz grains may have been derived from the Trias or directly from the source area of the Mercia Mudstone. A

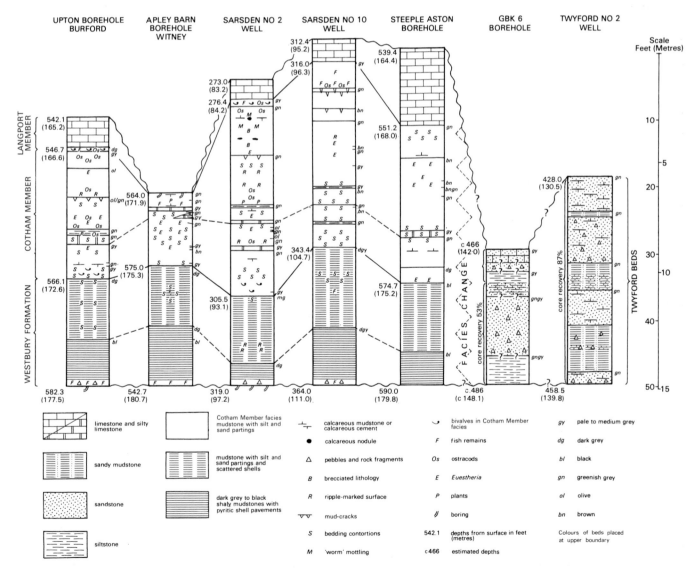

Figure 13 Comparative sections in the Westbury Formation, Cotham Member and Langport Member

single specimen of a Carboniferous ozawainellid foraminifer may indicate the presence of Visean or Namurian outcrops within the adjacent Triassic land area or could have been recycled from older Triassic rocks. The sediments are commonly cemented by carbonate, sparry calcite being dominant, although dolomitic and mixed carbonate cements may be present. Strong suggests that the low proportion of sand grains to matrix in some beds indicates that the carbonate in these cases was precipitated as a mud which was subsequently recrystallised.

The geophysical signature elsewhere produced by the typical massive Langport Member extends into the area where the Twyford Beds occur. In this area the signature is, however, produced by lime-cemented sandstones. These may occur at the same stratigraphic position as the Langport Member but no transitional lithologies have been recorded and, indeed, the Langport Member rarely contains any derived quartz. It is possible that the Twyford Beds are equivalent to the thin arenaceous beds of the Cotham Member and Westbury Formation. The evidence of borehole chippings and geophysical logs suggests that a thin sandstone may be present in the lower part of the Westbury Formation in the Deddington–Brackley area, where it is overlain by Penarth Group mudstones and typical Langport Member limestone. East of this the Langport Member is absent and the typical Twyford Beds calcareous sandstone facies is developed. In the type section (Twyford No. 1 Well, [6802 2569]) the Twyford Beds comprise a thin sandy limestone resting upon a patchily cemented gritty sandstone with a basal grit having a clayey matrix. The core recovered from this horizon in Twyford No. 2 Well [6760 2650] consisted of greyish green coarse sandstones with calcareous cement and pebble-rich horizons, interbedded with reddish brown and greenish grey mudstones. The sandstones differ from those at the base of the Mercia Mudstone Group and in the Bromsgrove Sandstone Formation to the west in their inferior sorting and in the presence of a calcareous cement. The mudstones resemble the poorly graded sandy mudstones of the Mercia Mudstone Group. Similar beds, probably of comparable age, were proved in the Noke Hill Borehole (Falcon and Kent, 1960). The Twyford Beds were absent in Marsh Gibbon No. 1 Borehole [6481 2374] and in the No. 3 and No. 4 Boreholes [6859 2659 and 6697 2561] at Twyford.

The Rhaetian age of the Twyford Beds is inferred from their stratigraphic position. They rest abruptly upon a bored surface of the Mercia Mudstone Group and are succeeded disconformably by beds in the upper part of the Lower Lias (Lower Pliensbachian). Macrofossils have not been found in them, though burrow-like structures have been recorded. A sample from Twyford No. 1 Borehole was reported by the late Mr J. M. Edmunds (personal communication) of Oxford University Museum to have contained Rhaetian spores, but the evidence has been lost and other samples from this and other boreholes have been barren. Dr G. Warrington (Appendix 2, p.131) has recovered microfloras indicative of a Rhaetian or early Jurassic age from samples from boreholes near Bicester.

A thin sandstone is recorded near the base of the Westbury Formation in the Cherwell Valley area and can be traced on geophysical logs into the marginal facies, suggesting that there the deposition of the Twyford Beds may have commenced whilst the Westbury Formation was being laid down. The presence of calcareous mud in the highest part of the Twyford Beds suggests that their accumulation may have continued whilst the Cotham Member was being deposited, and that the youngest part of the sequence may be contemporaneous with the Langport Member. Since the sandstones in the Twyford Beds have a granular spar cement, it is possible that sand deposition was completed synchronously with the Cotham Member, and that the upper parts of the Twyford Beds were cemented by waters percolating downwards from the Langport Member sea.

CONDITIONS OF DEPOSITION

In the district the earliest Penarth Group sediments rest unconformably upon the Mercia Mudstone, and finely conglomeratic sand lenses with fish debris fill very shallow channels at the base of the Westbury Formation. Dark grey pyritic argillaceous sediment, the 'Black Shale' facies, was soon being deposited in fairly shallow water throughout the district. Reducing conditions were probably present at a short distance below the sediment–water interface, but the evidence of sporadic bioturbated horizons and the prevalence of pavements with separated shells of bivalves suggest that stagnant conditions were not developed above the depositional interface. Gentle currents periodically swept sand along the sea floor, and sorted and transported shells and fish debris.

Various environments have been suggested, and the most likely is a shallow, possibly tideless sea, though accumulation in a muddy estuary cannot be precluded. This marine environment was succeeded, during the deposition of the Cotham Member, by a shallow brackish lagoon with freshwater and terrestrial phases and areas, and occasional marine incursions. The relatively quiet waters were periodically disturbed by gentle currents. The presence of brownish mudstone, fine-grained dolomite and calcareous bands, and some pseudo-brecciated mudstones and mud-cracked layers indicate complete desiccation and the occasional return of an environment more characteristic of Mercia Mudstone Group times. Poorly preserved marine bivalves indicate short-lived marine incursions, but the main marine phase set in after the transgression of the Langport Member sea. The Langport Member was deposited as a calcareous mud in a widespread shallow quiescent marine environment that was only rarely disturbed by periods of strong current activity and into which very small quantities of clay were washed.

Relative uplift of the central parts of the London Platform during Rhaetian times, possibly associated with climatic change, resulted in increased erosion and river flow; the transport of large quantities of rock debris into the peripheral zone of the Rhaetian sea led to the formation of the Twyford Beds. The sedimentary character of these beds indicates rapid deposition with very little reworking.

In the latest Rhaetian there was a major regression in this district. AH

CHAPTER 4

Lower Jurassic: Lias Group

Lower Jurassic rocks form the surface of most of the northern and south-western parts of the Chipping Norton district. The outcrop is mostly drift-free, but glacial and fluviatile deposits partly obscure it along the western margin of the district, in the Vale of Moreton, and in the Evenlode and Cherwell valley systems. Elongated inliers also occur in the deeply incised valleys of the River Dorn and River Glyme. Much of the information on the Lower Jurassic (and especially on the Lower Lias, of which only the uppermost 50 m crop out) has been obtained from The Gas Council's exploratory boreholes and from the BGS cored boreholes at Apley Barn, Steeple Aston and Withycombe Farm. A list recording the main faunal taxa found in the district is contained in Appendix 1(2).

LOWER LIAS

The major centres of sedimentation in Lower Lias times probably lay to the west and north-west of the present district. The Chipping Norton district lies on the south-eastern margin of the Worcester Basin, and is immediately adjacent to the former land area of the London Platform. The history of early Liassic sedimentation is one of progressive overlap on to this land area (Donovan and others, 1979) in four episodes; each of these was preceded by localised erosion at the edge of the basin and/or non-deposition, and so each is marked by a minor disconformity in the Liassic sequence and the absence of parts of one or more ammonite zones (Figure 14).

All the ammonite zones of the Lower Lias are present in the Stowell Park Borehole (Green and Melville, 1956, p.47) and are probably also present in the Stratford-upon-Avon (200) district where the basal Zone of *Psiloceras planorbis* and the pre-*planorbis* Beds have both been recognised.* These basal beds continue north-eastwards along the crop through the Banbury (201) district into the Market Harborough (170) district and south Nottinghamshire (Kent, 1937). The Lower Lias is thickest (Figure 15) where the fullest sequence of ammonite zones is present.

The extension of the area of Lower Lias deposition into the present district occurred at about the base of the *Schlotheimia angulata* Zone. A basal conglomerate of probable *angulata* age was found in the Withycombe Farm Borehole (Poole, 1978, p.8), and the lowest beds in the Batsford (Lower Lemington) Borehole may be of *angulata* or *Alsatites liasicus* Zone age (Williams and Whittaker, 1974, p.91). In the south-east of the district in the Steeple Aston Borehole (Poole, 1977a, fig. 5), the basal Lias conglomerate which rests disconformably upon the Langport Member, underlies beds with ammonites

* The Geological Society's Triassic Report (Warrington and others, 1980) recommended that the Triassic–Jurassic boundary be placed immediately below the lowest occurrence of *Psiloceras planorbis*. In the Chipping Norton district the *P. planorbis* Zone has not been proved.

of the *Caenisites turneri* Zone (Figure 45).

The second major stage of overlap took place during *Arnioceras semicostatum* Zone times. Beds of this age rest with marked disconformity upon Penarth Group strata in the Apley Barn and Upton boreholes (Poole, 1969, fig. 4), and may rest directly upon the limestones and conglomerate unit containing *Schlotheimia angulata* in the Withycombe Farm Borehole (Poole, 1978, p.8). This overlap is almost certainly that demonstrated by the geophysical logs to occur at the base of the Lower Lias in the vicinity of the GCN 94 Borehole (Figure 16) to the west of Deddington.

Throughout most of the area there is little evidence for the presence of the *Oxynoticeras oxynotum* Zone, and this represents a time of reduced deposition or regression. The zone is proved in the Sarsden area, and doubtfully established in the Steeple Aston Borehole. Subsequently, overlap continued (Figure 16). Thus, a limestone band, the '62 marker', which occurs low in the *Echioceras raricostatum* Zone, rests directly on the Twyford Beds to the east of the district. A further major extension of the area of Lower Lias sedimentation occurred during the *Uptonia jamesoni* Zone, the rocks of which overlap onto the Tremadoc shales of the London Platform in the Marsh Gibbon–Calvert area to the east of the district (Davies and Pringle, 1913, pp.320–322). In Twyford No.2 Borehole, just to the north of these boreholes, strata belonging to the *Platypleuroceras brevispina* Subzone rest directly upon the Twyford Beds. There is a basic difference in behaviour between the thickness variations within the Lower Lias below the '70 marker', which lies within the *brevispina* Subzone of the *Uptonia jamesoni* Zone (Horton and Poole, 1977), and those of the overlying units. The lowest division, below the '70 marker' (Sinemurian and Hettangian), thickens north-westwards towards the centre of the depositional basin (Figure 17A). This unit includes the four extensions to the area of deposition discussed above; the regional trend is principally due to this progressive overlap, the limited regression and possible local erosion producing disconformities within it.

In contrast the intervals between the '70' and '85 markers' (Figure 17B), the '85' and '100 markers' (Figure 18A), and the Lower Lias above the '100 marker' (Figure 18B), show irregular thickness variations which suggest that sedimentation during these periods was controlled by local factors rather than by regional ones. AH,EGP

Below the '85 marker' (concealed rocks)

The measures between the Langport Member and the '70 marker' contain many more thin impure limestone and cementstone bands than those above this level, and include the Blue Lias limestones. Generally the base of the Lias is sharp and erosive, the upper surface of the Langport Member being uneven, locally cavernous, coated with pyrite in places, and cut by pipes and borings extending down

50 mm into the limestone. A very thin pebble bed with tabular fragments of Langport Member limestone occurs locally, and a few of the pebbles show shallow molluscan borings.

The full sequence of the Lower Lias in the Apley Barn, Steeple Aston and Withycombe Farm boreholes has been discussed elsewhere (Poole, 1969; Poole, 1977; Poole, 1978; see also Table 1 for zonal details). In the Sarsden area additional information is available from The Gas Council

boreholes which show that here the basal 11 m of the Lias consist of mudstone with interbedded thin marls and limestones. These limestones are generally pale to medium grey, fine-grained micritic and argillaceous, with indefinite passage-type junctions, and are probably in part the result of secondary concentration of lime. They may be slightly silty and poorly laminated and are poorly fossiliferous, though *Chondrites*-type mottling with pyrite trails and pins occurs throughout. The mudstones are of two types, a pale grey

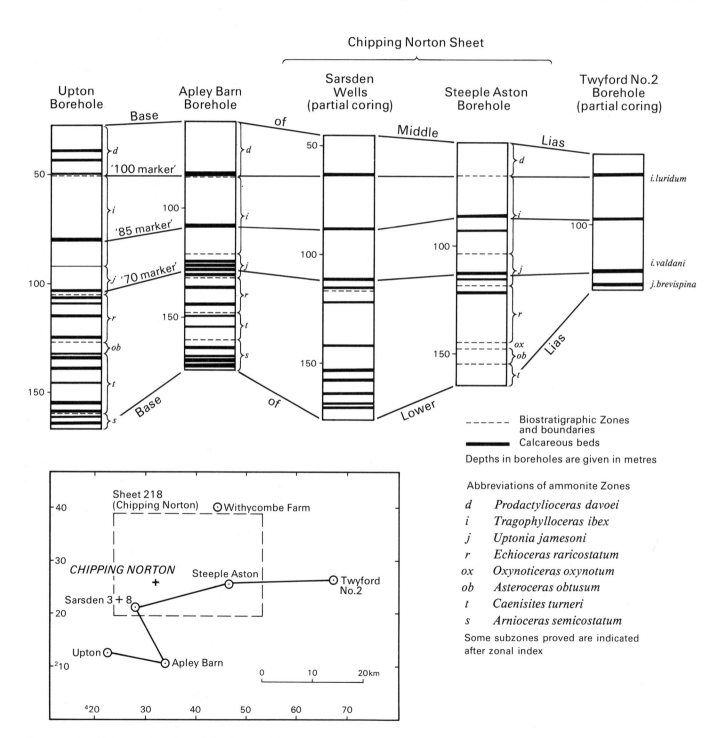

Figure 14 Lithostratigraphy of the Lower Lias

somewhat blocky calcareous mudstone and a darker shaly mudstone. The former may be weakly laminated, it contains scattered small pyrite granules, and is poorly fossiliferous. The proportion of silt to lime in this lithology varies and the beds may pass into limestone. The darker shaly mudstone is more fissile and consists of alternate laminae of bituminous olive-grey and medium grey mud which probably reflect variations in the proportion of organic matter. Junctions between the two lithologies may be abrupt or gradational.

The fauna of the basal Lias in this area is limited in species and abundance. It includes ammonites associated with a variety of free-swimming and bottom-living bivalves.

The age of the basal Lias in the Sarsden area is uncertain. Most borehole cores yield a number of poorly preserved arnioceratid ammonites which are indicative either of the *semicostatum* Zone or of the lower part of the *Caenisites turneri* Zone. In Sarsden No. 8 Well [2970 2097] a juvenile specimen of *Coroniceras* or *Paracoroniceras sp.*, found 10.85 m above the Langport Member, could indicate beds in the lower part of the *semicostatum* Zone. The zone is also present

above the Langport Member in Sarsden No.3 Well [28075 20744] (Figure 47).

The only other cores from the Lower Lias were drilled at the horizons of the three major geophysical marker horizons. The '70 marker' is the most important of these, being up to 2 m thick (Horton and Poole, 1977). It consists of interbedded argillaceous micritic limestones with marls and calcareous mudstones. The beds contain much shell debris and various fossils including burrowing forms. The underlying beds consist of a rhythmic alternation of pale grey calcareous mudstone with a basal shell layer and mottled fissile bituminous mudstone. Similar but much less fossiliferous beds overlie the '70 marker'. The '70 marker' lies within the *brevispina* Subzone of the *jamesoni* Zone; the immediately underlying beds at Upton and Steeple Aston belong to the *Phricodoceras taylori* Subzone, the upper limit of which is provisionally drawn at the base of the marker.

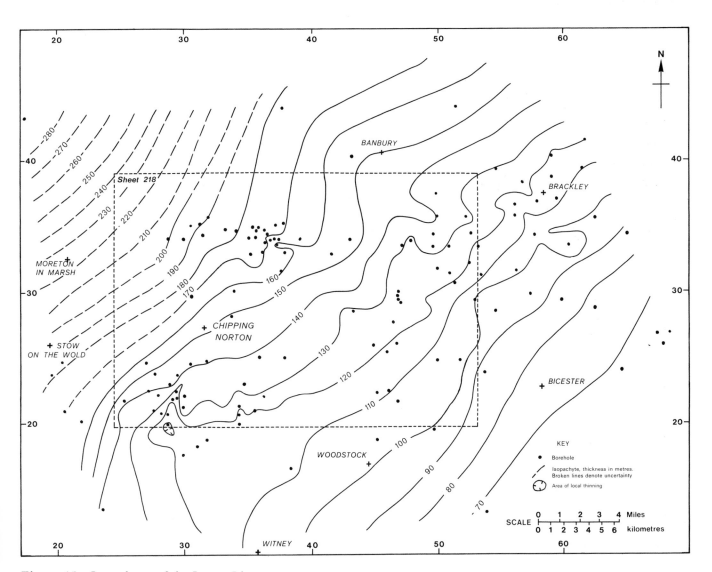

Figure 15 Isopachytes of the Lower Lias

Figure 16 Correlation of the Lias showing progressive onlap of the Lower Lias onto the Langport Member and Twyford Beds. Correlation based on gamma logs

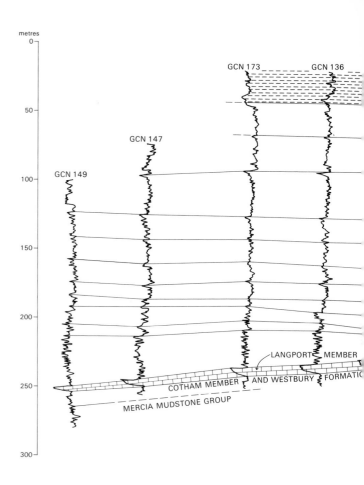

Above the '85 marker'

These measures form the surface of the low-lying ground of the Vale of Moreton and also occur in the north-western part of the district between Little Compton [265 303], Tidmington [260 383], Stourton [298 368] and Long Compton [290 330]. Farther south, the beds crop out in the valley of the River Evenlode and its tributaries, and eastwards they have an extensive outcrop south of the Barford faults between Swerford Heath [390 315] and the Cherwell Valley. The outcrop also extends northwards along the Cherwell Valley into the Banbury area, and along its tributary, the Sor Brook, to near Broughton [419 385].

Only the uppermost 50 m or so of the Lower Lias crop out within the district. These beds, which probably extend down to a horizon just below the '85 marker' in the *Tragophylloceras ibex* Zone, consist almost entirely of medium grey, finely micaceous mudstones which weather to pale bluish grey and brown mottled clay. Exposures are rare, and usually occur within the zone of surface weathering (3–4 m) in which most of the fossils and the mudstone structures are destroyed. Thin beds of limestone crop out locally, including the '85' and possibly the '100 marker'.

The '85 marker' comprises interbedded calcareous mudstones and argillaceous limestones. It is richly fossiliferous and shows evidence of rhythmic sedimentation. The idealised unit starts above a slight erosion surface overlain by a band of coarse well rounded shell debris with thick-walled shells. The proportion of shell debris decreases upward, burrowing bivalves appear and the lithology passes upward into a smooth *Chondrites*-mottled mudstone. The rhythm reflects a phase of decreasing current activity. The beds below the '85 marker' are medium grey slightly micaceous mudstones with small calcareous and ironstone nodules, whilst the beds above are medium to dark grey silty micaceous mudstones with a few thin silt partings. The '85 marker' lies near the top of the *Acanthopleuroceras valdani* Subzone of the *ibex* Zone (Horton and Poole, 1977). It is overlain by beds of *Beaniceras luridum* Subzone age.

The '100 marker', proved in boreholes, consists of up to 1 m of very fossiliferous mudstones, marls and argillaceous limestones. These beds commonly contain a high proportion of shell debris, which may be cross-stratified, and ferruginous nodules and impregnations. Derived phosphatic pebbles occur above a non-sequence which is marked by ferruginous grains and nodules and scattered shells, and is succeeded by pale to medium grey, poorly fossiliferous, silty

mudstones. The '100 marker' probably lies within the lower part of the *Prodactylioceras davoei* Zone, the widespread nonsequence at its base being taken as the top of the *luridum* Subzone of the *ibex* Zone (Horton and Poole, 1977). AH

The '85 marker' forms a prominent bench around Brailes Hill [295 387] at about 30 m below the arbitary line taken as the base of the Middle Lias. At Whichford [312 345] the feature is about 10 to 15 m below the Middle Lias, in the area south of the Barford faults it is about 15 m and in the valleys south-west of Chipping Norton only 3 to 6 m. Borehole evidence in the Whichford area suggests that the horizon mapped as the base of the Middle Lias may be the '100 marker'; it is probable, therefore, that the 'Middle Lias' of the district includes, in places, some silty mudstones of the *davoei* Zone. The '85 and 100 markers' also crop out in the Sarsden area between Bledington [247 226] and Sarsden [287 230]. AH, EGP

Details

Burmington – Barton – Stourton

In this area, much of the Lower Lias is concealed by drift deposits and exposures are uncommon. In Knee Brook [2488 3765], 275 m south-east of High Furze, 1.2 m of brown alluvial pebbly clay

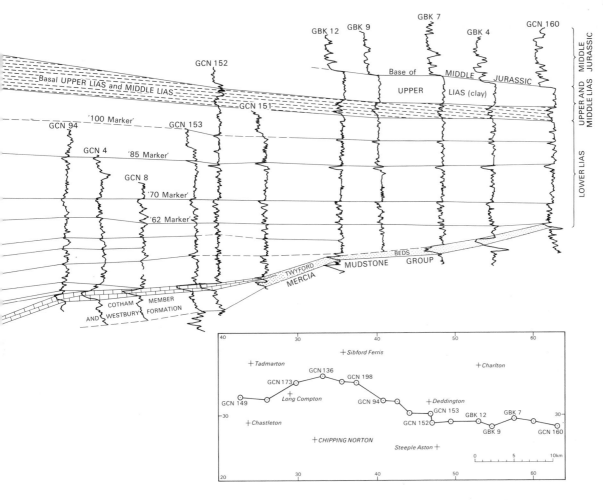

overlie 0.6 m of brown-weathered Lower Lias clay, and similar exposures occur in the banks of the small stream west of Great Wolford. Weathered Lower Lias clay was seen beneath boulder clay in the ancient earthworks east of Great Wolford village, and beneath brown alluvial clay in Nethercote Brook [2657 3336], SSE of Pepperwell Farm. In a borehole 794 m east of the farm, Lower Lias clays and mudstones were proved beneath 6.1 m of glacial drift to a depth of 45.7 m.

The best section in this area was noted south of Neakings in the north bank of a small brook [2700 3068], where 3.05 m of brown-weathering clayey shales overlie a 15 cm band of hard grey splintery cementstone. These beds are probably within 3.0 m of the base of the Middle Lias Silts and Clays.

To the north-east there are scattered exposures of Lower Lias clay in the banks and bed of the River Stour upstream from Mitford Bridge where up to 2.4 m of pale bluish grey clay, weathering dark grey, are visible beneath gravel and alluvial clay. The Lower Lias clay is well-bedded and contains many small shell fragments. Minor contortions and bedding-plane slickensiding occur within the section and are possibly due to ice action. A bed of small pale grey lenticular cementstone nodules is visible in the lower part of this exposure just above the normal summer water level of the river.   EGP

Around Brailes Hill the Lower Lias consists of flat-lying, bluish grey clay with a very few thin beds of limestone. A small feature about 30 m below the junction with the Middle Lias occurs on the western slopes of Brailes Hill and may mark a thin limestone bed.

To the east of Brailes Hill, clay is exposed in the floors of all the larger valleys.   EAE

Whichford–Long Compton

The village of Whichford is built on a slight bench produced by a thin, dark grey, argillaceous, oyster-rich limestone which occurs near the top of the Lower Lias. In fields immediately to the south of The Moat, Whichford, fragments of this bed are associated with fine-grained limestone nodules and bluish grey clay. The same horizon was recorded in the vicinity of the Methodist Chapel [3186 3478], where specimens of *Astarte, Camptonectes, Cardinia attenuata, Pseudolimea, Pseudopecten* and indeterminate ammonite fragments were obtained. A temporary section at the roadside immediately to the north of the Moat exposed 1.52 m of bluish grey, slightly micaceous clay with layers of selenite crystals and poorly-preserved fossils. The bed also contains bands of pyritic cementstone masses which weather to brown concentric ironstone nodules. Fossiliferous, micaceous blue clay was seen to a thickness of 0.91 m in a sewer trench [3224 3500] north of Ascott. Similar beds were exposed at several places in the village.

South of Yerdley Barn, the topmost 9.1 m of the Lower Lias consist of blue plastic clay, about 1.22 m of which are exposed in the banks of a stream [3062 3268]. The clay contained crinoid fragments and the bivalves *Mactromya* cf. *arenacea* and *Palaeoneilo galatea.*

Table 1   The Liassic sequence in the Chipping Norton district

Lithostratigraphic Unit	Stage	Ammonite Zone	Subzone
Upper Lias	Toarcian	Later Toarcian zones not present within district	
Local top of Upper Lias			*Catacoeloceras crassum**
		*Hildoceras bifrons**	*Peronoceras fibulatum**
			*Dactylioceras commune**
Cephalopod Limestone Member Fish Beds Member		*Harpoceras falciferum**	*Harpoceras falciferum** *Harpoceras exaratum**
Transition Bed		*Dactylioceras tenuicostatum**	*Dactylioceras semicelatum** (earlier subzones not proved)
Middle Lias Marlstone Rock Bed	Upper Pliensbachian	*Pleuroceras spinatum**	*Pleuroceras hawskerense* *Pleuroceras apyrenum*
			Amaltheus gibbosus
Middle Lias Silts and Clays		*Amaltheus margaritatus**	*Amaltheus subnodosus**
			*Amaltheus stokesi**
Lower Lias	Lower Pliensbachian		*Oistoceras figulinum**
		*Prodactylioceras davoei**	*Aegoceras capricornum**
			*Aegoceras maculatum**
'100 Marker'			*Beaniceras luridum**
'85 Marker'		*Tragophylloceras ibex**	*Acanthopleuroceras valdani**
			Tropidoceras masseanum
'70 Marker'		*Uptonia jamesoni**	*Uptonia jamesoni* *Platypleuroceras brevispina** *Polymorphites polymorphus*[1] *Phricodoceras taylori**
	Upper Sinemurian	*Echioceras raricostatum**	*Paltechioceras aplanatum** *Leptechioceras macdonnelli** *Echioceras raricostatoides** *Crucilobiceras densinodulum**
		*Oxynoticeras oxynotum**	*Oxynoticeras oxynotum** *Oxynoticeras simpsoni*
Local base of Lower Lias		*Asteroceras obtusum**	*Eparietites denotatus* *Asteroceras stellare* *Asteroceras obtusum*
	Lower Sinemurian	*Caenisites turneri**	*Microderoceras birchi* *Caenisites brooki*
		*Arnioceras semicostatum**	*Euagassiceras resupinatum* *Agassiceras scipionianum* *Coroniceras lyra*
		Arietites bucklandi	*Coroniceras rotiforme* *Vermiceras conybeari*
	Hettangian	*Schlotheimia angulata* *Alsatites liasicus* *Psiloceras planorbis*	probably not present within district

*Zones and subzones known to be present
[1]Evidence from other areas indicates that this and the overlying *brevispina* Subzone cannot be adequately separated

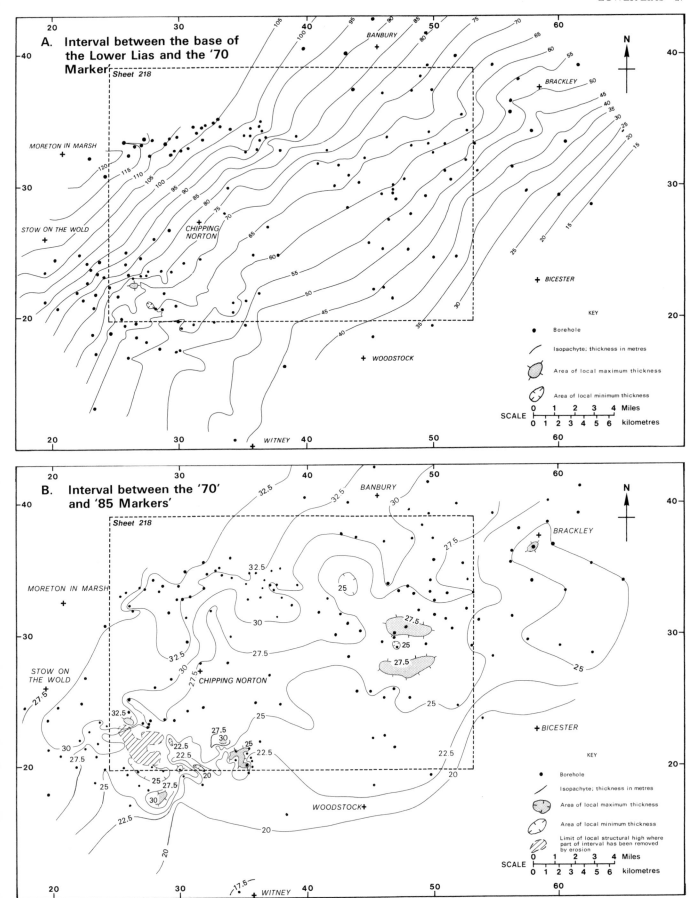

Figure 17 Isopachytes of stratal intervals within the Lower Lias

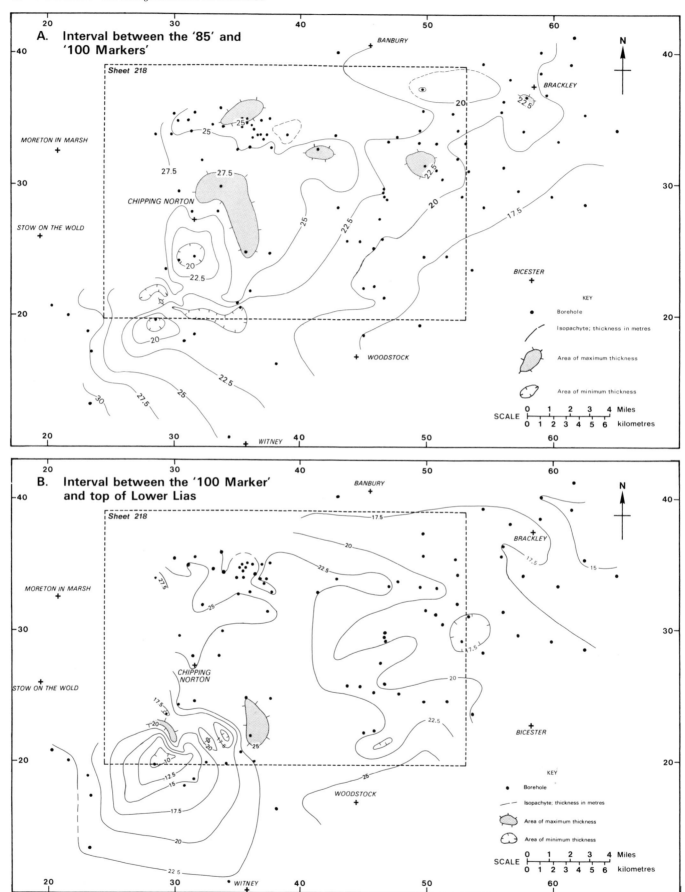

Figure 18   Isopachytes of stratal intervals within the Lower Lias

The following section totalling 7.56 m was recorded in a drainage ditch [3038 3257] situated west-north-west of Coombe Farm:

	Thickness m
Soil	0.30
Clay; bluish grey	1.22
Limestone; grey, weathering brown, shelly, slightly argillaceous, compact	0.10
Clay; grey, weathering to an ochreous clay	0.23
Limestone; grey, shelly, compact	0.18
Clay; bluish grey, partly obscured, with an impersistent band of fossiliferous olive-grey mudstone near the base	1.83
Limestone; dark grey, shelly, thinly bedded	0.03
Clay; grey, silty, ochreous-weathering	0.10
Limestone; olive-green, fine-grained cementstone	0.12
Clay; grey, partly obscured	1.52
Limestone; bluish grey, hard, shelly	0.03
Clay; grey	0.18
Limestone; bluish grey, shelly	0.05
Clay; grey, partly obscured	1.22
Limestone; bluish grey, shelly	0.15
Clay; grey	0.30

About 55 m farther north, beds slightly lower in the sequence are exposed in the same ditch [3037 3263]:

	Thickness m
Clay; grey plastic	0.30
Limestone; dully grey, silty, friable	0.13
Limestone; grey-hearted, massive, very fossiliferous, passes into	0.33
Limestone; grey, ochreous, silty, passes into	0.08
Mudstone; grey, weathering yellow, silty, calcareous	0.03
Limestone; olive-green, hard, shelly, impersistent	0.08
Clay; bluish grey	0.15

Both sections probably lie within the '85 marker'.

Kingham

A section in the eastern bank of the River Evenlode 2030 m north-west of St. Andrew's Church, Kingham, showed pebbly greyish brown clay (First Terrace), 2.1 m, overlying grey micaceous mudstone, 0.91 m. The present course of the Evenlode is controlled by a ridge, up to 3.05 m above the Alluvium, produced by the outcrop of a thin bed of argillaceous shelly limestone. This feature extends southwards from Bledington Heath to a patch of boulder clay lying to the north of Bledington village. A similar bed, but at a slightly higher level, produces a faint bench near a wind pump south of St. Leonard's Church, Bledington. A steep slope to the north, falling to the Westcote Brook, consists of heavy clay with limestone nodules. A borehole at Beckley House, Bledington [2433 2267], proved 61 m of Lower Lias, and another at the Station Garage, Kingham [c. 2564 2267], proved 21.6 m of Lower Lias consisting mainly of clay with two 0.91 m limestone bands at depths of 15.24 m and 17.98 m respectively. In both these boreholes the water was saline. In the vicinity of Kingham Station, downwashed pebbly loam appears to fill small pockets in the tenacious bluish grey Lower Lias clay. Around Kingham village the Lower Lias outcrop occurs on the lower part of the slope and exposures are few, with seepage from the overlying superficial deposits producing a belt of marshy pasture land. A temporary exposure [2579 2339] south of St. Andrew's Church, Kingham, was in 0.91 m of grey clay with small ironstone nodules. A flooded clay pit, 550 m north-

east of Rynehill Farm, once worked the Lower Lias but sections are no longer visible.   AH

In The Gas Council GS 5 Borehole [2688 2456] 1.2 km north-east of Kingham Church, Lower Lias clays with cementstone bands were proved to a depth of 108.81 m, and in the GS 25 Borehole [2791 2605], sited in the valley 0.5 km east of Hill Farm, almost the full thickness of the Lower Lias in the area was penetrated.   EGP

Foscot – Bruern

Deep weathering associated with solifluction of the superficial deposits has restricted the exposure of the Lower Lias in this area. Bluish grey clay with fine-grained grey limestone nodules was exposed during extensions to a cottage and stock yard [2430 2085] at Bould.

The Gas Council GS 26 Borehole [2429 2078] just south of Bould proved 112.47 m of Lower Lias, indicating a total thickness of approximately 128 m locally.

An exposure on the eastern side of the lane [2593 2640] west of Bruern Abbey showed 0.91 m of yellowish brown clay with quartzite pebbles (soliflucted boulder clay in part) resting on 0.61 m of ochreous-mottled, bluish grey clay. A borehole south-west of the road near the western extremity of Bould Wood [2599 1987] proved 2.1 m of boulder clay on 52.7 m of Lower Lias.

The Gas Council GS 10 Borehole [2630 2046] situated a little west of Bruern Abbey proved 91.44 m of Lower Lias.

Lyneham A grey, argillaceous, shelly limestone with associated nodular fine-grained limestone (cementstone) bands produces a distinct feature on the eastern side of Sars Brook, to the west-south-west of Sarsden House, whence it can be traced to near The Norrells [2816 2207]. These beds probably form part of the '85 marker'.

The Gas Council GS 24 Borehole [2844 2247], south-west of Sarsden House, proved the total thickness of the Lower Lias to be 97.84 m locally.

The outcrop of the Lower Lias south of Sarsden Lodge is largely obscured by small irregular patches of silty pebbly clay up to 0.6 m thick. Silty bluish grey clay with limestone nodules was seen ploughed in several places north of Lyneham. Fragments of dull grey fine-grained shelly limestone associated with bluish grey clay were seen in a ditch [2803 1982] east-north-east of All Angels Church, Lyneham.

Chipping Norton

Blue shales which contained 'fine specimens of *Ammonites capricornus, A. davoei, A. fimbriatus*' (i.e *davoei* Zone) were recorded during the excavation of the tunnel west of Chipping Norton on the Kingham to Banbury branch railway (Beesley, 1877, p.181). A temporary section [3055 2668] east of the Tweed Manufactory, Chipping Norton, showed 0.61 m of grey, slightly silty clay with a few fine-grained limestone nodules.

Bluish grey clay with a thin shelly limestone band and scattered small fine-grained limestone nodules was exposed in a drainage ditch [2778 2523] east-south-east of Churchill Grounds Farm. To the north-east, beds of similar character, but slightly thicker, produce a bench-like feature. These beds probably belong to the '85 marker'.   AH

Evenlode Valley south of Chadlington

The valley of the River Evenlode south of Chadlington is floored by Lower Lias clay. The formation is completely obscured by Alluvium and terrace gravels. The Gas Council GS 12 Borehole [3268 2130], south-south-east of Brookend, Chadlington, started in Lower Lias and proved 98.75 m of clay with cementstone bands. The total thickness of the Lower Lias here is thought to be about 107 m.

Swerford Heath – Nether Worton

The Lower Lias crops out in the area surrounding, and to the east of, the Marlstone plateau of Swerford Heath and Iron Down. Exposures are extremely rare in this low-lying heavy pasture land. In the banks of a small pond [4178 3232] south of Buttermilk Farm, 0.91 m of brown-weathering, bluish grey clay is exposed. In a stream bank [4127 3014], west of the church at Nether Worton, 0.61 m of silty stony alluvial clay rests on 0.61 m of blue Liassic clay. A short distance downstream, at 640 m W 15° N of Nether Worton church, 0.91 m of blue clay with greyish brown cementstone nodules is overlain by 0.30 m of grey shelly limestone, and that in turn by 0.91 m of silty stony alluvial clay.

Bodicote – Adderbury – King's Sutton

The Lower Lias occurs in the bottom of the valley of the Sor Brook, and in its tributary valley. No noteworthy sections exist.

Nether Worton – Deddington – Somerton

A slight feature occurs in the Lower Lias at a level about 15 m below the base of the Middle Lias to the west and north of Steepness Hill [435 317]. Field brash indicates that this is due to a cementstone band about 1.5 m thick, probably the '85 marker'.   BJW

Cherwell Valley

In the north-east of the district, dark clays of the upper part of the Lower Lias form outcrops of various widths along the lower slopes of the valley as far south as the Dane Hill Fault which crosses the valley in a SW–NE direction near Souldern Wharf. The upper limit of these clays is marked by scattered springs and by surface seepages or wet areas covered by strong tufts of sedge grass due to water draining from the more porous basal silty clays of the overlying Middle Lias. Crops and pasture are generally poor and ill-drained in these areas, though even a thin layer of overlying hill wash commonly makes the ground more workable. According to Woodward (1893, pp.162), old brick pits 230 m north-west of Aynho Station showed blue and brown clays with ironstone nodules, though no fossils are recorded.   VW

MIDDLE LIAS

The Middle Lias occurs throughout the district and comprises the Middle Lias Silts and Clays and the Marlstone Rock Bed. The latter is a hard ferrugimous limestone or ironstone that gives rise to extensive plateaux between Hook Norton, Deddington and Bodicote, which extend northwards into the Banbury district to culminate in the Edge Hill escarpment. Elsewhere the Rock Bed is thinner, and commonly produces a small bench on the steep slope that extends down from the base of the Middle Jurassic to the upper part of the Lower Lias. The Middle Lias, as a whole, shows a progressive south-eastward thinning (Figure 19).

Middle Lias Silts and Clays

The uppermost silts and silty clays of the *Prodactylioceras davoei* Zone of the Lower Lias pass up imperceptibly into the more arenaceous Middle Lias. At this level the sediments are rhythmically interbedded. An ideal rhythm starts with a coarse shell-debris horizon, which may contain glauconite and derived phosphatised ammonite fragments; this rapidly grades up into smooth mudstones. The base of the next unit may be marked by a non-sequence with evidence of erosion and burrowing. Superimposed on these variations is an overall upward increase in the silt and mica content of the mudstones.

In borehole cores, the junction of the Lower and Middle Lias can be drawn readily where there is evidence of non-sequence, marked by derived phosphatised *davoei* Zone ammonites. Several closely spaced non-sequences occur at this level. The one chosen is that which lies closest below the first occurrence of the amaltheid ammonites of the Upper Pliensbachian. In other cases the junction has had to be arbitrarily taken at a less defined horizon. In the field the junction is taken at the change in slope, commonly marked by seepage lines probably at the base of the more permeable silts of the Middle Lias, but possibly locally including some silty beds in the upper part of the *davoei* Zone. The junction probably lies at a lower level than that chosen using geophysical evidence in boreholes.

The Middle Lias Silts and Clays form a steep slope beneath the feature produced by the Marlstone Rock Bed. A number of steep-sided, flat-bottomed, tributary valleys and hollows incise the outcrop. It is probable that these valleys originated by spring-sapping and backward retreat during earlier, wetter and colder climatic phases. The Middle Lias Silts and Clays give rise to a greyish brown loamy soil which supports thickets of gorse and broom in many places.

The Middle Lias Silts and Clays have an estimated maximum outcrop thickness of 30 m in the Long Compton–Whichford area, where a borehole [2980 3390] south-west of Whichford Wood and starting below the Marlstone Rock Bed proved 26.2 m of Middle Lias. At Edge Hill, in the Banbury district, the formation may exceed 45 m in thickness. It thins to the south-east, but superimposed on this regional trend are local variations. Some of these are depositional, but others may be the result of inaccurate estimation of thickness at outcrop due to cambering; for example the unusually thin sequences in the much disturbed outcrops on the high ground east of Lyneham (Figure 19).

The beds are pale to medium grey micaceous silts and silty clays which become more arenaceous upward. Large ferruginous nodules occur throughout, and exhibit a box-ironstone type of weathering in the upper part of the sequence. The coarser beds are distinctly laminated and some show indefinite cross-lamination and shallow channel structures. Shell beds, some with shell debris, occur as bands and lenses, and may have formed by current winnowing (lag conglomerates). Some beds are weakly cemented and thin limestones occur in the upper part of the sequence. Differential cementation results in the formation of nodular limestones and extremely hard rounded concretionary masses up to 3.6 m diameter, such as have been recorded near Heyford railway station. The limestones are sandy bioturbated rocks with irregular wispy bedding, commonly pale grey but weathering to brownish hues. Some of the limestones contain a basal layer of ironstone and phosphatic pebbles. Rocks of this type occur immediately below the Marlstone Rock Bed in the Duns Tew Borehole [4632 2773], and were recorded at outcrop some 6 m below the Rock Bed at Long Compton. In the Whichford area, a leached and oxidised ferruginous siltstone occurs just below the Rock Bed, and a cross-stratified, thinly bedded sandy limestone occurs at a slightly lower level. Three calcareous beds occur near the top of the Middle Lias Silts and Clays near Salford. The highest, some 2 m below the Marlstone Rock Bed, consists of a leached and oxidised ferruginous siltstone packed with internal moulds of fossils. This distinctive band contains many amaltheid ammonites and can be traced from Sarsden to Hook Norton. The limestones in the lower part of the Middle Lias are readily distinguishable from the Marlstone Rock Bed above by their distinct fauna, greater siltiness, lower lime content and paler greenish grey colour when fresh.

The fauna of the Middle Lias Silts and Clays is diverse; it includes bottom-dwelling sessile and burrowing forms as well as free-swimming species. Brachiopods and ammonites are present but bivalves are dominant. The beds are intensively bioturbated; large burrows and the trace fossil *Chondrites sp.* occur throughout.

The Middle Lias Silts and Clays probably lie entirely within the Zone of *Amaltheus margaritatus*. The *Amaltheus gibbosus* Subzone has not been proved, but the underlying *Amaltheus subnodosus* Subzone, extending up to at least 0.84 m below the Marlstone Rock Bed, has been recognised in the Duns Tew Borehole (Appendix 4).   AH

Details

Chastleton area

The silts and clays of the Middle Lias form the lower slopes of the hills trending SW–NE south of Chastleton village. They are rarely seen except in a few temporary excavations due to their easily weathered nature, but many springs rise within the formation at the junction of more permeable sandy beds on less porous silts and clays. In the Chastleton area the formation is thought to be about 18 m thick and to thin slightly southwards into the Kingham area. The Workshops Borehole at Kingham Hill School proved 17.37 m of the formation, mainly consisting of sand and sandstone.

Long Compton

North-eastwards from Chastleton, the Middle Lias Silts and Clays thicken gradually; they are thought to be about 23 m thick at Barton Hill, north of Little Compton [262 317], and up to 30.5 m thick between Barton Hill and Long Compton [290 330], north-east of which the beds thin slightly to about 24.5 m in the vicinity of Traitor's Ford [337 364]. Good exposures are rare, but the base of the Middle Lias is commonly marked by a wet line with springs issuing at intervals.

Beds high in the sequence are seen in a trackside south-east of Redliff Hill Barn [299 334], where 0.15 m of brown, ferruginous, conglomeratic, calcareous sandstone is overlain by 0.43 m of brown, silty mudstone and 0.61 m of brown, sandy conglomeratic ironstone.

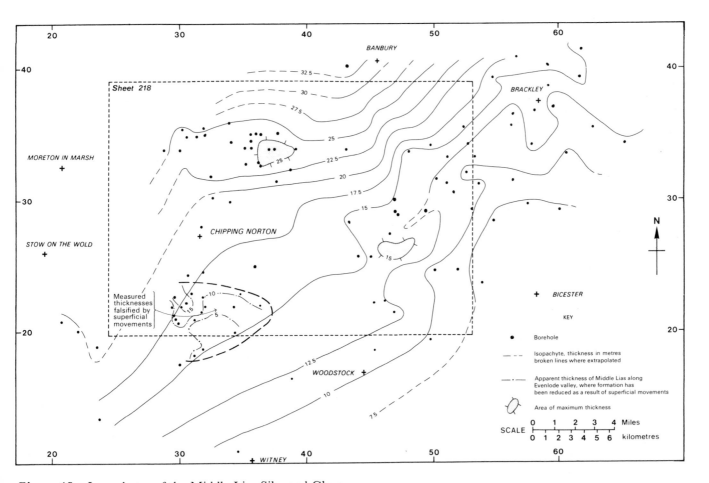

Figure 19   Isopachytes of the Middle Lias Silts and Clays

Similar high measures occur in a small stream east of Chinslade Farm [332 370] where bluish grey, silty micaceous clay is overlain by 0.79 m of bluish grey, hard, calcareous, lenticularly-bedded, shelly siltstone (passing laterally into softer, silty micaceous mudstone), then 2.1 m of brown-weathering sandy silt, and 0.91 m of bluish grey, sandy, ferruginous limestone with a small dark conglomeratic limestone bed lie about 6 m below the Marlstone Rock Bed.

Pale grey, silty micaceous clay immediately overlain by the Marlstone Rock Bed is visible in the south bank of the River Stour near a bend 230 m west of Traitor's Ford.   EGP

Northern margin of the district

At Brailes Hill buff-yellow silts and silty clays, commonly micaceous, overlie the Lower Lias and give rise to a seepage line at their base. On the western slopes they contain a few thin bands of limestone and calcareous sandstone. Their outcrop is characterised by gorse and broom. These beds are up to 34 m thick in Brailes Hill, but thin eastwards through 30.5, to 21 m at Holloway Hill, to about 18 m in the valley [405 387] north-west of Fulling Mill Farm, and eventually to 9 to 12 m in the River Cherwell valley.   EAE

Whichford

In this area the outcrop of the Middle Lias produces a very steep bank. South-west of Whichford, the Marlstone Rock Bed forms a plateau attaining 200 m above OD. Cambering of the Marlstone Rock Bed and the feature-producing upper part of the Middle Lias make an accurate estimate of the thickness difficult, but it is thought that the formation is at least 30.5 m thick hereabouts. Pale grey silty micaceous clay and silt lie immediately beneath the Rock Bed and rest upon a decalcified reddish brown ferruginous siltstone up to 0.91 m thick. This overlies several metres of grey silty clay, which in turn rest upon a calcareous siltstone with ferruginous ooliths, locally sufficiently flaggy to be called a tilestone. The remainder of the Middle Lias consists of grey silts and silty clay with a few limestone and siltstone bands; the latter are uncommon in the lower half of the formation. The lower parts of the Middle Lias slope are marked by lines of seepage and irregular hummocky ground. At a trackside [3084 3329] north of Yerdley Barn grey silty clay was augered above 0.61 m of brown ferruginous limestone. In fields [305 319] to the west-north-west of Hill Barn, ploughing revealed silty micaceous shelly limestone up to 0.61 m thick, overlain by about a metre of greenish grey, silty, micaceous clay, and succeeded by the Marlstone Rock Bed. The shelly limestone is pale grey when fresh but weathers to pale brown, and is strongly false-bedded. It produces a much stronger feature than the overlying Marlstone Rock Bed. Hereabouts the Middle Lias is thought to be only 21 to 24.5 m thick but apparently increases to about 30.5 m near Gottenham. The Middle Lias becomes increasingly silty upwards, and this lithological variation causes a large number of springs which, together with the steep furze-clad slope, mark the outcrop to the north. A temporary section at the side of Traitor's Ford Lane [332 348] was in 0.3 m of dark grey limestone overlain by 0.61 m of ferruginous siltstone with grey clay at the top. From field evidence these beds appear to be overlain by about 3 m of clay which includes a thin ferruginous siltstone band. Ploughed land indicates the persistence of these two siltstone bands and the associated grey silts and clays eastward into the Cowpasture area [335 350]. The outcrop of the Middle Lias eastwards from Ascott is notable for the presence of several steep-sided U-shaped tributary valleys, each of which terminates in a steep and abrupt bank. These troughs are floored by Lower Lias and have been produced by spring-sapping from water thrown out at and near the base of the Middle Lias.

Churchill – Lyneham

There are very few exposures in this area. Hard Middle Lias siltstones in the upper part of the sequence together with the thin Marlstone Rock Bed, where present, produce a strong bench, and fragments are common in ploughed fields. The remainder of the Middle Lias crops on the steep slope below and is generally obscured by hillwash. The vertical interval between the siltstones and the Marlstone Rock Bed varies between 0.6 and 1.5 m, the minimum being noted in the valley north of Sarsden Glebe [292 238]. Widening of the road [285 226] south of Sarsden exposed 0.61 m of green clay overlain by grey silty clay, the beds being near the base of the Middle Lias. From Fairgreen Farm southward, fragments of ferruginous siltstone with fossil casts and an overlying grey micaceous silt were seen in several ploughed fields, as well as other ferruginous siltstones which probably occur slightly lower in the succession. In a ditch [2961 2005] west of Pudlicote House a ferruginous silty limestone is overlain by 0.61 m of ferruginous shelly limestone (Marlstone Rock Bed), but nearer Pudlicote House the Rock Bed rests upon 0.6 to 0.9 m of grey silt, which in turn overlies a ferruginous siltstone with a calcareous conglomeratic base. About 2 m lower in the sequence a feature is produced by a dull grey, ochreous brown-weathering, silty limestone. Locally the thickness of the Middle Lias Silts and Clays is thought to be about 18 m.

Salford – Chipping Norton

Finely laminated, pale brown, argillaceous silt, 0.91 m thick, with some hard siltstone fragments, probably lying about 1.8 m beneath the Marlstone Rock Bed, was exposed in a roadside cutting immediately west of the School House, Salford [2899 2813]. A shallow pit, 110 m to the east-north-east, showed 0.3 m of extremely fossiliferous calcareous siltstone overlain by grey argillaceous micaceous silt, the section being about 0.91 m beneath the Marlstone Rock Bed. The siltstone is pale greenish grey, hard and highly calcareous when fresh, but it weathers to a soft, ochreous brown rock, the fossils being represented by casts. This distinctive rock is widespread. A ploughed field 214 m W 19° N of Salford church contained fragments of this bed with *Astarte sp.*, *Bakevellia laevis*, *Camptonectes sp.*, *Protocardia truncata*, *Amberleya sp.*, and *Amaltheus sp.*, overlain by pale grey micaceous silt and the basal Marlstone Rock Bed conglomerate. A borehole [2912 2692] north-north-east of Cornwell Hill Farm proved at least 10 m of Middle Lias. In this area the total thickness is thought to be about 24 m. Scattered exposures along the ridge below Cornwell Hill Farm indicate the presence of at least three distinct calcareous siltstone bands. Ferruginous siltstones crop out at two levels on the valley side east of Salford; one lies about 2 m below the Marlstone Rock Bed and at about 58 m above OD; the other forms a small knoll [2844 2768] at about 143 m above OD, where it is terminated by a branch of the Swerford Fault system. Farther north-east scattered exposures in grey silts and silty clays were seen but there are few exposures along the grass-covered slopes of the valley west of Chipping Norton. A trench in The Leys, Chipping Norton [3085 2678] showed the Marlstone Rock Bed resting on variegated grey silty clay with ferruginous streaks and small nodules. In the tunnel cutting north of Chipping Norton railway station [3022 2779] dark grey micaceous laminated clay is exposed. A ditch section 215 m W 42° N of Chipping Norton church exposes 2.74 m of deeply weathered medium to dark grey micaceous silt, the uppermost part of which was locally a dull grey fossiliferous limestone with *Chlamys sp.*, *Arieticeras nitescens* and *Arieticeras sp. nov.* A temporary section [3142 2783], to the west of the road and south of Over Norton, exposed a ferruginous siltstone like those of the Salford area with *Grammatodon sp.*, *Oxytoma inequivalvis*, *Pseudopecten dentatus* and *Amaltheus sp.*

The Gas Council GS 18 Borehole [3147 2799], in the valley north of Chipping Norton, proved 6.4 m of silty clay, suggesting a total thickness of 18 m for the Middle Lias. About 82 m to the north-east on the eastern side of the road, 0.91 m of ochreous yellow argillaceous silt is overlain by about 1.2 m of ironshot grey clay with small hollow ironstone nodules, which is overlain by 0.91 m of waxy micaceous grey clay.   AH

Evenlode Valley south of Chadlington and Spelsbury

The clays and silts of the Middle Lias occur in two fairly narrow strips, one on each side of the Evenlode Valley. The beds are very poorly exposed, and proved extremely difficult to separate from the Lower Lias, largely due to the presence of spreads of river gravels and Alluvium, but a weak spring-line marks their base south-westwards from Chadlington.   BJW

Heythrop – Enstone

The uppermost part of the Middle Lias is exposed in the north side of a drainage ditch [3731 2841], west of Little Tew church, where at least 0.15 m of soft ochreous-weathering siltstone packed with casts of fossils is overlain by the Marlstone Rock Bed. Exposures are few in the valleys of the River Glyme and its tributaries north of Enstone. The Marlstone Rock Bed forms a strong feature capping the steep, commonly wooded slopes which mark the outcrop of the Middle Lias. The grey silts and clays are frequently seen in the banks of the streams, and blocks of ferruginous siltstone form small crags on the steep valley sides. A thin ferruginous siltstone crops out at stream level [3631 2581] at the bridge south of Heythrop College.

Hook Norton

Scattered small sections in the valley west of Scotland End show the increase in thickness of the siltstone and limestone bands that characterises the upper part of the Middle Lias.

The following section can be seen in the stream banks [3408 3347] south-east of Oatleyhill Farm:

	Thickness m
Clay; grey, silty, micaceous with ferruginous particles, base not seen; apparently resting on	0.91
Siltstone; soft, ochreous, deeply weathered, extremely fossiliferous, the individual fossils now represented by casts	0.99
Section obscured	c.0.30
Limestone; grey, silty, fine-grained, scattered fossils	0.05–0.10
Siltstone; olive-green, micaceous, weathering to soft ochreous silt	c.1.22
Limestone; pale bluish grey, slightly ferruginous, with a dull brown-weathering patina	c.0.91
Siltstone; pale grey, compact, calcareous with ferruginous bands; passing down into	0.10
Silt; bluish grey, micaceous	

At a small waterfall [3416 3355] east-south-east of Oatleyhill Farm, 1.07 m of grey micaceous clay with pot lid concretions and poorly preserved fossils are overlain by 0.84 m of pale bluish grey silty limestone with scattered fossils, the limestone becoming less silty upwards. These beds are about 0.9 m beneath the base of the Marlstone Rock Bed. On the banks of the stream [3420 3362] north-north-east of the above exposure the following section was recorded:

	Thickness m
Siltstone; greyish green, ferruginous, thin to moderately well bedded; weathered to soft micaceous ochreous rock	0.71
Siltstone; grey, very hard, compact, fossiliferous	0.15
Siltstone; greyish green in part, almost completely weathered to friable ochreous silt with ferruginous veins and concretions	0.18
Silt; pale grey, micaceous, argillaceous; scattered fine-grained calcareous concretions	0.61

Grey silty micaceous clay, 1.68 m thick and stratigraphically immediately below this section, was seen 44 m farther south at the junction with the main stream. On the south bank of the stream at Scotland End, a hard ferruginous silty limestone, locally siltstone, produces a distinct feature about 0.9 m beneath the Marlstone Rock Bed. It seems to overlie grey silty clay, which appears to rest on the following beds, seen on the south bank of the stream [3478 3326] adjacent to Hook Norton Brewery:

	Thickness m
Siltstone; dull khaki to green, micaceous, now largely decalcified; at 25 mm from the top a thin band with small regular echinoids was recorded; at 0.84 m from the top a greyish green silt parting is present	1.83
Limestone; greyish green, silty, massive, fossiliferous	0.61
Siltstone; grey, calcareous; very hard and compact in top 0.15 m, decalcified to soft ochreous friable rock below	0.30

About 165 m downstream, on the south bank [3492 3318] and at the same horizon, the following section was visible:

	Thickness m
Soil and subsoil	0.61
Limestone; dark mauve-tinted brown to grey and greyish green, very silty, hard with irregular thin bedding; very fossiliferous; weathering to an ochreous hue in basal 0.05 m	0.20
Siltstone; greyish, micaceous, ferruginous, with scattered fossils; soft and ochreous in top 0.30 m, khaki-tinted grey, weathered to soft ochreous rock below	0.76

Scree obscures the section from this point, but grey micaceous clay is exposed in the stream bed 2.4 m below. A trench dug north along the road from a crossroads [3491 3473], south-east from Fodge Farm, exposed grey silt and silty clay which is faulted against Marlstone Rock Bed near Sixash Farm [3486 3493]. A pit at the crossroads is reported to have passed through 2.4 m of grey silt and siltstone.   AH

Hook Norton – Wigginton

The Middle Lias Silts and Clays floor the three valleys which form the headwaters of one of the tributaries of the River Swere immediately east of Hook Norton, but outcrops are largely obscured by alluvium. In the fault-bounded areas around Cradle House [379 325] and Swerford village [379 311], the base of the overlying Marlstone Rock Bed forms a strong feature, silts and clays being, as usual, infrequently exposed.

Swalcliffe

The clays and silts of the Middle Lias are poorly exposed in a narrow strip running south-eastwards from the village, bounded by the Swalcliffe Fault on the north-east and the Marlstone Rock Bed to the west. A short distance to the south, the Middle Lias comes to the surface again in the floors of three small east–west valleys, reaching an estimated thickness of 11 m in the steep-sided valley [387 370] south-east from Swalcliffe church.

Swerford – Iron Down – Great Tew

Due to the general steepness of the slope, the Middle Lias Silts and Clays have a narrow outcrop around the broad plateau formed by the Marlstone Rock Bed. The base of the formation is marked almost everywhere by a slight change of slope and a prominent spring line.   BJW

On the north bank of the stream [3739 2998] north of The Meetings, 0.61 m of green fossiliferous calcareous siltstone is overlain by the basal conglomerate of the Marlstone Rock Bed. Farther downstream 1.02 m of calcareous siltstone are overlain by 0.91 m of ferruginous limestone, the junction being obscured. In a small quarry [3770 2975] on the south side of the river, 185 m to the south-east, the following section is visible:

	Thickness m
MARLSTONE ROCK BED	
Limestone; green and grey-tinted, ferruginous, with shell-fragmental bands and lenses; scattered fossils	2.15
Section obscured	c.0.10
Limestone; reddish brown, shell-fragmental	0.04
MIDDLE LIAS SILTS AND CLAYS	
Clay; green to dull green, micaceous, with scattered minute yellow ferruginous grains	c.0.18
Mudstone; dark olive-green, micaceous, with ochreous grains scattered throughout, casts of fossils common	0.08
Siltstone; yellowish green, weathering to reddish brown, ferruginous, slightly calcareous, fossiliferous with abundant casts of fossils	0.61

Pipes and gulls of bluish grey Upper Lias clay commonly fill joints and bedding planes.   AH

Broughton – Adderbury – Bloxham

The silts and clays of the Middle Lias crop out on the sides of the valleys of the Sor Brook and its tributary which flows eastwards from Bloxham. Exposures are few but a borehole at Greenhill House [4719 3646], East Adderbury, proved 12.5 m of Middle Lias between the Marlstone Rock Bed and the Lower Lias.

Swere Valley and Barford Trough

Immediately north of the Barford St. John Fault, between Wigginton and the River Cherwell, a narrow strip of Middle Lias Silts and Clays south of the plateau formed by the Marlstone Rock Bed around Milcombe and Milton was proved by several abortive boreholes for ironstone. There are few exposures, but a road cutting [4672 3386] north-east of Bloxham Bridge showed 1.2 m of grey silty clay with thin nodular ferruginous sandstone bands.

Hempton – Deddington

The Middle Lias Silts and Clays border the Deddington outlier, and their base forms a good spring line. In a road cutting [4652 3266] west of Field Barn, 2.44 m of grey sandy clay were seen; 18 m farther south 0.61 m of grey clay rests on 1.2 m of grey silty clay with thin ferruginous highly weathered sandstone ribs.

Great Tew – Cherwell Valley

A good spring line lies at the base of the largely gorse-clad slope of the Middle Lias outcrop between Great Tew and the Dane Hill Fault near Coldharbour Farm.   BJW

Cherwell Valley

The Middle Lias Silts and Clays crop out along both sides of the Cherwell Valley in the eastern part of the district; in the north they form the middle slopes but they gradually fall in height southward. There are now no exposures. During the last century when the railway from Oxford to Banbury was being made these beds were seen in numerous cuttings between Kings Sutton Hill and Upper Heyford. In a cutting 275 m east of King's Sutton Hill about 3.4 m of sandy shales with concretionary blocks resting on laminated blue clays were recorded (Beesley, 1873, p.15). A section was formerly visible in an old pit close to Twyford (Canal) Wharf, 1785 m north-west of King's Sutton church, where about 5.5 m of grey and blue sandy, micaceous clays with a hard calcareous band were recorded by Woodward (1893). These beds are evidently in the lower part of the Middle Lias since Lower Lias clays were proved beneath them (Beesley, 1873; see also de Rance, 1872).

The branch railway from King's Sutton through Chipping Norton to Kingham also revealed some interesting details in a cutting 1.6 km south-east of Adderbury church and just north of the main road to Aynho. Woodward (1893, p.224) recorded 2.75 m of Marlstone Rock Bed on 2.29 m of micaceous sandy and ferruginous beds, on 0.91 m of harder rock with grey sandy nodules at the base and containing various fossils, on 1.22 m of yellow and blue sandy loam. He also recorded about 5.18 m of (predominantly) shales with hard concretionary limestone bands beneath 3.35 m of Marlstone Rock Bed in a trial pit put down in Adderbury Park. Farther south, similar Middle Lias Silts and Clays were exposed in an old brick pit south of Deddington where Woodward (1893, p.225) recorded 9.14 m of beds as follows: 'Brown and pale grey ferruginous and micaceous sands and sandy clays, with indurated calcareous brown and grey shelly sandstone in places, 10 ft; on blue sandy micaceous clay, passing down into blue micaceous and calcareous clay with cementstones and septarian nodules 20 ft'.

Buff and grey silty clays are seen in the east bank of the shallow railway cutting adjoining Souldern Wharf and in a railway cutting 1325 m north of Somerton church. About 2.4 km south of Somerton the railway runs in a cutting in the Middle Lias Silts and Clays on the west bank of the river before reaching Heyford station. When this cutting was made, Woodward (1893) noted the presence in these beds of roundish flattened, exceedingly hard, concretions 10 to 12 ft (3 to 3.6 m) in diameter.   VW

Marlstone Rock Bed

The Middle Lias Silts and Clays are abruptly succeeded by the Marlstone Rock Bed, a hard massive limestone, blue- or green-centred when fresh but readily weathered to a rich brown and reddish brown hue (Plate 2). In some areas the limestones are sufficiently ferruginous to have been exploited as an ore. At outcrop the bed gives rise to a reddish brown loamy brash which can be readily distinguished from the clay soils of the basal Upper Lias.

The Rock Bed contains two main facies; chamositic sideritic oolith- and shell-fragmental limestones, and thinner more sideritic, sandy limestones that may be more marginal in origin. Both facies are usually well stratified and well sorted, and usually cross-bedded. Thin chamositic mudstone partings and lenticular beds or iron-deficient shelly limestones are locally present. The main facies are arbitrarily separated on the basis of their iron content. The former constitutes the economic ore, the Banbury Ironstone; the latter facies somewhat resembles that of the local Northampton Sand which has a similar marginal relationship to the Northampton Sand Ironstone.

In detail there are rapid changes in lithology, both vertically and horizontally, and thus no constant succession. There are, however, two minor beds that persist over wide areas. At the base, and overlying a non-sequence that has been recorded from Dorset to the Humber, there is a generally persistant conglomeratic band, up to 0.3 m thick, consisting of tabular pebbles of more or less phosphatic or ferruginous limestone and mudstone, ranging in size from small grains up to fragments 0.15 m in diameter; rolled belemnites, shells and rare worn corals; set in a sandy shell-debris ferruginous matrix. Some pebbles show lithophagid-type borings. At the top of the formation is a distinctive hard greenish oolitic limestone up to 0.2 m thick. This bed, which may form part of the Transition Bed (p.42), was thought to be generally absent west of the Cherwell valley, though

similar beds have been recorded at the same level in quarries near East Adderbury and Lower Brailes (Whitehead and others, 1952, p.60). These authors considered that they formed by penecontemporaneous reworking of the unconsolidated uppermost part of the Marlstone.

The Rock Bed has been described in detail by Whitehead and others (1952, pp.140–201), and its petrography in the northern (Banbury) part of the Marlstone ironstone field has been dealt with by Edmonds (Edmonds and others, 1965, pp.62–82). In the Chipping Norton district the most ferruginous strata are chamosite-oolites with varying proportions of shell debris (Appendix 3).

The outcrop is extensively cambered, and thickness estimates based on it can be unreliable. The isopachyte map (Figure 20) has drawn on borehole data, surface exposures and estimated outcrop thicknesses. It shows an area of maximum thickness extending northwards and north-eastwards from Swerford Heath to Swalcliffe and Broughton, and thence through Shutford to Edge Hill in the Banbury district (Whitehead and others, 1952, fig. 20). The thickest local development, 7.6 m, has been recorded north-west of Bloxham. From there the formation thins rapidly eastward and westward, and more gradually to the south.

Plate 2 Redlands Quarry, Hook Norton [360 347]. Marlstone Rock Bed overlain by Upper Lias Fish Beds Member with clay and fissile limestones (A 9817)

Pringle (*in* Lamplugh and others, 1920, p.120) suggested that the north-eastward attentuation of the Rock Bed results from lateral passage of the basal beds into the sandy micaceous clays and thin limestones of the highest Middle Lias of Northamptonshire, but this view is no longer tenable since it is now appreciated that there is a widespread discontinuity, marked by an erosion surface, at the base of the Marlstone Rock Bed. On a broader scale Whitehead and others (1952, p.150) attempted to relate the area of maximum development of the Marlstone Rock Bed to the positions of axes of uplift along which movement occurred during Liassic times, axes that might have produced shoals, which may have produced the special conditions under which the ironstone was deposited (Cayeux, 1922, p.934; Whitehead and others, 1952, pp.150–151, p.164). Similarly Edmonds (*in* Edmonds and others, 1965, p.40) has suggested that the thinning of the Rock Bed to the west and east may have been related respectively to the Vale of Moreton Axis and the London Platform. He also suggested that some of the thinning may result from pre-Upper Lias erosion, pointing to the presence of a conglomerate locally at the base of the Upper Lias in a railway cutting [438 419] in the Banbury district, and it is notable that the Marlstone is represented only by a thin conglomerate at the base of the Upper Lias in the Apley Barn Borehole (Poole, 1969, p.8). However, this horizon and some intraformational conglomerates recorded from the Marlstone in the Banbury district are not laterally persistent, while the thickness variations are more complex than the above theories alone would predict. It now seems more likely that the Middle Lias was deposited at a time of progressive lowering of the sea level, presumably resulting in a widespread regression. By 'Marlstone Rock Bed times' a generally shallow-water environment probably extended from the London Platform to the Severn Basin, irrespective of the position of positive axes. It seems likely that the Marlstone Rock Bed accumulated in several small interconnecting basins, and that variations in its thickness are largely depositional. The areas of good-quality ironstone tend to coincide with the maximum thickness of the member.

Weathering is extremely important in controlling the value of the Rock Bed as an ore. The apparently recent weathering by oxygenated ground water involves the oxidation of chamosite and siderite to the hydrated iron oxide limonite and the leaching of carbonate. The most heavily limonitised material contains higher proportions of iron, silica and alumina, and less lime, than the fresh chamosite-siderite rock (Whitehead and others, 1952, pp.167–168). The most deeply weathered zone lies at outcrop; alteration decreases down-dip under the Upper Lias mudstones. At depth the movement of ground water is controlled by joints, fissures and bedding planes, many of which may have been opened by superficial movements. Thus in the lower parts of the Rock Bed, oxidation has penetrated downwards and inwards, and many joint blocks have hard unweathered cores. In the upper beds this form of weathering results in the production of box-ironstone structures and the deposition of secondary limonite veins. The massive shelly calcareous beds are the least oxidised. The overall result is that the exploitable ore lies on the exposed plateaus; with increasing overburden the degree of oxidation decreases and exploitation becomes uneconomic.

The fauna of the Marlstone Rock Bed is dominated by brachiopods and bivalves. Fragments of crinoids abound locally and indistinct cylindrical burrows occur throughout.

Figure 20
Isopachytes of the Marlstone Rock Bed

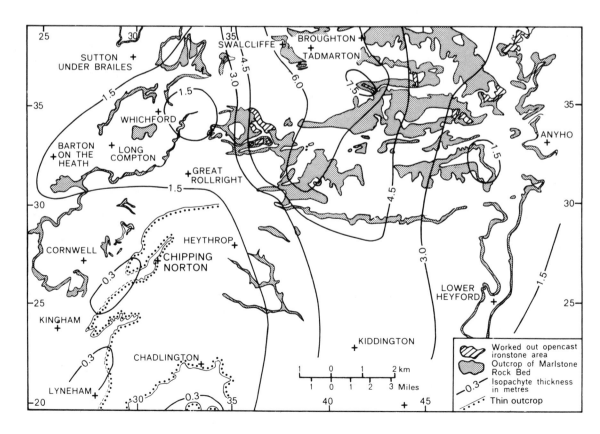

Most of the fauna are sessile bottom-dwellers, which colonised the sea floor during quiescent intervals. Burrowing bivalves are scarce, possibly because the shifting oolith sands of more turbulent phases provided unsuitable habitats. The Marlstone Rock Bed is thought to lie essentially within the zone of *Pleuroceras spinatum*. The zonal index fossil is rare, but one was found in Redlands Quarry, Hook Norton [362 347] and also a *Pleuroceras* cf. *solare* in the railway cutting north of Aynho Station. The presence of dactylioceratid ammmonites in the highest part of the Rock Bed indicates that the unit extends into the overlying *Dactylioceras tenuicostatum* Zone of the Toarcian (Howarth, 1973; see also Appendix 1(2)).　　AH

Details

Chastleton

South of Chastleton, the Marlstone Rock Bed caps the hilltop extending westwards from Peasewell Wood [249 287]. Old workings in the western part of the wood, which probably supplied local building stone, reveal up to 1.8 m of rubbly ironstone, almost certainly the full thickness of the formation hereabouts. Southwards towards Daylesford [244 259] the bed forms a prominent feature up to 1.8 m high.

Small digs showing up to 1.22 m of ironstone are visible immediately north-west of Slade Farm [262 259]. This farm stands on a north-east-trending anticline, the axis of which is visible in the Marlstone Rock Bed 365 m north-east of the farm. In the Workshops Borehole [2679 2615] at Kingham Hill School, the Marlstone Rock Bed is thought to be 2.21 m thick.

Long Compton

North-eastwards from Chastleton, the bed makes a well defined feature up to 1.2 m high with much ironstone brash on the hillside south of Little Compton [265 300]. To the north of this village, it caps the cambered plateau of Barton Hill where it is estimated to be about 2.4 m thick. Old workings, from which the stone was probably won for local building materials, occur at the side of the road 190 m and 660 m south of Barton Hill Farm [263 317], but these are now mostly obscured. Hull (1857, p.20) thought that the bed hereabouts was probably up to 3.7 m thick but it would seem more likely that the apparent increase in thickness is due to cambering (Figure 38).

Eastwards towards Long Compton, the bed is probably nowhere more than 1.8 m thick. At the top of a bank [2790 3179] west of The Hollow, Long Compton, the following section is visible:

	Thickness m
Upper Lias	
Limestone; cream, flaggy	0.05
Clay; grey, soft	0.25
Middle Lias	
Marlstone Rock Bed	
Ironstone; brown, flaggy in upper part becoming massive with depth	1.52
Middle Lias Silts and Clays	
Clay; greyish brown, soft	0.08

Farther east in a small exposure [2911 3128] south of The Hollow, a massive post of sandy brown-weathering ironstone 1.05 m thick is exposed below a spring which presumably issues from the basal Upper Lias limestones and flaggy Marlstone Rock Bed noted in the preceding section.

To the north of Long Compton, the Marlstone Rock Bed is traceable along the northern slopes of Harrow Hill and Stourton Hill where it is probably about 1.5 m thick. On the hillside south of North Leasow [315 359] the bed apparently consists of only one band of conglomeratic ironstone 0.61 m thick, but thickens again eastwards and in the south bank of the River Stour [336 364] it consists of massive brown ironstone 1.8 m thick. The westernmost exposures seen at the bend in the Stour here are almost horizontal, but 37 m to the east the beds dip at 40° to the south under the influence of the Stour Valley Fault.

Between Traitor's Ford, Chinslade Farm and Combslade, the Marlstone Rock Bed forms a large dissected plateau; it may be 2.4 m thick but there are no exposures. On the west bank of the road near Traitor's Ford [3365 3636], 0.91 m of brown-weathering, bluish grey-hearted, sandy, shelly ironstone rests on greyish green, sandy, micaceous clay. These beds dip S17°W at 50° due to the proximity of the Stour Valley Fault (Figure 3). To the north-east of Traitor's Ford, the Marlstone Rock Bed crops out in a limited area west of Sibford Ferris, and a good section dipping S24°W at 5° is seen in the south-west bank of a stream [3461 3737] west of The Colony:

	Thickness m
Alluvium	
Clay; reddish brown with ironstone fragments	1.52
Middle Lias	
Marlstone Rock Bed	
Ironstone; reddish brown, rather flaggy and rubbly weathering, with large rhynchonellids	1.22
Middle Lias Silts and Clays	
Clay; greyish brown, silty and micaceous	0.30

Up to 0.91 m of ironstone is exposed in the north-west bank of a small stream immediately opposite The Colony; the bed in this area is thought nowhere to exceed 3.05 m.　　EGP

Brailes Hill

The Marlstone Rock Bed on Brailes Hill comprises 1.5 m of sandy ferruginous oolite. It thickens and becomes less sandy and more ferruginous eastwards, and is 3.6 to 4.6 m thick to the north of Tyne Hill.

An old quarry [382 389] in a faulted inlier 0.4 km west of Tadmarton Hill shows:

	Thickness m
Limestone; bedded, shelly, calcitic, limonitic chamosite-oolite	0.43
Ironstone; bedded, porous, oolitic showing box-structure; locally of shelly, sideritic, calcitic chamosite-limonite-siderite-oolite but much oxidised to limonitic limonite-chamosite-oolite	1.04
Limestone; thicker-bedded oolite with streaks of limonite and shelly patches; locally of highly calcitic chamosite-oolite	0.91

A quarry section [386 386], west-north-west of Lower Lea Farm, exposes:

	Thickness m
Ironstone; bedded, calcitic, limonitic, chamosite-oolite with limonite streaks and local shelly bands of calcitic chamosite-limonite-oolite	0.74
Ironstone; massive and thickly bedded, blue-hearted calcitic siderite-chamosite-oolite with limonite streaks; locally shelly	1.14

Adjoining Upper Lea Farm [391 389] is a small quarry:

	Thickness m
Ironstone; bedded, limonitic chamosite-oolite with limonite streaks and some calcareous bands; locally shelly	1.22
Ironstone; thicker-bedded, green-hearted, limonitic, chamositic limonite-oolite with limonite streaks and box-structure; locally a calcitic chamosite-limonite-oolite	0.91
Ironstone; thickly bedded and massive limonitic chamosite-siderite-oolite with limonite streaks; shells locally	0.74

A quarry [394 383] east-south-east of Lower Lea Farm is much overgrown; it contains about 5.5 m of ironstone, the joints within which trend E–W. Trial holes about 0.8 km east of these last two sections proved up to 5 m of Marlstone Rock Bed.

Some 2 to 2.7 m of ironstone are exposed in the roadsides at Broughton [420 384] and about 2.5 m in an old quarry at the nearby alms-houses [422 383].   EAE

Swalcliffe

The greater part of the village stands on the Marlstone Rock Bed, the only exposure being in an old quarry [3804 3794] east of the church. South of here the ironstone forms a slightly undulating area between two faults, with three separate small strongly cambered outliers immediately to the south, which contain scattered old pits. A trackside exposure [3898 3706] shows 1.83 m of flaggy highly-jointed ironstone resting on 1.83 m of more massive weathered ironstone. Cambering and the proximity of the Sibford Fault have caused the high and variable dips seen in the slickensided jointed flaggy ironstone in old pits on the southernmost inlier.   BJW

Whichford

Up to 0.91 m of ironstone caps the hill south of Whichford Wood. Extensive cambering, probably associated with dip-and-strike faulting, causes Middle Lias silts to be exposed near the summit on the west and central parts of the ridge. Eastward and north-eastward from The Hollow, the Marlstone Rock Bed has a narrow sinuous outcrop, expanding locally to cap small spurs on the sides of the valley. A well [3058 3163] dug during 1959 is said to have penetrated 3.05 m of Upper Lias clay with limestones, resting on 2.44 m of 'rock' (the Marlstone Rock Bed and some Middle Lias siltstone), and 17.37 m of silty shale, with a 0.61-m band of hard limestone at the base. A ditch section [3079 3191] west of Hill Barn showed the Marlstone Rock Bed to be affected by dip-and-fault structures; three normal faults with downthrows to the north of between 0.6 m and 1.5 m were seen within 32 m, the rocks dipping to the south at between 10° and 30°. The section shows pale fawn, thinly-bedded siltstone overlain by about 0.91 m of pale greenish grey micaceous clay, and the basal conglomerate of the Marlstone Rock Bed which consists of green and fawn, highly rounded, platy, argillaceous cementstone pebbles up to 8 cm in diameter, set in a green-hued ferruginous-calcareous matrix. The Marlstone Rock Bed is about 1.2 m thick and consists of coarse ferruginous limestone with a thin coarse crinoidal almost non-ferruginous band at the top. It is overlain by the Cephalopod Limestones of the Upper Lias. To the north near Gottenham the thickness of the Rock Bed increases to 1.8 m, but decreases to about 0.9 m immediately to the west of the Traitor's Ford lane, where it consists of grey fossiliferous crinoidal limestone with a very low iron content. West of the lane, in the Cowpasture area, no trace of the ironstone is visible except in a small ditch [3360 3445] north-east of Oatleyhill Farm, where

0.30 m of grey clay with ferruginous nodules rests upon 0.15 m of decalcified reddish brown rock and 0.15 m of grey silty clay. The outcrop is terminated by a small E–W fault.

Salford – Little Rollright

Several faulted outcrops occur near Salford. The Marlstone Rock Bed, thought to be about 0.9 to 1.2 m thick, forms strong features on both sides of the valley west of Salford church. Reddish brown ironstone brash and the basal conglomerate can be readily recognised. The Rock Bed was reached in a 1.8 m pit at the School House, Salford [2898 2805]. Excavations during 1959 for the new Village Hall revealed 0.61 m of deeply-weathered ironstone overlain by Upper Lias clay with poorly-preserved ammonites. The Marlstone Rock Bed hereabouts is a good ironstone about 1.5 to 1.8 m thick. It produces a strong feature on both sides of the valley south of Little Rollright church.

No trace of the Rock Bed were seen in the vicinity of The Common, to the west of Chipping Norton, and it is very thin, possibly absent, south of The Common. It thickens rapidly to the north and east, being at least 1.5 m thick in the Worcester Road Cemetery, and 1.2 m of decalcified ironstone were seen in a temporary section in The Leys [3086 2667]. A ditch north-west of Chipping Norton church is dug through 1.5 m of poor quality ironstone and 1.8 m of deeply-weathered ironstone were seen in a temporary section at Ash Pollard [3143 2782]. To the north of the A44 at least 0.91 m of ferruginous limestone is present. The Marlstone Rock Bed thickens to the north-east and produces a strong feature with much ferruginous oolitic and shell-fragmental limestone brash. From this brash crinoid fragments, *Gibbirhynchia muirwoodae*, *Lobothyris punctata*, *Tetrarhynchia tetrahedra*, *Camptonectes* cf. *mundus*, *Liostrea sp.*, *Plicatula spinosa*, *Pseudopecten dentatus* and indeterminate belemnites were collected. Small faulted outcrops including the basal conglomerate occur within the Salford–Swerford Fault Trough (Figure 3) north of Hull Farm.

East of Walk Farm the Marlstone Rock Bed crops out in a narrow trough and is thought to be 1.8 m thick.

Churchill – Lyneham

In fields to the south-west of The Mount, the Marlstone Rock Bed is about 0.9 m thick and forms a distinct bench but thins northwards. It is about 0.6 m thick near the ruined church [2791 2445] at Churchill where it consists entirely of ferruginous pebbly oolitic limestone. To the north of the road to Sarsden Halt, the thickness is further reduced, and the Rock Bed is probably absent locally. In a ploughed field, 410 m north-east of Churchill Grounds Farm, at least 0.15 m of ironstone was seen. North-eastward there is no further trace of the bed except for a few fragments noted in a field east of Meads Farm [2985 2629].

South of Churchill the Marlstone Rock Bed is at least 0.6 m thick and can be traced along its outcrop along the northern side of Sars Brook valley. To the east of Churchill it is thought to be about 0.3–0.6 m thick. Its thickness is no more than 0.3 m near Sarsden Glebe, and it is absent farther south, though the boundary between the Middle and Upper Lias can be readily traced. A very thin silty ferruginous limestone lies at the horizon of the Rock Bed near Merriscourt Farm. The Bed is also seen in a ploughed field [2817 1943] south-east of Tithe Farm, Lyneham, where it is represented by about 0.3 m of ferruginous oolitic conglomerate which lies beneath the Upper Lias clay. Near Starveall [2817 1922], in the adjacent Witney district, about 0.6 m of ferruginous limestone is present.

Hook Norton – Swerford

In a stream bed [3382 3334] south-east of Oatleyhill Farm, the

Marlstone Rock Bed consists of 0.18 m of grey fossiliferous limestone with bands of well-rounded mudstone and calcareous siltstone pebbles; it is overlain by a few centimetres of ochreous clays. Near Fant Hill to the north-east the basal conglomerate is overlain [3437 3365] by about 1.2 m of typical ironstone. The Bed continues to thicken eastward, and at Scotland End, Hook Norton, about 3 m of good quality ironstone are present.　　　AH

The area to the immediate east and north of Hook Norton has been extensively worked for ironstone, large worked-out areas occurring near the village. The working faces of the now abandoned Redlands (north of Banbury road) and Park Farm (west of Butter Hill) quarries were described in their 1945 state by Whitehead and others (1952, pp.192–194). These faces are now largely obliterated by later working, restoration and downwash, as are the old workings around Hook Norton Grounds Farm. At the northern end of Redlands Quarry, however, the contact with the Upper Lias was seen in 1958 (Plate 2), in part of the face which was still standing [3622 3470]. The section was:

	Thickness m
Upper Lias	
Clay; grey with thin limestone bands, many ammonites, becoming darker grey downwards, sandy with ironstone nodules in the basal 0.20 m. Irregular base	3.05
Middle Lias	
MARLSTONE ROCK BED	
Ironstone; reddish brown, marly, oolitic	0.15
Ironstone	0.91

From a section in one of the old workings [3647 3367], the fossils collected included: serpulids, *L. punctata*, *Gibbirhynchia*?, *T.* aff. *tetrahedra*, *C. mundus*, *Entolium liasianum* and *Oxytoma inequivalvis*.　　　BJW

Little Tew – Great Tew

A faulted inlier of the Marlstone Rock Bed crops out in the valley running south-east from Showell Farm. It has been worked to a depth of 1.8 m in a quarry, now overgrown, about 1.2 km west of Little Tew church. In a ditch section [3732 2842] about 64 m to the south-east the basal beds are visible:

	Thickness m
MARLSTONE ROCK BED	
Limestone; greenish grey, weathering reddish brown, massive to irregular bedding, scattered shells and shell fragments	0.25
Limestone; khaki-coloured, silty, with pentacrinoid columnals	0.03
Limestone; dark grey, crystalline when fresh; thinly bedded, with shell fragments, ochreous ooliths and argillaceous pellets aligned parallel to the bedding. Only slightly ferruginous	0.18
Clay; dark greyish green	0.015
Limestone; very thinly bedded, silty, oolitic in top 15 mm; coarse shell-fragmental type with many belemnites and ostreids; scattered platy dull greenish brown oolitic silty mudstone pebbles	0.28
MIDDLE LIAS SILTS AND CLAYS	
Limestone; grey to ochreous, very silty with shell debris and small well rounded mudstone pebbles	seen 0.08

The central part of Little Tew is built on an inlier of Marlstone Rock Bed. About 2 m of deeply-weathered ironstone dipping 4° to the south were exposed in a ditch [3860 2862] immediately to the east of the vicarage.

To the south-east of Pomfret Castle the Rock Bed is thought to be about 2.4 m thick; it produces a strong feature on both sides of the valley, particularly in the north where a bench covered with the basal beds of the Upper Lias is present. In a small quarry [3770 2975] north-east of The Meetings the section is:

	Thickness m
MARLSTONE ROCK BED	
Limestone; green but khaki-brown weathering, ferruginous, medium- to fine-grained, shell fragments scattered throughout, coarse shelly crinoidal lenticles and secondary iron veins in basal 38 mm	0.295
Limestone; greenish grey, brown-speckled, coarse shell debris and crinoid fragments	0.065
Limestone; greenish brown, coarse, shell-fragmental, very hard	0.065
Limestone; greenish khaki, medium-grained but with coarser bands and lenticles, ferruginous, fossiliferous with worm tubes throughout	1.73
Obscured	0.08–0.10
Limestone; ruddy brown, shell-fragmental, worm tubes, ferruginous	0.038
MIDDLE LIAS SILTS AND CLAYS	
Clay; green to dull green, micaceous, with scattered minute yellow particles	0.18
Mudstone; dark lime-green, micaceous, coarser ochreous particles scattered throughout, numerous casts of fossils	0.08
Siltstone; ruddy brown, ferruginous and calcareous, fossiliferous; topmost 8 cm are secondarily enriched with iron	seen 0.61

About 135 m to the north, several small exposures occur on the steep northern bank of the stream which rises near Pomfret Castle. To the south of Buttercoombe [380 302] the ironstone is about 3.6 m thick. A disused quarry [3900 2947] shows about 3 m of massively bedded shell-fragmental ironstone. It has been suggested (Whitehead and others, 1952, p.195) that building stone was worked here.　　　AH

Southampton – Chadlington

The Marlstone Rock Bed, which is 0.6–1.2 m thick hereabouts, consists of a very ferruginous shelly limestone. It can be traced as a narrow band on the hillside north and west of Pudlicote House [313 205].

Heythrop – Enstone

A borehole at Miller's Barn [3402 2596] is said to have proved 2.29 m of limestone at a depth of 36.58 m. Examination of the chippings showed the presence of grey argillaceous limestone (presumably the basal beds of the Upper Lias), brown siltstone pebbles, and fragments of conglomeratic limestone and silty limestone, probably the Marlstone Rock Bed.

In a drainage ditch [3450 2556] north-east of the farmhouse at Old Chalford, 0.74 m of fossiliferous silty limestone, the top 0.28 m of which is decalcified, is overlain by 0.30 m of conglomeratic limestone. The latter, probably the Marlstone Rock Bed, has an irregular base and consists of well rounded pebbles of siltstone and mudstone set in a matrix of reddish brown sandy limestone, locally rich in fossil debris and with scattered belemnites and rhynchonellids. It is overlain by the basal beds of the Upper Lias. On the south bank of a stream [3480 2529] south-east of Old Chalford, the conglomeratic top of the Marlstone Rock Bed is seen in a down faulted block dipping into the valley at between 10° and 63° beneath the basal Upper Lias which occupies the low ground. The Marlstone Rock Bed crops out in the stream east of Heythrop church. Southward it produces a very strong feature, particularly within Foxberry Wood [363 271]. It has been worked, probably for building stone, in a small pit [3692 2700] near the western extremity of West Wood. Locally the thickness is about 1.5 m to 1.8 m and the surface debris suggests that it is an ironstone of workable quality. A ditch section [3723 2619] shows 1.83 m of ferruginous limestone with crinoidal and shell-rich bands.

In the valley of the River Glyme west of Enstone, the Marlstone Rock Bed is estimated to be about 0.9 m thick (Figure 20) and makes a small feature.

A well at Drystone Hill Farm [3839 2457] proved 2.29 m of ironstone, and south-south-west of the farm about 1.5 m of it are exposed in the northern bank of the River Glyme. Farther east, near Cleveley, well records suggest that the ironstone may be up to 2.4 m thick.

Glympton

The Marlstone Rock Bed is brought to the surface in a valley bulge (Figure 2) north-west of Killingworth Castle Inn [4382 2028]. The bed may be as much as 4 m thick hereabouts. EGP

Broughton – Bloxham

The Marlstone Rock Bed forms bench-like spurs along the hillside south of the Sor Brook, expanding into a plateau around Bloxham Grove, and continuing westwards to Bloxham. Amongst scattered exposures is one [4176 3749] where 1.8 m of current-bedded sandy ironstone were seen, and another [4270 3700] in which 3.05 m of brown oolitic ironstone were recorded.

In an old working [4462 3656] north of Oldbarn Farm, the following section was seen:

	Thickness m
Ironstone; very calcareous and oolitic	1.22
Ironstone; calcareous	0.91
Limestone; decalcified, ferruginous, thickly bedded, well jointed, spheroidal weathering. Limonitic enrichment in places, especially around spheroidal masses and along thinly bedded partings	1.52

Hereabouts the top bed of the ironstone is succeeded by 0.61 m to 0.91 m of brown, fine-grained Upper Lias limestone with, in places, up to 0.08 m of intervening clay. In an old quarry [4551 3655] south-west of Bloxham Grove the following section was recorded:

	Thickness m
Upper Lias	
Soil; brown loamy clay	0.38
Clay with limestone fragments; greyish brown, possibly made ground up to	0.30
Clay; grey, weathering yellowish brown	0.23
Limestone; brown, fine-grained, nodular	0.61–0.91
Middle Lias	
MARLSTONE ROCK BED	
Ironstone	0.91

In the north side of the railway cutting, 604 m east of Bloxham Station, 1.2 m of brown clay rest on 0.25 m of cream limestone with ammonites, on 2.44 m of reddish brown oolitic ironstone. The sections in a large abandoned quarry [423 358] on the western edge of Bloxham were described and figured in detail by Whitehead and others (1952, p.189).

Wigginton – Milcombe – Milton – West Adderbury

The Marlstone Rock Bed forms a broad plateau between the valleys of the Sor Brook and River Swere, and the base of the formation is cambered towards these streams. In an old quarry [3888 3400] north of Wigginton church, 2.4 m of thickly bedded slightly calcareous ironstone were seen. An abandoned quarry [4010 3414] near Lessor Farm yielded the following section:

	Thickness m
Upper Lias	
Clay; grey with calcareous nodules in lowest 0.30 m	1.22
Limestone; brown, slightly ferruginous with ammonites	0.08
Middle Lias	
MARLSTONE ROCK BED	
Ironstone rock; flaggy, sparsely oolitic	1.83

Farther east, an old pit [4214 3460] east of Milcombe church, showed 3.7 m of brown, highly weathered, decalcified ironstone, whilst another old working nearby [4214 3481] contained 3.0 m of sandy ferruginous limestone, the upper part probably being oolitic and decalcified, the lower part more calcareous but with fewer ooliths. The mineral railway cutting [4466 3537], south of Oldbarn Farm, was excavated through a cambered outlier of the Rock Bed and laid bare the following section:

	Thickness m
MARLSTONE ROCK BED	
Ironstone; sandy flaggy, limonitic, with shaly base	1.27
MIDDLE LIAS SILTS AND CLAYS	
Mudstone; grey	0.41
Sandstone (or decalcified sandy ironstone); soft, ferruginous	0.61
Limestone; flaggy, ferruginous	0.18
Sandstone; hard, calcareous, slightly ferruginous, shelly	0.25
Clay; greyish brown, sandy	0.61

The section in a quarry [4676 3462] west-south-west of Adderbury Station (New College Quarry) has been described by Whitehead (1952, p.190).

Swerford – Iron Down

The Marlstone Rock Bed is thought to be about 4.9 m thick in the small outlier on which Swerford is built. To the south-east of the Swerford Fault the Rock Bed outcrop widens rapidly eastwards to form the dissected plateau of Swerford Heath – Iron Down, and is markedly cambered on the borders of the plateau. Exposures are rare but the thickness may approach 6.1 m in the Swerford Heath area. In an old quarry [3742 3024] at Buttercoombe Farm, 1.27 m of weathered, thickly bedded, sparsely oolitic ironstone were seen, whilst at the southern end of Iron Down [418 312] old shallow digs, probably for dry-walling stone, showed calcareous oolitic ironstone debris. In this same area an old pit [4177 3140] south-west of Irondown Farm, contained 0.36 m of flaggy ironstone, on 0.84 m of thickly bedded, calcareous ironstone, on 0.51 m of limonitic thickly bedded calcareous ironstone, on 0.36 m of massive hard ironstone.

Hempton – Deddingon

This outlier forms a plateau capped by a cambered sheet of Marlstone Rock Bed with an overlying veneer of Upper Lias towards the eastern end. Exposures are few, but it is thought that the Rock Bed thins eastwards from 4.6 m to less than 1.5 m. An old quarry [4497 3097] north-west of Tomwell Farm reveals 0.74 m of broken weathered ironstone resting on 0.91 m of sandy oolitic ironstone with a little secondary limonite. Westwards towards Steepness Hill the conglomeratic sandy basal bed of the ironstone is frequently brought up by ploughing.

The Barford Trough

To the east of South Newington, in the faulted syncline which comprises the Barford Trough, the ironstone crops out in several small areas, as far as the Cherwell Valley. Many small old pits show that the Marlstone Rock Bed was worked as a building-stone, but good exposures are rare. In an old quarry [4159 3282] near Buttermilk Farm (South Newington), 1.52 m of weathered sparsely oolitic ironstone with shelly bands were seen; 3.05 m of weathered, dark reddish brown ironstone were recorded in the bank of a lane [4368 3261] east of Barford St. Michael church, and 1.52 m of ferruginous shelly limestone were seen in a small pit [4592 3346] north-north-east of Deddington Mill.

Great Tew – North Aston

Between Great Tew and the Duns Tew Trough the Marlstone Rock Bed crops out along a narrow strip to the south of a valley draining eastwards to the Cherwell from the ground south of the Swerford Heath – Iron Down and Hempton – Deddington plateaux. Scattered old stone-pits occur, but few good exposures. An old pit [4486 2926], south-east of Lower Farm, Duns Tew, showed:

	Thickness m
Ironstone; broken and weathered	0.46
Ironstone; rather soft with harder calcareous patches, some strings of secondary limonite along bedding, and films on joints	0.91
Ironstone; hard and massive, with a little limonite	0.61

Cherwell Valley

The Rock Bed has a very narrow outcrop on both flanks of the River Cherwell south from the North Aston Fault to near Northbrook. Some small workings are seen, amongst them an old quarry [4797 2774] near Grange Farm, Middle Aston, where the section is:

	Thickness m
Ironstone; brown with calcareous lenses and some secondary limonite	0.61
Ironstone; calcareous, shelly, with very calcareous lenses	0.30
Ironstone; brown, less calcareous, with limonite in strings and films	0.61

Some 3.2 km to the south, another old quarry [4818 2540] showed 1.4 m of broken ironstone, on 0.15 m of calcareous rock with much limonite in veins and strings, on 0.30 m of highly calcareous, blue-hearted, shelly ironstone. BJW

In the northern reaches of the River Cherwell, along the eastern side of the valley, the Marlstone Rock Bed crops out near Buston Farm on the northern margin of the district and extends south-west through a number of worked-out areas to Cobblers Pits Spinney (Whitehead and others, 1952, p.181). At Kings Sutton village the Rock Bed outcrop extends along both sides of the small valley running to the north-east from the village of Upper Astrop, but there is no evidence of any workings in this area. However, between Kings Sutton and Nell Bridge are the former Nell Bridge Quarries which were in operation during 1870 – 74 (Tonks, 1961, pp.240 – 241). To the south of Walton Grounds, the Marlstone Rock Bed crops out continuously southwards through Aynho Grounds until it is cut off by the north-east-trending Dane Hill Fault south of Aynho Park. There a are few sections of 0.30 m or more in ditches and drains. A small outlier of the Rock Bed occurs around Nellbridge Farm, and about 0.9 m of Marlstone Rock Bed ironstone on 1.8 m of pale silty shale were recorded in cuttings to the west and south of the farm when the Oxford to Banbury railway was constructed. To the south of Aynho Grounds the Rock Bed is cut out by the Dane Hill and North Aston faults that trend north-east along a small valley running from near Souldern Wharf towards Croughton. To the west and south-west of Souldern the Rock Bed, 1.8 to 2.4 m thick, forms a wide platform, but its outcrop narrows about 0.8 km north of Somerton and continues southwards through Upper Heyford and Lower Heyford until the Bed disappears under the Cherwell alluvium about 1.6 km south of the latter village. A well defined small outlier of the Rock Bed occurs around Chisnell Farm, about 1.6 km north of Somerton, with partial exposures in a nearby railway cutting at about 455 m south-east of the farm and again at 450 m west-south-west of Somerton church.

In the north, the Sor Brook runs eastward to join the Cherwell a short distance below Nell Bridge; the area north of this brook, from Bodicote south-eastward, is a plateau formed of the Marlstone Rock Bed. Some 410 m west of Twyford Wharf 1.5 m of the ferruginous calcareous sandstone are visible at the northern end of a large old quarry, and another 1.5-m face occurs in a small exposure about 230 m farther north-west. The south-east extremity of this plateau has been extensively worked in the past, both to the south-west and north-east of the Adderbury to Aynho road. The former locality is thought to be the site of the 1859 – 61 East Adderbury Pits, while the latter is that of the Sydenham Pits, originally opened in 1914. No ironstone has been won from these areas since 1926. Whitehead and others (1952, pp.187 – 188) and Tonks (1961, pp.242 – 243) all described the workings, and the following account deals solely with such other sections as are still available.

Immediately south-west of the Adderbury to Aynho road and south-east of East Adderbury East End as far as the railway, most of the ironstone has been won and only one old face, showing 2.13 m of ore overlain by weathered Upper Lias clay, now remains at some 230 m south-east of 'The Lawn'. The Sydenham area, between the Adderbury to Aynho road and the Cherwell valley to the east, was extensively worked from 1914 to 1926. A quarry about 410 m north-north-east of 'The Lawn', East Adderbury East End, shows 2.13 m of brown, current-bedded, calcareous ironstone in which the direction of the current-bedding is towards the south-east. A few metres to the south of this quarry is the supposed upthrow fault mentioned by Whitehead (Whitehead and others, 1952, p.188); at the time of the resurvey there appeared to be little or no evidence for this fault.

This area east of East Adderbury is gently cambered towards the Sor Brook valley and the Cherwell valley, and a fine example of dip-and-fault structure associated with this cambering is visible in an old working face near the main road 650 m west-south-west of Sydenham Farm. VW

UPPER LIAS

The Upper Lias consists predominantly of medium to pale grey mudstones which weather to pale greyish brown clays and overlie a thin, dominantly calcareous, unit that crops out on the gentle slopes above the Marlstone Rock Bed. Much of the formation has a narrow outcrop on the steep hillsides, protected beneath the Middle Jurassic limestones. The outcrop is poorly drained and was at one time generally laid down to pasture; with improved farming methods many areas are now ploughed.

The Upper Lias is divided, in ascending order, into the Transition Bed, the Fish Beds Member, the Cephalopod Limestones Member, and an unnamed argillaceous unit.

The outcrop of the **Transition Bed** (Walford, 1878, p.2) (Thompson, 1910, p.462) appears to be restricted to the northern and eastern parts of the Chipping Norton district, within an area bounded by Aynho, Lower Heyford, East Adderbury and Banbury (Figure 21). The Transition Bed may be represented by 0.13 m of silty limestone in the Steeple Aston Borehole (Poole, 1977, pp.5, 56). Within the district it consists of grey or cream-coloured, marly, oolitic limestone with thin seams of ferruginous sandy clay or clayey sand. Where it rests directly on the Marlstone Rock Bed, the two are in places cemented together, the Transition Bed filling irregularities in the upper surface of the Rock Bed. However, Howarth (1980, p.64) considers that the Transition Bed is not a distinct lithostratigraphic unit but the altered top of the Marlstone Rock Bed. He suggests that the changes, which consist mainly of oxidation and leaching of the ferrous iron of the Marlstone Rock Bed, occurred prior to the deposition of the overlying strata, although locally the process may have continued in recent times.

The Transition Bed is characterised by the high-keeled ammonite *Tiltoniceras antiquum*. This species (as *T. acutum*) was once thought to be of sufficient importance to be used as zonal index, e.g. by Walford (1899). Thompson (1910, p.461), though recognizing its Upper Lias affinities, placed the Transition Bed ('*Acutus* Zone') in the Middle Lias. Arkell (1933, p.179) included the *acutum* Subzone as the basal division of the *Dactylioceras tenuicostatum* Zone. Spath (see Whitehead and others, 1952, p.148) included these beds within an undivided *tenuicostatum* Zone, but Dean, Donovan and Howarth (1961) have concluded that the limited geographical distribution of the index species does not justify the recognition of an *acutum* Subzone. More recently Howarth (1973) showed that the species is invalid, and that the Transition Bed here equates with the top of the *tenuicostatum* Zone not the base (Howarth, 1978). Subsequently Howarth (1980) confirmed that the *tenuicostatum* Zone, the basal zone of the Toarcian, is represented by both the Transition Bed and also the upper part of the Marlstone Rock Bed of this account, or the upper part of the Rock Bed as defined by him which includes the Transition Bed. Although this important biostratigraphic boundary lies within ironstones of the Marlstone Rock Bed the traditional lithostratigraphic boundary, at the top of the Marlstone Rock Bed, between Middle and Upper Lias formations, is retained here.

The **Fish Beds Member** consists of slightly pyritic, bituminous, somewhat calcareous, laminated shales and limestones containing abundant fish fragments, rare ammonites, bivalves and some plant fragments. When fresh the rock shows marked fissility in bands of green and brownish grey reflecting the varying organic content of the laminae. It weathers to a pale cream hue, though in places with purplish tints. Uneven cementation locally results in the production of very hard dogger-like nodules.

These beds were first described as the 'Fish Bed' (Brodie, 1845, p.55) but have subsequently been called the 'Fish Beds' by Thompson (1910), this term including his 'Inconstant Cephalopod Bed', and most recently the Fish Beds Member (Horton and others, 1974). The Fish Beds may locally lie partly within the *tenuicostatum* Zone, but mainly belong to the *Harpoceras exaratum* Subzone of the *H.falciferum* Zone. The *exaratum* Subzone has been recognised near Upper Astrop [500 378] and south-west of Brailes [322 386], but appears to be absent near Hook Norton. Throughout most of the western part of the district, however, the Fish Beds form the basal Upper Lias deposit and probably lie within the *falciferum* Zone.

The **Cephalopod Limestones Member** has been variously called: the Serpentinus Beds (Judd, 1875), the Upper Cephalopod Clay and Lower Cephalopod Marl (Thompson, 1910, including the Upper and Lower Cephalopod Beds), the Cephalopod Limestones (Edmonds and others, 1965, p.41) and the Cephalopod Limestones Member (Horton and others, 1974).

The member comprises brownish grey-weathering, fine-grained, slightly oolitic limestones with slightly darker grey marly clays and mudstones. Phosphatic ooliths occur throughout the sequence (Horton and others, 1980) but are particularly evident in the limestones. Ammonites abound in certain beds and are associated locally with belemnites and bivalves, while crinoidal debris is common at some levels. The member is the most richly fossiliferous of the Upper Lias divisions. The limestones commonly show distinct *Chondrites*-type mottling but larger burrows are rare. At Neithrop [438 419], near Banbury, a conglomerate lies at this level (Edmonds and others, 1965, p.52) and is immediately overlain by beds containing *falciferum* Subzone ammonites. It is probable, however that the Cephalopod Limestones Member represents much of the *falciferum* Subzone and may continue upwards into the base of the *Dactylioceras commune* Subzone of the *Hildoceras bifrons* Zone. The *falciferum* Subzone has been proved in several places including some of the ironstone pits. The *commune* Subzone has been proved near Little Rollright and Hook Norton within the Cephalopod Limestones. North of Hook Norton towards Brailes, where the *exaratum* Subzone is present, this subzonal index occurs within 0.3 m of the top of the Marlstone. It is probable that the *commune* Subzone extends above the Cephalopod Limestones Member, and *D.* cf. *commune* was found 0.64 m above the 'Upper Cephalopod Bed' in the Steeple Aston Borehole (Poole, 1977).

An **Unnamed unit** occupies the remainder of the Upper Lias. It comprises medium grey mudstones with silty partings and thinly scattered nodules of both ferruginous and phosphatic types. Unweathered cores show a distinct very fine lamination marked by shades of grey. These beds (the Unfossiliferous Beds of Richardson, 1923) contain very few macrofossils; immature bivalves and ammonites are most common. *Peronoceras sp.* was found in the lower part of the unit in the Duns Tew Borehole, proving the *Peronoceras fibulatum* Subzone of the *bifrons* Zone. *Crassicoeloceras* aff. *crassum* and *Frechiella subcarinata* were found during the excavation of the Fritwell Tunnel and *P. fibulatum* in the railway cutting at Hook Norton. Crustacean remains and the characteristic rod-like crustacean faeces are relatively common. Trace-fossil burrows are rare and usually of the *Siphonites* type. See Appendix 1(2) for fauna of Upper Lias.

These mudstones probably lie entirely within the *Hildoceras bifrons* Zone. The *commune* Subzone has been recorded from clays in the Ardley-Fritwell Tunnel and adjacent cuttings, in the railway cutting at Hook Norton, and in the Steeple Aston Borehole. The *fibulatum* Subzone containing *H. bifrons* has also been recognised at Hook Norton where it may include the greater part of the poorly fossiliferous beds generally present in this part of the sequence. The highest division of the *bifrons* Zone, the *Catacoeloceras crassum* Subzone, may occur in the Ardley–Fritwell Tunnel; and Richardson (1922, p.111) suggests that it may be present at the top of the Upper Lias to the north of the Chipping Norton–Banbury road.

The maximum local thickness of the Upper Lias was proved in boreholes north of Chipping Norton (48.8–53.0 m) and near Great Rollright (50.6 and 51.6 m). A borehole at Sharp's Hill [3380 3592], slightly farther to the east, proved 57.9 m of Upper Lias; this is significantly larger than expected and may be due to local structural causes. The apparent thickness of the formation at outcrop is usually much less due to cambering. Thus boreholes on the ridge west of Chadlington give thicknesses for the complete Upper Lias ranging from 19.8 m on the summit to 3.9 m on the edge of the cambered Clypeus Grit outcrop. The camber structures are localised, and the orientation and trend of the changes in apparent thickness may mask the regional thickness variations. At outcrop the isopachytes of the Upper Lias are, therefore, unreliable, but it is probable that the trends found down-dip to the east and south-east of the Chipping Norton district, will persist into the present district.

Part of the south-easterly thinning (Figure 21) may be related to depositional features such as the progressive onlap

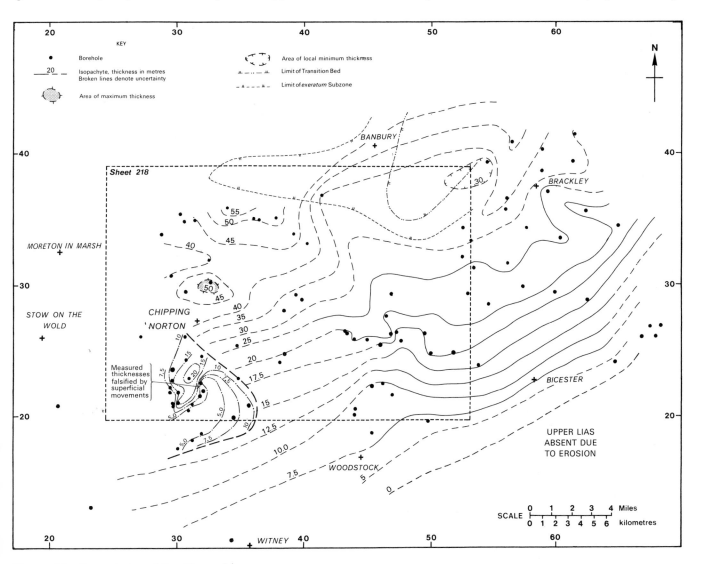

Figure 21   Isopachytes of the Upper Lias

of the Upper Lias during the post-Marlstone transgression; the greater part, however, is related to pre-Aalenian erosion which resulted in a widespread planar truncation of the Lias. The isopachtyes trend east-north-eastward and parallel the assumed trend of the London Platform. They thus provide some support for Richardson's suggestion (1922) that the youngest Upper Lias occurs in the north-west of the district.

AH

Details

Chastleton

Southwards from Chastleton, the Upper Lias crops out in a narrow band along which fresh exposures are extremely rare and mainly confined to temporary excavations. Due to cambering of the overlying Inferior Oolite limestones it is difficult to estimate the thickness of the formation with accuracy, and in places it appears to be only 7 m thick. In the Workshops Borehole [2679 2615], at Kingham Hill School, the Upper Lias totalled 4.86 m and consisted of the following beds: 4.33 m of bluish grey clay, on 0.23 m of dark greenish coloured clay full of fossils, on 0.30 m of hard shaly 'slate' and clay—the latter beds probably being the basal Cephalopod Limestones.

Long Compton

North-eastwards from Chastleton, the Upper Lias has a narrow sinuous outcrop on the higher slopes above Little Compton that becomes increasingly obscured with sandy downwash from the overlying Northampton Sand. It thickens north-eastwards, and on the hillside south-west and south of Long Compton is estimated to be at least 30.5 m thick, although in places this is reduced somewhat by cambering of the overlying strata.

At Harrow Hill [283 337] north of Long Compton, the Upper Lias is apparently only about 18 m or less in places, probably due to squeezing adjacent to the Whichford Fault.

EGP

Northern margin of the district

The Upper Lias is about 30.5 m thick at Brailes Hill and to the south-east of Lower Brailes near Holloway Lane. On the east of this lane, the basal limestone and clays rest on the Marlstone Rock Bed in an old quarry [324 387], and limestone debris was noted east of Combslade Farm [337 381]. An old overgrown brick pit [331 388] north-north-west of the farm shows bluish grey clay.

The thickness of the formation near Sibford Gower is 36.5 m. This diminishes eastwards to about 30.5 m at Tyne Hill and Tadmarton Hill [375 386], and the formation has a similar thickness farther east-north-east at Crouch Hill within the Banbury district.

EAE

Lyneham – Churchill

To the south of Lyneham Barrow the formation is thought to be about 13.7 to 15.3 m thick, but near Churchill it is impossible to fix the upper limit of the formation accurately, due to cambering of the overlying Clypeus Grit. To the north-east of the village the thickness may be 15.3 m. The Cephalopod Limestones persist along the outcrop from Churchill to Sarsgrove Farm [302 245] and then southward through Sarsden to Lyneham. South of Fairgreen Farm [2927 2126] the outcrop is locally obscured by Clypeus Grit rubble.

Salford – Chipping Norton

To the north of Salford the Upper Lias is thought to be at least 30.5 m thick. In this area the Cephalopod Limestones and associated Fish Beds are well developed though there are no sections. Clay was dug from a pit 550 m west-north-west of Salford Church.

North of The Common, Chipping Norton, fragments of the Cephalopod Limestones are rare. In the northern cutting for the railway tunnel west of Chipping Norton, Beesley (1877, p.180) notes a 'few feet of black Upper Lias Clay..., but without any bands of concretionary argillaceous limestone'. No fragments were seen in the fields to the north-east. In a field [3339 2988] north-west of Hull Farm, fragments of the Cephalopod Limestones associated with grey clay rich in ammonite fragments and large blocks of the Fish Beds can be seen.

The formation crops out on the higher slopes of the valley west of Chipping Norton. A temporary excavation [3145 2781] south-south-west of Ash Pollard revealed clays with limestone bands of the *falciferum* Zone which yielded *Pseudopecten dentatus* and *Nodicoeloceras sp.*, and, at a slightly lower level, *Dactylioceras sp.* and *Harpoceras sp.*

In this area the thickness is thought to be not more than 24.4 m. A borehole [3034 2607] on the north side of the Chipping Norton to Churchill road proved about 13.7 m of Upper Lias clay, but the thickness may have been reduced locally by cambering. In the vicinity of Meads Farm [296 263] and Churchill Grounds Farm [285 256] cambering has further reduced the outcrop thickness. The base of the formation can be readily determined by the scattered fragments of the Cephalopod Limestones seen in ploughed fields. AH

Whichford – Great Rollright

The formation crops out on the higher slopes of the valley and east of Long Compton. The general valley-ward slope is broken by hummocks and small benches; these are thought to be the result of solifluction of the Upper Lias clay, assisted by the seepage of water from the base of the overlying Inferior Oolite. At the base of the formation in the fields north and east of Hill Barn [3128 3167], fragments of pale grey, fine-grained limestones of the Cephalopod Limestones and pale fawn to grey, finely laminated, tabular Fish Beds were seen. These distinctive lithologies can be traced northwards to the vicinity of Gottenham [3182 3360]. The Upper Lias is thought to be about 30.5 m thick at Hill Barn and about 35 m east of Gottenham.

Fragments of fine-grained argillaceous limestone with *Dactylioceras sp.*, *Harpoceras sp.*, *Hildoceras sp.* and *Nodicoeloceras sp.*, which are indicative of the *bifrons* Zone (*commune* Subzone) and *falciferum* Zone and Subzone, were revealed during widening of the road 650 m west-north-west of Choicehill Farm [3064 2961]. Some 275 m farther north-east, fragments of these beds were found on the surface of the bench produced by the Marlstone Rock Bed. To the east bluish grey clay was seen in post holes and drainage ditches. Near Little Rollright the formation is thought to be at least 33.5 m thick. East of Great Rollright small outcrops occur abutting the Swerford Fault.

AH

Sutton under Brailes – Traitor's Ford

Near Rectory Farm [315 377] the Upper Lias is estimated to be about 30.5 m thick, though in places the full thickness of the formation is greatly reduced by the cambering of the Northampton Sand. Cambering also occurs between North Leasow [315 359] and Traitor's Ford and on the outcrop west of The Colony.

In a borehole [3493 3517] east of Fodge Farm, the Upper Lias was 38.7 m thick and consisted of: clay 17.4 m; resting on clay with traces of sand 6.1 m; clay 12.65 m; very hard rock 0.23 m; clay 0.24 m; rock 0.15 m; clay with rock layers 1.98 m. The rock bands in the lower part of this section are thought to be the basal Upper Lias limestones.

EGP

Sibford Gower – Swalcliffe – Tadmarton

The Upper Lias of this area is confined to small tracts much affected by faulting and, in many places, obscured by sandy downwash from the Northampton Sand. Exposures are rare. To the west of Swalcliffe [375 380], the only part of this area where the base of the Upper Lias is reached, the thickness is approximately 30.5 m.

In Tadmarton (Camp Farm) Borehole [4068 3783], 5.79 m of Upper Lias were proved between 46.33 m and the bottom of the borehole at 52.12 m. The junction with the Northampton Sand was faulted. (Appendix 4, p.139).

Hook Norton

To the north of Oatleyhill Farm [333 340] the narrow outcrop of the Upper Lias produces a steep slope; to the east the slope is gentler. In this area a gently undulating bench with a general southward fall is produced by the outcrop of the basal Cephalopod Limestones and Fish Beds. The following section [3377 3337] in basal Upper Lias was recorded along the banks of a stream, south-east of Oatleyhill Farm:

	Thickness m
Upper Lias	
Clay; bluish grey plastic, uneven texture, weathering to brownish hue, scattered ammonites	0.91
CEPHALOPOD LIMESTONES MEMBER (c.1.75) Cementstone; pale grey, hard, compact, weathering to brownish grey rock, the more intensely cemented pieces remaining to give a 'conglomeratic' appearance; abundant ammonites seen on weathered surfaces; belemnites	0.05 – 0.07
Clay; dull grey to khaki with rare ammonites: passing down into	0.03
Clay; blue, flaky texture, plastic	0.51
Cementstone; pale grey, compact with abundant ammonites; belemnites also present	0.10
FISH BEDS MEMBER (c.1.7 m) Clay; pale grey with irregular darker laminations, flaky texture	1.07
Limestone; massive, very pale dull cream, fine-grained, very finely laminated, coarser bands; shiny brown fish remains	0.08 – 0.115
Shale; dark green-speckled, finely laminated 'paper shales'; scattered fish remains.	seen to 0.15
Unexposed; probably as above but lowest bed appears to be an ochreous ferruginous clay	c.0.38
Middle Lias	
MARLSTONE ROCK BED Conglomeratic limestone; pebbles up to 0.05 m maximum diameter, well rounded low sphericity clay-limestone nodules set in a fine-grained grey calcareous matrix. Abundant rhynchonellids and belemnites	3.73

Deeply weathered clay of the *falciferum* Zone and Subzone with *Harpoceras exiguum* was seen in a ditch 505 m N 29° E of Oatleyhill Farm. In the vicinity of the farm the Upper Lias is at least 35 m thick, but south of Hook Norton it is only about 30.5 m.

Hook Norton – Swerford

A roughly triangular patch of Upper Lias clay rests on the flat-lying Marlstone Rock Bed to the north of Hook Norton [350 335]; the thickness on this small outcrop does not exceed 3.0 m. The Upper Lias crops in a poorly exposed belt around the margins of South Hill, south of Hook Norton, though the railway cutting at the southern end of the Hook Norton Tunnel offers good exposures of the highest beds. At the back of a small landslip on the east side of the cutting [3583 3158], near the south portal of the tunnel, 1.2 m of blue shaly clay with flattened ovoid limestone nodules are exposed and yielded the following fossils: *Dacryomya ovum*, *Grammatodon* aff. *insons*, *Meleagrinella substriata*, and *Thracia?*. The weathered surface of the west slopes of the cutting 27 m from the south portal of the tunnel yielded the following assemblage from the *fibulatum* Subzone of the *bifrons* Zone: *D. ovum*, *Peronoceras* cf. *andraei* and *Peronoceras sp*.

Richardson (1911, p.214), in his description of exposures now no longer visible in the west side of the cutting at the north end of the tunnel [3595 3202] recorded 9–12 m of Upper Lias as follows: 'Clay, blue, with curiously-shaped, hard grey-blue limestone-nodules; *Peronoceras fibulatum* (J. de C. Sow.), *Harpoceras subplanatum* (Oppel), *Nuculana ovum* (Sow.), *Inoceramus dubius*, Sow., *Orbiculoidea reflexa* (Sow.), etc'. This suggests that the Upper Lias thins south-eastwards from Hook Norton to 15 to 18 m beneath South Hill and in the small outcrop in the Swere valley north of Swerford [373 313]. The Upper Lias is thought to be about 16.7 m thick around Pomfret Castle, south of Swerford, where it is not exposed.   BJW

Heythrop – Enstone

The formation has a narrow outcrop on the sides of the valleys of the Glyme and its tributaries. The thickness at outcrop has been greatly reduced because of the cambering of overlying formations.

A borehole [3402 2595] at Miller's Barn, north-west of Old Chalford, is said by the driller to have passed through 27.0 m of blue clay on 2.3 m of limestone. Chippings of the latter were typical of the Cephalopod Limestones and the Marlstone Rock Bed, indicating a thickness of about 27.4 m for the Upper Lias in this area. To the east-south-east a borehole [3405 2581] at Old Chalford proved 27.4 m of 'blue Lias clay' beneath the Inferior Oolite. Another borehole [3458 2569] farther to the south-east proved 23.8 m of 'blue Lias clay' with a thin limestone band resting on 10.1 m of blue clay with limestone layers. The true thickness of the Upper Lias locally is thought to be 27 to 29 m.

The following section can be seen in a drainage ditch [3451 2556] south-east of Old Chalford farmhouse:

	Thickness m
CEPHALOPOD LIMESTONES MEMBER	
Clay; grey with some brown ironstone nodules; belemnites and *Dactylioceras sp*.	0.30
Limestone; lilac-tinted grey cementstone, the basal portions partly decalcified; belemnites and poorly preserved ammonites including *Harpoceras sp*.	0.115
Clay, variegated yellow and grey, ochreous	0.03
FISH BEDS MEMBER (0.24 m)	
Limestone; pale grey cementstone with a layer of fish fragments near the centre; the basal 13 mm is iron-rich with ferruginous veins	0.08
Limestone; olive-tinted grey, silty, finely laminated with several layers of fish fragments near the base	0.033
Clay; dark grey, silty with yellow ferruginous partings; scattered belemnites and shell fragments; variegated ochreous sandy clay base	0.13
MARLSTONE ROCK BED	
Conglomerate; pebbles of silty mudstone up to	

4.5 cm in diameter set in a pale to dark brown sandy ferruginous matrix; abundant specimens of *Tetrarhynchia tetrahedra* in the top 5 cm.
Apparently resting on an uneven surface   0.30
Limestone; brown ferruginous, decalcified, silty, abundant fossils in top 0.28 m, greenish grey and less weathered below   seen to 0.74

Beds of the *falciferum* Zone and Subzone are exposed in the bed of a stream [3550 2782] south-south-east of Dunthrop where 5 cm of greyish green argillaceous limestone with *Dactylioceras* cf. *consimile*, *Dactylioceras sp.*, *Harpoceras falciferum*, and *H. sp.* overlie 8 cm of pale fawn, finely laminated, fine-grained limestone with abundant fish remains which rest on yellow silty clay.

A borehole drilled from the bottom of a 15.9-m well at the Mill near Foxberry Wood passed through 14.63 m of blue and yellow clay, indicating a total thickness of the Upper Lias of about 33.5 m. About 1.6 km to the south, the apparent thickness at outcrop varies from 4.5 to 8.2 m due to cambering. A borehole at the Vicarage, Enstone [3802 2506] proved 11.28 m of blue clay resting on brown stone and marl, which suggests a thickness of 11.6 to 12.2 m for the Upper Lias.   AH

In the valley of the River Glyme east of Lidstone [356 248] the Upper Lias occupies a narrow outcrop which is somewhat obscured by cambering and downwash on the higher slopes of both sides of the river; its apparent thickness rarely exceeds 3.05 m. A more accurate assessment of the thickness is given by the records of three wells: (i) at Slade Farm [3769 2487], Church Enstone, where 10.7 m of Upper Lias, base at 18.39 m, were recorded; (ii) at Jolly's Ricks [3801 2387], where 10.4 m of clay, base at 33.5 m, were encountered; and (iii) at Drystone Hill Farm [3839 2457] where the formation was 11.9 m thick, base at 19.2 m.   EGP

Little Tew – Great Tew

The Upper Lias is poorly exposed in the valley west of Little Tew. To the south-west of The Meetings at least two thin bands of nodular fine-grained argillaceous limestone occur within the top 1.5 m of the formation. A borehole [c. 3774 2802], west-north-west of The Lodge, Little Tew, proved 15.24 m of clay, and a well [3820 2789] in the garden of The Lodge passed through 6.10 m of clay on rock. These provings indicate a thickness of about 16.8 m for the Upper Lias. In a ditch [3860 2861] immediately to the east of the Vicarage, Little Tew, the following section was recorded:

	Thickness m
CEPHALOPOD LIMESTONES MEMBER	
Clay; grey, blocky	0.33
Limestone; completely weathered to a soft ochreous yellow argillaceous material; poorly-preserved ammonites	0.03
?FISH BEDS MEMBER	
Mudstone; olive-green to purple, shaly, micaceous with harder partings	0.195
Limestone; intensely weathered; yellow, argillaceous with cavities in top 2.5 cm, purple-tinted with flaggy weathering below; poorly-preserved ammonites	0.20
MARLSTONE ROCK BED	
Limestone, ochreous yellow-weathered to matrix with 'residual' ironstone nodules in top 0.20 m, partly decalcified ferruginous shelly limestone below	0.28

The Upper Lias crops out on the steep sides of the valley running eastwards from the vicinity of Pomfret Castle. Exposures are few, partly due to the solifluction of the plastic clay. The Cephalopod

Limestones form a persistent horizon near the base of the formation. To the north of The Meetings the estimated outcrop thickness is about 9.1 m, but a borehole at Home Farm, 1050 m to the east, passed through 24.4 m of blue clay, almost the complete Upper Lias succession.

The section in a disused quarry [3900 2947] north-west of Great Tew church was recorded by Whitehead and others (1952, pp.196). From ammonites collected from a limestone 0.20 to 0.25 m above the Marlstone Rock Bed at the south end of the quarry, Dr L. F. Spath assigned the bed to the *falciferum* Subzone.   AH

Wigginton Heath – Milcombe – Bloxham – Adderbury

Near Council Hill [373 343], the Upper Lias is about 30.5 m thick, and the basal beds are exposed in many places along the eastern edge of the disused Redlands Quarry to the east of Hook Norton. At a place [3622 3471] west-south-west of Nill Farm, 3.05 m of brown clay overlie 0.91 m of ironstone, but basal Cephalopod Limestones and associated beds are obscured by downwash.

North of Tadmarton Heath, a stream section [3900 3648] exposes 0.91 m of brown clay overlain by a thin calcareous tufa. At Holy Well [3929 3565], 1.22 m of blue shaly clay are exposed beneath the Pump House. A boring at Tadmarton House [4124 3677] proved 34.8 m of Upper Lias; farther east, between Hobb Hill and Bloxham Grove, only the basal 3.0 m or so of clay overlying the Marlstone Rock Bed are seen. At a disused quarry [4471 3626], 310 m north of Oldbarn Farm, 0.61 m of brown clay overlies 8 cm of brown limestone with ammonite fragments which rest on the Marlstone Rock Bed.

In the north bank of the railway cutting [4320 3538] east of Bloxham Station the following section was recorded: 2.44 m of Marlstone Rock Bed; overlain by 0.25 m of cream-coloured limestone with *Entolium sp.*, *Dactylioceras* cf. *consimile*, *Hildaites sp.*, *Lytoceras crenatum*, *Nodicoeloceras sp.*, and belemnite fragments; overlain by 1.52 m of brown clay containing *Chlamys* cf. *textoria*, *Dactylioceras consimile*, *D. vermis*, *Harpoceras falciferum*, and belemnite fragments.

The Upper Lias does not exceed 3.7 m in thickness along the poorly exposed, elongated tract of Upper Lias stretching eastwards from Milton Airfield [440 340].

The Barford Trough and Deddington

The Upper Lias clay crops out in small poorly exposed areas in the Barford Trough between Wigginton and Bloxham Bridge. The thickness of the formation is thought to be about 30.5 m around Wigginton; at least 29.3 m of clay were recorded in a borehole [4029 3320] west-south-west of St. Peter's Church, South Newington, but the formation thins eastwards to about 15.24 m near Deddington Mill [455 330].

Ledwell – Duns Tew and the Bartons

Eastwards from Great Tew, the Upper Lias is poorly exposed, but has been penetrated in several boreholes. In a boring at Heath Farm [4372 2834] 25 m of Upper Lias were recorded; 19.8 m of Upper Lias were proved in another borehole [4322 2641] north of St. Edward's Church, Westcott Barton; in a nearby borehole [4331 2625] the Upper Lias was 19.2 m thick. The formation thins eastwards towards the Cherwell Valley.   BJW

Glympton – Wootton

Brown-weathering clay of the Upper Lias crops out in a valley bulge immediately north-west and south-east of Glympton Park [424 218]. Though it is not possible to assess the thickness of the formation at these localities, it was 9.9 m thick in the Killingworth Castle

Inn Borehole (base at 47.2 m), and 9.45 m thick (base at 39.9 m) in a borehole at Manor Farm, Wootton [4367 1983].   EGP

Cherwell Valley; North Aston – Northbrook – Somerton

The Upper Lias outcrop in this part of the Cherwell Valley forms narrow strips on both sides of the valley above Northbrook [490 220]. Exposures are few, but evidence of the thickness of the formation is furnished by several water wells and boreholes. In one [4770 2547], north of The Beeches, 15.5 m of Upper Lias clay were penetrated. The thickness is considered to remain at about 15 m south from here to Northbrook, and on the eastern side of the valley northwards to Upper Heyford, where a borehole [4953 2603] north-east of St Mary's Church, starting about 1.83 m below the top of the Upper Lias, proved 13.7 m of Upper Lias clay.   BJW

Cherwell Valley; north of the North Aston Fault, east bank

The Upper Lias clays crop out continuously from the north-east extremity of the district near Buston Farm southward to Northbrook where they disappear beneath the alluvium. As the working faces of the Marlstone Rock Bed progressed eastward in the old Astrop mines, an increasing thickness of Upper Lias overburden was encountered. Details of these basal beds in the Cobblers Pits Spinney section are given by Whitehead (Whitehead and others, 1952, p.181). From here the outcrop of these clays extends widely to the north of Upper Astrop and then passes southward to form the higher slopes of the south-east flank of the Astrop valley. Throughout this area many field ditches show small exposures of these clays and, towards the base of the formation, debris of the basal earthy limestones with fragmentary fossils litters the ploughed fields. The outcrop passes east of Walton Grounds and west of Aynho village, and then swings eastwards to underlie most of Aynho Park. It is then cut out by the Dane Hill and North Aston Faults near the brook south of the Park, but it forms another broad outcrop west of Souldern.

Cherwell Valley; north of the North Aston Fault, west bank

Only a few small outliers of the basal beds covering the cambered Marlstone Rock Bed plateau remain. The most notable is in the old ironstone workings near East End and around Sydenham Farm where up to 1.8 m of basal Upper Lias clay overlies the ore (Whitehead and others, 1952, p.188). Another outlier forms an irregular area north of Deddington and extends south-eastward between Deddington and Clifton. There are no exposures though debris of the Cephalopod Limestones is abundant.   VW

Chadlington

The Upper Lias was cored in Sarsden No. 9 Borehole [2966 1739], but only 20 per cent was recovered. The geophysical logs suggest that the junction with the overlying Clypeus Grit lies at about 11.9 m. The topmost Upper Lias (below 12.34 m) consists of dark grey finely micaceous clay with scattered calcareous ferruginous nodules. Below 14.33 m the fragmentary cores come from the basal Cephalopod Limestones, at least two limestone beds being present. The upper one, some 0.18 m thick, consists of pale grey, argillaceous, micritic limestone with pale fawn ?pseudo-ooliths, a few wisps of shell debris, ammonites, belemnites and bivalves. It appears to occur above a crinoidal shell-debris marl band, with a minimum thickness of 2.5 cm. The lower limestone bed is at least 0.18 m thick and is of similar lithology, but with fewer ooliths and shell fragments and with coarse *Chondrites* burrows. These limestone beds are separated by at least 0.48 m of medium-grey, finely laminated mudstone with silt partings, weakly sideritic and phasphatic bands and mottled *Chondrites* horizons. The base of the formation has been taken arbitrarily at 17.37 m.

Around Chadlington the Upper Lias outcrop is largely covered by soliflucted Clypeus Grit and Chipping Norton Limestone rubble.   AH, BJW

CHAPTER 5

Middle Jurassic: Inferior Oolite Group

In the North Cotswolds, a threefold sequence of Lower, Middle and Upper Inferior Oolite has long been established (Buckman, 1901). Richardson (1907; 1929) showed that attenuation and overstep of the Lower and Middle Inferior Oolite occur progressively northward and eastward, until near Icomb in the Moreton-in-Marsh district the Upper Inferior Oolite oversteps onto the Upper Lias. The present survey has confirmed that this relationship holds for that part of the Chipping Norton district that lies south of a line from Whichford through Hook Norton to Great Tew and Tackley, though elsewhere the Lower Inferior Oolite is preserved beneath the disconformity (Figure 22). Attenuation and internal discontinuities so complicate the sequence, however, that these subdivisions have not been used in the following account.

The district lies across the boundary between the Cotswold and Midlands provinces of the Inferior Oolite Group. Its maximum thickness within the district is 28.5 m—much less than in the central zone of the Cotswold provinces where it is 110 m at Cleeve Hill, Cheltenham, though similar to that at Northampton and Lincoln. The sequence comprises the Northampton Sand (which passes south-westwards into the Scissum Beds), the 'Lower Estuarine Series', and the Clypeus Grit. The last is part of the Upper Inferior Oolite; the older beds belong to the Lower Inferior Oolite (Figure 22).

NORTHAMPTON SAND AND SCISSUM BEDS

This combined division has yielded rare ammonites (pp.53, 126) within the district which are indicative of the *Leioceras opalinum* and *Ludwigia murchisonae* zones of the Aalenian Stage. The Scissum Beds represent the maximum carbonate development at this stratigraphical level. To the south and west of Chipping Norton and extending north-eastwards to Hook Norton, the formation consists of yellowish grey and pale orange-weathering sandy limestones identical with those along the main outcrop of the Scissum Beds in the North Cotswolds (Richardson, 1922, p.112), though it is commonly too thin to depict on the one-inch map. Small (less than 1 cm) derived phosphatic pebbles occur at its base. Irregular variations in its thickness may not be original but a result of pre-Clypeus Grit erosion.

To the north of Chipping Norton, quartz grains in the deposit increase in importance, and the sandy limestones are associated with calcareous sandstones and slightly ferruginous oolitic limestones that are more typical of the Northampton Sand. Brown sandy limestones and sand are present in the Whichford area, whilst at Traitor's Ford, near Sharp's Hill, the formation is even more arenaceous; sandstones and calcareous sandstones are associated with shelly limestones and thin mudstones. The maximum local thickness of the Northampton Sand is around the Wigginton

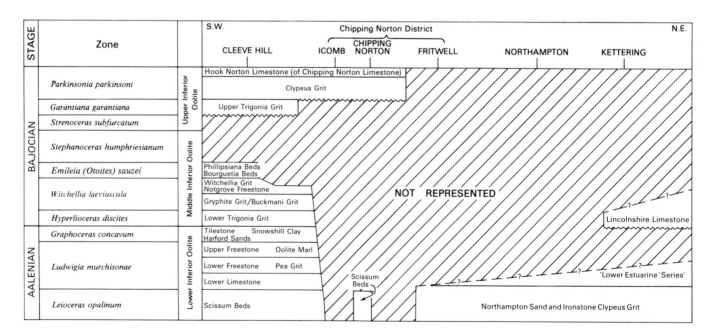

Figure 22 Stratigraphy of the Inferior Oolite Group

Heath area, the thickest individual sequence (11.2 m) being in the Hook Norton Borehole. Traced northward and eastward from the Whichford–Wigginton areas the formation becomes still more ferruginous and less calcareous, and the rocks resemble those at Northampton.

The Northampton Sand has not been recognised in the Barford Fault Trough to the east, although it may be present there, but it has a continuous outcrop along the Cherwell Valley where it contains a high proportion of oolitic and shell-fragmental ferruginous limestones. At Steeple Aston the iron content was sufficient for it to have been exploited as an ore for a short period (Woodward, 1894, p.163).

Surface oxidation and leaching have destroyed many of the original characters of the Northampton Sand and at outcrop the formation yields a reddish brown loam subsoil with rare stone fragments. The lack of surface exposure means that most of the details of the sequence come from the BGS's

boreholes at Hook Norton, Charlton, Duns Tew and Tadmarton, all of which lie in the north and east of the district. Detailed graphic logs of the first and last of these are given in Figures 23 and 24 respectively; see also Appendix 4.

Limestones constitute about 97 per cent of the formation proved in the four boreholes. Sandstones and calcareous sandstones form most of the remaining 3 per cent. They are usually fine- to medium-grained and invariably contain some carbonate grains and shell debris. The arenaceous beds tend to show horizontal and wispy bedding, the finer partings being enriched with mica and plant detritus, but much of the original bedding has been destroyed by bioturbation. Argillaceous material forms a very small part of the sequence and pure mudstones are absent.

Detailed examination of the cores shows a variety of non-skeletal particles in the limestone, principally quartz, ooliths and superfical ooliths, pellets, composite particles,

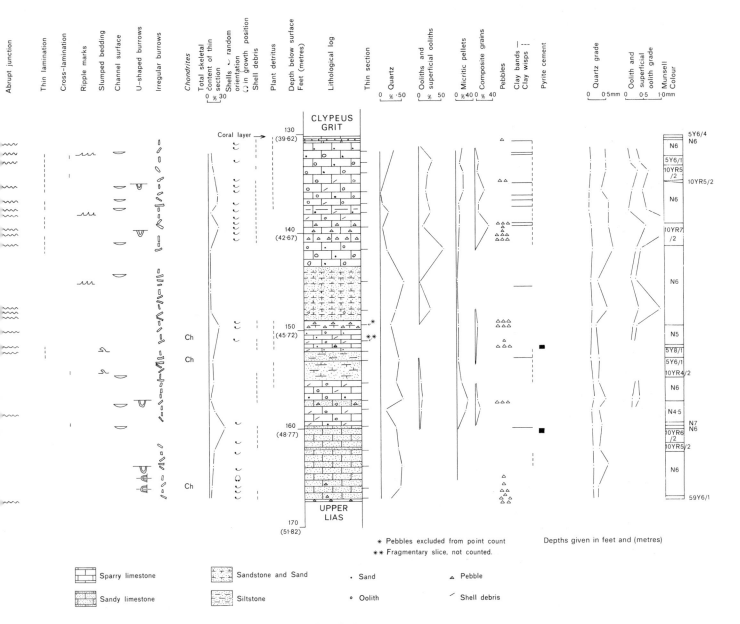

Figure 23   Northampton Sand in the Hook Norton Borehole

phosphatic and limestone pebbles: skeletal particles, mostly of molluscs and echinoids, are only a minor component. The particles are generally cemented by calcite spar though rarely a sideritic matrix is present. Most of the formation comprises grainstones (Dunham, 1962). Figures 23 and 24 also show the proportions of the main components as determined in thin sections taken from the Hook Norton and Tadmarton boreholes. Three triangular diagrams (Figure 25) show the interrelation of the various component particles. The sandy limestones and those containing dominant non-skeletal carbonate particles fall into separate clusters (Figure 25).

Two major lithologies have been recognised in the two boreholes:

(i) Sandy sparry limestones and calcareous sandstones: These account for about 57 per cent of the total thickness (of which 3 per cent are sandstones). Terrigenous sand grains, which form up to 69 per cent of these rocks, generally core the superficial ooliths. These rocks tend to be pale grey when fresh, but readily weather to pale yellowish brown and on

complete oxidation to varying shades of reddish brown. Usually massive when fresh, they readily become loose and friable on exposure, since they consist of medium- to fine-grained sand set in a sparry calcite matrix with minor proportions of small derived pebbles and shell debris. Rarely, they are fissile and cross-stratified, but generally bedding traces have been destroyed by the numerous burrows.

(ii) Mixed shell-fragment, oolith, pellet and composite particle sandy sparry limestones: These make up the remaining 43 per cent of the succession. The triangular diagrams show that non-skeletal carbonate particle limestones are very common, whilst the proportion of ooliths and superficial ooliths exceeds the proportion of pellets. Shell-fragmental sparry limestones usually have coarser easily recognisable organic fragments but the recognition of the non-terrigenous non-skeletal particles is extremely difficult in hand specimen. All these limestones have a speckled appearance when fresh, due to the particles being brown-tinted and paler than the matrix which is usually medium pale grey. The bedding varies from

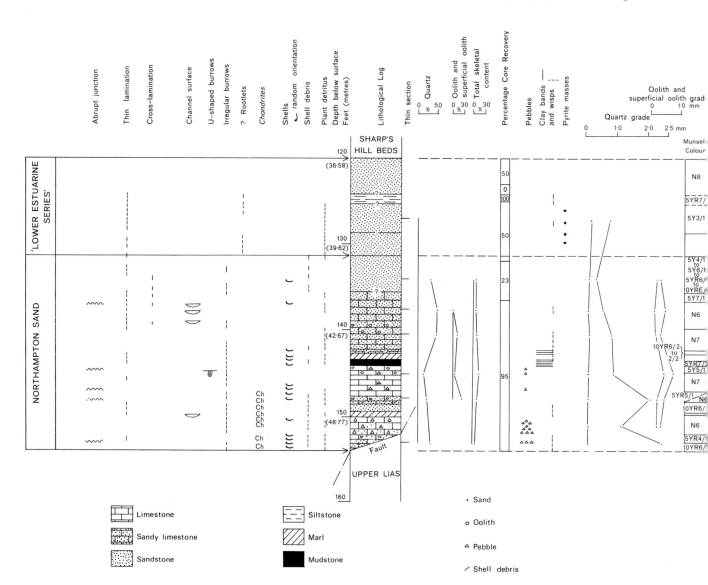

Figure 24 Northampton Sand and 'Lower Estuarine Series' in the Tadmarton Borehole

extremely thin units to beds up to 1 m thick.

Two minor lithologies occur, but are so subordinate that they have been excluded from the percentage count.

(iii) Conglomeratic limestones: A phosphatic pebble conglomerate is everywhere present at the base of the formation (Plate 5). There are homoiolithic conglomerates at higher levels, the matrices of which are mostly similar to the two main lithologies, though some have a higher clay content.

(iv) Sideritic micritic and sparry limestones: Using the nomenclature established for the Northampton Sand Ironstone (Taylor, 1949, p.5) these rocks are sideritic mudstones, sideritic-calcite-mudstones and siltstones. They usually form thin partings, up to 1 cm, but thicker beds are present in the Fritwell Cutting (sometimes called Ardley-Fritwell) (p.56). They are pale brown to brownish greyish red when fresh but weather reddish brown.

In the deeper boreholes the onset of oxidation is marked by a change from greyish colours to olive-tinted or yellowish brown ones. In the shallower boreholes and at outcrop the rocks are deeply weathered. The weathering process is identical to that described from the Northampton Sand Ironstone (Taylor, 1949). Siderite, the dominant iron mineral, is readily replaced by limonite. Progressive oxidation results in the redistribution of iron and the formation of ramifying oxide veins of crystalline character. Leaching of the granular calcite matrix first produces a porous greyish to dark yellowish orange rock in which carbonate particles still persist. Further weathering results in the solution of the remaining carbonate, leaving a soft friable sandstone indistinguishable in places from the overlying 'Lower Estuarine Series'. Differential leaching and redeposition of calcium carbonate produce hard massive doggers, each with a thin zone (up to 2.5 cm) of weathered material around a core of coarsely crystalline poikilitic calcite. The finer grained sparry matrices are more readily leached.

The Northampton Sand is not richly fossiliferous, either in terms of species or numbers of individuals. Almost all the shells are disarticulated, and skeletal debris is scattered throughout. Bivalves dominate the preserved fauna and are associated with echinoids, crinoids, brachiopods, gastropods, rare ammonites, belemnites, serpulids, foraminifera and corals; see Appendix 1(3). Trace fossils are present throughout. With the exception of one burrowing bivalve and the colonial annelid *Sarcinella*, only trace fossils are thought to have been preserved in their original habitat.

The fauna can be divided into the nekton, or forms swimming in the water above the sediment; the epifauna, living on the surface of the sediment; and the infauna, which lives within the sediment. The nekton includes ammonites, nautiloids and belemnites, all of which may have been transported into the area. Motile epifauna includes bivalves such as *Camptonectes, Entolium, Pseudolimea* and *Propeamussium*, the separated valves of which now lie convex-upward and cover some bedding planes. Sessile attached forms include *Liostrea, Lopha*, and probably *Modiolus*. Crinoids and the encrusting serpulids were stationary. The irregular echinoid *Holectypus* probably occupied shallow burrows. Of the infauna, *Gresslya, Plagiostoma, Trigonia* and possibly *Inoperna* were all suspension feeders that burrowed into the sediment.

The rest of the infauna includes trace fossils, four distinct types of which have been recognised:

(i) The most common consists of cylindrical tunnels arranged at all angles, but most usually steeply inclined to the bedding. These were probably feeding burrows.

(ii) Regularly ramifying tunnel structures (*Chondrites*), up to 1 mm diameter, occur in some of the finer-grained beds. The infilling sediment is identical with the parent rock, but paler in colour.

(iii) The largest trace fossil consists of U-shaped burrows with tube-diameters of 1 to 3.5 cm, separations of 2 to 5 cm, and lengths of up to 15.5 cm. The most common dimensions are about 1 cm diameter and about 3 cm separation. Generally the burrows are orientated in the vertical plane with the aperture uppermost, but some lie along the bedding. Both types have been interpreted as the tunnels of sediment eaters. The vertical burrows may be referred to *Diplocraterion*, whilst the bedding plane variety is called *Rhizocorallium*.

(iv) The fourth type is shallow (less than 1 cm) cylindrical to sac-like borings in both derived Liassic and homoiolithic pebbles. They are probably made by lithophagid bivalves.

The sedimentary features of the formation are indicative of deposition in shallow marine water. They are intermediate between those of the equivalent strata in Northamptonshire, where the sequence is richer in iron, and those to the south-west where the Scissum Beds reach their full development; energy levels appear to have been comparatively low. AH

Details

Chastleton – Hook Norton

The Scissum Beds have a narrow outcrop beneath the Clypeus Grit north-east of Hill Farm [2586 2890]. A short distance to the north they seem to be about 1.2 m thick and to consist of brown sandy limestone; angular fragments are present in the sandy clay soil. A small exposure [2747 3051] in a trench south-west of Oakham shows pale grey Upper Lias clay overlain by 0.76 m of sandy brown limestone and sand. These beds are closely overlain by the Clypeus Grit.

On the hillside east of Neakings, the formation thickens abruptly to about 4.6 m; white and brown sandy limestone of Scissum Beds type and sandy clay are ploughed up hereabouts, and the beds camber down the hillside to the north to obscure the upper part of the Upper Lias. At a place 1190 m east of Neakings, however, they disappear, and near South Hill Barn [2831 3116] the Clypeus Grit rests directly upon the Upper Lias.

To the north of Long Compton, the Northampton Sand is apparently thin in the vicinity of Long Compton Woods and on the north-east side of Harrow Hill [284 337] where large flaggy blocks of coralline shelly brown limestone and sandy brown limestone are ploughed.

North-eastwards along the hillside above Weston Park Farm, the formation thickens, and reaches some 6 m around Stourton Hill [301 354], where ploughing has revealed red and brown sandy soil with blocks of Scissum Beds limestone. EGP

The Scissum Beds have been recorded in a section [268 270] near a spring in a small valley west of Cornwell (Richardson, 1911, p.230). The beds were said to be overlain by sandy limestones rich in specimens of *Propeamussium* cf. *laeviradiatum*; they have been correlated with the Lower Limestone of the North Cotswolds (Richardson, 1911, p.230; 1922, p.113). Fragments of fine-grained sandy limestone with scattered pebbles were dug in a post hole [2768 2696] south of Cornwell Rectory and in a field immediately north-east of Glebe Farm where the formation is thought to be less than 0.6 m thick. Temporary excavations at Fisher's Barn [2807 2829], west-north-west of Salford, exposed about 0.9 m of pale grey sandy limestone with a fine-grained pebbly calcareous sandy band near the base. Similar beds, though probably not *in situ*, can be seen beneath the Clypeus Grit at a spring 905 m north-west of Salford church. In a roadside ditch north-east of Choicehill Farm [307 296], 0.3 m of fawn-weathering silty limestone rests directly upon the Upper Lias, and a ferruginous sandstone occurs beneath the Clypeus Grit in a ploughed field 820 m north of the farm.

Fragments of sandy limestone and ferruginous silty oolitic limestone occur beneath the Clypeus Grit in a cutting [306 317] on the A34, though no trace of them was found at the outcrop to the north and south. Similar beds can be seen in ploughed fields [331 311] to the south and west of Cardwell Farm near Great Rollright. To the north of the village, the Northampton Sand thickens, and appears to consist of ferruginous sandstones and limestones which readily weather to reddish brown sand. Solifluction of the latter produces thin sheets of Head which locally obscure the outcrop. The formation was once exposed at Oatley (Otley) Hill, where 1.22 m of sandy ferruginous limestones were recorded overlain by a coralline conglomeratic limestone (Woodward, 1894, p.157). Richardson correlated the latter with the 'Pea Grit Series' (1911, p.211) or possibly the Lower Limestones (1925, p.139) of the North Cotswolds; comparison with the Sharp's Hill area to the north suggests, however, that it may be the Clypeus Grit.

North-east of Court Farm [331 329], brown sandy limestones produce a strong feature at the summit of the Upper Lias slope. Similar beds were ploughed beneath the Clypeus Grit on the small hills to the east. South of the farm, the Northampton Sand is much thinner but can be traced intermittently to the vicinity of Fanville Head Farm [347 324]. AH

The following section and classification of the beds exposed on the now obscured west bank of the railway cutting at the north end of Hook Norton Tunnel was given by Richardson (1911, p.214):

	Thickness m
NORTHAMPTON SAND (SCISSUM BEDS) ('Upper Coral-Bed and Clypeus-Grit equivalent Scissum Beds')	
'Ammonite-Bed' Limestone; *Lioceras opalinum*, *L. thomsoni*, *Hammatoceras* aff. *newtoni*, *Volsella sowerbyana* *Pleuromya sp.*, *Gresslya abducta* etc.	0.46
Limestone; massive, often joined on to the bed below; *Trigonia brodiei*, *Rhyn. cynocephala*, *Astarte elegans*, *Belemnites spp.*, *Isocrinus* ossicles etc	0.43
Limestone; massive	0.81
Limestone; massive	0.67
Seam of sand; not very conspicuous	0.08
Non-sequence	—
Upper Lias	—

The fossil identifications have not been revised, and the authors of the taxa quoted have been omitted in this and subsequent quotations. BJW

Whichford – Brailes Hill – Tadmarton

Several scattered and faulted outcrops of the Scissum Beds were identified from field brash to the east and north of Whichford. A temporary section at Stourton Hill Barn [3035 3487] is reported to have shown white and brown sand. The thickness varies but appears to increase to the north and east. AH

A wide expanse of reddish brown, slightly ferruginous sandstone, locally calcareous and oolitic, forms the upper slopes of Brailes Hill and caps several small hills to the east. Between Sibford Gower and Sibford Heath these sands are up to 4.6 m thick. Still farther east they also form small hill caps. EAE

Judd (1875, p.1718) records 'about 2.4 m of calcareo-siliceous rock' in a quarry near the summit of Brailes Hill. These beds, which have yielded 'Ammonites Murchisonae', belong to the Northampton Sand, as does the overlying 'good ironstone' and possibly part of the succeeding brown sand, the bulk of which may be within the 'Lower Estuarine Series' (p.57). The highest beds in this sequence, comprising slightly siliceous oolitic freestones, are now considered to be Chipping Norton Limestone. AH

An outlier of Northampton Sand caps the summit of Mine Hill [319 378] and cambers over the Upper Lias clay making an estimate of its thickness very difficult. It is probably at least 6 m thick, and from the evidence of field brash, appears to consist of hard brown sandy Scissum Beds limestones overlain by soft, sandy and argillaceous beds. A large patch of cambered sand occurs immediately north of Rectory Farm and a copious spring issues from its base.

To the south, the Northampton Sand crops out on the hillside north-east and south-east of North Leasow [3148 3590]. The basal beds crop out in a scar just west of Bright Hill Barn [3183 3539] where 0.91 m of hard brown sandy limestone and soft sand is visible. The base of the formation is usually marked by a strong spring line.

Farther north-east, 0.91 m of massively-bedded, yellowish brown, calcareous, shelly sandstone crops at a copious spring 275 m south-east of Traitor's Ford. This exposure lies very close to the Stour Valley Fault, and the sandstone is slickensided, broken and jointed with many calcite veins along the joints and bedding planes. Similar broken yellowish brown sandstone occurs on the south bank of the Stour 300 m E32°S of Traitor's Ford.

In Sharp's Hill Quarry [338358], south-west of Leys Farm, the following section was measured:

	Thickness m
CLYPEUS GRIT	
Limestone; brown, coarse-grained, pisolitic	0.36
NORTHAMPTON SAND (SCISSUM BEDS)	
Sandstone; brown, fairly hard, calcareous, with *Sarcinella* and *Astarte*	0.36
Sandstone; brown, hard, calcareous	0.15
Sandstone; brown, micaceous, soft, ferruginous, with iron-pan veins and plants. Weathers to loose sand. Pale fawn pellets occur in thin conglomeratic bands	0.15
Limestone; brown, sandy, hard, with reddish brown iron-rich concentrations and streaks. Abundant shells, plants and echinoid spines, *Arcomya* aff. *crassiuscula*, *Camptonectes laminatus* and *Liostrea sp.*	0.79
Sandstone; brown, soft, decalcified, weathering to bright yellowish brown loose sand. Scattered nodules of calcareous sandstone containing shell and plant fragments. Thin clayey bands and greyish green mottling	0.61
Sandstone; purple-tinted, soft, micaceous, nodular, rubbly	0.91
Sandstone; purple and brown mottled, medium-grained, harder, calcareous with scattered ooliths and shell fragments—many ooliths in lowest 13 mm	0.79
Limestone; grey-hearted, brown-weathering, hard, sandy and oolitic, with many fossils including *Montlivaltia lens*, *Millericrinus?* echinoid indet., *Sarcinella* cf. *plexus*, *Kallirhynchia*, terebratulid and rhynchonellid	

fragments, bivalves including *Propeamussium* cf.
laeviradiatum; gastropods—*Aptyxiella subconica*,
Cossmannea (Eunerinea) sp.; also *Bredyia* cf. *subinsignis*
and belemnite fragments   0.30

The lowest bed is probably within 1.5 m of the Upper Lias, and
the high dip (48° to W10°N) is probably due to valley bulging
(Hollingworth *in* Whitehead and Arkell, 1946, p.17). This exposure
correlates closely with another in the wooded southern bank of the
Stour 355 m east of Leys Farms.

About 90 m east of this last-mentioned section, good exposures
occur in the river bank where the following section was measured:

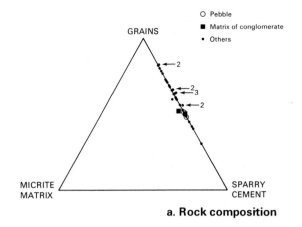

a. Rock composition

	Thickness m

NORTHAMPTON SAND (SCISSUM BEDS)

Sandstone; reddish brown, fine- to medium-grained,
micaceous and calcareous, with small carbonaceous
plant fragments and mud-filled tubes; rubbly and
ferruginous   0.91

Mudstone; yellowish brown, ferruginous, sandy and
micaceous, with grey mud flakes and pellets;
weathers to fine sand   0.25

Sandstone; reddish brown and yellow, fine-grained,
micaceous; rubbly-weathering, with thin ferruginous
bands   0.30

Sandstone; yellowish brown, ferruginous, soft and
argillaceous (almost a sandy mudstone); weathers to
yellowish brown sand   0.25

Sandstone; purple-tinged, fine-grained, fairly hard,
calcareous, with iron-rich bands   0.30

Sandstone; yellowish brown, hard, calcareous, flaggy,
fine-grained, with plant and shell fragments   0.46

Sandstone; yellowish brown, fine- to medium-grained,
hard, calcareous, with abundant fossils, including
brachiopods, *Montlivaltia lens*, and crinoid fragments.
Bands of coarse ferruginous pisolite similar to
Clypeus Grit occur in the lowest 50 to 80 mm   0.91

Sandstone; brown, soft and badly weathered, oolitic,
with ferruginous veins and carbonaceous plant
fragments   0.15

Limestone; grey-hearted, sandy and micaceous   0.97

Mudstone; purple and brown, soft, micaceous and
sandy   0.15

Sandstone; grey-hearted, hard, highly calcareous, with
belemnites, serpulid tubes, nautiloid fragments,
corals and shell fragments   0.46

Mudstone; brown-weathering, sandy, calcareous and
shelly   0.30

Sandstone; brown, fine-grained, hard, calcareous,
with round brown pebbles up to 13 mm diameter   0.13

Upper Lias

Clay; bluish grey, soft   0.91

Farther east, overturned Scissum Beds rest on Upper Lias in a
valley bulge at the bend of the Stour 530 m E19°N of Leys Farm:

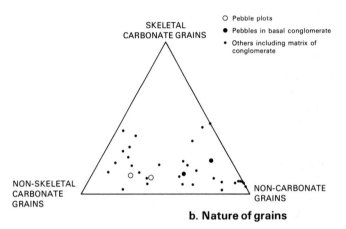

b. Nature of grains

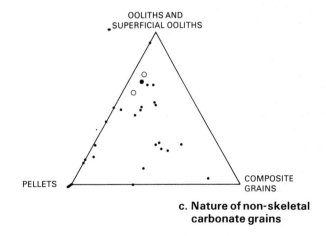

c. Nature of non-skeletal
carbonate grains

	Thickness m

SCISSUM BEDS

Limestone; brown, sandy, fairly coarse-grained, with
purple and reddish brown ferruginous veins and
bands. *Montlivaltia lens* and *Mactromya*   0.23

Limestone; brown-weathering, pale grey-hearted,
flaggy, very sandy, with many bivalves including
Astarte, *Entolium corneolum*, *Lopha* and *Propeamussium* cf.
laeviradiatum   2.44

Figure 25 Petrographical composition of the Northampton Sand

Limestone; grey, coarse-grained and oolitic, with
belemnites and shells   0.10
Limestone; blue-hearted, brown-weathering, medium-
grained, with small, dark grey, rounded limestone
pebbles up to 13 mm diameter; a few shell fragments
and mud-filled tubes   0.61

Upper Lias
Clay; bluish grey, weathered, slickensided   1.52

Round Hill [337 373] is capped by Northampton Sand which also
has a large outcrop, extending north and south through Ryehill
Farm [3413 3765], within which ferruginous reddish brown sand
with shelly limestone fragments occurs. A similar outcrop lies north
of Woodway Farm [3491 3656], and there is a smaller, down-
faulted outcrop in the Stour valley south of the farm.   EGP

In the Hook Norton Borehole [3565 3588] the Northampton Sand
is 11.20 m thick, and consists mainly of bioturbated sandy
limestone and sandstone with a conglomeratic basal layer rich in
phosphatised pebbles. The Northampton Sand occupies extensive
upland areas, much cambered at the plateau edge, around the
villages of Sibford Gower and Sibford Ferris.

In an old quarry [356 364] east of Woodway Farm, the following
section was recorded:

	Thickness m
Sandstone; pale brown, flaggy	0.76
Sandstone; pale reddish brown, with much white shelly material; probably decalcified	0.36
Sandstone; reddish brown	0.08

Limestone; brown, decalcified, very shelly oolite, with
maroon staining   0.15
Sandstone; pale brown passing upwards into grey hard
shelly limestone   0.53
Sandstone; reddish brown   0.05
Sandstone; pale brown, with shelly fragments,
maroon-stained ribs, probably originally calcareous   0.38

The fauna includes: *Sarcinella sp., Camptonectes laminatus, Entolium
corneolum, Inoperna plicatus, Propeamussium sp., Pseudolimea interstincta*,
belemnites and fish fragments.

Strata at about the same level are exposed in a small quarry at
Old Grange Farm [367 370], (Plate 3) where the sequence is:

	Thickness m
Sandstone; reddish brown, ferruginous, flaggy; basal 0.30 m very soft and weathered	1.22
Limestone; pinkish grey, hard, massive, sandy and calcareous, shelly in parts	0.36
Sandstone; brown, ferruginous, shelly, calcareous, weathered, with boxstone structure	0.30
Limestone; hard, grey, shelly, with some fragments of fossil wood	0.18
Sandstone; pale brown, weathering to a rusty yellowish brown with mauve horizontal bands	0.20
Limestone; hard, grey, compact	0.56
Sandstone; crumbly, rusty yellowish brown	0−0.08
Limestone; grey, shelly, rather sandy	seen 0.30
Upper Lias	0.30

The thickness over most of this area is about 6 m, though in places
as much as 8 – 9 m may be present.

Plate 3   Quarry at Old Grange Farm, Sibford Ferris [367 370]. Basal Northampton Sand
(Scissum Beds) overlying Upper Lias (beneath overhang) A9821

The high ground around Wigginton Heath and Rye Hill is also capped by Northampton Sand. The base of the formation is commonly marked by a strong spring line. One of the few exposures is found in an old quarry [3814 3525] west of Wigginton Heath crossroads, where 1.22 m of brown flaggy ferruginous sandstone are exposed.

Near Tadmarton, the Northampton Sand is difficult to separate in the field from the 'Lower Estuarine Series', but is thought to be about 7.6 m thick. The outliers at Tadmarton Lodge, Hobb Hill and Fern Hill, and adjacent smaller ones, are all poorly exposed. In some the areas mapped as Northampton Sand may include thin representatives of Chipping Norton Limestone and possibly of 'Lower Estuarine Series'.   BJW

In the Tadmarton Borehole, the Northampton Sand was faulted and the junction with the overlying 'Lower Estuarine Series' was not recovered. On the evidence of the gamma-ray log, the top of the formation has been taken at 40.06 m, and the formation continues downwards to a small fault which throws it against the Upper Lias at 46.91 m. The sequence is mainly composed of grey sandy limestones with brown sandstones rich in shell debris and plant fragments, with much bioturbation at some levels.   AH

Lidstone

The following section [3436 2565] was recorded behind a landslip on the south side of the valley 560 m N61°W of Old Chalford Farm:

	Thickness m
CLYPEUS GRIT (see p.64)	
Limestone; cream, argillaceous, oolitic	1.22
?NORTHAMPTON SAND	
Limestone; oolitic, extremely sandy, weathered to reddish brown sand	0.30
Limestone; pale cream, sandy oolite, with plant fragments	0.15
Limestone; pale cream, sandy fine-grained oolite, with plant debris and shell fragments, iron-stained and locally decalcified	0.53

No other exposures were seen in this area. Farther west and south the Clypeus Grit rests directly upon Upper Lias clay.   AH

Wigginton – Deddington

Thin Northampton Sand may be present below the Chipping Norton Limestone and Clypeus Grit in the outcrops of Chipping Norton Limestone in the Barford Trough. Fragments of oxidised ferruginous sandstone with secondary limonite veins and rare blocks of sandy oolitic limestone with *Propeamussium* were visible in spoil heaps in churchyards at Wigginton [3907 3330] and South Newington [4072 3335]. A roadside exposure [4068 3335] at South Newington shows about 0.5 m of ferruginous sandstone with box-ironstone structures above the Upper Lias.

West of the Cherwell Valley

The Northampton Sand, probably less than 6.1 m thick, has a narrow outcrop on the sides of the Cherwell valley beneath the 'Lower Estuarine Series'. A sand pit [455 272] north-east of Horsehay Farm, Duns Tew, exposes 2.8 m of reddish brown fine-grained sand and poorly cemented sandy shell-fragmental limestone. Laterally the limestones are decalcified to form brown sand. The bedding is prominent, with thin gentle cross-stratification, a few clayey bands and secondary limonite ribs. Boxstone-weathering is well developed. Astartid bivalves are abundant in the top 0.6 m, which is thinly bedded.

Elsewhere the outcrop tends to be covered by downwash from the overlying 'Lower Estuarine Series'.   BJW

In the Duns Tew Borehole [4632 2773] the junction with the 'Lower Estuarine Series' was not recovered due to the friable nature of the beds. The remainder comprised 3.82 m of sand, sandstone, silt and limestone resting on Upper Lias at 19.37 m. The estimated maximum thickness is about 5.4 m. The beds generally contain shell debris, with plant remains and bioturbation structures at certain horizons. The lowest beds consist of 0.60 m of olive-grey fossiliferous calcareous silty mudstone with scattered phosphatised pebbles at the base.   AH

East of the Cherwell Valley

Southwards from Farthinghoe Lodge these beds give rise to rich pale brown, sandy arable land. A section [5274 3827] south of the Lodge exposes 2.74 m of rotten friable brown sandstone and sand resting on Upper Lias clay. A copious spring issues from the junction.

To the west of Farthinghoe Lodge an outlier of these sands caps the hill around Astrophill Farm, but there are no exposures. An old pit in a small spinney 410 m north-north-east of St James' Church, Newbottle, shows 3–3.7 m of friable sandstone, and small overgrown pits lie on each side of the road some 275 m south-west of the church.   VW

Woodward (1894, pp.175–176) first described a now overgrown section in the vicinity of Newbottle Spinney [517364]. It was also described by Richardson (1923) and Thompson (1924). Their generalised sequence (with only the classification revised) was:

	Thickness m
TAYNTON STONE (UPPER ESTUARINE LIMESTONE)	
Limestone; brown, shelly, oolitic and gritty	0.61
Limestone; pale, marly and slightly oolitic, with *Modiola*, echinoid spines, etc	0.76
Marl; brown, shelly, with nodules of earthy limestone. 'Ostrea sowerbyi, Cyprina, Modiola, Trigonia and Rhynchonella'	0.61 to 7.6
SHARP'S HILL BEDS ('UPPER ESTUARINE SERIES')	
Clay; black, bluish grey, brown and greenish coloured, with an irregular basal junction	0.76
'LOWER ESTUARINE SERIES'	
Sand and clay; white and grey, the sand, white, brown and purplish coloured, with ochreous nodules	seen to 2.74
NORTHAMPTON SAND	
Limestone; brown and ferruginous, micaceous and sandy, with false bedding. Blue-hearted in parts. Some beds are very hard and fissile, others are softer and more calcareous and slightly oolitic in some places, with shelly layers and plant remains. Hard pebbly concretions or pebbles in places	seen to 3.05

A small exposure in Newbottle Spinney [5175 3635] revealed 1 m of pale brown sandy sparry slightly oolitic limestone with some shell debris and scattered bivalves. A thin pebbly bed occurs in the middle of the sequence and includes bored Upper Lias pebbles and homoiolithic pebbles. At surface the massive Northampton Sand limestones show flaggy weathering.   AH

South of Souldern the outcrop gradually narrows and the beds appear to degenerate into a brown sand which persists through Somerton and Upper Heyford to Northbrook.   VW

The local Inferior Oolite sequence was exposed during the excavation of the railway cutting south-east of Fritwell [514 290]. The sequence was first described by Odling (1913, p.491), but it was subsequently more fully described (Arkell and others, 1933, pp.346–347) and, for convenience, is given in full below with the published bed numbers. The original classification is shown in brackets after the present usage.

		Thickness m
Sharp's Hill Beds (Upper Estuarine Clay)		
9	Grey blue soapy clay (Bed 5 of Sharp's Hill?)	0.10
8	Peat Bed: Black carbonaceous seam: (Bed 6 of Sharp's Hill)	0.05–0.46
Non-sequence		
(**Chipping Norton Limestone Series, Swerford Beds or White Sands**)		
7	Grey and brown mottled sandy clay with white papery shell fragments, many gastropods of the *Cerithium* type	0.30
'Lower Estuarine Series'		
6b	Yellow sand, white when weathered	1.52
6a	Black sand, with 'iron' seeping out; seen below aqueduct to 1.83 m but cutting down in deep channels into the bed below to at least	4.57
Marked unconformity accompanied by channelling.		
Northampton Sand (Hook Norton Beds)		
5	False-bedded, doggery, laminated, brown sand and sandstones. Maximum thickness about	3.66
4	Flaggy red sandy limestone interbedded irregularly with brown argillaceous sand. Some of the limestone layers contain abundant *Pseudomonotis lycettii* Rollier	1.52
3	Pebble Bed: Sandy limestone with rolled fragments of the bed below and smaller pebbles of Upper Lias limestone with *Serpulae* attached, as in Newbottle Spinney: *P. lycetti, Camptonectes sp.,* [*Trigonia signata*—J. Pringle], small *Ostrea sp.* and *Clypeus* (fragments)	0.30
2	Hard grey sandstone	0.46
Major non-sequence		

Upper Lias

| 1 | Dark shaly clay [with *Dactylioceras* J.P.] | seen to 1.83 |

The lowest bed now exposed is a 0.45-m bluish grey oolith sparry limestone with a basal conglomerate bed. The largest pebbles seen are 50 mm in diameter, and consist of bored angular to rounded fragments of Upper Lias cementstone. These are associated with smaller pebbles of pale fawn sandy oolith limestone which macroscopically resemble the overlying Northampton Sand. This corresponds to Bed 3 of the above section; it forms a prominent overhang and appears to rest directly on the Upper Lias. The middle part of the formation is not exposed. The highest beds form a bench on the slope of the cutting. They consist of grey sandy sparry limestones with some shell debris and rare ooliths; in places a lenticular band of fine-grained sideritic mudstone appears at this level. Near the tunnel portal these limestones are overlain by weathered ferruginous sandstone, but to the south-east a bed of very thinly laminated and gently cross-stratified sandy shell-debris sparry limestone (tilestone) with some fine plant debris appears; differential leaching has given a rounded dogger-like appearance to this bed. The 'Lower Estuarine Series' fills a channel cut into the

Northampton Sand, and the rock on which it rests has been leached and oxidised to red sand, the alteration extending beyond the margins of the channel. According to the original records of the cutting and tunnel shafts, the thickness of beds which would now be grouped as the Northampton Sand ranges from 2.13 to 5.94 m. Arkell and his co-workers suggested a thickness of 6.1 m, whilst a current estimate at the south portal of the tunnel is 3.5 m.   AH

'LOWER ESTUARINE SERIES'

In the northern and north-eastern parts of the district, some 3 to 6 m of pale grey and brown sands overlie the Northampton Sand and locally overstep on to the Upper Lias. They produce a narrow belt of brownish sandy soil on the higher valley slopes and, in more dissected areas, form small hill-top plateaux. Mapping suggests that these sands equate with the 'white sands' of the Northampton district, and they were originally grouped with the Northampton Sand (Aveline and Trench, 1860), and thus considered to be part of the Lower Inferior Oolite. Some occurrences within the district have, however, been considered to equate with the appreciably younger Swerford Beds, an arenaceous facies of the Chipping Norton Limestone (Richardson, 1911; Arkell, 1947a; Sellwood and McKerrow, 1974). The two sands are, however, distinctive, and the former view seems preferable (Horton, 1977), although in the absence of diagnostic fossils that could place the sands in either the Aalenian or the Bathonian, the problem cannot be conclusively resolved. The sands die out north-eastwards of the Clypeus Grit, which would otherwise establish their correct stratigraphic position, though the believed presence of the latter overlying 'white sands' at Westcott Barton and Middle Barton favours the preferred hypothesis.

Within the district the 'Lower Estuarine Series'[1] generally rests with apparent conformity on the Northampton Sand, though locally this is a disconformable relationship as in the Fritwell railway cutting [514 290], where the lower part fills a channel up to 3 m deep in the Northampton Sand (Arkell and others, 1933, pl. 34A). Where secondary iron-enrichment in the basal beds of the 'Lower Estuarine Series' is associated with intensive leaching of the underlying sandy limestones, the precise junction with the underlying Northampton Sand is difficult to define. The top of the formation is also difficult to determine where the overlying 'Great Oolite Series' contains reworked sandy sediments at its base. In general, however, the formation is distinguished from the overlying and underlying beds by the absence within it of any calcareous skeletal remains. Exposures are few and borehole information is limited because it is difficult to recover cores from the sands.

In detail there are minor, but rapid, thickness variations along the outcrop. The maximum recorded is in Horsehay Quarry, Duns Tew [455 272], where the formation thickens from 7.3 to 9.7 m along the line of a channel cut into the Northampton Sand; in Duns Tew Borehole [4632 2773], only 915 m to the north-east, the thickness is 6.4 m. Similarly in Salmon's Pit, Lower Tadmarton [400 376], the form-

---

1 Since the geological survey was completed the formation has been renamed the Grantham Formation.

ation is about 8.6 m thick (Richardson, 1922, p.119), but in Tadmarton Borehole [4068 3783], some 730 m to the east, it is only 3.5 m (Figure 24). In quarries at Newbottle Spinney [517 364], in the extreme north-east, 2.7 m were recorded (Woodward, 1894), and 3 m were present in Charlton Borehole [5291 3487]. In the Fritwell railway cutting, 8 km farther south, up to 6.4 m were noted (Arkell and others, 1933, pp.346–347). The formation thus thins south-westward, and dies out along a line that extends from north of Kiddington towards Kirtlington. Any southward extension of the formation is buried beneath younger Jurassic rocks east and south of the Cherwell valley.

The 'Lower Estuarine Series' is predominantly arenaceous. Two types of sandstone are present. The first and most common consists of moderately compact, massive sandstone, varying from greyish yellow to yellowish orange or brown and reddish brown, according to the content of iron and its degree of oxidation. Bedding structures are difficult to recognise, but include mudstone wisps and bands, and beds with thin parallel cross-lamination commonly marked by partings of carbonaceous detritus. In hand specimens the quartz grains appear to be well rounded and medium- to fine-grained, but thin sections show them to be mainly subrounded to subangular, and only the larger ones are spheroidal. Most of the grains consist of quartz though rare chert and metamorphic quartzites are present. Plagioclase and microcline felspars form less than one per cent of the rocks. Heavy minerals are uncommon but include tourmaline. Limonite occurs as grains, and also as secondary veins and cement. The sandstones contain a varying proportion of clay matrix, and grade from the more common mature orthoquartzites ('white sands') to sub-greywackes. The second sandstone type is finer grained, apparently unbedded, friable in texture, and very pale grey ('white') or pale yellowish grey except where an abundance of plant detritus gives it a darker grey shade. A few sandstones are intermediate between the two main types.

Mudstone bands, up to 76 mm thick, can occur throughout the sequence. Locally, thicker beds of dark grey, unbedded plastic clay lie at the top of the formation and are commonly associated and interbedded with ill-sorted olive and pinkish grey silts, many of which are thinly laminated and contain a little plant debris. These clays and silts weather to purple tints and form a readily mappable band.

Pyrite occurs both as small spheroidal cemented masses within the sandstones and disseminated throughout the finer grained beds. At outcrop, weathering has redistributed the original pyrite and limonite into limonitic surfaces or joint stains and secondary veins.

Plant remains are common throughout the 'Lower Estuarine Series' and are generally concentrated on the bedding planes. Some plant-rich and lignitic clays are present. Rootlets are present locally throughout the formation, but are most common in the more argillaceous upper beds (see Figure 24 for example). They are variously filled with clay, silt or sand and, therefore, vary in prominence according to the lithology of the bed being penetrated. Where the filling is the same as the surrounding matrix, the rootlets can often be distinguished by the presence of carbonaceous markings.

No other fossils have been recorded locally from the formation. This may, however, not be an original feature but the result of later leaching.

Ferruginous shelly sands and decalcified sandy limestones underlie the 'white sands' in the Fritwell Cutting and in Horsehay Quarry, Duns Tew. These beds have been included in the Swerford Member (= Beds) by Sellwood and McKerrow (1974), but it seems more probable that the sandy limestones are a facies of the Northampton Sand.

The 'Lower Estuarine Series' sequence is similar to that in Northamptonshire which Taylor (1963) considered to have formed in a fluviatile swamp and marsh. The present district comprises the most south-western occurrence of this coastal facies.   AH

Details

Sibford Gower

Pale buff yellow sand and sandstone overlie the Northampton Sand on the top of Brailes Hill to the north and south of Highwall Spinney [2955 3900], and may belong to this formation.   EAE

Wigginton Heath – Tadmarton

In the outlier capping Wigginton Heath there are several old sand pits; in one of these [3840 3508] 2.44 m of pale brown fine-grained sand, with ferruginous sandstone courses and iron-stained bands, are exposed. In the faulted area north of Lower Tadmarton, a large pit [3997 3786] east of St Nicholas' Church, Tadmarton, exposes bluish grey to white and yellow, fine-grained sand with lignitic fragments, beneath Sharp's Hill Beds.   BJW

In Tadmarton Borehole [4068 3783], the 'Lower Estuarine Series' was approximately 3.5 m thick. Because of the friable character of the beds, core recovery was only 49 per cent, and the base of the formation was taken at 40.06 m.   AH

Ledwell – Duns Tew

The 'Lower Estuarine Series' crops out on high ground around Heath Farm, where it emerges from beneath the Chipping Norton Limestone, and in two outliers to the east, capping small hills. To the south, around Downhill Farm, a sand pit [4362 2692] is in 2.44 m of mainly white fine-grained sand and poorly cemented sandstone, with lilac, brown and blue streaks and patches, well-bedded parts, and thin clayey bands up to 13 mm thick (Plate 4).   BJW

In Duns Tew Borehole [4632 2773] the formation was approximately 6.4 m thick (p.139). Core recovery was only 32 per cent.   AH

North Aston – Northbrook – Upper Heyford

Between the North Aston and Dane Hill faults on the west bank of the Cherwell there are two small tracts of 'Lower Estuarine Series'. In the westernmost one, an old pit [4612 2895] shows 0.30 m of pale brown marly shelly sandstone (Sharp's Hill Beds) resting on 1.83 m of lilac and brown fine-grained sand. Southwards the formation occupies a substantial area, in which there are many old overgrown sand pits. A good exposure at Horsehay Quarry [455 272] shows:

Thickness
m
—

SHARP'S HILL BEDS (see p.81)

'LOWER ESTUARINE SERIES'
Sand; pale bluish grey to buff fine-grained well-sorted
  clean sand with planar bedding. Colour-banded, with

darker and lighter bands, coarse-grained bands and
ferruginous ribs. A few clay bands, including an
80-mm thick impersistent blue clay, 1.42 m above
the base   9.75

NORTHAMPTON SAND   —

                                                                                              BJW

The pit was enlarged in 1975 and showed pale brown slightly
ferruginous sandstone passing up from the Northampton Sand and
giving way to pale grey sand and sandstone. The bedding is
irregular with fine-scale gentle cross-stratification and shallow
channel structures. Beds of dark blue and purplish clay are
interbedded with purplish brown sand laminae which contain clay
galls, plant debris and seeds. A bed of purplish brown sand at the
top contains abundant plant debris. The 'Lower Estuarine Series' is
overlain non-sequentially by the Sharp's Hill Beds.   AH

The outcrop of the formation continues down the west side of the
Cherwell valley to the vicinity of Nethercott and forms a narrow
outcrop on the eastern bank through Lower and Upper Heyford.
                                                                                              BJW

The formation appears to be about 3 m thick in a railway cutting
[4840 2213] 2 km south of Rousham. The lowest beds exposed
comprise a reddish brown chamositic sandstone which is succeeded
by about 0.6 m of uncemented fine-grained white sand. At a higher
level there are fragments of brown limonitised chamositic sandstone
with rare clay galls and secondary box-ironstone structures. The
highest beds exposed are deeply weathered limonitised coarse
brown sandstone with bright red sandy clay mottling in lenses and
pockets.

Somerton – Charlton

The 'Lower Estuarine Series' is partly exposed in the Fritwell Cutting [514 290]. The channel recorded during the initial excavation is
still visible (Arkell and others, 1933, pp.346 – 347). It is probably
about 25 m wide, and runs at a slight angle to the cutting for some
95 m before turning abruptly away from the excavation. The lowest
beds seen consist of pale fawn to lilac-tinted brown, fine-grained,
thinly-bedded sandstone with plant debris. The laminae drape the
walls of the channel which extends down for at least 2 m into the
Northampton Sand. Rootlets are present at the top of these beds.
They are succeeded by about 2 m of ferruginous sand, which are
dark brownish grey with abundant rootlets in the basal 0.3 m but
become paler with fewer rootlets and an irregular concentric type of
weathering structure in their topmost 0.5 to 1.0 m. The highest bed
consists of at least 1.2 m of white well sorted fine-grained sand.

In the Charlton Borehole [5291 3487] the formation consists of
black and grey clay and silt overlying yellow and brown sand and
sandstone, in all some 3 m thick with its base at 9.75 m. These beds
are rich in plant fragments and rootlets.   AH

CLYPEUS GRIT

The Clypeus Grit is the sole representative of the Upper Inferior Oolite within the district. It has a disconformable base
that lies above a major non-sequence which cuts out the
Middle Inferior Oolite. To the north of a line through Little
Compton, Great Rollright and Wigginton the formation
rests upon the Northampton Sand; elsewhere it overlies the

Plate 4   Quarry [436 269] in 'Lower Estuarine Series' near Downhill Farm, Westcott Barton
(A 9844)

Upper Lias though there are local intervening pockets of the Scissum Beds.

The Clypeus Grit has a narrow outcrop along the margins of the upland plateaux and falls south-eastwards to the valley bottoms. The most south-easterly exposures are near Glympton, where the Grit is introduced by valley bulging. It attains its maximum thickness of about 7.5 m around Chadlington and Charlbury (Figure 26), but thins out to the north and east of a line joining Whichford, Great Tew, Steeple Barton and Tackley. Beyond this line it has been recorded only in isolated sections at Sharp's Hill Quarry [338 358], Hook Norton, and in the Hook Norton and Ledwell boreholes (see also Figure 29). Fragments of marly limestone overlying the Northampton Sand at Fern Hill [407 353] north of Milcombe (Richardson, 1922, p.131) may well be the most north-easterly record of the formation. Small isolated patches of the typical lithology have been recorded between Ledwell and Middle Barton, to the east of the main pinch-out.

The Clypeus Grit comprises cream to pale buff, rubbly-weathering, shelly, oolitic and pisolitic limestones with cream to pale brown carbonate grains set in a pale olive-green-tinted micrite matrix. When fresh the grains are dark grey, and the matrix paler grey. Where it is thickest the formation can be separated into lower micritic (lime-mud) limestones and marls, with abundant coarse carbonate particles including pisoliths and ooliths, and upper skeletal pisolitic and oolitic limestones. The lower beds are the more widespread and can be traced throughout the outcrop. As the formation thins, however, a distinct marginal facies of shell-fragmental oolitic and iron-shot limestones appears and forms an increasingly important part of the succession.

An unusual condensed sequence in the Hook Norton Borehole is thought to belong to the Clypeus Grit. Its base is formed by a thin encrusting coral layer which covers borings and cavities in the underlying Northampton Sand. The overlying conglomerate consists of three units which are separated by uneven, possibly erosional, surfaces. The dominant pebbles in the basal unit are calcarenites which are associated with pebbles of siderite-mudstone derived from the Northampton Sand; the middle unit also contains phosphatic pebbles; in the upper unit there are pebbles of oolitic sparry and micritic limestones together with flakes of mudstone. The matrix of these units is unlike that of the thin Clypeus Grit nearby at Sharp's Hill (p.64), but the evidence of a major break at the base, the nature of the constituent pebbles, and the presence at the base of the overlying Chipping Norton Limestone of a homoiolithic conglomerate resting on a non-sequence suggest the correlation.

The major rock constituents as determined from thin sections are summarised in Figure 27: they comprise diverse skeletal remains, detrital grains, ooliths and superficial ooliths, pellets, composite grains and algal particles, including pisoliths, in a micrite or micrograined calcite matrix. At least five distinct rock types have been recorded in these sections:

(a) Conglomeratic limestones. A basal conglomerate is ubiquitous (Plate 5). It contains up to three varieties of pebbles: namely, small spheroidal phosphatic pebbles and grains, well rounded sandy limestone pebbles of Northampton Sand type, and abraded nodules of Upper Lias micritic limestone. The first type is always present, whilst the other two are commonest in the attenuated marginal facies. In the latter, sandy limestone pebbles occur at several levels, and in the most marginal outcrops the sequence consists entirely of conglomerates. In addition, small well rounded quartz pebbles and a very few homoiolithic pebbles have been recorded.

(b) Shell-fragmental limestones. Most of these limestones have either cryptograined or micrograined calcite matrices. In some, the coarser calcite occurs in pockets, suggesting that the matrix precipitated as micrite and was subsequently recrystallised. Most of these rocks fall within the mud-supported or packstone category (Dunham, 1962), although high-energy grainstones are important in the marginal facies.

Figure 26 Isopachytes of the Clypeus Grit

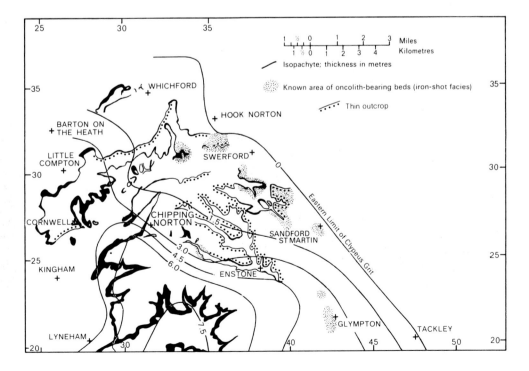

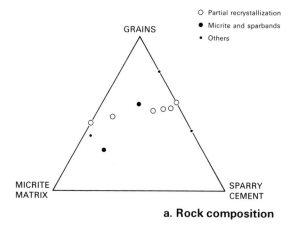

a. Rock composition

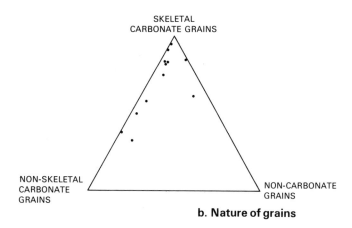

b. Nature of grains

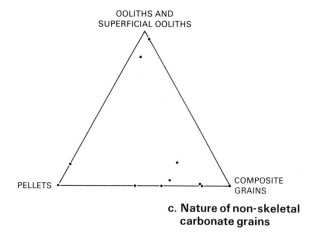

c. Nature of non-skeletal carbonate grains

Figure 27 Petrographical composition of the Clypeus Grit

(c) Oolith micritic limestones and composite grain-pellet micritic limestones. Oolith limestones are common in the upper part of the formation in the south. They usually contain a high proportion of shell debris. Pellets and composite grains are invariably present, but few in number.

(d) Pisolith micritic limestones. These include the characteristic iron-shot limestones of the marginal facies. They usually contain a significant proportion of shell debris, which forms the cores of the pisoliths.

(e) Mudstones and marls. Quartz rarely forms more than 2 per cent by volume of the Clypeus Grit. Clay is always present in the limestones, though usually only in traces. As its proportion increases the micritic limestones grade into marls. At some outcrops in the marginal facies area, mudstones can constitute half the thickness of the formation. Much of the depositional structure has been destroyed by bioturbation, but partings and lenses of winnowed shell debris can still be recognised.

Bivalves are the most abundant fossils, whilst brachiopods are locally common; echinoids, corals and free-swimming ammonites also occur. The sessile fauna includes the brachiopods *Kallirhynchia*, *Rhactorhynchia* and *Stiphrothyris* and the byssate *Modiolus*; these are associated with *Sarcinella*, *Liostrea* and *Placunopsis*. The motile and semi-motile epifauna includes the bivalves *Astarte*, *Barbatia*, *Camptonectes*, *Chlamys*, *Limatula*, *Meleagrinella*, *Plagiostoma*, *Pseudolimea*, and the semi-burrowing forms *Trigonia* and *Myophorella*. The irregular echinoids *Clypeus*, *Holectypus* and *Pygurus* also lived in shallow burrows. Fossils in growth positions are rare and most belong to the burrowing genera *Arcomya* and *Pholadomya*. Cavities of the rock-boring *Lithophaga* are common in most of the large pebbles although the shells are rare. Indefinite bioturbation structures occur throughout, and two well-defined types of burrows are present: firstly, narrow tubular burrows preserved in pebbles; secondly, 'U-shaped' burrows similar to those in the Northampton Sand (see pp.51).

Plate 5 Polished cores of Clypeus Grit and Chipping Norton Limestone, Hook Norton and Ledwell boreholes × 0.75

a. Chipping Norton Limestone on Clypeus Grit. The Chipping Norton Limestone comprises 50 mm of bluish grey medium-grained shell fragmental oolith limestone with traces of bedding marked by differential grain size banding. Small pebbles are present near the base where it rests on an uneven surface of the Clypeus Grit, the pebbles in which stand out above the matrix. The Clypeus Grit is a darker bluish grey conglomeratic coarse shell fragmental sparry limestone. The largest pebbles are sandy silty shell fragmental rocks, others present, include oolith sparry limestones, micritic limestones, micritic limestones and at the base black phosphatic types. Irregular masses of reddish brown sideritic micrite may represent poorly consolidated pebbles. Many of the pebbles have be reworked from the Northampton Sand and show lithophagid borings, others have been derived from the Lias. Hook Norton Borehole, junction at 39.6 m (129ft 11in), natural size.

b. Clypeus Grit. Pale fawn-weathering bluish grey hearted oolith micritic limestone. Soft and argillaceous at the top becoming more calcareous downward with unevenly distributed limonitic ooliths and shell debris. Bivalves are scattered throughout and are associated with large compound grains and small pebbles. Ledwell Borehole, 15.9 m (52ft 3in), natural size.

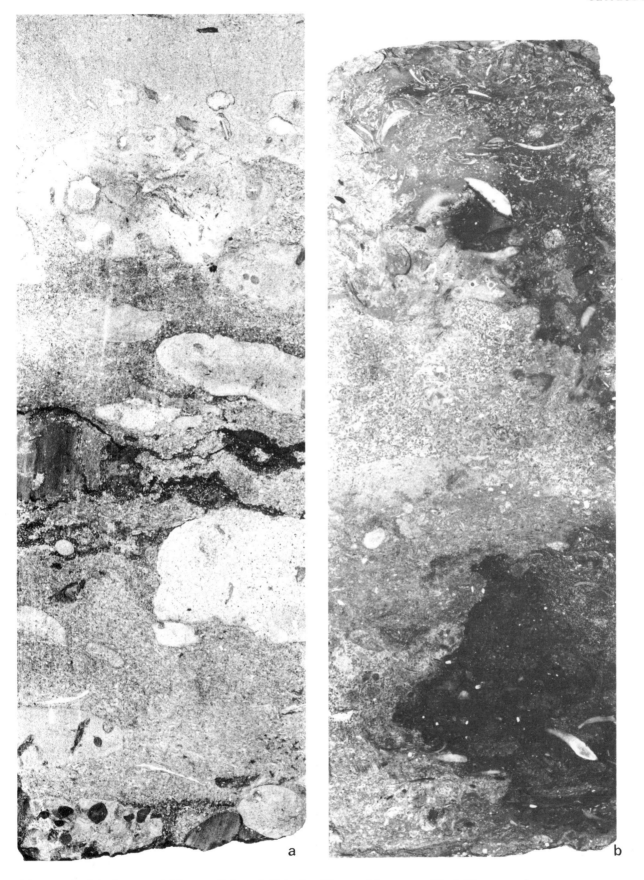

Plate 5 Polished cores of Clypeus Grit and Chipping Norton Limestone, Hook Norton and Ledwell boreholes. For details, see opposite·

Corals have been collected from the Clypeus Grit at Hook Norton (p.63) and Sharp's Hill (p.64), and from field brash at Oatley Hill. The solitary coral *Dimorpharea* is associated with compound forms: both types are unabraded. The compound corals form disc-like masses up to 50 mm thick, and are of particular interest because of the pholid-type borings which are confined to the upper surface or sides of the colony. The unworn character and the distribution of the borings indicate that the colonies are either in or very near to their growth positions. Colonial corals have also been recorded from near the top of the Clypeus Grit in the Ledwell Borehole. The fauna is listed in Appendix 1(3).

A marine transgression preceded the deposition of the Clypeus Grit. It accumulated in relatively shallow quiet water with a stable bottom habitat. Precipitation of lime mud was important; the ooliths and pisoliths were swept in from adjacent areas. To the north and east, where the deposit thins out, iron-shot conglomeratic limestones accumulated.

AH

Details

Chastleton – Long Compton

The Clypeus Grit is estimated to be at least 3 m thick in this area. In an old quarry [2482 2683] east of Adlestrop church, 2.4 m of rubbly pisolite are overlain by the Chipping Norton Limestone. There are similar exposures in two other quarries [2574 2627; 2694 2682] to the east. Close to the latter quarry, above a spring [2691 2711] west of Cornwell Manor, 3 m of Clypeus Grit rubble occur above fragments of Scissum Beds found at the bottom of the bank.

Farther north, there is much coarse pisolite brash along the hillside between Hill Farm [2586 2890] and Oakham [2747 3051] with sporadic exposures showing up to 1.82 m of the formation. Eastwards, on the hillside north of the Rollright Stones [2963 3133], the Clypeus Grit locally thickens to 3.7 m and forms two good features, but to the east of Hill Barn it appears to thin to 2.4 m. North of Long Compton from Harrow Hill to Stourton Hill the Clypeus Grit thins rapidly, and there are few exposures and little field brash.

EGP

To the north of Whichford Wood, the Clypeus Grit is also very thin, and consists of a rubbly-weathering pisolitic cementstone and marly pisolitic limestone. North of Whichford it is less than 0.6 m thick, the outcrop being obscured in most places by downwash.

Churchill – Chipping Norton

South of Lyneham Barrow, the formation is about 6.1 m thick, field brash suggesting that the lower part is a coarse pisolitic and shelly limestone and the upper part a uniformly medium-grained pale cream oolite. Near Churchill, it is estimated to be about 4.9 m, and a basal conglomerate, with pebbles of quartz, fine-grained fawn limestone and Liassic limestone, is frequently ploughed. A borehole [3034 2607] south-west of Chipping Norton church proved 5.94 m of limestone, almost the whole thickness of the Clypeus Grit.

The basal conglomerate is again present near The Common, Chipping Norton. Overlying rubbly marly oolitic and pisolitic limestones have been ploughed north of Primsdown Farm [3038 2700], and contain *Rhynchonelloidea* and *Stiphrothyris*. Cream marly pisolite brash in a field [3050 2815] west of Over Norton contains *Clypeus* cf. *ploti*, *Stiphrothyris birdlipensis* and *S. tumida*. The formation progressively thins along the outcrop to the north. A drainage ditch [3048 2969] along the roadside at Choicehill Farm exposed only 0.6 to 0.9 m of Clypeus Grit. The thickness is about 1.2 m near Hull Farm [329 296], and slightly less in a small outcrop at Walk Farm [3379 2997] within the Swerford fault trough. The formation could not be mapped south of Coldharbour Farm [347 301].

The Clypeus Grit is believed to be about 5.8 m thick in Sarsden No.9 Borehole [2966 1739] in the Witney district. The cores were fragmentary but consisted in the upper part of pale fawn medium-to fine-grained oolitic micritic limestones with scattered shells and shell debris, overlying pale fawn, medium to coarse, shell-fragmental oolitic micritic limestones with coarse pisolith composite grains and greenish and brown argillaceous pipes.

Cornwell – Great Rollright – Hook Norton

The Clypeus Grit is probably about 3 m thick near Park Farm [274 278], but is slightly thicker east of Cornwell Manor. Fossiliferous rubbly oolitic limestone was exposed in a temporary section [2808 2883] north-west of Salford church. The following fossils were collected: *Sarcinella sp.*, *Chomatoseris porpites*, *Holectypus hemisphaericus*, *Stiphrothyris birdlipensis*, *Rhactorhynchia sp.*, *Camptonectes sp.*, *Chlamys (Radulopecten)* aff. *vagans*, *Entolium corneolum*, *Limatula* cf. *gibbosa.*, *Liostrea (Praeexogyra) acuminata*, *Modiolus imbricatus* and *Cossmannea (Eunerinea)* cf. *eudesii*. At a spring [2891 2930] east-north-east of Hirons Hill Farm, coarse pisolitic marly limestone rubble rests upon 0.46 m of massive shelly limestone (probably the basal Clypeus Grit), which overlies the Upper Lias.

Near Little Rollright the Clypeus Grit is about 3 m thick and has a conglomeratic band at its base. Hard bands appear in a road cutting [306 311] south-west of Hill Barn, where scattered exposures show rubbly argillaceous coarse oolitic limestones, shell-fragmental limestones and a thin pebbly limestone resting above a bored bed, which probably belongs to the Scissum Beds. The basal beds are also seen in a drainage ditch [3182 3127] west of Great Rollright, where 150 mm of greenish grey argillaceous limestone with brown limonitised pisoliths and shell fragments rest on 50 mm of fossiliferous pisolitic limestone with small pebbles largely derived from Upper Lias limestones.

North of Great Rollright the Grit is thinner. Woodward (1894, p.157) recorded 'a hard sandy oolitic bed with bored stones and corals; pebbly at base' resting on 'Northampton Sand' in a quarry, now overgrown, west of Hotley Hill Farm (now Oatleyhill Farm).

Fragments of bored limestone, conglomerate, pisolitic limestone and coralline limestone are ploughed in fields to the south-west and south-east. Near Fanville Head Farm [347 324] the thickness is less than 0.6 m, and the formation cannot be separately mapped.

A reservoir 185 m east of Cardwell Farm was dug into Clypeus Grit; fragments of shelly argillaceous oolite and a coarse, slightly sandy, shell-fragmental oolite are still visible; the former is of particular interest since the ooliths are entirely limonitised, having a lustrous appearance that contrasts strongly with the greenish grey marly matrix. To the east scattered outcrops occur immediately to the north of the Rollright Fault, where the thickness is thought to be about 1 m at Duckpool Farm [350 314].

AH

The most easterly exposure of the Clypeus Grit in this area is in the railway cutting at the southern end of the Hook Norton Tunnel (Plate 6). At the back of a small landslip on the east side of the cutting [3583 3158], the following section is exposed:

	Thickness m
CHIPPING NORTON LIMESTONE (see p.69)	—
CLYPEUS GRIT	
Limestone; brownish grey, sandy, oolitic, rather flaggy, with some small black limestone pebbles. The ooliths are ferruginous and limonitised in their outer layers. Much shell debris, making up most of the rock in some patches. A few large flat wood fragments	0.25
Marl; mauve-coloured, sandy, passing upwards into brown clay; bands of white shell fragments including *Cucullaea sp.*, *Liostrea* cf. *hebridica*, *Vaugonia (Orthotrigonia) gemmata*, *Plicatula sp.*	0.18

Limestone; bluish grey to brown weathering, with a few small black limestone pebbles; *Dimorpharea defranciana, Chlamys viminea, Cucullaea sp., Liostrea (P.)* aff. *acuminata, Liostrea sp.* and *Procerithium vetustus-majus*   0.10–0.15

Limestone; brown, weathering grey, with black limestone pebbles up to 25 mm across. Large flattened compound corals; highly fossiliferous with *Montlivaltia trochoides, Thamnasteria sp., Barbatia pulchra, Chlamys* cf. *viminea, Liostrea* cf. *hebridica,* and *Pseudolimea sp.*   0.10–0.15

Limestone; brownish grey, and marly clay with black limestone pebbles, and much shell debris. Fossils include *Montlivaltia trochoides, Thamnasteria sp., Chlamys viminea, Liostrea sp.* and *Modiolus sp.*   0.08–0.10

Upper Lias   seen to 1.2

The lowermost three beds of this section are possibly equivalent in age to the Upper Coral Bed (Richardson, 1911, p.213). In a now inaccessible section in the west side of the cutting at the northern end of the tunnel [3596 3227], the following section (with authors of taxa omitted) was recorded by Richardson (1911, p.214); the original lithostratigraphic classification is shown in brackets after the current usage:

Thickness
m

CHIPPING NORTON LIMESTONE ('HOOK NORTON BEDS') (see p.69)   —

CLYPEUS GRIT ('UPPER CORAL BED AND CLYPEUS GRIT equivalent')

Limestone; very hard, somewhat ferruginous, with a very irregular under surface, forming a kind of cap to the Conglomerate-Bed; *Astarte minima, Trigoniae, Acanthothyris* sp.   about 0.15

Conglomerate-Bed. Pebbles, water-worn, bored by *Lithophagi* and often covered with oysters and *Serpulae,* in a brown, rather sandy marl with bleached oysters and well-rolled shells. Where this bed is thicker and less conglomeratic, the Coral-Bed comes in at the base. *Rhynchonella* cf. *subtetrahedra,* common, *Gresslya abducta, Pleuromya* cf. *goldfussi* and other species, *Pholadomya sp., Myoconcha, Cucullaea, Alectryonia, Pteria inaequivalvis, Serpulae,* etc.   average 0.13

Limestone; very hard   0.13

Limestone; hard, iron-speckled, with irregular under surface   0.10

SCISSUM BEDS   —

Plate 6   Clypeus Grit resting on Upper Lias mudstones, Hook Norton railway cutting [358 316] A9820

Richardson (1922, pp.121,131) also recorded 0.51 m of Clypeus Grit at crop at Fern Hill, near Bloxham [407 352]; the section is no longer visible.

BJW

In the Hook Norton Borehole [3564 3588] a 0.46-m limestone conglomerate band (base at 39.75 m) may be the Clypeus Grit. Superficial oolith limestone, siderite mudstone, calcite mudstone, phosphate, fine-grained conglomerate and calcarenite pebbles were recorded from it, and burrows in the underlying Northampton Sand had been sealed by encrusting corals prior to the deposition of the conglomerate.

AH

Traitor's Ford

The Clypeus Grit is not mappable in this area but it forms a bed 0.36 m thick beneath the Chipping Norton Limestone in Sharp's Hill Quarry [338 358], where it consists of brown, coarse-grained, pisolitic limestone with many fossils and abundant plants. Among the fossils were *Meleagrinella lycetti, Modiolus sp., Plicatula sp.* and *Trigonia sculpta cheltensis*.

EGP

Heythrop – Enstone

The Clypeus Grit forms a narrow sinuous outcrop along the valleys of the River Glyme and its tributaries. It appears to thicken to the south-south-west. A specimen of *Parkinsonia schloenbachi* of the early Bathonian *Zigzagiceras zigzag* Zone was collected from pisolitic marly limestone brash in a field east of Priory Farm [336 281], Over Norton. About 0.30 m of limestone, consisting of pale fawn ooliths and shell fragments set in a greenish grey micritic matrix, with *Pseudomelania sp.* and *Protocardia sp.*, rests on Upper Lias in a ditch north-west of Castle Farm [362 282], Heythrop. A rubbly coarse pisolitic micritic limestone with *Pygurus michelini* was exposed in a pipe trench west of Heythrop College.

The formation is seen in two small exposures in the Glyme valley. The first [3436 2565] shows 1.22 m of cream, rubbly-bedded argillaceous oolitic limestone with *Chomatoseris porpites, Clypeus ploti, Globirhynchia subobsoleta, Arcomya crassiuscula, Ceratomya sp., Chlamys (Radulopecten) sp., Entolium corneolum, Limatula gibbosa, Pholadomya deltoidea, Plagiostoma sp., Pleuromya subelongata, Protocardia* cf. *lycetti, Pseudolimea duplicata* and wood fragments, resting on 0.61 m of pale brown sandy limestone; the second shows 0.13 m of ferruginous pisolitic marly limestone beneath the Chipping Norton Limestone.

AH

Enstone – Glympton

The Clypeus Grit thickens eastwards from about 3 m near Lidstone to at least 4.6 m near Cleveley. Its base is commonly marked by seepages.

To the south, around Taston [360 220] the Clypeus Grit thickens to at least 6.1 m. To the east, in the Glyme valley, a small outcrop of Clypeus Grit occurs in a copse [4141 2273] south-west of Whitehouse Farm, Kiddington, where about 0.3 m of soft, nodular-weathering, pale fawn limestone with large, brown-weathering, ferruginous pisoliths is brought to the surface by valley bulging. Fossils collected include: *Kallirhynchia acutiplicata, Cucullaea, Entolium, Liostrea, Opis, Pholadomya* cf. *ovulum, Pleuromya uniformis, Trigonia* cf. *sculpta* and *Vaugonia sp.*

Farther to the south-east, the hall and church at Glympton Park stand on Clypeus Grit, which is brought to surface by valley bulging

(Figure 3). The formation has a small outcrop to the north-west and south-east, within which numerous minor exposures occur. Two further small isolated outcrops [428 205; 425 210], near Hill Farm, are also due to valley bulging.

EGP

Charlbury

Mr R. J. Wyatt has recorded almost 5.6 m of marly oolitic and shell-fragmental limestones in the Town Quarry, Charlbury [3687 1985] (see p.71).

The Tews – Sandford St Martin

Near Showell Farm [359 291] the formation is thought to be about 1.2 m thick; it consists of the typical pale yellow to cream ooliths and pisoliths set in a greenish grey micrite matrix. This lithology persists along the outcrop to the east-south-east, but when traced eastward along the northern side of the valley and also eastward from the vicinity of Pomfret Castle [367 303] field brash shows a marginal iron-shot facies which consists of thinly cross-bedded limonitised pisolitic and shell-debris limestones, platy limonitised shell-debris limestones, pisolitic shelly micritic limestones and rare coral-bearing limestones. In thin section a complex history of limonitisation and reworking is revealed. The zonal index *Parkinsonia parkinsoni* was collected from field brash [3713 2968], north-west of The Meetings.

South of Great Tew the thickness is only 0.6 to 0.9 m, but farther south it increases to about 1.5 m in the mill race at Tracey Farm [3983 2690], where the beds are poorly exposed in an anticline. The basal bed (resting on Upper Lias) is 0.15 m of pale fawn, fine-grained oolitic conglomeratic limestone with pebbles of Upper Lias cementstone, oolite and phosphate. It is overlain by a weathered rubble of oolitic micritic limestone and a limonitised-pisolith shell-fragmental micritic limestone which yielded *Astarte minima, Camptonectes* cf. *comatus, Cucullaea minchinhamptonensis, Entolium corneolum, Grammatodon sp., Isocyprina* cf. *sharpi, Liostrea* cf. *hebridica, Plagiostoma sp., Pseudolimea* cf. *duplicata, Pseudolimea sp., Tancredia brevis, Trigonia sp.*, fish teeth and fragments of wood.

In the Ledwell Borehole [4093 2821], the Clypeus Grit was 2.29 m of shelly limestones and mudstones. Scattered pebbles lie at various levels, and the formation is overlain by the Chipping Norton Limestone. To the south-east, two small exposures of Clypeus Grit near Sandford St Martin lie near the original limit of the formation. In a small ditch [4138 2737] east of Beaconsfield Farm, 50 mm of pisolite are overlain by 0.30 m of flaggy shelly limestone, possibly also part of the Clypeus Grit and, in turn, by 150 mm of brown sandstone, representing a sandy facies of the Chipping Norton Limestone. In a stream bank [4215 2613] near Sandford St Martin, the Upper Lias is overlain by 0.30 m of pisolite, which lies beneath the Chipping Norton Limestone.

BJW

A few fragments of typical Clypeus Grit have been recorded from hill-wash in a field [4225 2602] west of the Manor House, Westcot Barton. A single fragment was reported in the spoil from a roadside ditch [4434 2592] east of Middle Barton. Rare fragments of micritic limestone and shelly shell-fragmental limestone, possibly Clypeus Grit, were found in a post hole [4350 2702] at Downhill Farm: the bed appears to separate white sands of the 'Lower Estuarine Series' from the Chipping Norton Limestone.

The Clypeus Grit has not been recorded east of the Dorn Valley Fault.

AH

CHAPTER 6

Middle Jurassic: Great Oolite Group

Much of the Middle Jurassic succession has been traditionally grouped together as the 'Great Oolite Series'. This term does not conform with modern stratigraphic practice, and is replaced by Great Oolite Group. The division covers all the strata between the base of the Chipping Norton Limestone and the top of the Cornbrash. The stratigraphical terminology employed in this account is that used on the 1:50 000 map. Most of the units have been subsequently called formations (McKerrow and Kennedy, 1973). The sequence is largely of Bathonian age (Figure 28).

CHIPPING NORTON LIMESTONE

The name Chipping Norton Limestone was introduced by Hudleston (1878) to cover the strata lying between the top of the Clypeus Grit and the largely argillaceous beds now referred to as the Sharp's Hill Beds. Walford (1883) used the term in a different sense, restricting it to the limestones lying above the Trigonia signata Bed, a horizon he considered to have correlative value. Richardson (1911), Arkell (1933, 1947a), and Sellwood and McKerrow (1974) employ variants of this scheme but, because of the difficulty in

establishing the continuity of the critical marker bed, the present account reverts to the original definition.

The Chipping Norton Limestone attains its maximum thickness around Chipping Norton where it is 10.7 m thick and gives rise to extensive plateaux. To the north-east and east it thins steadily, being only about 5 m thick in Sharp's Hill Quarry, some 8 km to the north, and in the Ledwell Borehole, about 14 km to the east-north-east. In the extreme north, and again near its eastern limit, it overlaps the Clypeus Grit, resting on horizons as low as the Upper Lias. It is absent from the eastern part of the district, dying out roughly along a line from Sibford Ferris to Steeple Aston. It also dies out westwards and south-westwards from the district where it passes into the Fuller's Earth. Sellwood and McKerrow (1974) suggested that the formation is thickest in two areas, one centred about Chipping Norton and the other in the north Cotswolds, and that these areas were separated by a thinner sequence overlying the Moreton-in-Marsh Swell. There are, however, too few data to confirm the thickness trends in detail.

A typical vertical section of the unit is given in Figure 29 (see also Figure 31). A small outcrop of clay at or near the base of the formation north-east of Lyneham may represent

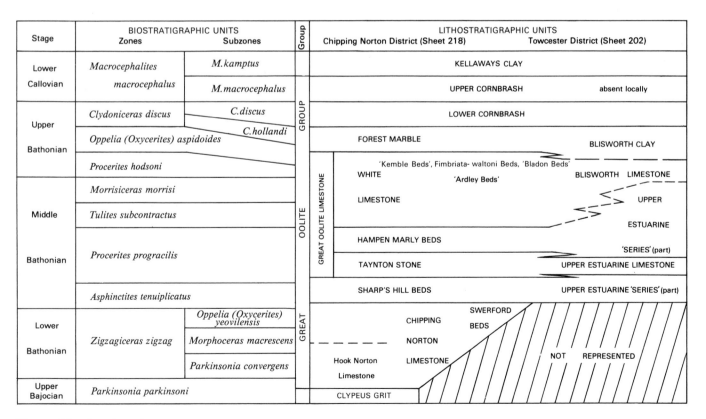

Figure 28 Stratigraphy of the Great Oolite Group

the Roundhill Clay which locally underlies the limestone in the district to the north; it has been included in the main formation. Throughout much of the rest of the district the limestone rests with apparent conformity upon the Clypeus Grit.

In its eponymous area the bulk of the formation consists of fine- to medium-grained, pale fawn to cream-speckled oolitic limestone with shell-fragmental bands: non-calcareous lithologies are restricted to a few thin mudstones and marls up to 75 mm thick. The limestones are of the spar-cemented and grainstone types (Dunham, 1962). Ooliths and superficial ooliths are the dominant rock constituents, associated with varying proportions of shell debris, pellets, composite grains, quartz and pebbles. Thin conglomeratic limestones occur throughout the formation. Homoiolithic pebbles are the most common, though difficult to recognise in the field; some of them have been bored into by *Lithophaga* and encrusted by oysters. They are commonly associated with well-rounded pebbles of quartz up to 13 mm in diameter. The

skeletal limestones contain few whole shells and are commonly comparatively coarse grained. The matrix is generally sparry. Individual beds have sharp bases and locally show graded bedding, burrows and clay wisps. The composition of representative limestones is shown in Figure 30.

When fresh the limestones appear to be thickly and poorly bedded; locally they are freestones. Weathering, however, produces flaggy textures, and reveals tabular beds affected by gently inclined or, more rarely, steeply inclined cross-stratification. Ripple-marked surfaces are uncommon, but there are many weak erosional surfaces and thin conglomerates overlie some of these.

A hard massive sandy limestone with bored and oyster-encrusted pebbles has been termed the Trigonia signata Bed (Richardson, 1911), but it is not now possible to verify that all such records represent the same horizon. Beneath these occurrences the limestones ('Hook Norton Limestone' of Walford, 1883) are slightly argillaceous with rubbly flaggy weathering; they contain more plant debris, shell remains

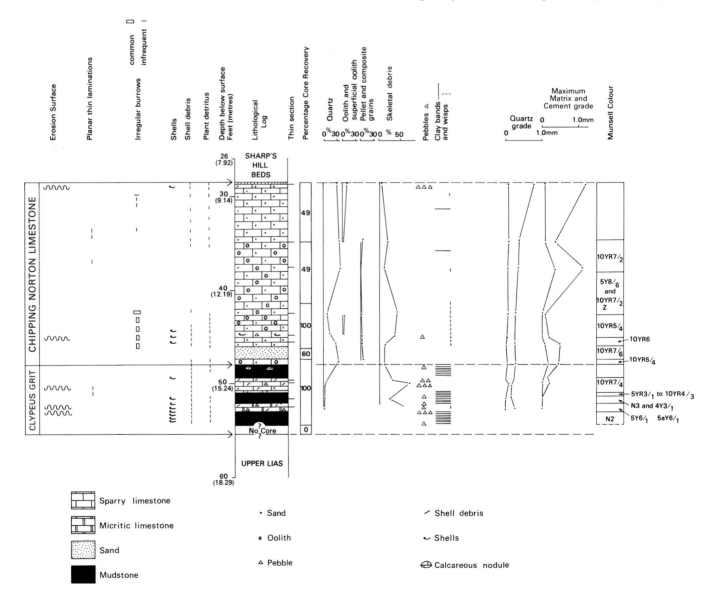

Figure 29 Clypeus Grit and Chipping Norton Limestone in the Ledwell Borehole

and clay-filled pipes than do the beds above.

Around Swerford and Great Tew the formation changes appreciably in character: ooliths are much less common in the limestones, and quartz forms up to 30 per cent of the rock. Indeed at outcrop, due to decalcification, the rocks can be mistaken for sands. These sandy limestones have been called the Swerford Beds (Richardson, 1911). Richardson assigned them to a position high in the sequence, but it seems more probable that they range significantly downwards and they may represent the beginning of a north-eastwards passage into a sand facies. The Swerford Beds have not been mapped separately because their limits are so transitional.

Near Sarsden and Chadlington, at Swerford Quarry [370 317], and in the Hook Norton Borehole, micritic limestones with some interbedded marls cap the more characteristic lithologies. Some authors have included these within the Chipping Norton Limestone, but the present account treats them as the basal beds of the Sharp's Hill Beds with which they have much in common.

The Chipping Norton Limestone rarely yields well-preserved macrofossils, and few of these are diagnostic of age. The fauna is of shallow marine type. It is dominated by bivalves, particularly thick-shelled taxa: sessile epifaunal forms such as *Liostrea* abound, and are associated with *Lopha*, *Modiolus* and *Plicatula*; mobile species include *Camptonectes* and *Chlamys*; shallow-burrowing species such as *Astarte*, *Cucullaea*, *Myophorella*, *Plagiostoma*, *Pleuromya* and *Trigonia* occur, but are rarely found in growth position. Brachiopods, gastropods and serpulids form an insignificant part of the fauna, as do echinoid and crinoid fragments. In contrast corals and trace fossils are rare, except for inclined or vertical cylindrical burrows filled with clay, which are particularly common in the lower part of the limestone. Few ammonites have been recorded from the district. The recorded faunas are summarised in Appendix 1(4) and related to the Lower Bathonian zones and subzones in Figure 28.

Both lithology and fauna suggest that the Chipping Norton Limestone accumulated in a shallow sea which was bounded to the south-west by deeper and quieter water in which the Fuller's Earth was laid down. The shoreline lay across the north-eastern part of the district. Near it the sea transgressed across the 'Lower Estuarine Series', some of the sediments of which were possibly incorporated in the basal limestones and in the Swerford Beds (Horton, 1977). Indeed, Sellwood and McKerrow (1974) considered that the latter and the 'Lower Estuarine Series' form a single unit.

The environment seems at first to have been one of moderate energy with a subsequent increase in current activity. The general lack of grading within the tabular beds and their sharp junctions suggest that they originated as sheet deposits, while the steeply cross-stratified units probably represent truncated mega-ripples or avalanche foresets forming part of a landward-prograding shoal (Sellwood and McKerrow, 1974). Most of the shells are concentrated into layers in which the valves are largely disarticulated and some abraded; these beds are lag conglomerates produced by winnowing of the contemporary sediment. Unstable substrate conditions with continued abrasion and reworking seem to be responsible for the many beds of skeletal debris, and for the mixture of ooliths and coated and non-coated sand

grains. The lack of diversity and the paucity of the fauna together with the rarity of burrowing organisms confirm the presence of unstable substrate conditions, particularly in the upper part of the sequence. AH

Details

Chastleton – Long Compton

The Chipping Norton Limestone is estimated to be at least 6.1 m thick on the hills to the east of Chastleton and Adlestrop. On Chastleton Hill, up to 3.7 m of fairly coarse, brown-weathering, oolitic, sandy limestone is exposed in old roadside quarries [2559 2841]. To the south, the uppermost beds of the Chipping Norton Limestone can be seen in another old quarry [2576 2782] where 1.83 m of hard, yellow, sandy, massively bedded, medium-grained, oolitic limestone is overlain in turn by 1.83 m of coarse, cream, flaggy oolitic limestone and by the Sharp's Hill Beds: the rocks dip to the south-east at 6°. Similar beds occur in the old Chastleton Hill quarry [2621 2867].

A quarry [2535 2705] north-west of Hill Farm, Daylesford, exposes 1.52 m of coarse, brown, shelly, oolitic flags resting on 0.61 m of hard, brown, sandy limestone with scattered ooliths. In this general area, 1.22 m of flaggy oolitic limestone overlie the Clypeus Grit in a temporary excavation [2546 2656] near Hill Farm.

The best section hereabouts is in a quarry [2573 2628] south of Hill Farm:

	Thickness m
CHIPPING NORTON LIMESTONE	
Limestone; cream, rubbly and flaggy, oolitic	1.83
Limestone; brown, massive, sandy and oolitic with many shells at the base	0.84
Clay; dark brown with lignite and shells	0.03 – 0.05
Limestone; brown, fine-grained, sandy, rather flaggy	0.61
Limestone; brown, massive sandy and oolitic with lignitic fragments	1.52
Limestone; brown, flaggy, sandy, passing into	0.61
Limestone; brown, massive, coarsely oolitic	0.61
CLYPEUS GRIT	
Limestone; brown, massive, pisolitic and fossiliferous	0.91

Most of the old quarries on Whitequarry Hill (Richardson, 1911, p.230) are now overgrown, but in one [2676 2708], west of Cornwell Manor, 2.74 m of whitish cream, hard, massively-bedded, oolitic, sandy limestone with a few flaggy bands are overlain by 0.3 m of cream flaggy oolitic limestone. The basal beds are exposed in a nearby quarry [2695 2682] where the Clypeus Grit is overlain by 1.22 m of flaggy, sandy, brown oolitic limestone. EGP

In working quarries to the north and south of the A44 at Cross Hands [2701 2889] there are several sections which show up to 3.8 metres of fawn, fine-grained oolitic flaggy limestones, with bands of coarse oolite layers, rich in shells, and in the lower part, large plant fragments. These are overlain by the Sharp's Hill Beds in the latter quarry which also expose the base of the formation. AH, EGP

Another disused quarry [2744 2888] east of Cross Hands shows beds high in the sequence dipping south-east at 12°:

	Thickness m
Soil, brown clayey	0.15
Limestone; cream, coarse-grained, oolitic, flaggy, with much shell debris	1.52

Limestone; cream, sandy, massively bedded and
hard;   seen 0.30

Farther north, yet another disused quarry [2748 2974] is in
1.52 m of massive, brown, sandy limestone overlain by 1.52 m of
flaggy, brown, coarse-grained, oolitic limestone which dips west-
north-west at 20°.

There are good sections of the Chipping Norton Limestone
overlain by the Sharp's Hill Beds in several quarries at Oakham.
The highest limestones are flaggy oolites, and these rest on massive
sandy oolitic limestones. *Oppelia (Oxycerites) limosa* has been collected
from the easternmost quarry [2825 3070] (Richardson, 1911, p.228;
Arkell, 1951–8, pp.60–61). The northernmost [2810 3093] shows
the following section:

	Thickness m
Soil; brown, clayey with limestone fragments	0.30
Limestone; cream, thinly bedded, flaggy, coarsely oolitic, highly contorted in places	0.91
Limestone; cream, flaggy, coarse-grained and oolitic	1.22
Limestone; brown, massive, hard, sandy, oolitic with some small shell fragments, gently current-bedded,	1.22

North of Long Compton the Chipping Norton Limestone
occupies a wide outcrop from Harrow Hill [285 337] north-
eastwards to Margett's Hill [296 348], with scattered old workings.
A roadside quarry [2862 3402], north-east of the Weston Park
Lodge, exposes 1.98 m of fine-grained, whitish-weathering, brown-
hearted, very sandy limestone containing a few shell fragments,
overlain by 2.44 m of fine-grained, white-weathering, brown-
hearted, ripple-marked, very soft calcareous sandstone with bands
of very coarse oolite in the upper parts. The north-north-west face
shows up to 3.7 m of fairly massive, gently current-bedded
sandstone or sandy limestone, which is finely oolitic in places and
dips north-east at 10°.

Similar sections can be examined in small diggings and quarries
nearby [e.g. 2903 3424].   EGP

Whichford

The Chipping Norton Limestone crops out on the ridge trending
north-east from Harrow Hill to Margett's Hill and Whichford. The
following section is visible in an old quarry [3067 3475]:

	Thickness m
Limestone; white, shelly oolite	0.08
Limestone; flesh-coloured sandy oolite with pale ochreous brown clay wisps and pipes, irregular thin platy bedding; increasingly argillaceous downward with shell debris and plant fragments	0.66
Limestone; pale fawn, speckled, oolitic, with clay wisps and scattered shell and plant fragments; irregular flaggy bedding	0.23
Limestone; largely decalcified, consisting of fragments of pale fawn-tinted grey, fine-grained oolite set in a coarse, soft, argillaceous oolitic matrix with plant and shell fragments; most of the fragments are angular but there are a few rounded pebbles of ferruginous brown shell-fragmental pisolite	0.20
Limestone; very sandy with scattered ooliths, plant and shell fragments and argillaceous wisps, passing down into an oolitic calcareous sandstone which weathers to an ochreous sand	0.66
Limestone; pale cream, sandy, oolitic, with plant fragments and clay wisps	1.02

Section obscured	c.0.71
Limestone; shell-fragmental passing down into a sandy conglomerate with oolite pebbles	0.20
Limestone or calcareous sandstone; deeply weathered to sandy shelly rubble with secondary ferruginous veins	0.56
Limestone; very sandy, oolitic with clay wisps	0.58

Cornwell – Rollright

To the east of Cornwell, the Chipping Norton Limestone has been
brought down into the valley by the Swerford Fault. Some 1.52 m of
cream sandy oolite can be seen in a small quarry [2785 2703] south-
south-east of Cornwell church.

There are several small quarries to the east and south-east of
Hirons Hill Farm, Salford. The best exposed [2806 2913] shows the
following sequence:

	Thickness m
Soil; brown loam with pebbly limestone debris	0.30
Limestone; white to pale cream speckled, coarse shell-fragmental and oolitic, irregular flaggy bedding, sparsely fossiliferous	2.44
Limestone; white, finely oolitic with shell fragments; the proportion and grain size of the ooliths and shell debris vary, resulting in a banded appearance; massive, in two beds, the lower being the thinner and containing bivalves	1.09
Limestone; white, oolitic	0.61
	EGP

East of the King's Men (Rollright Stones) the Chipping Norton
Limestone can be divided into a lower unit of fawn to pale brown
coarse shelly and argillaceous oolite and fine-grained oolite with
abundant plant fragments (Hook Norton Limestone facies), and an
upper one of cream to white well-sorted sandy oolitic limestones:
the lower is exposed in grassed banks at the crossroads west-south-
west of Hill Barn. Limestone has been dug at various points on the
ride east of Oatleyhill Farm, but sections are no longer visible
although Richardson (1911, p.211) recorded 2.44 m of brown sandy
limestones with fragments of brown lignite and fossils in a quarry
[326 336] south-west of the farmhouse.

A temporary section [3311 3291], immediately south of Court
Farm, is notable for exposing lithologies typical of the lower part of
the sequence (Hook Norton Limestone):

	Thickness m
Soil	0.10
Limestone rubble; fragments of pale grey sandy and oolitic limestone with plant debris and argillaceous bands	0.30
Limestone; off-white, shell-fragmental with scattered quartz grains and limonitised ooliths, plant fragments and a few clay-filled burrows	0.30
Limestone; grey speckled, argillaceous, shell-fragmental, slightly sandy, plant fragments, some green clay pellets	0.18
Limestone; dull grey; speckled, sandy with clay wisps, shell fragments, scattered plant debris and grey clay-filled burrows	0.28

To the north of Rollright Heath Farm the upper part of the
formation is extremely sandy and large blocks of coarse oyster-rich
limestone can be seen.

The Chipping Norton Limestone crops out at several points

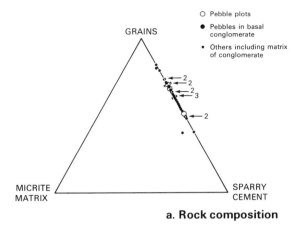

a. Rock composition

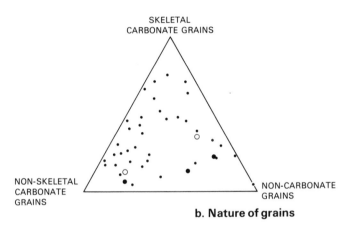

b. Nature of grains

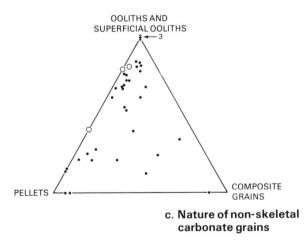

c. Nature of non-skeletal
carbonate grains

Figure 30 Petrographical composition of the Chipping Norton Limestone

within the Swerford Trough to the south-west of Great Rollright.

A complete section was formerly exposed in a quarry [3144 3021] to the north-north-west but has never been recorded in detail; the section is now largely obscured, but fragments indicate that the Hook Norton Limestone facies must be at least 3 m thick. There are numerous small exposures along the road to the north-west showing pale-coloured, false-bedded, sandy limestones with a few bands containing pebbles of oolitic limestone and the following section [3130 3047] was recorded on the east side of the A34 road:

	Thickness m
Soil and limestone rubble	0.91
Limestone; off-white oolitic and siliceous with rare shell fragments; generally fine-grained but with coarser bands; irregular platy bedding with secondary iron-rich layers, hard and compact but weathering to yellow sand	0.66
Limestone; pale cream, oolitic with shell fragments; medium- to fine-grained, slightly argillaceous with coarser bands	0.71
Limestone; cream-coloured with black speckling, shell-fragmental and oolitic with grey clayey patches	0.23
Limestone; cream, fine-grained, shell-fragmental and oolitic, with clay patches, irregular bedding	0.43

There are several small outcrops along the southern margin of the Swerford Trough. The best in Richardson's Swerford Beds, is behind a garage [3332 2997] at Priory Mill:

	Thickness m
Limestone; off-white to pale fawn, sandy, oolitic, strongly false-bedded, flaggy	3.66
Limestone; dull cream, slightly sandy, oolitic, thinly-bedded; becoming pale yellow, and weathering to sand downwards	0.5
Limestone; sandy, conglomeratic, with well-rounded homoiolithic pebbles, scattered oysters and *Trigonia*	0.18
Sand; yellow, patchily calcareous	0.13
Limestone; dull cream, sandy, oolitic, scattered oyster fragments, very thinly bedded, weathering to sand in basal 0.15 m	0.30
	AH

Hook Norton – Swerford

The railway tunnel piercing South Hill provides good sections in its approach cuttings. In the southern cutting the succession is:

	Thickness m
Limestone; hard, grey oolitic with reddish brown ooliths, and black lignitic fragments	1.22
Clay; brown, sandy with marly fragments	0.05 – 0.15
Limestone; greyish brown, oolitic with brown flattened ferruginous ooliths. Very shelly in parts with a band of mauve clay up to 50 mm thick near the top. Serpulid tubes, bivalves including *Catinula* aff. *matisconensis*, *Cucullaea* and *Vaugonia* cf. *producta*, wood fragments	0.38

The most complete section was recorded by Richardson (1911, p.213) from the northern cutting [3596 3227] and is given below with only minor changes (the original stratigraphic classification is given in brackets):

	Thickness m
CHIPPING NORTON LIMESTONE ('SWERFORD BEDS' OF RICHARDSON)	
Limestone; flaggy white oolitic (horizon of Plant Bed)	0.61
Sand; weathering white and very conspicuous	1.07
Limestone; bored in places by annelids	0.53
Sand; brown and yellow ⎤ with *Ostrea calceola* and	0.28
Limestone; sandy ⎱ *Lima* according to	0.10
Sand; brown and yellow ⎦ Walford	0.13
Limestone; sandy with incipient 'pot-lid' structure at the base	0.69 – 0.91
Sand; yellow and brown; *Serpula* and *Ostrea*	0.03
Limestone; sandy. The top surface of this bed is often well water-worn and pitted and covered with oysters	0.56
Sand; coarse gritty	0.05
('TRIGONIA SIGNATA BED' OF RICHARDSON)	
'Old Man Limestone'; hard, brown, sandy, with a water-worn surface covered with oysters, pebbly at the base	0.38
('HOOK NORTON BEDS' OF RICHARDSON)	
Sand; brown and yellow, with occasional 'knots'	0.05
Limestone; brown, shelly; *Pteria inaequivalvis* and shell fragments	c.0.58
Clay; dark, with a brown layer	0.18
Limestone; shelly	0.13
Clay; arenaceous	0.05
Limestone; hard sandy, brown but blue-centred, with numerous pieces of lignite	0.30
PLANT BED (of Walford): Limestone; brown sandy, full of brown fragments of lignite	0.10
Clay	0.06
Limestone; brown, shaly and marl	0.61
CLYPEUS GRIT (see p.63)	seen 0.51

Towards the eastern end of the Swerford Trough, the Chipping Norton Limestone is exposed in the bottom of the Swere valley, between Swerford Park [363 313] and Swerford village. On the north side of the valley 1.5 m of sandy oolite are exposed in a quarry [371 317] that has been fully described by Richardson (1911, p.216). On the south side of the valley, an old quarry [365 309] is in 2.74 m of sandy oolitic limestone which yielded *'Peronidella'?*, and a variety of bivalves, especially *Myophorella signata* and species of *Tancredia*. BJW

Churchill – Chadlington

Conglomeratic bands are exposed in the south-east corner of a quarry [2905 2522] south of Boulter's Barn:

	Thickness m
Limestone; pale fawn to cream, oolitic with minor shell debris and scattered grit-size pebbles (as below); irregular flaggy bedding	0.33
Limestone; medium-grained, sandy and oolitic with angular shell debris and bands with well rounded pebbles; the dominant pebbles are oolites of Chipping Norton Limestone type and of white vein quartz; there are a few pebbles of fawn oolith cementstones and one of blue-grey cherty sandstone; the matrices of the pebbly bands tend to be recrystallised, the rest	

	Thickness m
of the bed is friable; scattered oysters, trigoniids and crinoid columnals	0.36
Limestone; pale fawn, oolitic shell-fragmental, passing down into	0.15
Limestone; sandy oolitic, conglomeratic, as above, irregular honeycomb weathering	0.74
Limestone; off-white to cream, fine-grained oolitic, hard, compact, massive, flaggy weathering	0.53

About 3.7 m of shell-fragmental oolites lower in the sequence are poorly exposed on the north face (see Richardson, 1911, p.225). They are poorly fossiliferous, but contain *Liostrea hebridica*, *Lopha gregarea* and *Nanogyra crassa*.

The upper part of the Chipping Norton Limestone is well exposed in a quarry [313 250] east of Walterbush Farm where 1.07 m of Sharp's Hill Beds overlie 2.74 m of cross-bedded sandy oolites of the Chipping Norton Limestone. The same beds are visible in a nearby quarry [3141 2500]. The topmost beds of the Chipping Norton Limestone have been documented in another quarry [3000 2260] by Richardson (1911, p.223).

A thin band of dark blue clay resting on green clay was traced for several hundred metres in a field 180 m west-north-west of Lyneham Barrow. It appears to be about 1.5 m above the base of the Chipping Norton Limestone and resembles the Roundhill Clay recorded from the base of the formation south of the district (Richardson, 1929, pp.82–83).

The following section is visible in a quarry [297 210] to the south of Lyneham Barrow:

	Thickness m
?SHARP'S HILL BEDS	
Soil and angular limestone debris	0.36
Limestone; cream to pale brown, speckled, fossiliferous shell-fragmental, oolitic, irregular-weathering	0.79
Marl; pale brown, with white oyster valves, passing laterally into grey argillaceous limestone with ochreous ooliths and shell fragments	0.05 – 0.08
CHIPPING NORTON LIMESTONE	
Limestone; pale fawn, fine-grained, shell-fragmental and oolitic, with black dendritic markings; semi-porcellanised in top few centimetres	0.51
Limestone; cream, oolitic, friable	0.30
Limestone; fawn to cream, shell-fragmental, oolitic, friable in top few centimetres, flaggy weathering below	2.03
Limestone; fawn and dark cream mottled, medium-grained oolite with layers of large trigoniid shells seen on vertical faces, differential cementation, massive- to rubbly-weathering	0.83
Limestone; pale fawn, oolitic, very hard, massive, well-jointed	1.26

The fauna included: *Astarte?*, *Liostrea sp.*, *Modiolus sp.*, *Myophorella?* and *Vaugonia* cf. *moretoni*. AH

Most of the old quarry sections described by Richardson (1911) from the northern slopes of the Evenlode valley around Chadlington and Spelsbury are no longer visible. His account of the Hawk Stone Quarry [3415 2337], Dean, recorded beds now regarded as Sharp's Hill Beds resting on the Chipping Norton Limestone.

Richardson (p.221) also described a broadly similar succession in East-end Quarry, Chadlington [3323 2269]. In the reopened Town Quarry [3687 1985], Charlbury, Mr R. J. Wyatt records the following section (the higher parts of the section appear on p.78).

	Thickness m

CHIPPING NORTON LIMESTONE
Limestone; cream to white, fine- to medium-
grained, shell-fragmental and oolitic, with pale
fawn sparsely oolitic beds; individual beds show
small-scale cross-stratification and rippled
surfaces; hard, brownish and recrystallised in
top 0.3 m 3.00
Limestone; pale cream, very fine-grained, sandy,
finely oolitic; thickly-bedded and compact 3.10
Sand; orange-brown, marly with impersistent
limestone ribs; shell debris and shells; 0.10–0.15

CLYPEUS GRIT
Limestone; cream, marly, medium to coarse
ooliths and scattered pale orange pisoliths 1.80
Limestone; pale orange to cream, soft, marly,
shell-fragmental 0.00–0.10
Limestone; yellowish cream, marly oolitic and
shell-fragmental with many brachiopods and
bivalves 0.50–0.75
Limestone; creamy fawn, marly, fine-grained
with scattered ferruginous grains and sparse
ooliths; many brachiopods, bivalves, some
gastropods; includes two thin bands of orange-
brown shell-detrital sand 2.13
Limestone; pale brown and buff, soft, very
marly, shell-fragmental, sparse coarse ooliths ... 0.90
Limestone; brown, hard, marly, sparsely oolitic
shell-fragmental with scattered ferruginous
grains and a sparry cement .... seen 0.25
                                                          BJW

Chipping Norton

The outcrop of the Chipping Norton Limestone forms the high
ground to the north and east of the town. It is difficult to determine
its total thickness because of cambering, but it may be about 7.6 m.
Pale cream to white sandy shelly oolites were seen in several old
quarries around Over Norton [e.g. 3143 2911].

Excavations for a swimming pool at Chipping Norton Grammar
School [3153 2658] were in 1.52 m of thinly bedded, well jointed,
pale brown, black-speckled, well sorted, medium-grained oolite. The
following section was recorded in a nearby quarry [3172 2692]:

	Thickness m

SHARP'S HILL BEDS
Soil; brown clay with oysters 0.30
Clay; greenish brown, disturbed, scattered oysters,
sandy and ochreous with limestone fragments near
the base 0.38

CHIPPING NORTON LIMESTONE
Limestone; fawn to cream, medium-grained, oolitic
and shell-fragmental, cross-stratified, flaggy 1.09
Limestone; fawn, medium to coarse, oolitic with shell
debris sorted in coarse and fine layers, massive but
tending to flaggy bedding 1.12
Limestone; oolitic, shell-fragmental with coarse shell-
fragmental band near the base; slightly argillaceous,
locally decalcified 0.23
Limestone; pale fawn, oolitic, shell-fragmental with
bands of varying grain size 0.76

About 275 m to the north is the well-known Padley's Quarry
where Woodward (1894, p.324) recorded 3.66 m of 'brown and
pale oolite, sharply jointed, current-bedded, the lower beds tougher

and siliceous'; the sections are now overgrown. The formation is
well exposed, however, in the Oxfordshire County Council Quarry
[3184 2748]:

	Thickness m

Limestone; yellow to cream, oolitic, shell-fragmental,
with coarser bands of shell-fragmental limestone up
to 76 mm in thickness; well rounded quartz pebbles
with a few limestone pebbles at three levels; thin
false-bedding 1.55
Limestone; pale cream, variegated, fine-grained oolitic ... 1.02
Limestone; cream, oolitic, very fine-grained, thinly
bedded with dendritic markings, darker in lower
0.36 m 0.56
Limestone (? Knotty Bed or Trigonia signata Bed);
pale cream, oolitic fine-grained, massive, with large
trigoniids 0.91
Limestone; pale yellow, marly 0.03
Limestone; cream, fine-grained oolitic, with plant
fragments; in two massive beds 1.22

The following were collected from the section: *Kallirhynchia sp.*,
Rhactorhynchia obsoleta, *Bakevellia*, *Liostrea*, *Myophorella signata*,
Plagiostoma subcardiiformis, trigoniids and plant fragments. AH

A quarry [385 250], south of the airfield at Enstone (Plate 7),
shows:

	Thickness m

Soil with brash 0.3
Limestone; pale brown ooliths and shell debris set in a
pale grey spar, slightly sandy, flaggy 1.22
Limestone; pale fawn, sandy, rich in shell debris,
oolitic locally decalcified 0.32
Limestone; pale fawn, sandy, shell-fragmental oolite,
medium to fine-grained bands, massive 3.35
                                                 EGP, AH

There are several large overgrown quarries north-west of
Heythrop, which expose broadly similar sections [e.g. 3477 2798].
About 130 m to the east-north-east of the latter section the
succession includes a lens of very coarse oyster-rich massive
limestone up to 1.52 m thick. AH

Traitor's Ford

The best section in the area is in Sharp's Hill Quarry [338 358]
where the complete thickness of 4.5 m is visible. The highest beds of
the Chipping Norton Limestone and their junction with the Sharp's
Hill Beds are best seen in the western face; the lower beds are best
seen in the south-eastern face. The following is a composite section
of these exposures (after Richardson, 1911, p.209):

	Thickness m

SHARP'S HILL BEDS (see p.79) .... —

CHIPPING NORTON LIMESTONE
Limestone; brown, rather flaggy with a few large
shells, worm tubes and plant fragments 0.46
Clay; greyish brown, fairly tough 0.03
Limestone; pale grey and cream, rubbly, oolitic shelly
flags 0.61
Limestone; brown, rubbly, sandy flags 0.79
Limestone; (Trigonia signata Bed); pale grey, very
hard, finely oolitic and sandy-weathering to loose
sand with trigoniids 0.25

Limestone; brown, sandy, with plant fragments and shells	0.25
Limestone; brown, very sandy, oolitic with flaggy bands, ferruginous veins and sand partings	1.07
Limestone; brown, hard, massive and oolitic	0.33
Limestone; brown, flaggy, weathering to soft clay	0.10
Limestone; brown, sandy, massive, with plant fragments	0.46
Limestone; brown, argillaceous	0.15
CLYPEUS GRIT (see p.72)	—

EGP

In the Fulling Mill Farm – Broughton Park area creamy-white, generally oolitic, limestone rests directly on Upper Lias clay. A quarry [408 386] north of the farm has the Chipping Norton Limestone in the base. At the north end of the quarry some 1.68 m of the bottom limestone is exposed; the lower half grades into a cream oolite, tinged with pink in the basal 0.30 to 0.46 m. To the east, creamy white oolitic limestone, locally with pinkish ooliths, is exposed in several shallow excavations in Broughton Park.   EAE

Enstone – Glympton area

The Chipping Norton Limestone is sporadically exposed in the bottom of a steep-sided valley [4097 2206 to 4228 2074] near Over Kiddington, and also in the Glyme valley east of Hill Farm. Similar small exposures occur in the steep-sided valley south of Wood Farm [4089 1993] near the southern margin of the district.   EGP

Barford Trough

The Chipping Norton Limestone gives rise to a pale brown sandy soil, and crops out in large areas around the villages of Wigginton and South Newington, with small patches elsewhere. Former exposures were recorded by Woodward (1894, p.162) and Richardson (1922, p.123).   BJW

Great Tew

There are two disused quarries near Great Tew; the section of the first [3944 2908], was described by Richardson (1911, p.218) and has been reclassified and summarised below:

	Thickness m
CHIPPING NORTON LIMESTONE	
('SWERFORD BEDS' OF RICHARDSON)	
Limestone; pale brown, hard, rubbly	0.53
Limestone; similar, rubbly mixed with sand, in the southern face becoming a white and yellow sand with a 'shelly-bed' about the middle	1.37
Limestone; hard, massive, with an extremely shelly bed and (with *Trigoniae*, *Lucinae*, etc) joined on to the bottom limestone	0.97
Limestone ('Old Man' of Richardson); sandy, rubbly, mixed with sand	0.46
Limestone; massive, sandy, in three layers, ferruginous and shelly; water-worn pebbles, bored by *Lithophagi* and with oysters on them, are embedded in the top portion of the bed, which has a very irregular nether surface	0.69
('HOOK NORTON BEDS' OF RICHARDSON)	
Sand; brown and grey-streaked	0.25
Calcareous sand-rock; hard, passing into soft brown sand	0.23
Sandy rock; brown, *Syncyclonema demissum*	0.18

Plate 7   Cross-stratified Chipping Norton Limestone, Quarry [385 250] east of Enstone (A 9837)

Sandy rock; somewhat hard, bluish grey-centred, shelly   0.10

Only the uppermost 2 m are exposed at present.

A quarry [3946 2860] south of the Little Tew–Ledwell road (Plate 8) begins at about the same stratigraphical level, and shows 1.75 m of sandy oolitic limestone, with a basal homoiolithic pebble bed, resting on fossiliferous shell-debris oolite.

Excavations in a disused mill race [3983 2690] at Tracey Farm exposed a faulted asymmetrical anticline; the following section was recorded along its southern limb:

	Thickness m
SHARP'S HILL BEDS (see p.80)	
Clay; pale grey with yellow mottling, very silty and finely sandy	0.43
CHIPPING NORTON LIMESTONE (7.72 m)	
Limestone; pale fawn with local greenish argillaceous patches now largely decalcified	up to 0.30
Limestone; pale fawn, sandy, well rounded quartz grains set in a fine-grained crystalline matrix; hard, weathered surfaces show very thin current-bedding	c.0.30
Limestone; oolite with minor shell fragments, interbedded current-sorted layers, very sandy, ?sand-centre ooliths in top 0.61 m, locally weathering to yellow sand	seen 0.15
Section obscured; probably yellow sand with rubbly limestone fragments	c.2.13
Limestone; white to fawn, oolitic, shell-fragmental	
and sandy, with minor secondary ironstone veins	seen 0.20
Limestone; very sandy, oolitic, scattered shell fragments; largely decalcified, locally recrystallised, no visible bedding, rubble set in a fawn sand matrix	1.73
Limestone; pale fawn speckled, oolitic, sandy, minor secondary iron-rich veins, scattered plant fragments and ostreids, flaggy-weathering	0.58
Sand; pale ochreous yellow, fine- to medium-grained, a few limestone nodules, abundant ostreids	0.30
Limestone; fawn to grey, speckled, sandy with shell fragments and a few ostreids; thin argillaceous bands and lenses, plant fragments increasingly common downward	0.81
Limestone; pale fawn and grey, extremely fossiliferous, the shell-fragmental lenticular lumachelle passes laterally into grey-speckled, sandy plant-rich limestone	0.08
Limestone; fawn to grey, sandy with a few small pebbles, sparsely oolitic, abundant plant fragments, some secondary iron-rich veins and local replacement of calcite	0.28
Sand; fawn to pale ochreous, abundant lignitic plant fragments, scattered large ostreids	0.20
Limestone; greyish brown, soft, argillaceous, largely decalcified, abundant lignite fragments and a few plant stems	c.0.25
Limestone; dull greyish brown, sandy with abundant lignite fragments and a few plant stems, scattered ostreids	0.05
Clay; brown ochreous, sandy with lignite fragments	0.05

Plate 8   Rubbly weathering sandy Chipping Norton Limestone, Swerford Beds facies, Great Tew 'sand' pit [3946 2860] (A 9842)

Limestone; pale brown, sandy, sparsely oolitic, some
bands of shell debris and fossiliferous layers,
abundant lignite fragments, a few clay-filled worm
tubes, traces of ultra-fine current-bedding, locally
decalcified to brown sand   0.58

CLYPEUS GRIT (see p.64)   —

The following fossils were collected from the lowest 2.3 m of the
section:
Kallirhynchia sp., *Camptonectes (Camptochlamys)* cf. *rosimon*, *Chlamys
sp.*, *Liostrea* cf. *hebridica*, *Modiolus sp.*, *Myophorella signata*, *Plagiostoma*
cf. *cardiiformis*, and *P. subcardiiformis*.   AH

To the south, the Chipping Norton Limestone crops out on the
southern slopes of the Glyme valley between Lidstone and Cleveley.
The old Bell Inn Quarry [3782 2406] shows 1.83 m of mostly
obscured, sandy, brown limestone, but the best section hereabouts
is in a quarry [3811 2401] 275 m to the east:

	Thickness m
SHARPS'S HILL BEDS	—
CHIPPING NORTON LIMESTONE	
Limestone; cream and brown, hard, massive bed of coarsely oolitic, coralline limestone	0.36
Limestone; cream-coloured, softer, oolitic with fossil fragments	1.22
Obscured	1.52
Limestone; brown, sandy, oolitic	0.30

Veins of tufa are well developed along joints in the quarry, and
the beds dip E24°S at 3°.
Farther south, two quarries near Fulwell expose good sections in
Chipping Norton Limestone. The first [3713 2331] west of Fulwell
shows:

	Thickness m
Limestone; fawn, medium-grained, flaggy, sandy, oolitic	0.30
Limestone; honey-coloured, coarse-grained, massive but becoming flaggy laterally; sandy and oolitic, with shell fragments	0.81
Limestone; honey-coloured, very coarse, with shells and pebbles up to 25 mm diameter, coarsely oolitic; very soft and easily eroded	0.13
Limestone; honey-coloured, coarse, oolitic, sandy and flaggy, with many shell fragments	0.91

The second [3753 2305], south-west of Fulwell (Fulwell Quarry,
Richardson 1911, p.220), exposes 3.66 m of poorly fossiliferous
limestone with rare ostreids; the upper part consists of flaggy, fawn,
current-bedded, sandy oolite and the lower part of massive, fawn,
sandy, medium-grained limestone.

Radford – Glympton

Small overgrown quarries [4056 2451; 4066 2465] on the east side of
the valley north of Radford show mainly flaggy oolitic sandy
limestone. A good section of Chipping Norton Limestone overlain
by Sharp's Hill Beds lies in an old quarry [4103 2373] south of Radford church, where 3 m of hard sandy limestone with flaggy bands
are succeeded by clays with limestone. A similar section is exposed
in another old quarry [4102 2373] nearby. In yet another quarry
[4268 2173] 4.57 m of hard, massive, brown, sandy limestone lie
beneath 3 m of Sharp's Hill Beds; the strata dip south-eastwards at
10°.   EGP

Ledwell – Sandford St Martin – Middle Barton

In the Ledwell Borehole [4093 2821] the Chipping Norton
Limestone was 5.89 m thick (p.139). It consisted mainly of beds of
yellowish brown and pale yellow sandy limestone with superficial
ooliths, shell debris and plant remains.   AH

Eastwards from Great Tew the Chipping Norton Limestone has
a broad outcrop extending to the vicinity of Downhill Farm, and is
separated from a parallel outlier to the north and east around Heath
Farm by a valley cut into the Upper Lias. It thins rapidly eastwards.

Around Sandford St Martin and Middle Barton, the formation
crops out on the valley sides. In a small quarry [4187 2678] north-
west of Sandford Park, 1.52 m of flaggy, brown, lignitic, very sandy
limestone rest on 1.52 m of brown sandy limestone.

On the eastern side of the Dorn Valley Fault, the field evidence
suggests that the formation consists of very sandy limestones.   BJW

SHARP'S HILL BEDS

These strata were first called the Neaeran Beds (Walford,
1906, p.2), but after several minor revisions of definition,
the term Sharp's Hill Beds was applied to all the fossiliferous
limestones, muds and clays between the Chipping Norton
Limestone and the Taynton Stone. McKerrow and Kennedy
(1973) have proposed that these beds be described as the
Sharp's Hill Formation. The base is taken at the lowest
richly fossiliferous stratum above the underlying oolitic
limestones of the Chipping Norton Limestone.

The Sharp's Hill Beds rest conformably on the Chipping
Norton Limestone except in the east where they overlap on
to the 'Lower Estuarine Series'. They are thickest in a belt
running south-eastwards from Lower Brailes towards
Steeple Aston, the thickest records being 4.67 m in the
Ledwell Borehole and 4.60 m in the type section at Sharp's
Hill [338 358]. Over most of the district their thickness
exceeds 1.5 m, but between Chadlington and Churchill it is
locally less; they are very thin and even absent locally in the
Cherwell valley. They thin northwards into the Banbury
district (Edmonds and others, 1965), where they have also
been called the 'Upper Estuarine Series' as they have in
Northamptonshire.

At Sharp's Hill Quarry, the type section has 0.7 m of clay
at the base. More generally the sequence begins with a thin
sand seam that rests on the Chipping Norton Limestone or,
near Steeple Aston, on the sands of the Lower Estuarine
Series. This seam of sand is absent in the Hook Norton
(Figure 31) and Tadmarton boreholes. The basal unit is then
a limestone; where this rests on the Chipping Norton
Limestone, it can be recognised by its more micritic nature.

The remainder of the sequence, although generally
argillaceous, is extremely variable in detail (Figure 32). It is
impossible to establish whether any of the constituent beds
are laterally persistent, though certain of them have been
claimed to be so. In particular, Richardson (1911) introduced names for almost every bed in the sequence (see
Details). For example, he recognised a distinctive grey,
brown and black clay at the top of the sequence, which he
believed could be traced north-eastwards into the basal beds
of the 'Upper Estuarine Series', and termed it the Upper
Estuarine Clay. He also noted a pale marl beneath this clay
which he called the 'Viviparus Marl'. However, marls containing *Bathonella* [*Viviparus*] have been recorded at various

levels within the Sharp's Hill Beds, and it is hard to be certain of the identity of any one of them.

Various types of greenish mudstones make up about 70 per cent of the sequence. Well graded mudstones are uncommon and when present are generally thin. More typically the mudstones are slightly silty, weakly calcareous, and contain a little shell debris. They commonly contain scattered bivalves, in places preserved as brown-stained casts. The greenish grey mudstones grade imperceptibly into paler marls with better preserved fossils. Shells are locally common and the valves remain articulated, in contrast to those in the lumachelles. Olive-grey mudstones are less common and are usually less calcareous and silty than the greenish grey varieties. Oyster lumachelles are preserved at some levels and are comparable with the oyster mudstones of the 'Upper Estuarine Series'; most of the shells are disarticulated and tend to be horizontally arranged. Calcareous silt particles are scattered throughout, and in places form thin partings and beds giving rise to indistinct colour banding. As the silt content increases, the lithology passes into 'clay with lenticles';

this description denotes a greenish grey mudstone with layers or lenses of silt showing pronounced micro-cross-stratification and common sole structures. These silts are well sorted, and originated as isolated silt ripples. As the size of the ripples increases they coalesce into more continuous silty limestone beds.

The most vividly coloured of the mudstone lithologies are seatearths and carbonaceous clays. Scattered rootlets occur in the silty mudstones, but they abound in certain dark green-grey and brownish grey variegated mudstones, which also contain much plant detritus, especially carbonaceous laths. Like the seatearths of the Coal Measures they contain listric surfaces and scattered ironstone nodules. Many are strongly pyritic, and fresh specimens soon disintegrate on exposure. Some rootlets also occur in the more argillaceous sandstones.

Coarse siltstones and sandstones occur mainly towards the base of the sequence. They are of two main types; greenish grey silts, which grade from the silty mudstones, and siltstones which range from carbonaceous orange-black sandy

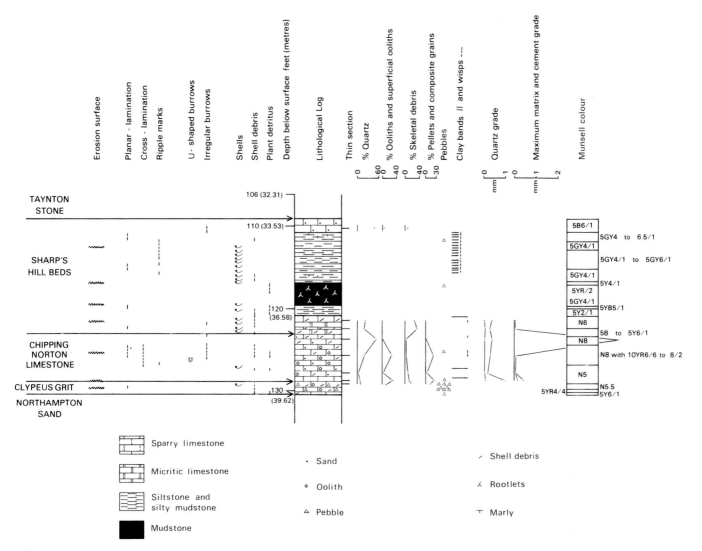

Figure 31 Clypeus Grit, Chipping Norton Limestone, and Sharp's Hill Beds in the Hook Norton Borehole

siltstones to pale grey sandstones containing comminuted plant debris. Some of the beds are weakly calcareous and contain shells. Conglomerates have been recorded from at least two horizons. They commonly underlie the beds of Viviparus marls, and one overlies such a band in Castle Barn Quarry (see p.78).

Thin porcellanous and fine-grained gastropod limestones (cementstones) are also present. As the proportion of skeletal particles increases these grade into wackestones. Grainstones are the least common variety of limestone, and most of these are shell-fragmental, sandy and oolitic.

The Sharp's Hill Beds are extremely fossiliferous. Bivalves are dominant with an abundance of byssate epifaunal species. Ostreids are so common at some levels that they form lumachelles. The motile epifauna includes *Camptonectes* and *Chlamys*, while the burrowing bivalves include active forms such as cardiids, cyprinids and trigoniids, and less active ones such as the myids and pleuromyids. A few brachiopods, corals and echinoids also occur. The proximity of land is suggested by the presence of much plant debris and the bones of *Cetiosaurus*, while the presence of gastropods including *Bathonella* and freshwater ostracods suggests marked fluctuation in salinity. None of these forms is diagnostic of a precise age. Arkell (1951–58) has correlated the Sharp's Hill Beds with the Stonesfield Slate, which has yielded ammonites diagnostic of the *Procerites progracilis* Zone of the Middle Bathonian. More recently Torrens (*in* Cope and others, 1980) equated them with the older *Asphinctites tenuiplicatus* Zone of the Lower Bathonian and the *progracilis* Zone (Figure 28).

Although the mixed lithologies of the Sharp's Hill Beds suggest rapid variations in the detailed depositional environment, the presence of organisms tolerant of low salinity and, in particular, the presence of seatearths, shows that water depth was periodically shallower than when the Chipping Norton Limestone was laid down, and periods of emergence were not uncommon. Between these emergent episodes the fauna ranges to fully marine. The water was generally shallow and quiet, only intermittently disturbed by currents. These general characteristics point to a pronounced regression, but Sellwood and McKerrow (1974) consider that the formation marks a transgression because it apparently oversteps the Chipping Norton Limestone towards the London Platform. The latter interpretation raises the general problem of the possible diachronism of such marginal facies as they are traced landwards. It is clear, however, that an origin in a coastal lagoon is probable. AH

Details

Numerous sections in the Sharp's Hill Beds described by Richardson are no longer available. Quotations from Richardson and other authors have been simplified, the bed numbers and authors of taxa are generally omitted. Taxa quoted have not been revised. The stratigraphic boundaries have been re-interpreted.

Chastleton – Little Rollright

A small patch of brown clay, probably not exceeding 0.9 m in thickness and containing lenticular limestone bands rich in oyster shells, occurs on the hilltop [258 282] south of Chastleton Barrow. The only fresh exposure is in a small quarry on the north-west of the outcrop, where 0.3 m of brown clay with thin lenticularly bedded

bands of coarse grey shelly limestone was seen. No exposures of Sharp's Hill Beds are now visible in the Chastleton Hill Quarry [2618 2864] where Richardson (1911, p.229) recorded a section, given here in slightly modified form:

	Thickness m
SHARP'S HILL BEDS	
Ostrea and Rhynchonella Bed: Clayey marl; greenish grey, with *Ostrea, Terebratula, Rhynchonella concinna, Trapezium, Pholadomya, Nerinaea*	c.0.15
Limestone; pale yellow, rubbly, oolitic; *Ostrea, Trapezium,* and *Nerita pseudocostata* at the base	0.30
Clay; dark greenish grey; *Ostrea*	0.08
Limestone; hard, brownish, in two layers; a water-worn top	0.66
Marl; pale yellow	c.0.13
Clay; tough	0.05
Sand and marl; brown sand, patchily cemented, passing laterally into marl with *Placunopsis socialis*	0.25–0.46
Clay, tough, dark;	up to 0.05
CHIPPING NORTON LIMESTONE	
Limestone, top bed (? = 'Plant-Bed'): very hard and gritty	seen 3.66

To the south, Richardson (p.229) recorded 0.99 m of basal Sharp's Hill Beds in Pointed Heath Quarry [2537 2703], and (p. 230) over 2.4 m in an old quarry at Whitequarry Hill [264 264]: he collected *Cuspidaria ibbetsoni* and *Liostrea acuminata* from the former. These beds are no longer visible.

To the north-east, exposures of Sharp's Hill Beds occur in the north-eastern corner [2727 2926] of Cross Hands Quarry, west of Hirons Hill Farm. Up to 0.6 m of brown-weathering dark bluish grey clay with lenticular cream, nodular-weathering limestones is seen, many of the limestone lenses being rich in compound corals and shells including *Isastraea limitata, Thamnasteria lyelli, Clypeus?,* rhynchonellid and terebratulid fragments, *Isognomon (Mytiloperna) murchisonii, Liostrea hebridica, Modiolus imbricatus, Pholadomya?, Placunopsis socialis, Pleuromya sp.,* and *Trigonia pullus.* EGP

In the most southerly of the Oakham quarries [2785 3045], up to 0.46 m of brown clay with nodular, pale cream-weathering, rubbly, shelly limestones rests upon 2.44 m of Chipping Norton Limestone. There are similar exposures in the eastern face of the larger quarry to the north-north-east, where up to 1.2 m of greyish green clay with nodular limestones occur, and also in the easternmost quarry [2823 3068]. Richardson (1911, p.228) gives a more complete section of the southernmost Oakham quarry which has been somewhat simplified below:

	Thickness m
SHARP'S HILL BEDS	
Dark purple clayey subsoil	—
Clay; dirty green, and yellowish-blotched, with fragments of whitened ostreid shell	seen 0.30
Limestone; weathers rubbly, very shelly; *Ostrea, Quenstedtia, Volsella imbricata* very common, *Pholadomya, Nerinaea* spp., *Nerita pseudocostata,* at the base, *Turbo ?burtonensis, Ataphrus labadyei*	(not stated)
Marl; brownish; *Ostrea, Placunopsis socialis*	0.13
Limestone; rubbly shelly; *Pleuromya, Chlamys vagans, Grammatodon, Volsella imbricata, Nerinaea, Clypeus mülleri, Strophodus* (tooth), lignite, etc.	c.0.56
Clay; tough, greenish	0.10

Marl, brown, shelly, and stiff chocolate-coloured clay, often enclosing irregular masses of rotten marl; masses of brown gritty limestone 0 to 0.9 m thick at the base in places ... 0.61

CHIPPING NORTON LIMESTONES
Limestone; with plant remains and 'Oppelia fusca' (now O. (Oxycerites) limosa) ... 3.66

The Sharp's Hill Beds crop out on the ridge to the north-west of Hirons Hill Farm. There are oyster-rich clays and limestones near the base of the sequence, preserved in gulls within the Chipping Norton Limestone, in a small quarry [282 303], north-west of Hirons Hill Farm. Very small outliers and remanié patches of clay soil occur on the dip slope of the Chipping Norton Limestone immediately to the west of the farm. AH, EGP

Chipping Norton – Chadlington – Charlbury

Outliers of Sharp's Hill Beds occur north-east of Over Norton [312 286], south of Hull Farm, and south-west of Pomfret Castle; there are no sections. Richardson (1911, p.225) first described the section at Padley's Quarry [318 271], east of Chipping Norton, as follows:

Thickness
m

GREAT OOLITE LIMESTONE
Limestone; coarse, oolitic, shelly, with tendency to become flaggy at the base; *Trigonia pullus* ... 1.52

SHARP'S HILL BEDS
Ostrea Clay: Clay; dirty greenish grey and pale yellow, crowded with oysters; more clayey at the top and marly below; *Placunopsis socialis, Serpula,* pentacrinoid ossicles and echinoid radioles ... 0.46
Clay; greenish, tough, irregular; bones of *Cetiosaurus;* ... c.0.10
Marl; pale yellow, with 'race', *P. socialis* abundant ... c.0.08
Clay; shaly, dirty green, reddish brown with crowds of *Placunopsis socialis* ... 0.08
Clay; greenish brown, tough ... 0.10
Limestone; rotten, often reduced to white carbonate of lime ... up to 0.05
Sand and clay, yellowish, intimately associated with the irregular top of the beds below ... 0.20

CHIPPING NORTON LIMESTONE
Limestone ... —

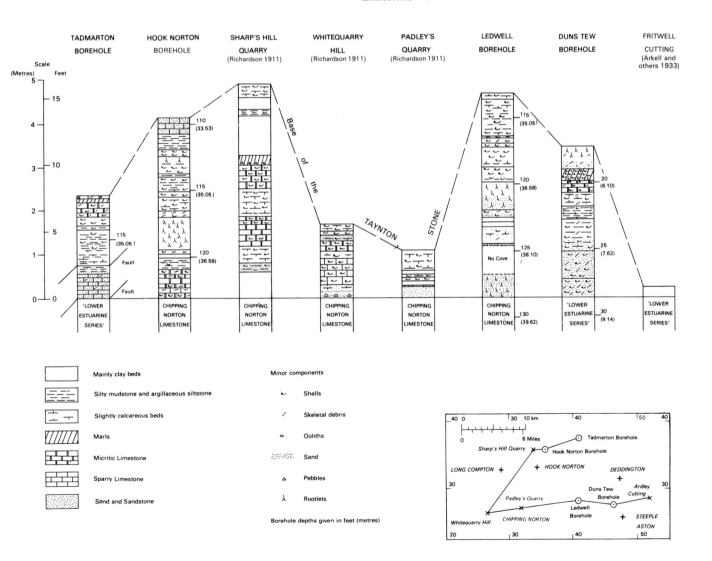

Figure 32 Representative vertical section of the Sharp's Hill Beds

There are two outliers of Sharp's Hill Beds on the ridge north-west of Enstone, where ploughed fields indicate the presence of white gastropod-rich cementstone beds associated with oyster-rich clays and limestones. Variegated clays, marls and oyster-rich limestones crop out south and south-west of Chipping Norton and on the upper slopes of the higher reaches of the River Glyme south-east of the town. A drainage sump [3177 2593] indicates a total local thickness of about 2.6 m. Amongst a variety of excavated lithologies was a well developed calcareous sandstone seatearth. South of Glyme Farm the thickness decreases to about 0.9 m, and it may thin further near Old Chalford, though much of the outcrop is masked by downwash.

The base of the formation is visible in a quarry [3141 2500] north-east of Walterbush Farm (see Woodward 1894, p.152):

	Thickness m
SHARP'S HILL BEDS	
Limestone; white to pale grey, sandy, oolitic, compact	0.36
Limestone; hard, white, micritic (cementstone), a rubbly band with gastropods at the top	0.20
Marl; dull grey, blocky, scattered ooliths, basal 0.15 m brown-stained and wet	0.58
Marl; brown, iron-stained, partly weathered	0.13
CHIPPING NORTON LIMESTONE	—

Fossils collected from the quarry include *Limopsis minima, Liostrea sp., Aphanoptyxis?, Fibula?, Katosira sp.* and *Nerinella sp.* The overlying argillaceous part of the Sharp's Hill Beds crops out in ploughed fields to the north.

To the south of East Downs Farm the Sharp's Hill Beds could not be separated from the overlying Taynton Stone. Near Fairgreen Farm the limits of the formation are uncertain and it is possible that the depicted outcrop includes clays of similar facies within the Taynton Stone.

The section in Castle Barn Quarry [3000 2262] has been described by Richardson (1911) and Arkell (1947). The present section is as follows:

	Thickness m
SHARP'S HILL BEDS ('TAYNTON STONE' OF RICHARDSON)	
Limestone; cream, shell-fragmental oolitic, with a few shells and wisps of green clay	0.10
Limestone; off-white, fine-grained, shell-fragmental oolitic, some mudstone flakes scattered throughout; coarser shell-fragmental banding showing micro-lamination; massive but flaggy-weathering and cross-bedded	0.46
Clay; dark greenish brown, tenacious, with scattered oysters	c.0.13
Marl; reddish brown, oolitic and oyster-rich, decalcified with small ironstone aggregates	0.11
Limestone; pale brown, fine-grained, oolitic, hard and massive, a few clay wisps and coarser oolitic bands, flaggy and cross-bedded	1.52
Limestone; medium-grained, oolitic and shell-fragmental, hard and massive with large marl pebbles and shells above an irregular base, the matrix filling cracks in the underlying beds	0.25–0.41
('SHARP'S HILL BEDS' OF ARKELL AND RICHARDSON)	
Clay; greenish and marly, with oysters; finely banded with oolitic and shell-debris partings	up to 0.1
Marl ('Viviparus Marl' of Arkell and	

Richardson); brownish grey but drying off-white, blocky weathering, with scattered shells and ooliths, soft and brown-stained in basal 180 mm. Passes laterally into a dull bluish grey marly tenacious clay and into harder white micritic limestone | up to 0.66 |
| CHIPPING NORTON LIMESTONE | — |

The Sharp's Hill Beds are extremely variable, and none of the beds recorded is laterally persistent even within the confines of the small quarry. In the case of the less indurated clay horizons this may partly result from squeezing, with the resultant development of pseudo-conglomerates and clay-filled joints. Beds slightly higher than the quarry sequence were exposed in a silage pit [2989 2234] some 30 m to the south-east. They consisted of greyish green clay with ripple-bedded silty limestone and skeletal oolitic micritic limestone.

Mr R. J. Wyatt recorded the following section (1976) in the reopened Town Quarry, Charlbury [3687 1985]:

	Thickness m
TAYNTON STONE	
Limestone; pale creamy grey, shell-fragmental and oolitic, fine-grained, compact, flaggy weathering	0.15
SHARP'S HILL BEDS (2.65 to 3.95 m)	
Limestone; greenish grey, marly, shell-fragmental and oolitic, weathering to buff marl; abundant rhynchonellids and some terebratulids, abundant oysters and other bivalves	0.40
Limestone; pale brown, oolitic and shell-fragmental, hard; small-scale cross-bedding with partings of coarse oyster-debris and a few khaki marly clay flakes; scattered rhynchonellids and oysters with coarse shell layer locally at base, uneven junction	0.20–0.25
Mudstone; bluish green with orange-brown to khaki mottling; scattered white shell debris at top but becoming more fossiliferous with rusty brown oyster-shell debris partings in lowest 0.05 m; uneven base 0.25–0.32	
Clay; black, peaty, with abundant white decalcified chalky oyster debris	0.02–0.03
Marl; pale brown, sandy, shell-fragmental; abundant terebratulids, oysters and other bivalves; scattered small carbonaceous fragments; indefinitely and unevenly bedded; passing down at 0.20 m into a more cemented shell-fragmental limestone with abundant oysters for 0.2 m; continuing below in marl	0.55
Limestone; bluish grey, shell-fragmental with crudely bedded oyster debris; in three beds separated by greenish grey clays with partings and lenses of oxidised shell debris; oyster-encrusted upper surface and thin layer of fibrous calcite ('beef') above abrupt base	0.30–0.35
Mudstone; dark bluish grey to black, marly, with carbonaceous plant fragments; partings of silt and fine- to medium-grained sand, particularly at top; a few layers of pale yellowish marly concretions ('race'); becoming slightly paler with white shell-debris partings at base	0.18–0.42
Limestone; greenish grey to buff, marly, sandy and shell-fragmental, passing into marl with dark grey clay patches; many bivalves	0.20–0.42
Mudstone; dark grey but weathering to rusty	

brown, scattered lenses of shelly shell-fragmental
and quartz sand; passing laterally into clay with
abundant bivalves. Up to 0.08 m of micritic-
limestone pebble conglomerate at base welded
on to uneven surface of underlying bed   0.15–0.33

Limestone; pale fawn, sparsely oolitic, micritic;
hard and porcellanous at top but with no signs
of burrows or borings; passing down into pale
grey more marly rock with scattered ooliths,
quartz grains and shell debris, and a few
gastropods; more shells and shell debris with
lignitic plant detritus at base in places. Uneven
undulating junction   0.40–0.90

The section continues downwards through 6.2 m of Chipping
Norton Limestone into the Clypeus Grit (p.71).   AH

The Swerford Trough

The Sharp's Hill Beds have a narrow outcrop within the fault
trough. They were well exposed during the construction of the Banbury–Cheltenham railway. Several authors have described the
section at Langton Bridge [316 300]. The most recent account
(Richardson, 1911, p.226) is given below in terms of the current
classification.

	Thickness m
SHARP'S HILL BEDS	
Limestone; compact, grey, crystalline and shelly	1.12
Marl; grey, with '*Pteroperna*', oysters and gastropods	0.51
Neaeran Slate: Limestone; fissile, with '*Neaera ibbetsoni*'	0.10
Marl; shelly and sandy	0.05
Clay; grey, rather sandy at the base, with '*Ataphrus*', '*Isastraea sp.*'	0.15
Bituminous clay; black but lighter in the lower part:	average 0.46
Viviparus Marl: Limestone; grey mortar-like, '*Nerinaea*', '*Viviparus langtonensis*'	0.91
Sand, red	1.22
CHIPPING NORTON LIMESTONE	—
	AH, BJW

Traitor's Ford area

A small patch of brown clay with nodular limestones lies on the
hillside south of North Leasow [3148 3590]. The formation also
crops out in a narrow belt on the hillside of North Leasow extending
eastwards above Farnicombe [3287 3626] to Traitor's Ford
Coppice, south-west of Traitor's Ford.

The type section of the Sharp's Hill Beds occurs in Sharp's Hill
Quarry [338 358] south of Traitor's Ford, where up to 3.7 m of
brown-weathering clay with grey and greenish grey, nodular, shelly
limestone bands are seen. The section was described by Richardson
(1911, pp.207–208), and is summarised below in terms of the
revised classification.

	Thickness m
SHARP'S HILL BEDS	
Reddish soil	up to 0.30
Rhynchonella and Ostrea Bed: Marls; yellowish, clayey, crowded with oysters, *Rhynchonella*; *Camptonectes annulatus*	0.30

('SHARP'S HILL BEDS' OF RICHARDSON)

Clay; brown and dirty greenish grey at the top, darker towards the base:	c.0.30
Ostrea Clay: Marly clay; crowded with whitened oysters	0.15
Clay; tough, dark brown, bluish and greenish, with a discontinuous bed of brown sandstone, up to 0.05 m thick near the top	0.76
Bituminous Clay: Clay; black (in places almost a coal-seam), overlying a seam of rich brown clay	c.0.15
Viviparus Marl: Marl; pale purplish, with numerous pebbles and concretions, some ochreous, others phosphatic; *Viviparus langtonensis*, *Ataphrus labadyei*, *Nerinaea* spp.	up to c.0.20
Upper Nerinaea Bed: Limestone; generally hard but rubbly in places, passing locally into a whitish grey marl; large *Nerinaea* of *eudesi* type common. *N.* cf. *voltzi*, *Nerita minuta* at the base, *Corbula buckmani*, *Arctica loweana* (dwarfed form), *Gervillia waltoni*, *Ostrea*, *Volsella imbricata*	c.0.53
Cyathopora bourgeti Bed: Marl; greenish grey, with numerous white concretions and irregular limestone layers. *Nerinaea voltzi*, *Gervillia waltoni*, *Perna mytiloides*, *Placunopsis socialis*, *Nucula menkei*, *Ostrea*, *Volsella imbricata*. *Cyathopora bourgeti* occurs principally at the base	0.64
Lower Nerinaea Bed: Limestone; pale green when freshly fractured with innumerable specimens of *Nerinaea*; at the western end represented only by an occasional nodule; *Cyathopora bourgeti* near the top, *Arctica loweana* (dwarfed form), *Rhynchonella concinna*, *Astarte*, *Nerinaea*,	up to 0.20
Irregular parting of clayey marl	0.05
Astarte oxoniensis Limestone: Limestone; variable in thickness and mixed with marl; pale green when fresh, though the harder portions are blue and shelly; *Perna* cf. *mytiloides*, *Nucula menkei* auctt., *Volsella imbricata*, *Exelissa* spp.	up to 0.20
Fairly persistent parting of greenish clayey marl:	up to 0.08
Exelissa Limestone: pale yellow or whitish exterior, blue-hearted; *Exelissa*, *Amberleya* aff. *nodosa*, '*Phasianella*' *pontonis*, *Protocardia buckmani* *Nucula menkei*	up to 0.25
Limestone;	0.13
Perna Bed: Marl and stone; pale yellow, greenish and bluish; *Perna oxoniensis P. mytiloides*, *Gervillia waltoni* [*G. richardsoni*], *Protocardia lingulata*, *Pleuromya* cf. *unioniformis*, *Volsella imbricata*, *Ataphrus labadyei*, *Exelissa* spp.,	0.46
Sand; reddish brown with nodules and masses of a blue shelly limestone; *Perna*, *Placunopsis socialis*, *Gervillia*, *Volsella*, *Exelissa*; numerous ostracods in the limestone	0–0.20
Clay; black and reddish brown	0.58
	EGP

The formation is also seen in a small quarry [3444 3631] west-
south-west of Woodway Farm:

	Thickness m
Clay; brown-weathering, somewhat obscured, with bands of white, flaggy, thinly bedded, oolitic	

	Thickness m
limestone and many fragments of *Liostrea*	c.1.20
Clay; brown-weathering with abundant *Liostrea*	0.04
Limestone; dark grey, medium-grained, compact	0.28
Clay; grey, with many shell fragments including *Liostrea* and rhynchonellids	0.30
Limestone; grey, rubbly-weathering, coarse-grained, shelly	0.30
Clay; poorly exposed, brown-weathering, with many *Liostrea* fragments	3.05

Tadmarton

Richardson (1922, p.130) also described the sequence in the Tadmarton Sand Pit [3997 3786]. This has been reclassified as follows:

	Thickness m
SHARP'S HILL BEDS	
Marls; clayey, with abundant *Ostrea acuminata*	
Marls; indurated, oolitic; *Terebratula globata, Rhynchonella concinna, Pleuromya* sp.,	0.91
Limestone; sandy, sparsely oolitic; *Ostrea sp.,* echinoid radioles	0.53
Marl; brownish, sandy, the marl particles being of a greenish colour	0.10
'LOWER ESTUARINE SERIES' (see p.57)	—
	BJW

Enstone – Middle Barton

To the north and east of Church Enstone the Sharp's Hill Beds consist of green and grey clays, and argillaceous and shelly limestones packed with oysters. Excavation in the Mill Race [3982 2689] at Tracey Farm revealed the following section:

	Thickness m
SHARP'S HILL BEDS	
Clay; pale dull grey, abundant oysters	0.61
Limestone; pale fawnish grey, slightly sandy, oyster-rich lumachelle	0.23–0.30
Clay; bluish grey, very stiff, with a lenticular band of greenish yellow shaly clay varying up to 0.1 m at the top; dull greyish brown, plastic, with abundant poorly preserved fossils below; dull brown, very sandy with some bright reddish brown areas for up to 50 mm at the base	0.38
Sand; pale reddish brown, ferruginous-coated, well rounded quartz grains; possibly decalcified, with casts of bivalves in fresher fragments	up to 0.08
Clay; lens of dull purple to lilac grey, sandy, up to 0.08 m at the top; very pale grey for 0.13 to 0.05 m below; yellow mottled pale grey silty clay, with fine-grained sand below 0.43	0.51–0.61
CHIPPING NORTON LIMESTONE (see p.73)	—

Fossils collected included: *Liostrea, Modiolus, Parallelodon, Placunopsis socialis, Protocardia?,* fish and wood fragments. AH

Spelsbury – Enstone – Glympton

To the east and north of Taston [360 220], the Sharp's Hill Beds are thin and unmappable. South-east of Taston, brown clay with oyster and rhynchonellid fragments has been ploughed in fields [3580

2114] above Conygree Farm and on the hillside above Clark's Bottom; the maximum thickness of the deposit probably does not exceed 1.5 m. Farther south, in the vicinity of Charlbury, the formation again thins and becomes unmappable.

In an old quarry [3754 2306] south-west of Fulwell, 1.22 m of brown-weathering grey clay rest on 3.66 m of Chipping Norton Limestone. The section was seen when fresh by Richardson (1911, p.220) who described it as follows:

	Thickness m
Dark green clayey subsoil with numerous *Ostreae*:	seen 0.30
5 a. Upper Placunopsis Bed: Clay; bluish grey, shelly, with occasional pieces of bluish limestone full of *P. socialis*	0.15
b. Clay; reddish brown, sandy and	
c. Sandy clay; greenish grey	0.10
6 Bituminous Clay	
(Beds 7 to 13 inclusive are absent)	
14 Lower Nerinaea Bed:	
a. Sandstone; very hard, calcareous; *Perna oxoniensis, P. mytiloides, Mytilus, Camptonectes lens, Volsella imbricata, Nerinaea* spp. *Rhynchonella concinna, Cyathopora bourgeti* etc.	0.08
b. Limestone; greyish white, rubbly, mixed with some marl; *Perna oxoniensis, Grammatodon* sp., *Tancredia* cf. *angulata, Ataphrus labadyei* etc.	0.15
[Beds 15 (the Astarte Bed), 16 (the Exelissa Limestone), 17 and 18 (the Perna Bed) are all absent]	
19 Clay; greenish grey, marly, with small concretions that weather into soft calcium carbonate, passing down into:	0.15
20 Clay, black, weathering bluish grey	c.0.20

CHIPPING NORTON LIMESTONE —

Richardson presented much faunal material to BGS. Specimens from the locality include: from Bed 5a, *Placunopsis socialis, Liostrea hebridica;* Bed 14, Lower Nerinea Bed (undivided), *Anisocardia truncata, Isognomon oxoniensis, I. (Mytiloperna) patchamensis, Modiolus imbricatus;* Bed 14a, *Camptonectes rigidus, Falcimytilus sublaevis;* Bed 14b, *Anisocardia* sp., and *Ataphrus heliciformis.*

The Sharp's Hill Beds in the Fulwell – Enstone area are estimated to be about 1.8 m thick, possibly thickening slightly towards the south-east. In the old Bell Inn Quarry [3783 2405], Enstone, the section was described by Richardson (1911, p.219). The section is broadly similar to others recorded above.

A borehole [3801 2387] just south of the Jolly's Ricks crossroads [3800 2392] penetrated 2.13 m of 'claystone', with its base at 8.23 m. To the north, in an old quarry north-east of this crossroads, the following beds overlie the Chipping Norton Limestone:

	Thickness m
Limestone; white, oolitic, flaggy; *Cossmannea (Eunerinea) eudesii, Eomiodon* cf. *angulatus* and *Liostrea* sp.	0.23
Marl; fawn-weathering, with abundant *Liostrea hebridica*	0.23
Clay; yellow-weathering, grey mottled, soft and sticky, with many *Liostrea hebridica*	1.07
Limestone; grey, compact, hard, coarsely clastic, with many shell fragments; probably lenticular	0.15
Limestone; brown, coarse-grained, oolitic, sandy, with many shell fragments including *Bakevellia* aff. *waltoni, Liostrea hebridica, Mactromya?, Modiolus* cf. *imbricatus,*	

Placunopsis socialis, Acrodus? and fish scales	0.36
Clay; fawn and yellow, with abundant *Liostrea hebridica*	0.15

To the north of Radford [410 240] green clay with oysters, pale grey shell-fragmental limestone, and dark bluish grey clay are frequently ploughed on the eastern side of the valley. The Sharp's Hill Beds hereabouts are estimated to be about 1.8 m thick. In an old quarry [4103 2373] south of Radford R.C. church, 1.07 m of fawn-weathering clay rest on the Chipping Norton Limestone. The clay contains a typical bivalve fauna, also *Kallirhynchia spp.*; *Burmirhynchia vagans* and *Liostrea hebridica elongata* occur high in the sequence. In another old quarry [4102 2312] farther south of the church, 1.58 m of fawn and grey clays with thin nodular and lenticular limestones overlie the Chipping Norton Limestone. They have yielded *Epithyris oxonica, Kallirhynchia* cf. *concinna, Liostrea hebridica elongata, Modiolus sp.* and *Placunopsis socialis.*

To the south-east, near Glympton, the formation is estimated to be about 3.0 to 3.7 m thick. The best section is in a quarry [4275 2175] south-west of Home Farm, where up to 3 m of brown-weathering clay with scattered limestone nodules overlie the Chipping Norton Limestone. These beds have yielded *Acrosalenia* cf. *hemicidaroides, Isocyprina* cf. *depressiuscula, Isognomon isognomonoides, Liostrea hebridica, Modiolus imbricatus* and *Placunopsis socialis.* The soil above yielded *Nucleolites griesbachii, Epithyris?, Wattonithyris?, Kallirhynchia sp., Camptonectes sp., Catinula* cf. *matisconensis, Chlamys (Radulopecten)* cf. *hemicostata, 'Corbula' buckmani, Liostrea hebridica* and *Pholadomya lirata.* In an old quarry 90 m to the east, up to 2.4 m of similar brown clay with limestone nodules are exposed.

Farther south-east, in the Killingworth Castle Borehole [4382 2028] the driller's record suggests that the Sharp's Hill Beds are 2.44 m in thickness. EGP

Cherwell Valley

The lower part of the formation is exposed in the Horsehay Farm Quarry, Duns Tew [455 272], where the sequence is:

	Thickness m
SHARP'S HILL BEDS	
Limestone; fawn speckled, shell-detrital and oolitic, cross-stratified, weathering to flaggy rubble (Possibly basal Taynton Stone)	0.97
Mudstone; greenish grey, hard, with scattered shell debris	0.91
Limestone; flesh-coloured with fawn speckling, shell-detrital and oolitic, lenticular	up to 0.30
Mudstone; greenish grey, with numerous oysters, rhynchonellids and much shell debris. Hard, more calcareous olive-grey marly band for 0.15 m at 0.46 m below top	1.83
Sand; soft brown, bedded but decalcified, with traces of fossils including corals. Uneven base filling hollows and cracks in underlying bed	up to 0.38
'LOWER ESTUARINE SERIES' AND NORTHAMPTON SAND (see p.57 and p.58)	—

In the Duns Tew Borehole, the formation comprised 3.46 m of mudstones and marls with shells and shell debris interbedded with oolitic shell-debris limestones, and with a shelly silt and sand at the base.

The formation was exposed during the excavation of the Fritwell Railway Cutting [514 290] (Arkell and others 1933, p.346). The sequence was as follows (with the revised classification employed):

	Thickness m
TAYNTON STONE	—
SHARP'S HILL BEDS	
11 Ostrea sowerbyi Bed; grey clay and marl, packed with *Ostrea sowerbyi*; some specimens large, but on the whole smaller than those so abundant in the Hampen Marly Beds	0.61
10 Hard limestone; containing small rounded pellets or pebbles; projects as a prominent ledge at the waterfall below the aqueduct (possibly the pebble bed in the Stonesfield Slate of Stonesfield and the Cotswolds)	0.30
9 Grey-blue soapy clay [bed 5 of Sharp's Hill?]	0.10
8 Peat Bed: Black carbonaceous seam; 50 mm in cutting [varying from a few centimetres to 0.45 m thick in pumping shafts, —JP] [Equivalent to Lower Nerinaea Bed 4 Sharp's Hill]	0.05
7 Grey and brown mottled sandy clay with white papery shell fragments [many shell fragments of the *Cerithium* type, —JP]	0.30
'LOWER ESTUARINE SERIES' (see p.58)	—

Parts of the sequence are still visible. The base of Bed 7 contains *Bakevellia?, Cuspidaria ibbetsoni, Eomiodon nortonensis, Protocardia sp., Aphanoptyxis* and wood fragments. The remainder of Bed 7 comprises grey silty sandy clay, whilst Bed 9 appears to include grey shelly and marly clay. These beds yielded *Isocyprina, Isognomon, Liostrea hebridica, Modiolus, Neocrassina, Placunopsis socialis* and *Protocardia.* Bed 10 also contained *Protocardia*, whilst Bed 11 contained *Epithyris?, Liostrea hebridica*, and *Modiolus imbricatus.*

The formation was not recorded in the Charlton Borehole [5291 3487]: core recovery was poor, and silty oyster-rich marls and silty shell clays classified as basal Taynton Stone may belong to the Sharp's Hill Beds. AH

GREAT OOLITE LIMESTONE

Within the district the Great Oolite Limestone comprises, in upward succession, the Taynton Stone, the Hampen Marly Beds and the White Limestone (including the Kemble Beds). These subdivisions have not been mapped separately, although the Hampen Marly Beds commonly floor low ground between the features formed by the two resistant limestones. The composition of the limestones in these three subdivisions is summarised in Figure 33.

Taynton Stone

The freestones of the Burford area have been known for many centuries as the Taynton Stone (Arkell 1947a, p.61). The term was first used formally by Woodward (1894, pp.306–307) for the lowest division of the 'Great Oolite'; more recently McKerrow and Kennedy (1973) have proposed that these beds be described as the Taynton Limestone Formation. In places, arenaceous strata occur at the base of the formation, and have been correlated in the past with the Stonesfield Slate. This correlation is far from certain, for though in its type area at Taynton in the Witney district the Taynton Stone overlies the Stonesfield Slate, the latter is overlapped northwards towards Chipping Norton where the Taynton Stone rests directly upon the Sharp's Hill Beds. Sellwood and McKerrow (1974, pp.192–193), however, consider that their Stonesfield Member (the Slate) constitutes the whole of the Sharp's Hill Beds at Stonesfield. Traced north-eastwards into the Towcester district the Taynton Stone probably passes into the Upper Estuarine Limestone (Horton and others, 1974, p.114).

The main escarpment, much interrupted by erosion, trends south-westwards from Newbottle [525 369] to Churchill [284 243], though there are scattered outliers north-west of this line. Along its main outcrop the Taynton Stone forms a plateau; towards the south-east it gradually descends to the valley floors.

The minimum thickness recorded within the district is 4.14 m in the Hook Norton Borehole [3565 3588]; at Langton Bridge [316 300] it is 5.31 m (Woodward 1894, p.331); in Tadmarton Borehole it is 5.80 m thick; in the Fritwell Cutting it is 6.10 m thick (Arkell and others 1933, p.346).

At outcrop the Taynton Stone comprises cream and buff-weathering, flaggy, shelly, oolitic and sandy limestones with thin argillaceous beds. In detail there are a variety of limestone types but no single one can be said to typify the formation, although cross-stratified shell-fragmental sparry oolitic limestones are dominant in the type sections: there seems to be no sequential relationship between the different lithologies. In borehole cores sparry calcite-cemented limestones or grainstones are slightly more common than micritic limestones. Except for a very few micritic limestones of wackestone type (calcareous mud), grains exceed the matrix in volume. Sandy limestones and superficial oolith limestones are also present. Conglomerates, generally with marl or clay flakes, but some with small calcareous pebbles, are rare, and form thin beds at the base of the coarser limestones.

In the Hook Norton Borehole, the cores of which have been examined in detail, limestones constitute two-thirds of the total thickness (Figure 34). The remainder consists of calcareous silt (about 14 per cent), marl (about 11 per cent) and mudstone (about 8 per cent). The limestone is well bedded, individual beds varying in thickness from 0.15 to 1 m; many are strongly grain-size banded, and some show fine-scale graded bedding. Pale grey colours are general, with bluish or olive tints; at outcrop these weather to orange-speckled, yellowish grey hues. In the Charlton Borehole limestones make up only 43 per cent of the formation; marls and calcareous silt, at 32 per cent and 20 per cent respectively, are more important than at other localities; mudstone is only 5 per cent. The limestones are generally silty with a variable amount of shell debris, less ooliths, and either micritic or spar matrices: individual beds rarely exceed 0.3 m in thickness.

Three main types of mudstone are present in the boreholes, all greenish or olive-grey when fresh: they are barren blocky silty mudstone, shelly mudstone or lumachelle, and mudstone with thin silt partings and wisps of shell debris. With increasing proportions of silt the latter merge into beds of laminated or striped siltstone, in which the coarser units show micro-cross-stratification and have erosional bases. Rippled lenses of silt occur in places and pass into silty and sandy limestones. The marls are generally poorly sorted with much quartz silt, skeletal remains and carbonate particles; the lack of sorting is probably a result of bioturbation.

The fauna is varied (see Appendix 1(4)); the better preserved fossils occur in the finer-grained sediments, comminuted and abraded shell predominating in the coarser beds.

Bivalves and, locally, gastropods are abundant and reflect a variety of habitats in this diverse calcarenite and lime-mud community. Echinoid and crinoid fragments are found, also some horizons with brachiopods; the latter include a variety of forms of *Kallirhynchia*. Some of these were given species status by Buckman (1918)—(*K. communalis*, *K. decora*, *K. deliciosa*); they form a plexus of forms which are (like those in the Hampen Marly Beds above) quite indicative of horizon but not readily separable into distinct species.

Around Taynton, the environment was a high-energy one with subaqueous oolith dune fields (Sellwood and McKerrow 1974, p.205). This was replaced north-eastwards by a less turbulent, oolitic, cross-stratified, shell-debris facies and then, near Charlton, by a shallow-water sequence in which silty and micritic shell-debris limestones, marls and mudstones were deposited. Klein (1965) considered that the cross-stratified limestones formed in intertidal channels, but there is no evidence of emergent structures.

Hampen Marly Beds

This formation was first described from Hampen in the Moreton-in-Marsh district, and named by Arkell (1931, footnote on p.612). McKerrow and Kennedy (1973) have proposed that these beds be described as the Hampen Marly Formation. Exposures are now scanty, since the road and rail cuttings and quarries sections have long been largely obliterated. At outcrop the estimated thickness varies between 6 and 9 m. In the Fritwell Cutting [520 285] estimates range from 8 to 10 m; in the Tadmarton Borehole 8.46 m was encountered, and in the Hook Norton Borehole it was 12.78 m thick. Some of these minor thickness variations may result from difficulties in defining the limits of the formation.

The Hampen Marly Beds comprise limestones and marls with thin mudstone, siltstone and sandstone bands. In the type area, the Hampen Marly Beds are entirely marine, but in the Chipping Norton district they contain rootlet beds, and are transitional to the alternately marine and brackish-water near-shore sediments forming the upper part of the 'Upper Estuarine Series', into which the formation passes farther north-eastward.

Detailed descriptions of the formation are based on cores and thin sections obtained from the boreholes at Hook Norton (Figure 34); (Plate 9) and Tadmarton. In these, three-quarters of the sequence is made up of limestones. Most consist of a micrite matrix with a varying proportion of silt-grade skeletal debris. Of these, the majority are packstones, though there are a few wackestones: some grainstones with a spar cement are also present. Skeletal microsparry limestones are most common in the lower part of the formation. The skeletal material ranges from complete shells down to fine detritus, and is set in a clear microgranular calcite cement. Sandy microsparry limestones are only slightly less common and merge with the previous group. In both types, sorting of the constituent grains by type or coarseness can produce stratification, including ripple-drift. In the micritic limestones, which include both packstones and wackestones, the proportion of matrix varies from about 30 to 90 per cent by volume, and ranges from pure cryptograined calcite to micrograined skeletal hash with quartz silt. Fine current lamination is locally present in the microskeletal micritic packstones. The coarser grains are usually skeletal fragments, but ?algal pisoliths, pellets or ooliths are also present. In a few cases quartz is dominant.

The marls are intermediate between the fine-grained limestones and the mudstones and siltstones. They are generally greenish or olive-grey in colour but become pale grey as their lime content increases. Fine skeletal debris with fine sand and silt are almost ubiquitous. Ooliths are uncommon and are restricted to the marls in the lower part of the sequence. The marls and associated fine-grained limestones yield the bulk of the fauna, many shells being in the position of growth. There are traces of original bedding but these structures are commonly destroyed by bioturbation or, less commonly, by slumping. Calcareous pseudo-nodules are present in some beds.

The siltstones and fine sandstones are typically greenish grey. Many are poorly sorted and argillaceous, and some contain a little fine skeletal debris. As their sorting increases, they become grey and pass into silty and sandy sparry limestones. 'Striped beds', consisting of pale silt interbedded with partings of clay, also occur, and some show compactional and slump distortion. Fossils are uncommon and are preserved as pale brown casts. Burrows are present, but more generally there is widespread bioturbation which produces a diffuse mottling.

Mudstones form a minor part of the sequence. They include olive-grey to greenish grey, unbedded or bioturbated varieties, which are slightly calcareous and commonly contain some silt and shell debris. Ooliths are rare. Bedded mudstones are also present, and some contain silt or shell-debris-rich partings, shell pavements or less commonly plant-debris layers. Darker olive or greenish grey seatearths with carbonaceous rootlets also occur.

A rich fauna was obtained from these beds (see Appendix 1(4)). Sporadic simple corals and some echinoids occur whilst rhynchonellids and epithyrid brachiopods are locally abundant. Determination of the rhynchonellids is difficult and a wide variety of morphotypes are attributed to *Kallirhynchia spp.* The fauna is more varied than that of the Taynton Stone. This reflects the predominantly quiet-water conditions under which these shelly lime-mud to lime-sand communities developed. Palmer (1979, pp.194–198) describes the Hampen Marly Bed sequence from Wood Eaton Quarry [534 123] immediately south-east of the present district where the fauna and flora suggest shallow swampy near-shore conditions. This contrasts with the more marine nature of the lime muds of the present district in which thriving marine bivalve-rich communities developed similar to those in parts of the overlying White Limestone.

The Hampen Marly Beds resemble the Sharp's Hill Beds (p.74) both in the variety of rock types and in the presence of rootlet-bearing seatearths, indicating periods of very shallow water and emergence. Three rootlet horizons were recorded in the Hook Norton Borehole but only one at Tadmarton, suggesting that these beds were of limited lateral extent. A rootlet-bearing horizon is also present at North Leigh [3829 1296] between Woodstock and Witney, to the south of

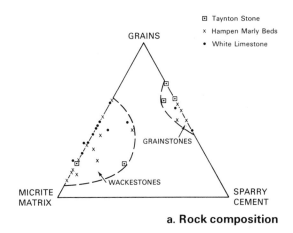

a. Rock composition

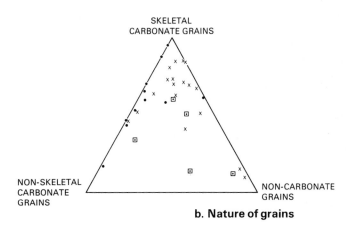

b. Nature of grains

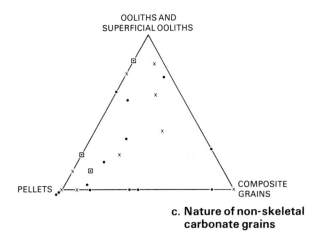

c. Nature of non-skeletal
carbonate grains

Figure 33 Petrographical composition of Great Oolite Group limestones in the Hook Norton Borehole

the present district. The tops of the seat earths are sharp, commonly bored, and one shows desiccation cracks. The capping sediments are highly variable though all show evidence of increased current activity, presumably after a break in sedimentation.

Clearly the depositional environment was one of very shallow water with brief episodes of emergence. Mostly marine conditions obtained, although the distinctive lithological and some faunal associations may suggest phases of varying salinity. No obvious rhythmic sequence of sedimentation is, however, discernible. Traced north-eastwards into Northamptonshire the formation passes into the 'Upper Estuarine Series', with its rhythmic interbedding of low-lying coastal marsh sediments and thin more marine beds. To the south-west marls and limestones constitute an increasing proportion of the Hampen Marly Beds. Although Palmer (1979) suggests that the local environment was one of marl deposition with oyster reef development, the latter generally occurs as oyster-rich beds which form only a minor part of the sequence. The remainder are bioturbated argillaceous limestones, marls and mudstones with varying proportions of shell debris and ooliths. This facies is more akin to the lime muds and muddy lime sands of the overlying White Limestone.

White Limestone

Hull (1857, p.13; 1859, p.19) called the youngest beds of his Great Oolite the White Limestone. Woodward introduced a division between his 'White Limestone' and the overlying Forest Marble, and named it the Kemble Beds. Subsequently Arkell (1947b, pp.42–44) grouped the Kemble Beds with the Forest Marble, and divided the White Limestone into the Ardley Beds and the Bladon Beds.

In the present account Hull's definition of the White Limestone has been used. This also retains Hull's original

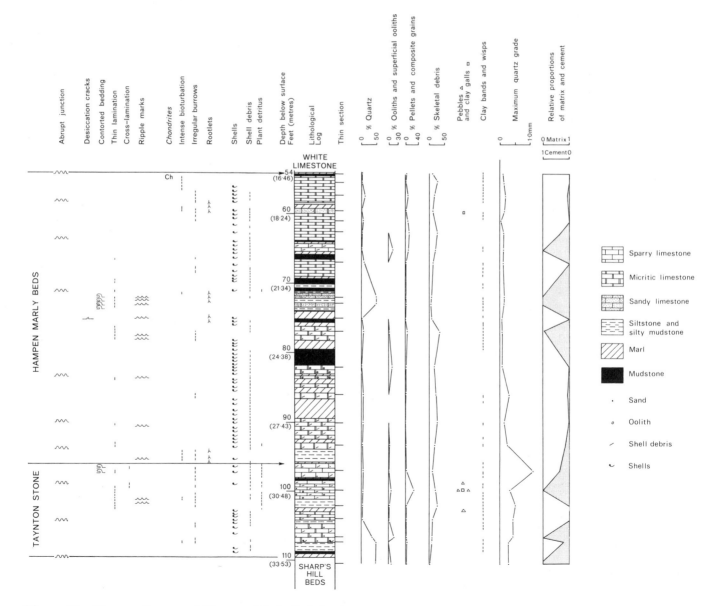

Figure 34   Taynton Stone and Hampen Marly Beds in the Hook Norton Borehole

definition of the Forest Marble as a distinct and laterally persistent lithostratigraphic unit. The survey preceded the subdivision of the White Limestone into three units (Palmer, 1979, Sumbler, 1984) which are in ascending order: the Shipton Member, the Ardley Member and the Bladon Member, and its formal description as the White Limestone Formation (McKerrow and Kennedy, 1973). These divisions were not delineated in the cores in the Hook Norton and Tadmarton boreholes which now provide the only complete local records of the formation (Appendix 4); (Plate 10). In these sequences the base of the White Limestone has been arbitrarily drawn at a minor change in lithology associated with an abrupt (?erosional) junction. The upper limit of the formation has been taken in the field at the first appearance of flaggy, coarse, shell-debris limestones and mudstones of the Forest Marble facies. In the Hook Norton Borehole a hardground occurs at this level, but at Tadmarton its position is less certain, and though an indurated surface occurs beneath a 0.41 m bed of limestone with pebbles and other derived grains, this bed has been included in the White Limestone. In the Swerford Trough brightly coloured clays probably equivalent to the Fimbriata-waltoni Beds, now included in the Bladon Member, can be recognised locally just below the Forest Marble and appear to be overlain by a bed of typical White Limestone lithology.

The White Limestone has long been considered to be equivalent to the Blisworth (Great Oolite) Limestone of Northamptonshire. The faunal evidence was recently summarised by Torrens (in Cope and others, 1980). It suggests that the lower part of the White Limestone may have been deposited during the *Tulites subcontractus* and *Morrisiceras morrisi* zones of the Middle Bathonian. The upper part of the sequence yields some evidence of a *Procerites hodsoni* Zone age and deposition may have continued into the younger *Oppelia (Oxycerites) aspidoides* Zone.

The White Limestone has an extensive outcrop on the plateau around Kiddington and Glympton, and east of the Cherwell between Caulcot and Fritwell. Smaller outcrops occur in outliers confined by the fault troughs south of Great Rollright and south of Swalcliffe. The numerous shallow quarries along the outcrop reflect the former importance of the formation as a source of lime. Few sections have proved the complete sequence but published accounts indicate that the maximum thicknesses occur to the south and south-west of the present district. The minimum thickness recorded is 7.98 m in the Tadmarton Borehole and the maximum 10.34 m in the Hook Norton Borehole. The detailed section of the latter hole is given in Figure 35. The formation was 9.4 m thick in the Fritwell Cutting [518 287] (Arkell and others 1933, pp.343–344); 8.51 m are exposed in the nearby Ardley Fields Farm Quarry [541 265]; in the Slape Hill Quarry, Wootton, immediately to the south of the present district, the formation is 11 m thick.

At outcrop the formation consists of well bedded white, cream and buff limestones and marls with thin mudstones. The limestones are mostly fine grained, with scattered ooliths, pellets and shell debris set in a calcareous mud matrix (see Figure 33). When weathered they have often been described as marly. Shell-detrital limestones are common but less important. The formation is relatively uniformly flat-bedded, but a few gently cross-stratified beds are pres-

ent. The bases of the detrital limestones are usually sharp in quarry sections and, rarely, include small pebbles.

Detailed examination of the Hook Norton and Tadmarton borehole cores forms the basis of the following petrographic description. The limestones may be roughly divided into three types. The first is of minor importance, and consists of micritic limestones which contain cryptocrystalline calcite, originally deposited as calcareous mud, with scattered grains and shell fragments. In the field they can described as calcite-mudstones (wackestones), but as the proportion of micrograined skeletal debris increases they grade into calcite siltstones (packstones).

The second comprises shelly limestones with a very pronounced bimodal grain-size distribution. In these rocks (packstones) the matrix consists of micrite which usually contains an abundance of micrograined skeletal debris, the whole forming more than 50 per cent by volume of the rock. Fossils abound and are usually articulated, some in growth positions. Shells and shell debris are the dominant components; pellets, ooliths and composite grains are less common. These limestones are unbedded with the grains 'floating' in the matrix. The irregular distribution of the grains is probably the result of bioturbation. Very irregular worm burrows are also present and U-shaped burrows occur throughout.

The third variety is less common than the micritic limestones. The matrices consist of sparry calcite of diagenetic origin, though bands and pockets of micrite may be present. These limestones contain varying proportions of ooliths, pellets, composite grains and abraded skeletal grains. In hand specimen they can be described as oolitic or pellet limestones, though when the grains are small they are easily mistaken for very fine quartz sand. These grainstones are commonly indefinitely stratified with bands of varying coarseness. Gentle cross-stratification can be seen at some levels. Burrows are uncommon. The bases of these limestones are usually sharp and some are marked by small pebbles.

The interbedded marls are intermediate between the limestones and the mudstones. They are usually medium grey or pale greenish or olive-tinted grey when fresh, and weather to pale orange or greenish grey hues. They contain a high proportion of shell debris and complete shells which are either scattered through the rock or present as winnowed layers or shell lenses.

Non-calcareous mudstones are very subordinate. They can be divided into: (i) medium to pale greenish grey mudstone which weathers to a yellowish brown and orange clay; lenses and layers of shell debris and shells occur, whilst shallow burrows and organic 'trails' may be present; (ii) dark greenish grey to black mudstones with race (secondary calcite nodules) and locally much lignitic material; these are known only at outcrop, and carry a limited fauna; they comprise the dominant lithology of the Fimbriata-waltoni Beds; (iii) 'clay with lenticles', where the lenticles consist of isolated ripples of silt and fine shell debris.

Since the survey was completed Palmer (1979) has studied the White Limestone of the Cotswolds. He has extended the research of McKerrow and others (1969) to the complete formation, confirming the relationship between sediment and fossils, and has recognised eight faunal–lithological associations within the White Limestone. These include coral beds (1) which consist of branching frame-building species. Sessile brachiopods and bivalves occur, associated with encrusting and boring taxa. The muddy lime sands (2), a major element in the sequence, contain a sedentary epifauna of brachiopods and bivalves together with burrowing bivalves. The faunal differences between Palmer's clean-washed lime sands (3) and cross-bedded lime sands (4) reflect the increased current activity in the latter facies. The former type is rich in nerineid gastropods and has rare epifaunal bivalves, but contains a variety of burrowing taxa; the mobile nature of the sediments of the latter type is reflected in their very reduced fauna, most of which is preserved in lag deposits. Pelletal lime muds (5), which are rich in *Aphanoptyxis* and shallow-burrowing bivalves, are important and form the major correlatable limestones which are characterised by their distinct gastropod faunas. These, in upward sequence, are the Aphanoptyxis excavata Bed, the Aphanoptyxis ardleyensis Bed and the Aphanoptyxis bladonensis Bed. The shelly micrites (6) are highly fossiliferous with both epifaunal and infaunal taxa. The near-shore lagoon deposits (7) include clays and marly limestones with a fauna similar to that of the lime-mud facies. The mud-flat colonising fauna is low in variety and is associated with freshwater species of gastropods, ostracods and charophytes and also reptile bones. The lagoon deposits contain much derived plant remains and also have rootlet beds (Palmer and Jenkyns, 1975, p.129). Klein (1965, p.177) suggested that the caliche-like 'race' nodules in these clays result from periodic exposure of mud-flats. Palmer (1979, p.221) also recognised several hardgrounds (8) with encrusting bivalves and boring organisms. Some of the rich and varied fauna of the White Limestone is listed in Appendix 1(4).

Palmer's major divisions of the White Limestone (1979, p.202–203) were each thought to represent a shoaling-upward rhythm which culminated in a hardground. This pattern was not recognised in the White Limestone core in the Hook Norton Borehole (Figure 35). Sumbler (1984) noted that thin clays locally overlie the hardgrounds and concluded that they represent temporary extensions of an estuarine environment into the mainly marine White Limestone facies. Klein (1965) suggested that graded beds form an important part of the facies and concluded that the latter was of intertidal origin. However, Palmer (1979, p.225) believes that areas of emergence were very limited and most of the formation 'was deposited in shallow, subtidal conditions'. The best developed emergent horizon, the highest hardground, contains a 'laminated vuggy micrite' (Palmer and Jenkyns, 1975) which was thought to form a barrier island in the White Limestone sea. However, Sumbler (1984) believes that similar lithologies occur in at least one of the other rhythms. Palmer (1979, p.225) interprets the environment as one of shallow water, probably subtidal or with very small tidal influence, such as is found today in Florida Bay or the Great Bahama Bank. Epithyrid-rich shell banks and very small coral-patch reefs developed locally in an area of extensive lime-mud and lime-silty-sand flats which was dissected by migrating channels. Little terrigenous material was introduced and only rarely were estuarine conditions established.

Details

Little Compton

About 1.5 m of Taynton Stone crops out on the summit of a hill [279 299] south-east of Oakham. The highest beds are white, coarse, shelly oolites which rest on pale grey oolitic limestones and false-bedded, sandy limestones. The regional dip is to the south-east.

EGP, AH

Whichford Trough

A few metres of the basal beds of the Great Oolite Limestone cap a small hill south of North Leasow [3148 3590]. To the east, a larger outcrop occurs south of Farnicombe and extends eastwards to Traitor's Ford Coppice where there are several small exposures. The lowest beds, which include bands similar to the Stonesfield Slate, are visible in a roadside exposure [3367 3633] south of Traitor's Ford, and dip south at 44° to 50°. The section is:

	Thickness m
TAYNTON STONE	
Limestone; brown-weathering, coarse-grained, coarsely oolitic, shell-fragmental	0.46
Clay; greyish green	0.18
Limestone; pale grey, coarsely oolitic, hard, fairly pure, with much shell debris	0.15
Limestone; brown-weathering, oolitic, flaggy, with shells	0.08
Limestone; grey-hearted, fairly coarse and oolitic, massive	0.53
Limestone; grey, fine-grained, thinly bedded, hard and sandy	0.38
Limestone; grey and brown, nodular-weathering, poorly exposed	0.38
Limestone; grey and brown, nodular and flaggy bands, coarsely oolitic and shelly	0.38

Plate 9 Polished cores of Hampen Marly Beds × 0.7

a. Hampen Marly Beds. Pale grey fine-grained shell-fragmental limestone with darker, pale greenish grey bands. Slightly silty and intensely bioturbated. Hook Norton Borehole, depth 16.8 m (55ft), natural size.

b. Hampen Marly Beds. Olive-grey shelly shell-fragmental marl. Abundant oysters in a variably cemented matrix. Hook Norton Borehole, depth 24.8 m (81ft 3in), natural size.

c. Hampen Marly Beds. Pale bluish grey fine-grained shell-fragmental limestone with fine-grained matrix at top. Becoming increasingly coarse grained downward, medium bluish grey with large bivalve and echinoderm fragments which show pronounced stratification. The lithologies are comparable with those shown in the Forest Marble the bed grading down from thinly bedded argillaceous limestone, through the section shown, to very coarse shell-fragmental limestone with rests abruptly on an eroded surface of medium dark grey clayey calcareous silt with rootlets. Hook Norton Borehole, depth 28.5 m (93ft 6in), natural size.

d. Hampen Marly Beds. Pale olive-grey shelly oolith shell-fragmental micritic limestone. Some of the oysters are in position of growth. Uneven distribution of grains and the matrix results from bioturbation. A singular burrow in the centre of the specimen shows peripheral concentration of grains in the cavity wall (collapsed). Hook Norton Borehole, depth 25 m (82ft), natural size.

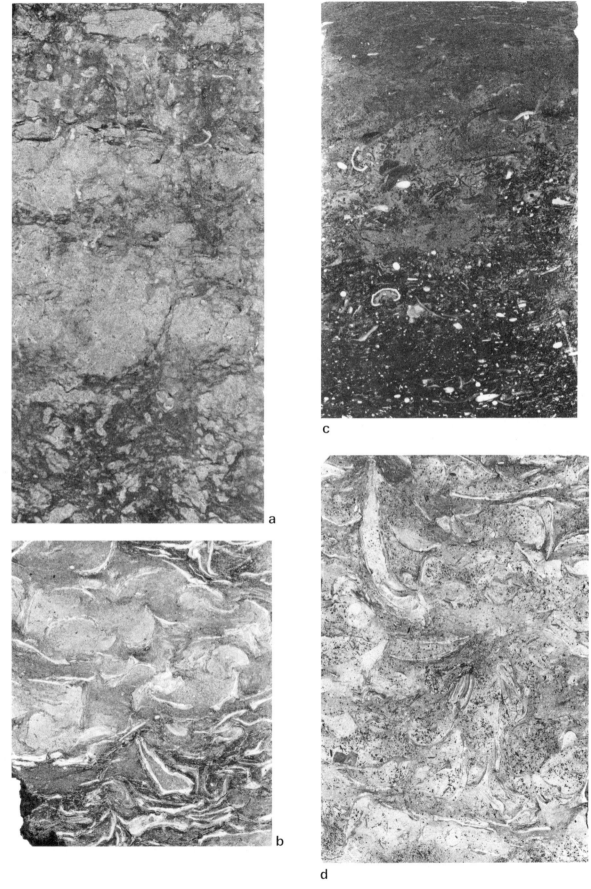

a

c

b

d

Plate 9 Polished cores of the Hampen Marly Beds. For details, see opposite

Limestone; brown-weathering, oolitic, thinly bedded
and shelly 0.10
Limestone; pale grey, fine-grained, hard, massively
bedded with strong joints 0.56
Limestone; brown-weathering, pale grey-hearted, very
hard and flinty, finely sandy and splintery 0.18

In the south-west corner of Traitor's Ford Coppice [3353 3622], the following section was measured in beds higher in the sequence:

	Thickness m
?TAYNTON STONE	
Limestone; grey, platy, very hard, with abundant shell fragments	0.46
Marl; grey and brown, with many shells	0.46
Clay; brown, soft and sticky	0.28
Limestone; brown-weathering, shell-fragmental	0.38
Limestone; cream, sparsely oolitic, hard, massively-bedded, with calcite veins and shell fragments	0.33

Fossils from this locality included: *Liostrea sp.*, *'Lucina' bellona*, *Modiolus sp.*, *Plagiostoma subcardiiformis*, *Cossmannea (Eunerinea)* cf. *eudesii* and *Nerinaea sp.*

Poor exposures of limestone slightly lower in the sequence occur in the Coppice to the north-east; in one old digging [3361 3625] bivalves included *Ceratomya concentrica*, and *Liostrea* aff. *hebridica*.

White oolite caps the hill south of Sharp's Hill Quarry [338 358] and has a large outcrop north of Fodge Farm [3457 3520] towards Temple Mills. In an old quarry 73 m north of Fodge Farm the following section high in the sequence was recorded:

	Thickness m
WHITE LIMESTONE	
Limestone; brown-weathering, grey, flaggy	0.61
Limestone (A. bladonensis Bed); cream, oolitic, massively bedded and shelly	0.91
Shale (Oyster Bed); dark grey, with abundant white-weathering ostreids	0.30

The Oyster Bed also crops out at the top of a bank on the eastern side of the road east of Fodge Farm. Similar beds are exposed in a small quarry [3471 3585] north of Fodge Farm.

The best sections hereabouts, however, are seen in the large Temple Mills quarries [347 359 to 347 363], where the upper beds of the Great Oolite Limestone are overlain by the Forest Marble (Figure 36). This section has been described by Whitehead and Arkell (1946, pp.16–18) as follows (the bed numbers given are those of Figure 36):

	Thickness m
FOREST MARBLE	
9 Kemble Beds: brown, ripple-marked, sandy flags and dark oyster limestone with many shaly partings, passing laterally into marl and clay,	Up to 3.66
8 Upper Epithyris Bed: marl, locally compacted, passing north into limestone; many *Epithyris oxonica*	0.30
WHITE LIMESTONE (Beds 2–7 = Fimbriata-waltoni Beds of S. Oxon)	
7 Limestone; weathering crumbly	0 (at south end)–0.41
6 Bladonensis Bed: white, porcellanous limestone full of *Aphanoptyxis bladonensis*,	

Gervillia waltoni, *Astarte fimbriata*	0.91
5 Oyster bed: marl full of *Ostrea hebridica*	0.15
4 Clay; green becoming purple and black downwards, with white pellets and lignite; channelling the beds below	0–0.46
3 Argillaceous limestone; blue-hearted, of flinty appearance, in up to six layers with marl partings	0–0.38
2 Cast bed: greenish marly limestone passing into marl, locally a mass of casts of same fossils as in bed 6	0.30
1 Limestone; white, with *Nerinea eudesii* and many lamellibranchs; *Ptygmatis bacillus* and corals in bottom course	2.13

A similar suite of fossils was obtained from those beds in the southern quarry [347 360].

To the north of Temple Mills an old quarry [3452 3646] exposes:

	Thickness m
WHITE LIMESTONE	
Limestone (possible A. bladonensis Bed); grey-hearted, hard shelly and nodular-weathering	0.25
Clay (?Oyster Bed); brown-weathering, with abundant *Liostrea*	0.08
Limestone; pale grey, oolitic and shelly	0.61

Similar beds, dipping south at 70°, are exposed in a small faulted inlier west of Woodway Farm.

In the Hook Norton Borehole [3564 3588], the Great Oolite Limestone was 25.59 m thick. The abbreviated log is given in Appendix 4.   EGP

Plate 10   Polished cores of White Limestone and Forest Marble × 0.75

a. White Limestone. Very pale grey gastropod-rich micritic limestone. Gastropods infilled with greenish grey marl and less commonly calcite spar. Some bivalves are present and the micrite matrix contains an abundance of fine-grained shell fragments. Burrow traces are rare. Hook Norton Borehole, depth 7.9 m (26ft), natural size.

b. Forest Marble. Medium bluish grey shell-fragmental limestone with irregular wispy pockets of olive-grey ?micritic matrix. Oyster shells dominant with other bivalve remains. Rare pebbles of micritic limestones up to 2 cm diameter with smaller carbonate grains and lignitic fragments. Weak stratification of shell debris. Tadmarton Borehole, depth 11.3 m (37ft), natural size.

c. White Limestone. Pale bluish grey shell-fragmental limestone. Many blue medium grained shell fragments in a pale grey micrite matrix with scattered more argillaceous wisps and occasional debris-free micrite-filled burrows. Hook Norton Borehole, depth 13.6 m (44ft 6in), natural size.

d. Forest Marble resting on White Limestone. Forest Marble comprises medium bluish grey shell-fragmental limestone with irregular pockets and bands of olive-grey micrite. The Forest Marble infills borings and penetrates down cracks in the White Limestone which consists of a pale grey micrite with scattered fine shell debris and some carbonate grains. Bivalves, some articulated, dominate the White Limestone fauna. The limestone becomes more olive-grey and argillaceous near the base. Hook Norton Borehole, depth of junction 6.15 m (20ft 2in), natural size.

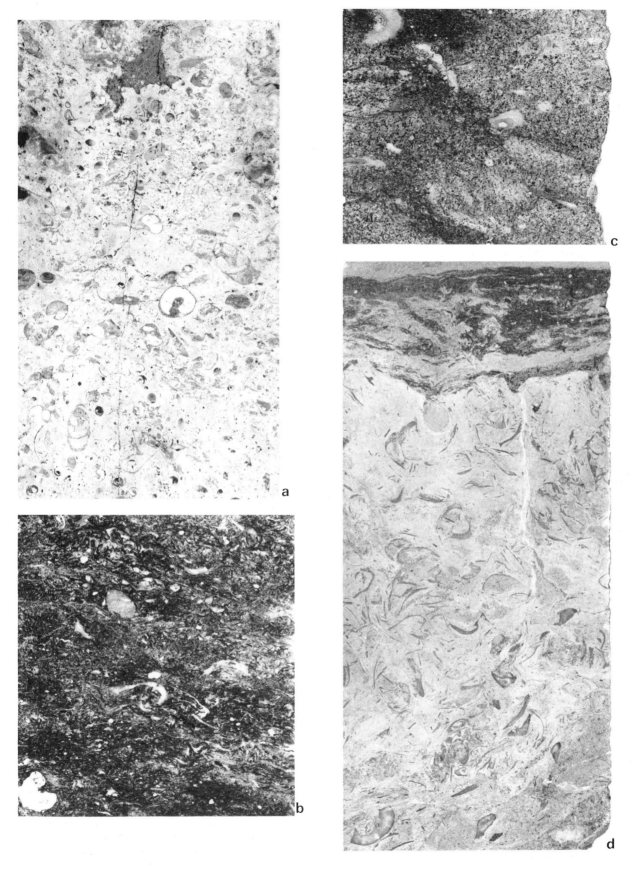

Plate 10   Polished cores of White Limestone and Forest Marble, Hook Norton and Tadmarton boreholes. For details, see opposite

The White Limestone crops extensively between the Sibford and Whichford faults between Belleisle Farm [354 356] and Stour Well [378 363], though locally field brash shows the presence of the Taynton Stone and the Hampen Marly Beds. An old quarry [3557 3579] near Belleisle Farm exposes:

		Thickness m
Forest Marble		
13	Limestone; brown, sandy, shelly in parts	0.61
12	Marl; yellowish brown, shaly, with thin blue and brown clay bands and sandy ribs	0.18
11	Clay; blue, with thin brown shell limestone bands	0.30
10	Calcite 'beef'; faintly greenish grey, vertically fibrous with an irregular base and regular top	0.13
9	Limestone; pale grey, blocky, marly and shelly, jointed, with irregular base	0.30
8	Marl; greyish brown, clayey, shell-fragmental, with nodular limestone masses	0.15
White Limestone		
7	Limestone; white, porcellanous, blocky and shelly, with echinoid spines, bivalves, nerineids, and fish fragments	0.61–0.91
6a	Sandy parting, impersistent	0.03
6	Limestone; brown, sandy, shelly, roughly false-bedded, with echinoid fragments, *Placunopsis sp.* and *Tancredia?*	0.30
5	Clay; brown	0.05
4	Mudstone; brown, clayey, packed with ostreids	0.13
3	Clay; black	0.10
2	Limestone; grey, shelly, rubbly, sparsely oolitic, shelly in parts with nerineids	0.41
1	Limestone; oolitic, pale grey, massive, shelly with nerineids	1.22

Many of the beds vary in thickness across the quarry; in such cases the maximum thicknesses are given. At the southern end of the quarry, Bed 13 (Forest Marble) cuts down to Bed 9.

Farther east, beds at about the same position are exposed beneath the Forest Marble in a large quarry [3768 3618] south-east of Stour Well (Plate 11). The succession is:

	Thickness m
White Limestone	
Limestone; bluish grey, hard, shelly, with *Liostrea hebridica, Modiolus imbricatus* and *Placunopsis socialis*	0.10–0.38
Clay; reddish brown, sandy, packed with ostreids	0–0.10
Marl; greyish, passing into marly clay, locally sandy basally, many ostreids	0.15–0.30
Clay; dark grey to black with brownish patches	0–0.15
Limestone; bluish grey, oolitic, with fine jointing; *Anisocardia, Eomiodon, Liostrea,* and *Protocardia, Endiaplocus* cf. *roissyi*	0.23
Limestone; pale brown, oolitic, hard	0.15
Limestone; pale pinkish brown, oolitic, hard, coarser and most fossiliferous at the base with *Aphanoptyxis sp.*	0.41
Limestone; greyish white, oolitic, hard and massive, *Eomiodon?*, '*Lucina*' *bellona* and *Modiolus*	0.36
Limestone; pale grey, oolitic, marly	0.30
Limestone; greyish white, oolitic, hard and massive	0.68

BJW

Great Rollright

The Great Oolite Limestone is preserved in the Swerford Trough to the south and east of the village. Numerous sections were visible during the building of the Banbury–Cheltenham railway; the most complete record is that of Woodward (1894, pp.300–301) who gives the total thickness of the beds as 22.6 m. The sides of the cuttings are now largely grassed over.

The Taynton Stone crops out in a narrow belt along the northern and southern edges of the Swerford Trough adjacent to the Rollright and Swerford Faults. It is 5.51 m thick and comprises pale grey, fissile, false-bedded limestones and white oolitic and shell-fragmental limestones. The basal beds are visible in a cutting at Langton Bridge [317 300]. A sandy false-bedded limestone with clay pellets and worm tubes forms a prominent rib on the wall of the cutting 146 m east of the A34 road bridge: crinoid, echinoid and rhynchonellid fragments, *Coelopis* cf. *pulchella, Falcimytilus sublaevis, Liostrea hebridica, Placunopsis socialis,* and *Procerithium (Xystrella) tancredi* were collected here.

Higher beds of the Taynton Stone are exposed in a small quarry [3222 3061] to the west of the A34.

	Thickness m
Taynton Stone	
Limestone; buff to cream-coloured, sandy, micaceous, fine-grained; very thinly bedded	0.15
Limestone; mostly white oolitic layers set in a fine-grained grey calcareous matrix; massive, with cross-bedded fine-grained sandy limestone partings	0.74
Limestone; pale to buff-weathering, sandy, fine-grained, finely laminated; irregular micro-cross-bedding visible on weathered surfaces	0.15
Limestone; buff, coarsely oolitic, the ooliths showing micro-cross-bedding set in a finer-grained matrix; fossiliferous, massive, but flaggy-weathering	0.66
Limestone; cream, fine-grained, oolitic, massive	seen to 0.46

These beds yielded: echinoid and rhynchonellid fragments, *Astarte squamula, Bakevellia waltoni, Eomiodon sp., Liostrea hebridica, Lopha gregarea* and *Placunopsis socialis.*

The Hampen Marly Beds have a narrow outcrop which is largely obscured by a wash of limestone rubble. From Walk Farm [339 300] to north of Coldharbour Farm they crop out against the main southern fault of the Trough. They have an estimated thickness of about 7 m, the basal beds, dipping at 25° to the north, being visible in a small quarry [3235 2992]:

		Thickness m
Hampen Marly Beds		
	Soil; brown loam with limestone fragments	—
5	Limestone; grey argillaceous cementstone, weathering to a rubbly marl; serpulid tubes and bryozoa encrusting *Liostrea hebridica*	0.38
4	Limestone; dull greyish green, weathering to brown marl; oolitic and argillaceous. The top of the bed contains *Epithyris bathonica, E. oxonica, E. oxonica transversa, Liostrea hebridica, L. hebridica elongata* and *Modiolus imbricatus;* the middle bed contains bryozoa, *Kallirhynchia spp. E. bathonica, E. oxonica, Anisocardia islipensis, Chlamys (Radulopecten) hemicostata, Liostrea hebridica, M. imbricatus* and *Pholadomya lirata*	1.27

TAYNTON STONE

3 Limestone, fawn-coloured, silty to sandy, micaceous, with scattered white ooliths and a few oolith layers; thinly false-bedded, some lignite fragments   0.57

2 Limestone; silty to sandy, fawn with grey clay pipes   0.05

1 Limestone; white to cream, medium-grained oolite with a small proportion of shell debris and scattered fossils; a few micro-cross-bedded bands of grey fine-grained compact limestone which contain layers of ooliths; massive, flaggy-weathering, ?cross-bedded   0.66

Dr Ivimey-Cook notes that there appears to be a complete transition between the two 'species' of epithyrids recovered from Bed 4: all forms are more highly punctate than the epithyrids found higher in the Great Oolite Group.

An adjoining quarry [3236 2995] exposes beds slightly higher in the Hampen Marly Beds, dipping north at 18°:

Thickness
m

Soil; brown, clayey with marly limestone fragments   —

Limestone; bluish grey, shell-fragmental oolite, speckled with fawn ooliths, small ochreous patches and greyish green argillaceous wisps   0.36

Marl; greyish green, weathering to greenish brown with ochreous hues; white and pink ooliths throughout; compact, silty; bryozoa, echinoid spines, *Kallirhynchia spp.*, *Anisocardia (Antiquicyprina) loweana*, *Camptonectes annulatus*, *C.* cf. *rigidus*, *Liostrea hebridica*, *Mactromya varicosa*, *Modiolus imbricatus*, *Parallelodon* aff. *bynei*, *Protocardia lycetti*, *Sphaeriola oolithica* and *Trigonia pullus*   0.69

Clay; brownish grey with abundant *Liostrea hebridica*   0.30

Marly; greyish green to khaki-green, dense, silty, with scattered ooliths; cidarid spine, *Kallirhynchia spp.*, *Anisocardia sp.*, *Liostrea hebridica*, *Modiolus imbricatus*, *Trigonia pullus*, *Vaugonia moretoni*   0.71

Limestone; grey, weathering brown, silty to sandy,

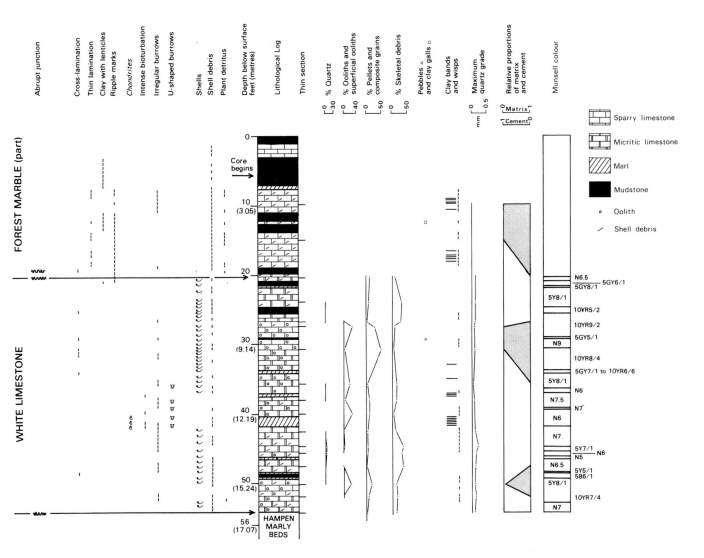

Figure 35   White Limestone and Forest Marble in the Hook Norton Borehole

fine-grained; sparsely oolitic with scattered ooliths, showing micro-false-bedding; becoming increasingly oolitic downward 0.18

Limestone; buff to pale buff, shell-fragmental oolite (white ooliths) with clays wisps along the bedding planes; *Kallirhynchia?* 0.53

Clay; dull ochreous brown, deeply weathered, silty, laminated and sparsely oolitic 0.25

Clay, dark greyish blue, fossiliferous 0.10

Limestone; dull grey to buff, sandy oolite with blue clay partings 0.13

Limestone; pale orange-tinted buff, sandy ... seen 0.08

The White Limestone is exposed in two quarries immediately to the north of the railway bridge at Limekiln Farm. The first, [323 303] to the west of the road, shows the following succession, dipping at 6° to S18°E:

	Thickness m
Limestone (cementstone); grey, shelly, hard, compact, flaggy-weathering	0.18
Limestone (cementstone); grey, shelly; now a rubble set in a pale brown marly matrix	0.51
Limestone; dark grey, argillaceous, with minor greenish grey clay wisps, passing laterally into a white marl; '*Corbula*' cf. *hulliana*, *Cuspidaria* aff. *ibbetsoni*, *Mactromya impressa*, *Modiolus londsdalei*, *Amberleya sp.*, *Aphanoptyxis bladonensis*, and a fish scale	0.05–0.18
Clay; greyish green, plastic, unfossiliferous; squeezed into the joints of the underlying bed	0.03–0.10
Limestone (cementstone); grey with pinkish mottling, fine-grained, argillaceous, yellow to ochreous ooliths locally concentrated, rubbly-weathering; the top is porcellanous and yields *Eomiodon* cf. *angulatus* and *Aphanoptyxis* cf. *bladonensis*; the remainder of the bed yields *A. (A.) loweana* and '*Lucina*' *bellona*	not recorded
Limestone (cementstone); pale grey with irregular pale pink-tinted areas, hard, compact, porcellaneous, sub-conchoidal fracture; finely laminated; recrystallised shell fragments	0.06
Limestone (cementstone); argillaceous with coarse buff to pinkish oolith limestone bands; upper part contains *Pleuromya*, *Aphanoptyxis* aff. *ardleyensis*, *A.* aff. *eulimoides* and *Eomesodon trigonus*; lower part contains *Anisocardia truncata*, *Astarte* cf. *oolitharum*, *Bakevellia waltoni*, *Ceratomya concentrica*, *Fimbria lajoyei*, '*Lucina*' *bellona*, *Mactromya sp.*, *Myophorella* aff. *signata*, *Pronoella lycetti*, *Pseudotrapezium* aff. *cordiforme*, *Pteroperna costatula*, *Sphaeriola oolithica*, *Trigonia pullus*, *Bactroptyxis bacillus*	1.04
Limestone (cementstone); very pale grey matrix with pale yellow to buff and white ooliths scattered throughout, argillaceous, a few fossils and shell fragments, massive, irregular weathering	seen 0.41

The second quarry [3252 3030], east of the road, shows a similar sequence though two thin marls are recorded.

The highest beds of the White Limestone crop out in fields south of the railway sidings [3272 3032] where they consist of green and bluish black clay. Brightly coloured clays with thin cementstones and oyster-rich limestones were excavated from a pit [341 305] on the bank of the River Swere, north-east of Walk Farm. In this tract the thickness of the White Limestone is estimated to be 10 m.

Chipping Norton – Sarsden – Enstone

The basal beds of the Taynton Stone are exposed in Padley's (*Cetiosaurus*) Quarry [318 272], east-south-east of Chipping Norton church where about 1.5 m of white false-bedded, shell-fragmental limestone yielded *Clypeus sp.*, *Kallirhynchia?*, *Liostrea sp.*, and *Ataphrus* aff. *heliciformis*.

To the south of the town, the Glyme Valley Fault brings the basal beds of the Great Oolite Limestone against the Clypeus Grit and the Chipping Norton Limestone. These basal beds have been dug in a number of small quarries. Field fragments are typical of the Taynton Stone. The overlying Hampen Marly Beds crop out near Walterbush Farm, to the west. Immediately to the north and east of the farmhouse, green and yellow clays and oyster-rich limestones and marls have been dug in drainage ditches. Temporary excavations at the farm revealed 0.61 m of very hard, compact, pale fawn variegated, shell-fragmental limestone containing *Clypeus* cf. *rimosus*, *Camptonectes rigidus*, *Falcimytilus sublaevis*, *Liostrea hebridica*, *Modiolus sp.*, and *Pleuromya*.

The Taynton Stone crops out near the Tumulus, east-north-east of Sarsden House, and forms the high ground to the south-east of Fairgreen Farm [2926 2226]. A disused quarry [2957 2214], east-south-east of the farmhouse showed:

	Thickness m
Soil and rubble	0.30
Limestone; pale fawn to brown-speckled oolite with greyish green marl pellets and argillaceous wisps; variable coarseness resulting in a banded appearance; irregular flaggy-weathering	0.43
Limestone; brown-speckled, coarse shelly oolite with argillaceous wisps in top 0.36 m, brownish green speckled below; massive to flaggy-weathering	0.74
Limestone; cream, fine-grained oolite with coarse oolite bands and argillaceous partings	0.43
Section obscured	0.61
Limestone; pale cream, hard, fine-grained oolite with some coarser bands	0.36
Limestone; pale cream, medium-grained oolite, locally decalcified, with friable oolitic patches; top 0.30 m rubbly-weathering, the remainder a massive freestone	1.98
Limestone; off-white, oolitic, with minor shell debris, false-bedded with flaggy-weathering	seen to 0.53

The lowest three beds of limestone are lithologically very similar to the Chipping Norton Limestone.

To the south, near the trigonometrical station [2995 2187], false-bedded sandy limestones and argillaceous oolitic and clay-pellet limestones of the Taynton Stone are overlain by thin clays and argillaceous limestones, probably the Hampen Marly Beds.

A quarry [2990 2130], in flaggy Taynton Stone, immediately to the south of the Camp, west of Barters Hill Farm, exposes about 2.1 m of limestone with khaki-green clay seams, from which *Kallirhynchia sp.*, *Liostrea* cf. *hebridica*, and *Placunopsis* cf. *socialis* were collected.   AH

The Sharp's Hill Beds are absent or very thin to the south and east of a line running from Lyneham Barrow [297 211] in the south via the Sarsden Tumulus to East Downs Farm [322 251], but the Great Oolite Limestone is usually separated from the underlying Chipping Norton Limestone by a band of calcareous cementstone. Most of the upland area north of Chadlington and Spelsbury is composed of Taynton Stone, which is exposed in a roadside quarry [3056 2139] east of Barter's Hill Farm.

The Great Oolite Limestone crops out on high ground to the north-east of Enstone.

The following section of the Taynton Stone was recorded in a disused well shaft [3948 2511] east of Quarrypiece Farm:

	Thickness m
Soil	0.03
Clay; greenish brown, with numerous ostreids and rare rhynchonellids, passing down into	0.30–0.60
Limestone; white-weathering, with pale orange ooliths, shell fragments, ostreids and rhynchonellids in a micritic matrix	0.56
Limestone; pale orange ooliths, shells and debris set in a white fine-grained matrix	0.19
Marl; green with ooliths and shells	0.01
Limestone; off-white, medium- to coarse-grained, shell-fragmental oolite, with bands and lenticles of shell debris	0.21
Limestone; white, coarse- to medium-grained, shell-fragmental oolite, massive, with irregular cross-bedding marked by coarser bands of white ooliths and shell debris interbedded with (particularly in top 50 mm) impersistent layers of greenish grey very fine-grained silty limestone with clay partings	1.47
	AH

Enstone – Glympton

The Great Oolite Limestone forms a somewhat dissected plateau which dips gently south-eastwards from the higher ground south of Enstone to Glympton and Wootton.

Between Lidstone [355 247] and Charlbury, the basal beds comprise brown, sandy, current-bedded, flaggy oolitic Taynton Stone which rests directly upon the Chipping Norton Limestone. There are several old quarries. The basal junction is seen in two of them [3625 2251; 3673 2230] near Taston Cross. The section in the former shows:

	Thickness m
TAYNTON STONE	
Limestone; fawn, rubbly, flaggy, current-bedded, sandy and oolitic	1.22
Limestone; fawn, flaggy in places, more massive than above, current-bedded, sandy, oolitic	0.97
CHIPPING NORTON LIMESTONE	
Limestone; brown, massive, sandy and oolitic, with a few thin flaggy bands	1.22

In another old quarry [3617 2053] 0.61 m of fine-grained, hard, brown, sandy, oolitic limestone with ostreids is overlain by 1.83 m of flaggy, brown, coarser-grained, current-bedded oolitic limestone. These beds are thought to be near the base of the Taynton Stone. To the east similar beds are seen in yet another disused quarry [3895 2170].

In the Ditchley Park Borehole [3907 2246], north of Ditchley Hall, the Great Oolite Limestone has been taken to extend to a depth of 13.7 m. Farther east, an old quarry [3997 2216] west of Asterleigh shows:

	Thickness m
Clay (Oyster Bed); brown-weathering with many shells	0.30

Plate 11 White Limestone (Great Oolite Limestone) quarry near Stour Well, Swacliffe [377 362] (A 9867)

Limestone; whitish grey, flaggy, coarse-grained, oolitic, gently current-bedded, with many fossils including echinoid fragments, *Kallirhynchia sp.*, *Camptonectes* cf. *annulatus*, *Ceratomya* cf. *concentrica*, *Chlamys (R.) hemicostata*, *Liostrea hebridica*, *Modiolus sp.*, *Tancredia extensa*, *Trigonia pullus*, *Vaugonia* cf. *moretoni* and wood fragments   3.05

The best section in the Great Oolite Limestone hereabouts is in the north-eastern face of Whiteway Quarry [421 247], north of Whitehouse Farm, where over 9.8 m of beds are exposed:

Thickness
m

WHITE LIMESTONE
25 Limestone; whitish grey, hard, fine-grained, splintery chinastone type—probably very pure—with many broken fossil fragments including *Anisocardia (Antiquicyprina) loweana*, *Eomiodon angulatus*, *Modiolus imbricatus*, and '*Cylindrites*' *sp.*   0.76
24 Limestone; pale grey, with scattered ooliths, fairly fine-grained and shelly with *Epithyris?*, *Anisocardia (A.) loweana*, *Bakevellia waltoni* and *Modiolus imbricatus*. Weathers to massive angular fragments   0.30
23 Clay; yellowish brown, finely sandy and silty   0.08–0.10
22 Limestone; grey, rubbly-weathering; well preserved fossils include *Epithyris oxonica*, *Anisocardia* cf. *islipensis*, *A. (A.) loweana*, *Bakevellia waltoni*, *Camptonectes annulatus*, *Costigervillia crassicosta*, *Modiolus imbricatus*, *Protocardia lycetti*, *Fibula phasianoides* and *Globularia morrisi*; pink-tinted in the lower part with scattered ooliths in a marly matrix   0.84
21 Limestone; fawn-weathering with pinkish weathering ooliths, hard and massive; *A. (A.)* cf. *loweana* and *Placunopsis socialis*   0.30
20 Mudstone; fawn and cream-weathering, calcareous; shaly in places, with scattered ooliths   0.23
19 Limestone; whitish grey, soft, rubbly and oolitic   0.18–0.20
18 Limestone; cream, soft and rubbly; made up mostly of bivalves and casts of gastropods including *Eomiodon* cf. *angulatus*, *Modiolus imbricatus*, *Aphanoptyxis ardleyensis*, *C. (E.) eudesii* and *Globularia* cf. *formosa*   0.10–0.20
17 Limestone; cream, marly, nodular-weathering   0.05
16 Mudstone; fawn and yellow-weathering, calcareous   0.10
15 Limestone; cream and fawn, oolitic, many gastropods and bivalves including *Anisocardia truncata*, *Pleuromya uniformis* and *Aphanoptyxis ardleyensis*   0.66
14 Mudstone; grey and cream, calcareous, with many large ooliths   0.15
13 Limestone; cream with pink tinges, oolitic, with many shell fragments. Shaly in lower part   1.22
12 Limestone; grey and cream with pink tinges, hard and compact, many oolites and shells including *Ceratomya?*   0.30
11 Mudstone; brown-weathering, soft, calcareous   0.13
10 Limestone; whitish grey, densely oolitic with reddish brown ferruginous stains along cracks and joints; numerous fossils including *Ceratomya concentrica* and *Trigonia* cf. *pullus*   0.28

9 Mudstone; deep brown-weathering, ferruginous and calcareous   0.10
8 Limestone; dark bluish grey and brown mottled, coarsely crystalline in places, rubbly-weathering; highly fossiliferous with echinoid spines, gastropods, *Barbatia prattii*, *Falcimytilus sublaevis*, *Modiolus imbricatus*, *Plagiostoma subcardiiformis* and *Vaugonia?*   0.25
6 Limestone; brown-weathering, hard and densely oolitic; many fossils including *Placunopsis socialis*   0.30
5 Limestone; cream, oolitic   0.91
4 Limestone; pale grey, hard, oolitic; highly fossiliferous, containing echinoid fragments and gastropods, *A. (A.) loweana*, *Modiolus imbricatus*, *Pleuromya sp.*, *Vaugonia?* and wood fragments   0.61
3 Sand; brown, medium-grained   0.03
2 Limestone; brown, hard, very sandy, with lignitic plant fragments   0.33
1 Sand; brown, medium-grained   0.08

Beds 1 to 5 of the above section were somewhat obscured at the foot of the main north-eastern face, but are well exposed in a small section along the northern margin of the quarry; it is possible that Beds 1 to 3 equate with the Hampen Marly Beds.

The uppermost beds of the Great Oolite Limestone and their junction with the Forest Marble are seen in a small disused quarry [4219 2470], on the eastern side of the road opposite the Whiteway Quarry. The section is:

Thickness
m

FOREST MARBLE
Limestone; grey, coarse-grained, flaggy, shelly, with green mudstone fragments; erosive base   0.46

WHITE LIMESTONE
Limestone; whitish cream, fine-grained with scattered ooliths, rubbly-weathering; highly fossiliferous with *Bakevellia waltoni*   0.61
Marl; whitish cream, with limestone nodules   0.61
Limestone; fawn, current-bedded, finely sandy and oolitic; many shells and large lignitic wood fragments   0.41
Clay; dark bluish grey—in places almost black, brown-weathering with many lignite fragments   0.46
Limestone; cream and fawn, rubbly-weathering, oolitic; many fossils including gastropod casts   seen 0.30

To the south-south-east, the Great Oolite Limestone is estimated to be over 30 m thick at outcrop; a borehole at Killingworth Castle Inn [4382 2028], Wootton, proved 26.2 m of these beds. The best sections hereabouts are just outside the district in a large working quarry at Slape Hill [424 196] 1.5 km west of Wootton. The section commences on the south face in the western corner of the quarry:

Thickness
m

WHITE LIMESTONE
Soil; deep brown, clayey, with limestone fragments   0.30
Limestone; pale grey, brashy and rubbly, fine-grained, splintery chinastone, many fossils   1.83
Limestone; cream and pale grey with a faint greenish tinge; fairly soft argillaceous, oolitic, many shells: *Ceratomyopsis undulata*, *Lopha costata* and *Protocardia* cf. *stricklandi* were collected from

beds 26 and 27	1.42
Clay; greenish grey, weathering brown	0.03
Limestone; grey with green tinges, hard and oolitic	0.10
Clay; brown, marly	0.03
Limestone; grey with green tinges	0.15
Clay; green	0.01
Gap—section continued c.18 m to the east:	c.0.30
Limestone; cream, oolitic, massive, abundantly fossiliferous with shells and corals	0.56
Limestone; brown, thinly bedded with clay partings	0.05
Limestone; cream, massive bed of hard oolite with shells	0.51
Limestone; flaggy parting	0.01
Limestone; pale grey and cream, green-tinged in places, oolitic and shelly	0.28
Limestone; whitish grey, brown-weathering, oolitic, scattered corals and shells including *Pseudomelania*?	0.81
Gap (section below in west face near centre of quarry):	c.1.00–1.50
Limestone; whitish grey, fine-grained, argillaceous and soft	0.20
Limestone; grey, fine-grained, hard, splintery, fossiliferous	0.13
Marl; pale grey, brown-weathering	0.20
Limestone; whitish grey, pink-tinged, fine-grained hard; many fossils including gastropods	0.81
Marl; green-tinged grey, with thin limestone bands	0–0.20

Limestone; whitish grey with pink tinges, and scattered oolites, highly fossiliferous with gastropods and *Liostrea sp.*	0.66
Gap	—
Limestone; cream and whitish grey, oolitic, with thin marly partings; highly fossiliferous with *Montlivaltia smithi, Anisocardia caudata, Bakevellia waltoni, Chlamys?, Isognomon isognomonoides, Liostrea hebridica, Lopha costata, Placunopsis* cf. *socialis, Vaugonia moretoni, C.(E.) eudesii, Nerinella sp., Pleurotomaria sp., Pseudomelania?* and wood fragments	2.74

HAMPEN MARLY BEDS

Silt; reddish brown, sandy, ferruginous, with shells	0.20
Limestone; green-tinged, oolitic	0.18–0.28
Marl; greenish grey and brown	0.13
Limestone; green-tinged grey, soft, argillaceous, rubbly weathering; many shells including *Acrosalenia sp., Anisocardia sp., Modiolus sp., Pholadomya lirata, Protocardia stricklandi*	0.97

The River Glyme has carved a steep-sided valley in Great Oolite Limestone near Wootton. There are two sections of note in the south bank. One is in an old quarry [4374 1943] (Plate 12):

	Thickness m
Limestone; buff, flaggy, oolitic	0.30
Marl; brown, soft	0.30

Plate 12 White Limestone (Great Oolite Limestone) quarry at Wootton village [437 194] (A 9858)

Limestone; pale brown, massive, with marly base;
Epithyris?, *A.(A.) loweana*, *Bakevellia waltoni*, *Liostrea
sp.*, *Modiolus imbricatus* and *Pleuromya subelongata*.   1.07
Limestone; pale buff, rubbly; *Cyathophora sp.*,
Isastraea limitata, *Thamnasteria sp.*, *Epithyris* cf.
bathonica, *E. oxonica*; *A. (A.) loweana*, *Astarte sp.*,
Isognomon isognomonoides, *Modiolus imbricatus*,
Praeconia rhomboidalis, *Protocardia lycetti*, *P. stricklandi*
and *Aphanoptyxis ardleyensis*   seen 1.33

The second [4400 1952] is somewhat lower in the sequence, and
shows:

		Thickness m
10	Limestone; white, rubbly and oolitic	0.91
9	Limestone; cream, massively bedded and oolitic	0.46
8	Limestone; brown and cream, soft, marly and oolitic	0.46
7	Limestone; fawn, hard, with many fossils	0.20
6	Clayey shale; fawn, calcareous and oolitic	0.05
5	Limestone; fawn and cream, hard, massively bedded and oolitic, with many fossils	0.30
4	Limestone; fawn, oolitic, with shells	0.08
3	Limestone; fawn and cream, with purple blotches, hard, massively bedded, oolitic, with many fossils	1.52
2	Marl; fawn and brown-weathering	0.20
1	Limestone; whitish grey, fawn-weathering, rather rubbly, many fossils including echinoid spines and bivalves	1.37

The fossils from Beds 3 to 8 include: *Anisocardia (Antiquicyprina)
loweana*, *Bakevellia waltoni*, *Modiolus imbricatus*, *Pholadomya sp.* and
Cossmannea (Eunerinea) eudesii. Beds 9 and 10 also yielded *Costigervillia
crassicosta*, *Isognomon isognomonoides*, *Modiolus imbricatus* and *Protocardia*
cf. *stricklandi*.   EGP

Sandford St Martin – The Bartons

East of the artificially-levelled Enstone Airfield [390 260], the Great
Oolite Limestone forms a poorly-exposed plateau, cambered into
the valley around Sandford St. Martin and with widespread White
Limestone debris on the highest ground. An old quarry [4120 2717]
shows 0.91 m of pale grey oolitic limestone beneath the Forest
Marble.

Duns Tew – Rousham – Tackley

An elongated down-faulted area between the North Aston and
Dane Hill faults is floored by Great Oolite Limestone. South of
Duns Tew village, an elongated outlier of Great Oolite Limestone
forms an expanse of high ground; the outcrops of the Taynton
Stone and the Hampen Marly Beds are largely obscured by
downwash from the overlying White Limestone. In an old quarry
[4613 2720] east of Horsehay Farm, 1.52 m of brownish weathered,
rather clayey, oolitic limestone are exposed, and in another quarry
[4648 2639], just north-east of Brasenose Farm, shows 1.83 m of
white, densely oolitic limestone. In the Tackley area the Great
Oolite Limestone exceeds 30 m in thickness.

Northbrook – Caulcott

To the east of the Cherwell the Great Oolite Limestone forms a
wide outcrop and, together with the White Limestone, forms the
high ground. Old quarries [499 224; 5180 2469] expose white oolitic
limestone.   BJW

FOREST MARBLE

The Forest Marble as defined by Hull (1857, p.68) comprises a variable sequence of false-bedded flaggy oolites,
oolitic freestones, sandy limestones, sands, marls and
mudstones. The base of the formation as first selected is
much higher than that used by subsequent workers. Hull
takes the boundary above an oolitic bed at the top of his
'White Limestone', whereas Phillips (1860) selected the base
of some brightly coloured clays that are now called the
Fimbriata-waltoni Beds. Woodward (1894, p.250) introduced the term Kemble Beds for a succession of false-bedded
oolites which rested upon his 'White Limestone'. They were
succeeded by the Bradford Clay which he selected as the base
of his restricted 'Forest Marble'. Traced north-eastwards
from Kemble, near Cirencester, Woodward considered that
the Kemble Beds were overlapped by the Forest Marble, but
Arkell (1931, p.594) suggested that equivalent beds lay
within the Forest Marble of Oxfordshire, and divided his
'Forest Marble' of North Oxfordshire into Kemble Beds,
Bradford Beds and Wychwood Beds. Arkell (1931, pp.566
and 572–573) also described a new unit, the Fimbriata-
waltoni Beds, within the Kemble Beds. Their faunal
assemblage and lithological character provide a firm marker.
In many places a non-sequence marks the base of these beds,
and this was used to define the base of the Forest Marble by
Arkell (1931). Subsequently (1947b, p.44) he transferred the
Fimbriata-waltoni Beds into the upper part of the Bladon
Beds and suggested that they pass westward into limestones.
The Fimbriata-waltoni Beds were placed in the Forest Marble by McKerrow and others, (1969) on faunal grounds.
More recently Palmer and Jenkins (1975) have again considered them as part of the White Limestone. In the present
account Hull's original definition has been followed. The
base of the formation, as thus defined, is marked by a non-
sequence (Sumbler, 1984), and the unit is equivalent to the
combined Bradford Beds and Wychwood Beds of Arkell.

The Forest Marble occupies a narrow outcrop in the
south-east of the district, and forms isolated outcrops farther
north. The formation is the overburden of many quarries in
the White Limestone; the best exposure is in the Temple
Mills Quarry [347 360], where the formation is 6.37 m thick
(Figure 35). Elsewhere, thicknesses range from 1.8 m to 3
m. Within the district it is entirely marine, but it is thought
to pass north-eastward into the more estuarine Blisworth
(Great Oolite) Clay of Northamptonshire.

The formation is highly variable, and consists of a mixture
of limestones and clays. In the Tadmarton Borehole, 31 per
cent was classified as limestone, a comparable proportion
was recorded in the Kirtlington Cement Works, but in the
Hook Norton Borehole (see Figure 35) limestones con-
stituted 48 per cent of the incomplete sequence proved.

The limestones are divisible into two types: medium to
dark grey, commonly blue-hearted, shelly and shell-
fragmental limestone; and medium grey thinly laminated silty limestone. The former is the commonest, and provided
much of the decorative stone (the original 'marble') once
worked in Wychwood Forest. It is generally very hard and
well bedded with pronounced cross-stratification, with well-
rounded, platy skeletal debris aligned parallel to the bedding. The fragments include mudstone and micrite pellets,

quartz sand, echinoderm debris and foraminifera; all are set in a fine-grained sparry calcite matrix with irregular bands of olive-grey micrite. The second type is finer grained and very finely laminated with pale greenish grey clay partings. The laminations show all variations from tabular to intense ripple-drift and undulatory bedding. The rock consists largely of quartz silt and fine shell debris in a sparry matrix. The partings may contain much plant detritus. A complete gradation occurs between the two limestone types.

Mudstones comprise the greater part of the remainder of the formation. They range from olive to dark grey and commonly contain fine silt partings. Clay-mica minerals constitute more than 75 per cent of ten insoluble residues examined by Mr R. J. Merriman using X-ray diffraction techniques; kaolinite formed up to 10 per cent of the remainder, whilst quartz never exceeded this amount in the samples tested. With increasing silt and shell debris, the mudstones grade into siltstones. A characteristic lithology is 'clay with lenticles' (see p.85). The thicker lenses may coalesce to form the 'biscuits' which are a distinctive feature in the soil. The silt partings locally include abundant plant debris; their basal surfaces carry the casts of the trails of bottom-dwelling organisms.

Burrows are rare and are usually marked by concentrations of silt and shell debris. Small and indefinite mottles occur in the less well bedded mudstones and may be due to bioturbation. Shells other than oysters are uncommon; those that occur tend to be concentrated as thin pavements and molluscan spat-rich layers. Plant debris is ubiquitous.

Lithological junctions are commonly abrupt, and channels occur throughout the sequence. Clay and marl pebbles or galls are common. The basal bed of limestone in the Tadmarton Borehole is unusual in that it contains pebbles, ooliths and superficial ooliths.

The fauna is indicative of a restricted shallow-water marine environment. It is limited in both numbers and species and is dominated by bivalves. It includes *Sarcinella plexus*, *Epithyris oxonica*, *Anisocardia (Antiquicyprina) loweana*, *Bakevellia waltoni*, 'Corbula' *hulliana*, *Costigervillia sp.*, *Liostrea hebridica*, *L. sp.*, 'Lucina'?, *Modiolus imbricatus*, *Placunopsis socialis* and *Pseudolimea sp.* In addition, a few fish fragments, ostracods, echinoid remains and a solitary rhynchonellid have been noted. The fauna is listed in Appendix 1(4).

The variable marine sequence bears the imprint of current activity, which introduced fine-grained terrigenous material

and plant debris. The mudstones, including the 'clay with lenticles', represent repeated winnowing in a relatively quiet environment, which was periodically crossed by channels in which grainstones accumulated. The district seems to be intermediate between the near-shore estuarine environment of the Blisworth Clay to the north-east and the increasingly deeper-water and quiescent environments of the south Cotswolds. AH

Details

Sibford Ferris area

The best sections in this area are in two large quarries near Temple Mills [347 359 to 347 363]. In the northernmost one, up to 3.66 m of brown-weathering clayey shale with hard, flaggy, brown-weathering, blue-hearted, shelly limestone bands, are exposed dipping E13°N at 6° to 8°. The Upper Epithyris Bed (up to 0.61 m in thickness) is locally present at the base of the Forest Marble, and rests unconformably on the White Limestone (Bed 8, Figure 36).

A gap of only 90 m separates the northern and southern quarries, but in the latter the Upper Epithyris Bed is absent and the basal Forest Marble comprises 2.74 m of pale brown-weathering, clayey mudstone overlain by 1.52 m of hard, flaggy, brown-weathering, lilac-coloured, coarsely oolitic, ripple-marked, clastic limestones rich in thin mudstone pellets which weather out to give a honeycomb texture. In the southern end of the southern quarry, the Upper Epithyris Bed re-appears as a coarse-grained, shelly, dark grey-hearted oolite with *Epithyris oxonica* and *Liostrea sp.*, and reaches a thickness of 0.46 m.

A gap of only 0.9 to 1.5 m separates the uppermost Forest Marble limestones in the quarry sections from the base of the Lower Cornbrash which outcrops to the east of the quarries. A temporary trench section [3488 3598] on the eastern side of the road south of Woodway Farm, exposed 0.91 m of grey clay beneath Cornbrash. EGP

Great Rollright

The Forest Marble was well exposed during the excavation of the railway cuttings to the south-east of the village. Woodward (1894, p.375) recorded the following succession:

	Thickness m
CORNBRASH	
Tough grey limestones	1.83
FOREST MARBLE	
Hard calcareous sandstone and sandy shale	0.30

Figure 36 Sequence in the Temple Mills—Gibraltar Farm area, south-west of Sibford Ferris

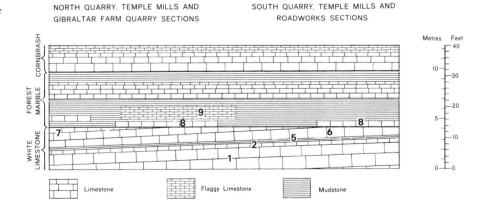

NORTH QUARRY, TEMPLE MILLS AND GIBRALTAR FARM QUARRY SECTIONS

SOUTH QUARRY, TEMPLE MILLS AND ROADWORKS SECTIONS

Limestone   Flaggy Limestone   Mudstone

Irregular cross-bedded series of bluish shales with thin
  beds of sandy limestone, and inconstant beds of
  oolitic limestone and calcareous sandstone: with
  much lignite   4.72
Blue shelly oolitic limestones with lignite   0.91
Yellowish marly clays with hard lumps of marl   0.76

On the south side of one cutting [3331 3051], 0.91 m of bluish grey shale with very thin, hard, bluish grey, silty limestone bands is exposed. The limestones are very finely laminated with argillaceous wisps and lignite fragments along the bedding planes.

The following section was recorded in the cutting [3402 3075] south of Rollright Heath Farm:

	Thickness m
Clay soil and subsoil with limestone debris	—
Limestone; fawn, sandy with rare grey clay wisps, scattered lignite and small shell fragments, sparsely oolitic, hard, compact	0.08
Limestone; bluish grey, shelly with abundant shell debris, oysters dominant, scattered ooliths and lignite fragments, ?fish remains	0.33–0.38
Limestone; bluish grey, speckled brown-weathering, coarse shelly and shell-fragmental, scattered ooliths and grit-size material, clay wisps and argillaceous lenticles, hard	0.66

AH

Westcott Barton area

In an old quarry, now a refuse tip [422 246] south-west of Westcott Barton, a small, down-faulted inlier of Forest Marble is exposed. In the easternmost part of the quarry, the basal flaggy limestones are mainly replaced by brown-weathering, green and blue-grey clays.

EGP

CORNBRASH

The main outcrop of the Cornbrash lies in the south-east of the district, with outliers west of the Cherwell around Tackley Heath and west of Tackley. To the north and west, small outliers occur in the Swerford Trough, in the Whichford Trough, and east of Tadmarton.

The Upper Cornbrash (Callovian) has not been recognised within the district, although it may be present in the main outcrop (Douglas and Arkell 1932). The outliers apparently consist entirely of Lower Cornbrash (Bathonian), and fossils diagnostic of both the *Obovothyris obovata* and *Cereithyris intermedia* zones have been recorded during the survey.

The local Cornbrash is composed of beds of bluish grey, massive, commonly oolitic, shell-fragmental limestone, with some softer argillaceous and sandy limestones. The weathered rock is a rubbly reddish brown limestone which forms an abundant and characteristic stone brash at outcrop. Thicknesses range from 1.5 to about 3 m. Faunal details are given below and in Appendix 1(4).

AH

Details

Sibford Ferris

In an old quarry [348 362] near Gibraltar Farm, up to 1.52 m of rubbly, brown-weathering, cream-hearted, shelly limestone overlie a 0.61 m post of more massive, oolitic, compact limestone. The fossils collected include: *Acrosalenia* cf. *hemicidaroides*, *Nucleolites clunicularis*, *Dictyothyris sp.*, *Obovothyris magnobovata*, *O. obovata*, *Ornithella* aff. *rugosa*, *Catinula sp.*, *Ceratomyopsis sp.*, *Chlamys (Radulopecten) hemicostata*, *Homomya gibbosa*, *Limatula?*, *Lucina sp.*, *Meleagrinella echinata*, *Modiolus* cf. *lonsdalei*, *Pleuromya uniformis*, *Pseudolimea duplicata* and *Pseudotrapezium sp.*

Rubbly limestone was well exposed in a trench dug for some 275 m along the road southwards from Gibraltar Farm. About 450 m south of Woodway Farm the rocks yielded a typical bivalve fauna and also *Obovothyris magnobovata* and *O. obovata*. The junction with the Forest Marble was exposed in this trench [349 363], south of Woodway Farm.

EGP

Great Rollright

Five small outliers of Lower Cornbrash are preserved within the down-faulted Salford–Swerford trough to the south-east of the village. The most north-westerly outcrop was exposed during the excavation of the Banbury and Cheltenham Direct Railway (Beesley, 1877, p.177). The following section is visible on the south side of the cutting:

	Thickness m
Obscured; fragments of dull greenish grey shell-fragmental limestone with pale green argillaceous wisps	c.0.76
Limestone; pinkish brown, fine-grained, sandy, with pale greenish grey partings of argillaceous limestone	0.03
Limestone; bluish grey, weathering pale brown, oolitic shell-fragmental limestone with large pipes of greenish grey argillaceous limestone, argillaceous bands with plant fragments; variation in coarseness of the shell debris produces a banded appearance within the massive bed	0.43
Limestone; bluish grey, fine-grained, sandy, scattered lignite fragments, rubbly-weathering	seen to 0.15

Cereithyris intermedia, indicative of the lowest part (*intermedia* Zone) of the Lower Cornbrash, was collected from the highest beds. The regional dip is 10° to the south, but superimposed on this is a gentle synclinal flexure plunging to the east-south-east.

AH

Tackley – Kirtlington – Middleton Park

A small exposure in Tackley Wood [4722 2210] revealed 1.07 m of massive cream-hearted brown-weathering limestone with thin shelly courses. The full thickness of 2.97 m of Lower Cornbrash is exposed in Kirtlington Cement Works Quarry [4950 1988] (Douglas and Arkell 1932, p.124). A borehole at Slade Farm [5095 2209] penetrated 3.50 m of brown clay and stone, interpreted as Cornbrash, and another borehole at Park Farm [5149 2049] penetrated 3.35 m of Cornbrash.

BJW

CHAPTER 7

Upper Jurassic

KELLAWAYS BEDS AND OXFORD CLAY

The outcrop of these formations within the present district is restricted to a small area around Kirtlington and Kirtlington Park, and a small outlier at Tackley Heath, both in the south-east. The formations are poorly exposed, but comprise brownish green-weathering, bluish or greenish grey stiff clays with thin shell bands. It was not possible to distinguish the Kellaways Sand because there are no exposures and augering was impracticable. Surveys in the Witney (236) district suggest that both the Kellaways Clay, 1 to 4 m of dark grey mudstone, and the Kellaways Sand, 2 to 4 m of buff silty sand, underlie the Oxford Clay around Kirtlington Park.

BJW

Details

Tackley Heath

A temporary section [4677 2138] at Tackley Heath revealed 1.07 m of stiff brownish green shaly clay.   BJW

CHAPTER 8

Quaternary—Pleistocene and Recent

The district is remarkably free from Quaternary deposits. There are small patches of Boulder Clay and Glacial Sand and Gravel on low ground in the extreme west, and remanié erratic pebbles on the plateau to the east. Younger Quaternary deposits are confined to the valley sides and floors where Head, River Terrace Deposits, Peat, Calcareous Tufa and Alluvium are sporadically preserved.

Despite the limited area occupied by these deposits they are of considerable interest for they provide a link that is pertinent to a correlation between the extensive glacial deposits of the Midlands and the terrace sequence of the Upper Thames. No critical data have, however, emerged from the resurvey and, although this region has attracted much research for over a century, the chronology of the Quaternary sequence is still only imperfectly understood.

REMANIÉ DRIFTS

Widely scattered erratics, notably of quartzites, vein-quartz, schorl rock, Palaeozoic rocks, including quartzitic sandstones (some up to 1 m across) and worn yellow flints are spread across much of the high ground in the central parts of the district. Their presence indicates the former existence of at least one ice sheet that overtopped this part of the Cotswolds. The erratics point to a northerly or north-westerly provenance, though the source of the flints is uncertain.

Typical of the scattered erratic pebbles are those on the hills south-east of Little Compton [279 298] where they have been found at over 244 m above OD (Kellaway and others, 1971, p.3). There are a very few small associated patches of pebbly clay, as at Margett's Hill [2955 3470], where about 0.3 m overlies the Chipping Norton Limestone at over 200 m above OD. None of these patches is large enough to be mappable.

The residual nature of these pebbles and clays, and their preservation on the highest ground marks them out as the earliest Quaternary deposits within the district. They have long been included within the omnibus term of 'Northern Drift' (Hull, 1855; Arkell, 1947a; Kellaway and others, 1971). Their absolute age (or ages) cannot be determined; nevertheless, at Sugworth, near Oxford, a Cromerian fauna and flora have recently been recorded (Shotton and others, 1980) from a terrace that contains Bunter erratics[1]; it follows that at least one of the glaciations that introduced these pebbles is pre-Cromerian.

BOULDER CLAY

Several small patches of boulder clay lie on low interfluves between the tributaries of the northward-flowing Stour and flank the valley of the southward-flowing Evenlode. Most, though not necessarily all, are outliers of a larger spread around Moreton-in-Marsh, some 4 km west of the district, which caps the interfluve between the Avon and Thames catchments at a general height of about 135 m above OD.

The clast content of the boulder clay varies considerably. In places Bunter-derived pebbles are dominant, together with fragments of Welsh slates, the clast content is thus identical with the remanié drift and such boulder clays therefore fall within the 'Northern Drift'. In other localities flints are comparatively abundant, and some chalk is present locally. It is far from clear whether two contiguous ice sheets are involved, or whether two separate glaciations are represented by these small patches of boulder clay.

Tomlinson (1929) separated the different patches of boulder clay into quartzite-rich 'Plateau Drift' (the Northern Drift of earlier authors) and flint-rich 'Moreton Drift', though the latter also includes Bunter-derived pebbles. Nowhere have two boulder clays of different clast content been recorded in superposition, though there is evidence in places of chalky boulder clay overlying Bunter-rich gravels. It follows that at least one ice advance from the north predated the advent of the ice that laid down the chalky boulder clay.

The absolute ages of both the boulder clays are still uncertain. An isolated patch of gravel at Stretton-on-Fosse, 3 km west of the extreme north-east of the district, has yielded a modest vertebrate fauna that Shotton (1973) believes to be Hoxnian in age. It is overlain by up to 4 m of chalky-Liassic till which, if the faunal attribution is correct, is presumably Wolstonian. If this chalky till is of the same age as the main part of the Moreton Drift, then the age of the latter is established. Bishop (1958) has suggested that Wolstonian ice advanced from the north-east to a terminal moraine at Moreton-in-Marsh, slightly later than the advance of north-western and western ice into the region; the conclusion is that the latter ice was also Wolstonian. Nevertheless, because the Moreton Drift is separated from the extensive till sheets that lie to the east and north, and that may once have existed to the west, by many miles of drift-free ground the correlation is at best speculative and, if correct, raises many problems that have never been addressed.   EGP

Details

Tidmington – Great Wolford

Sandy pebbly boulder clay caps ridges near Tidmington in the extreme north-west; its base is at about 107 m above OD. Tomlinson (1935, p.427) has identified Welsh erratics in the deposit.

Sandy clay with many Bunter-derived quartzite pebbles and a

---

1 'Bunter erratics' are pebbles of quartz, quartzite, metamorphic rocks, tourmaline rocks, etc, all of which are thought to have been derived from the Sherwood Sandstone Group (Triassic) of the Midlands, and in particular from the conglomeratic division, formerly known as the Bunter Pebble Beds.

few flints caps a hill at Lower Farm, Todenham [244 368]. Farther south, similar boulder clay extends along the western margin of the district from Great Wolford southwards for over 3 km, being co-extensive to the west with the large sheet which covers Wolford Wood and extends westwards into the north-eastern part of the Moreton-in-Marsh district where it has been termed the Moreton Drift (Tomlinson, 1929, pp.157–196). In the northern part of the outcrop, flints are relatively abundant, but farther south they become rarer. Bunter-derived pebbles are ubiquitous, and fragments of Welsh slate have been found. In places the clay matrix is reddish brown, and possibly contains much material incorporated from the Mercia Mudstone Group; in other places, for example north-west of Gravels Coppice [245 326], the matrix contains much bluish grey clay probably derived from the Lower Lias. At Gravels Coppice and to the north of Stanford Brook, the clay overlies sands and gravels, and is locally very sandy due to incorporation of the underlying material. Around Barton-on-the-Heath [255 325] the deposit is very gravelly with many flints, and is probably at least 6.1 m thick. The northern part of the clay outcrop extending through Little Wolford [262 353] is also very gravelly with many flints and Bunter-derived pebbles. At the northern end of the out-crop, the deposit is probably no more than 3 m thick, but it thickens southwards and in a borehole east of Pepperwell Farm [265 341] it is 6.1 m thick. The bankside south of Pepperwell Farm shows stiff red-dish brown and drab grey clay with pale grey, brown, red and black flints and cherts, Bunter pebbles, coal, grey Welsh slate fragments, Old Red Sandstone pebbles and a fragment of grey mica-schist.

To the south and south-east of Burmington [264 379] there are two small areas of boulder clay, probably not more than 3 m thick. They contain abundant flints and Bunter-derived pebbles. The out-crop south of Burmington apparently overlies sand and gravel, seen only in a small sand pit at its eastern end.   EGP

Kingham area

A deposit of boulder clay, consisting of sandy clay with Bunter-derived pebbles and a few limestone and ironstone fragments, pro-duces a slight ridge north of Kingham. Locally at the base very sandy clays and loams are developed. Grey sandy boulder clay caps a low ridge north-north-west of Rynehill Farm [270 228]; here the matrix appears to be local Lias clay. The relation to the associated sands and gravels is uncertain. Boulder clay caps a knoll [247 235] between the stream north of Bledington and the Evenlode. Pebbles of quartzite and sandstone are abundant and are associated with yellow flints, metamorphic rocks including schorl, local limestones and nodular ironstone, all being set in a matrix of sandy loam or clay. A large quartzite erratic (almost 1 m across) has been placed in a hedgerow at a site [246 238] near the Evenlode.

Bruern – Lyneham

A substantial tract of boulder clay forms the high ground south-east of Bould but there are few exposures. Excavations [2584 1995] south-west of Bruern Abbey, were in dark red and brown variegated, sandy clay with abundant Bunter pebbles. Nearby dig-gings are said to have entered an underlying bed of finely laminated grey silt. A borehole [260 199] proved 2.13 m of 'yellow clay', prob-ably boulder clay, resting on Lower Lias clay. At the southern end of Bruern Wood the basal boulder clay becomes increasingly gravelly.

There are three small deposits of boulder clay north of Lyneham, the highest being at about 131 m above OD. South of the village, one of two small patches forms a small knoll [279 198] at about 113 m above OD, and consists of gravelly loam with Bunter-derived clasts up to 0.3 m in diameter; the deposits are all of 'Northern Drift' type.   AH

GLACIAL SAND AND GRAVEL

Small patches of sand and gravel are associated with the deposits of boulder clay south-east of Great Wolford and those south-east of Kingham. In the former area the gravel is overlain by boulder clay. A section [247 328] shows clayey flint and Bunter-derived gravel beneath stony clay, and Bishop (1958, p.295) records that it rests on purple-chocolate 'lake-clay'. About 1.5 km to the north-east, sand and gravel are again overlain by flinty boulder clay. Nevertheless, it ap-pears premature to erect a consistent stratigraphy from such isolated exposures. South-east of Kingham the relationship to the boulder clay is uncertain. The sand and gravel deposit contains abundant quartzite and ironstone fragments, and becomes increasingly terrace-like in form southwards, with a surface level at about 125 m above OD. The spreads may be the remnants of a fluvioglacial train fed by the north-western ice.   EGP

Details

Barton-on-the-Heath

Dirty gravel composed mainly of Bunter-derived pebbles with flints and limestone fragments underlies boulder clay at Gravels Coppice [248 325] and extends northwards and north-eastwards to Rectory Farm [254 337]. Its maximum thickness probably does not exceed about 9 m. In an old pit north of Gravels Barn [247 328], 1.22 m of roughly stratified clayey gravel with many flints, including very large ones, and Bunter-derived pebbles are overlain by 0.61 m of reddish brown stony clay (possibly a lake deposit), which apparently succeeds the gravel conformably except where it has soliflucted over it at the western end of the pit. The gravel is said by Bishop (1958, p.295) to rest upon purple-chocolate lake clay [256 334].

Sands and gravels with a much lower clay content extend around Pepperwell Farm, Little Wolford; they probably do not exceed 4.6 m in thickness. In an old gravel pit [266 344] north-north-east of the farm, poorly exposed sands and gravels are overlain by 1.2 m of brown, flinty, stony boulder clay. In another old pit some 180 m to the north-east, 0.91 m of pale brown, very sandy stony clay ap-parently rests upon sand: this stony clay, which could be either water-lain or a glacial till, has been mapped as the latter. Tomlin-son (1929, p.161) thought it possible that 'Campden Drift' overlies 'Moreton Drift' in these pits, but a well 485 m east of Pepperwell Farm shows no evidence of any sand and gravel deposits, and the deposits in the pits may be very local.   EGP

Kingham – Lyneham

Glacial sand and gravel form a pronounced bench with a maximum height of about 125 m above OD near Rynehill Farm [270 228]. The deposit has a maximum thickness of 3.7 m and is well exposed in a disused pit 275 m south of the farmhouse where the following section was recorded:

	Thickness m
Sandy clay, pale ochreous yellow and fawn, mottled, scattered small pebbles, no bedding visible, uneven base (?Boulder Clay)	0 – 0.91
Sand, pale reddish brown, with pebbles scattered throughout, strongly current-bedded, with slightly more argillaceous bands; 0.15 m bed of hard sandy clay at the base locally	0 – 0.61

Sand, reddish brown, with irregular bands and
  stringers of pebbles, especially in top 0.61 m,
  irregular and impersistent bands of black sand seen
  to   0.91

The pebbles are predominantly quartzites with significant numbers of 'box' ironstone, ferruginous siltstone and silty limestone nodules. In a small excavation at the south-eastern extremity of the pit the sand is overlain by up to 0.91 m of unsorted loamy clay with scattered small pebbles, including small calcareous ?chalk pebbles.

To the south of the Sars Brook there is a substantial deposit which attains a mean height of about 125 m above OD, though at the north-eastern extremity the highest point is about 128 m above OD. There are several overgrown pits in it north-east of Sarsden Lodge. On the east side of the road [273 215] south of Sarsden Lodge impersistent springs are thrown out at the junction of the gravel with the underlying Midde Lias.   AH

FOURTH TERRACE

Apart from a single patch of gravel in the Cherwell Valley at Kirtlington, the only deposits assigned to the Fourth Terrace are in the Evenlode valley. Parts of Bledington, Kingham and Lyneham are built on this terrace, which has been called the Bledington Terrace (Tomlinson, 1929. p.173). The deposits consist largely of well-sorted Jurassic limestone and ironstone debris, together with pebbles of Bunter-derived quartzite, vein quartz, grit and schorl rock, that were probably derived from the 'Northern Drift'. Thin seams of silt and clay are present locally.

The deposit appears to have been laid down in a river that had cut into the glacial (or fluvioglacial) sands that extend southwards from Rynehill Farm, and so is clearly older than these. The surface of the terrace slopes downstream but on a gentler gradient than the present alluvium. Thus its profile seems to coincide with the present flood-plain above Daylesford, but is 21.3 m above the alluvium at Chadlington some 12 km downstream, where it has been called the Spelsbury Terrace (Arkell, 1947b). Farther south-east it appears to be the Hanborough Terrace which is some 30 m above the local alluvium.

Sandford (1924, p.26) described a warm-climate vertebrate fauna from the bottom of the Hanborough Terrace, but Briggs and Gilbertson (1974) have since discovered cold-climate molluscs within silt layers in the terrace deposits at Long Hanborough. An intensely cold period clearly occurred after the deposition of the terrace, for in many places ice-wedge casts extend down from its surface; there is, however, no certain evidence of the date of this cold episode.
                                                              AH

Details

River Evenlode and tributaries

The greater part of Kingham is built on an extensive spread of Fourth Terrace gravels. They produce a well defined bench rising to a height of 119 m above OD, the front of the feature being about 8.5 m above the alluvium. There are several disued pits south-east of the village, in one of which [262 238] 0.9 m of contorted imbricated limestone gravel was recorded. The pebbles are large and subangular and probably of very local origin, deposited as a fan at

the confluence of a tributary valley and the main river. Approximately 1.4 km to the north-east small patches of thin limestone pebble soil on the valley sides south of the Kingham Field may represent a former extension of this deposit.

At Bledington the Fourth Terrace is largely obscured by the overlying deposits of the Third Terrace (Figure 37). Gravel has been extensively worked in pits south-east of the village. In one pit [248 223] west of the road, 0.6 m of ill-sorted gravel consisting predominantly of subrounded limestone pebbles set in a coarse limestone sand is overlain by a clayey limestone gravel with many quartzite pebbles and by clayey pebbly sand and purplish brown sandy clay. The topmost beds probably form part of the Third Terrace. There are several pipes of purplish brown pebbly clay with a core of paler brown sandy clay. These pipes penetrate about 1.2 m into the limestone gravel. The pebbles within the pipes are almost entirely ironstone or of Bunter type; they compare well with the pebbles in the Third Terrace and the non-limestone part of the Fourth Terrace. There is no evidence of contortion in the limestone gravel at the edge of the pipes. Similar structures have been recorded in the gravels at Chadlington and Long Hanborough (Arkell, 1947b; Kellaway and others, 1971), farther downstream.

Temporary excavations at Foscot show limestone gravel apparently overlain by reddish pebbly sand of the Third Terrace. On the eastern bank of the River Evenlode near Lyneham the Fourth Terrace forms well-defined benches about 110 m above OD and 8.2 to 9.1 m above the alluvium. The most northerly patch [263 211] was worked in pits adjacent to the railway line and in a field to the east. Locally the limestone gravel is capped by up to 0.6 m of dark brown clay. Lyneham village is built on about 2.4 m of limestone gravel which was dug in the field immediately west of Lyneham church.   AH

There are extensive outcrops of Fourth Terrace deposits south of Chadlington; the once continuous sheet has been dissected by southward-flowing tributaries of the Evenlode, and now lies at about 21 m above the alluvium. The deposits have been extensively worked at Grove Lane [341 213] where they consist of about 4.6 m of coarse poorly-graded gravel, lacking regular bedding but with rare sandy seams, and locally near the base up to 0.9 m of brown and grey mottled silty clay. The gravels are overlain by silty clay, clay and unsorted clayey gravel (Kellaway and others, 1971).

Cherwell Valley

Kirtlington is built on a terrace flat which has been correlated with the Hanborough Terrace. The deposit is at least 6 m thick (Hull, 1859, p.116).   BJW

THIRD TERRACE

The third terrace of the Evenlode begins a little to the west of Daylesford, where the gravels were regarded by Tomlinson (1929. p.164) as part of the 'Moreton Drift'. Downstream its long profile parallels the alluvium, and thus crosses that of the gentler Fourth Terrace around Kingham and Bledington. Presumably the deposit choked the higher reaches of the valley, which has since been exhumed so that the Third Terrace deposits locally rest on those of the Fourth Terrace. Downstream there is no sign of the Third Terrace near Chadlington, but it is tentatively correlated with the Wolvercote Terrace of the Thames.

The gravels are characterised by a high proportion of quartzite and ironstone pebbles, but there are significant quantities of flints. Their poor sorting and the presence of beds of sand, silt and laminated clays suggest that they originated in a braided stream as an outwash from the flinty part of the 'Moreton Till'. Their absolute age is governed by the same factors that make the dating of that till difficult.

In the Cherwell Valley there are a few remnants of terrace gravels, similar in lithology to the Third Terrace of the Evenlode. Small patches occur between Somerton and Upper Heyford, and have been so assigned.   AH

Details

River Evenlode and tributaries

This terrace is well developed on the eastern bank of the Evenlode, south-east of Daylesford Church. The north-western face of an old gravel pit [244 255] south-south-east of the church shows up to 2.13 m of poorly-graded clayey gravel with sand bands. Angular brown and white patinated flints and rounded Bunter quartzites form the bulk of the gravel, with polished, millet-seed sand grains common in the sand. The north-eastern face shows 2.74 m of orange sand and silt with gravel bands. The top of this terrace is about 6.1 to 7.6 m above the top of the Evenlode alluvium.

There are extensive spreads of coarse gravel to the east of Kingham village. At the northern end of the railway cutting, west-south-west of Kingham church, Lower Lias clay is overlain by 0.61 m of gravel containing an abundance of limestone pebbles. Slightly farther south, the gravel is made mainly of quartzite and ironstone pebbles. Poorly sorted gravel with abundant box-ironstones and Bunter quartzite pebbles and with only a few limestone and flint pebbles is exposed in several places near Kingham church.   EGP

North of Churchill Heath Farm [262 225] the terrace produces a bench at about 110 m OD. There are no exposures, but ploughing reveals a hard iron-cemented band at the base (with local patches of limestone gravel), overlain by coarse gravel with quartzite, flint and limestone pebbles and seams of white and yellow sand. The greater part of Bledington village is built on this terrace, which reaches a height of 103.0 to 118.9 m above OD. Several disused pits north and east of the church are said to have proved up to 1.8 m of red pebbly sand. The widening of the road [247 227] near the village school exposed:

	Thickness m
Soil; brown sandy loam	c.0.30
Sand; reddish brown, moderately well sorted with strings of quartzite pebbles and a 0.05-m thick pebble band about 0.15 m from the base	c.0.45
Clay; purple to brown; scattered sand grains and a few small pebbles thoughout; irregular base, apparently contorted	up to c.0.38
Clay; mottled fawn to purplish brown, silty, with scattered sand grains, indistinctly laminated	c.0.30
Clay; mottled fawn to purplish brown, silty, with scattered sand grains, indistinctly laminated	c.0.30
Sand; ochreous brown, fine-grained, moderately well sorted	proved to 1.52

The relative proportions of the main pebble types are: Bunter-derived types, 42.0%; sandstone and grit, 16.9%; siltstone, 5.9%, flint, 5.1%; box-ironstone, 26.7%, with fragments of box-ironstone type forming the bulk of the pebbles smaller than 1 cm in diameter. The contact with the Fourth Terrace is nowhere exposed, but digging and augering at the southern extremity [248 223] of a gravel pit south-east of St Leonard's Church gave the following section:

	Thickness m
THIRD TERRACE DEPOSITS	
Sand; bright reddish brown, slightly argillaceous, a few small Bunter-derived pebbles and patinated flints, uncommon platy limestone pebbles; distinctly false-bedded near the base; ?channelled into underlying bed	0.76
Clay; purple-tinted chocolate brown, slightly silty with a few small pebbles; maximum augered	0.33
Sand; reddish brown, argillaceous, poorly sorted, scattered pebbles including quartzites and partings of box-ironstone fragments	c.1.52
Clay; dull reddish grey, sandy	0.03
Sand; fawn to red, well-sorted	0.10
FOURTH TERRACE DEPOSITS	
Sand; fawn to khaki, slightly argillaceous, a few small Triassic quartzite and limestone pebbles; thin seams of pale fawn sandy clay and a band of coarse gravel with oyster shells at base	0.69

Extensive but morphologically ill defined patches of the Third Terrace occur south of Foscot. A temporary section [247 217] exposed 0.61 m of ill sorted clayey gravel with abundant Bunter-derived quartzites and a few flint pebbles. There are three deposits of quartzite and flint gravel north of Fifield Heath, having ill defined terrace forms which reach a height of about 117 m above OD. The most northerly appears to be built against Glacial Sand and Gravel. It is impossible to separate the two deposits lithologically, and the extent of reworking is uncertain. On the north-east side of the River Evenlode two small patches of Third Terrace rest on Lower Lias in Churchill Heath Wood. Red pebbly sand with clay seams occurs south-west of Sarsden Lodge at a height of 116 m above OD. Farther to the south-east there are small patches of flint and quartzite gravel with a few blocks of iron-cemented gravel.

At Tithe Farm [277 201], Lyneham a thin deposit of red sand, correlated with the Third Terrace, rests upon limestone gravel of the Fourth Terrace.   AH

SECOND TERRACE OF THE EVENLODE

Very few deposits have been considered to belong to the Second Terrace of the Evenlode. Those that occur lie consistently at 1.8–2.4 m above the alluvium. They may correlate with the Second Terrace of the Upper Thames, though there is little pertinent evidence within the district to substantiate this correlation. In the Glyme valley, a small patch of limestone gravel has been taken to represent the Second Terrace.   AH

Details

The Second Terrace is poorly developed along the Evenlode and its tributaries. Narrow benches covered with gravelly loam occur between 1.83 and 2.44 m above the alluvium on both banks of the Evenlode west of Kingham. The most extensive grades into a broad expanse of stiff brown pebbly clay south-west of Slade Farm [262 259].

A small patch of sandy loam east of Lyneham Church [278 202] is tentatively correlated with the terrace.   AH

In the lower reaches of the River Glyme south-east of Hill Farm [423 207] there is a narrow strip of limestone gravel on the eastern bank, which has been taken to be the Second Terrace. The top of this gravel is about 3 m above the alluvium, and about 2 m above the top of the First Terrace.   EGP

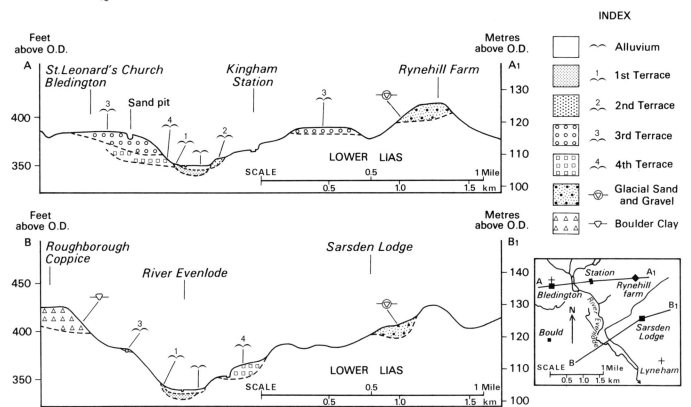

Figure 37   Cross-profiles of the drift deposits near Bledington and Sarsden

SECOND TERRACE OF THE STOUR

In the north-west, there are extensive spreads of the Second Terrace of the Stour. To the north this terrace grades into the Second Terrace of the Avon (Tomlinson, 1929), parts of which have been dated elsewhere by radiocarbon methods at 38 000 years BP, that is within the Devensian Stage. The terrace, therefore, corresponds broadly in age to the First Terrace of the Evenlode.   EGP

Details

In the extreme north-west the Second Terrace comprises gravel, or silt and gravel, spreads on both banks of the River Stour and its tributaries. It extends upstream from the northern margin of the district near Tidmington to Stourton [300 368], along Nethercote Brook to Long Compton [295 325], and along the smaller tributary streams in the vicinity of Todenham and Great Walford.

At Tidmington the terrace is up to about 460 m wide. It has been worked on a very small scale for sand and gravel.

South of Mitford Bridge [263 372] the terrace is well preserved at the junction of the River Stour and Nethercote Brook. Upstream along Nethercote Brook 1.8 m of brown gravelly loam rest on 0.9 m of Lower Lias. The top of the terrace is about 1.8 m above the alluvium, but this separation decreases upstream. The gravel in the terrace is mainly derived from local boulder clay and the Lower Lias; it contains quartzite pebbles, brown and white patinated flints, fragments of Lower Lias limestones and Lias-derived *Gryphaea*. The terrace covers a wide area west of Long Compton village, which may even have been a lake; a temporary exposure south-west of Long Compton church exposed 0.15 m of gravel

overlain by 0.61 m of brown silty clay. To the east of Long Compton there are small patches of thin gravelly soil which are probably residual traces of the terrace.

FIRST TERRACE

Small tracts of First Terrace gravel, adjacent to the alluvium, occur in the valleys of the Stour, Evenlode and Cherwell. These may correspond to the Floodplain Gravel complex of the Upper Thames. If so they may include deposits ranging from the mid- to late-Devensian.   AH

Details

River Stour and tributaries

Burmington House [262 381], north-north-west of Mitford Bridge, stands on a small patch of First Terrace which is 0.6 m above alluvium level and is composed of stony brown clay.   EGP

River Evenlode and tributaries

The First Terrace is present on both banks of the Evenlode between Daylesford and Kingham as narrow strips of gravelly clay about 0.6 m above the alluvium.

South and east of Churchill, sandy limestone gravel forms narrow benches 0.6 m above the alluvium on both sides of Sars Brook. The Gas Council GS 5 Borehole [2688 2457] proved 2.7 m of limestone gravel, though hand-augering shows only sandy and pebbly clay. South-east of Cornwell the First Terrace forms a broad tract of gravelly clay about 0.9 m above the alluvium. South of

Swilsford Bridge [282 264] a small spread of limestone gravel forms a bluff about 0.3 m above the alluvium: this can be traced northwards to a point west of Cornwell Hill Farm [290 268] where it is about 1.2 m above the alluvium. At several places along the stream west of Chipping Norton sandy loam rests on cemented limestone gravel. EGP

South of Bledington an extensive spread of gravel consisting of quartzite, limestone and flint pebbles lies on the west bank of the River Evenlode. North-east of Fifield Heath [256 206] the terrace forms a narrow spread of pebbly loam 0.9 to 1.2 m above the alluvium, and the upper reaches of the Sars Brook contain deposits which are largely contemporaneous with the First Terrace. To the south-west of Rynehill Farm a slight bluff formed by limestone gravel crosses the main valley at right angles. Silty clay rests on limestone gravel at several points upstream. In the vicinity of Lyneham a bench 0.3 to 0.6 m above the alluvium is covered by pebbly loam with local patches of limestone gravel. AH, EGP

River Glyme and tributaries

The First Terrace is not present between Lidstone [356 248] and Cleveley [390 240]. There is a tiny terrace patch of stony clay up to 0.6 m above the alluvium level 130 m south-east of Cleveley Farm, and a slightly larger patch about 0.9 to 1.2 m above the alluvium level at Kiddington [414 228]. Between Glympton and Wootton, several similar small patches of First Terrace occur. EGP

Cherwell Valley

There are very few terrace deposits in this valley. A small patch straddles the road from Banbury to Aynho just east of Nell Bridge, and a small hollow 0.6 m deep on the north side of the road shows it to be largely sand with pebbles of local rocks probably brought down by the nearby stream which drains the area around Charlton and ground farther to the north-east. On the west side of the Cherwell and east-north-east of Hazelhedge Farm there are two small patches of thin gravel in which brown flints and pebbles of purple Bunter-derived sandstone and white quartzite predominate.

Farther south around Aynho station there is an obvious terrace flat, but no section of the deposits. Again, about 915 m south of Clifton a terrace remnant of unknown thickness is made up of liver-coloured and white quartzites, brown-stained flints, grey limestones and much smaller box-ironstone debris in a sandy matrix.

Another small area of gravel, consisting mainly of flint pebbles, occurs on the Upper Lias about 15.2 m above the west bank of the river and 1050 m north-west of the church at Somerton. On the east bank of the river, and about 915 m west of the church, a terrace borders the alluvium and continues southwards for 1000 m. The deposit is mainly sandy loam with scattered flints. Two other small patches of thin pebbly loam occur near the railway cutting at Somerton. BJW

ALLUVIUM

The alluvium comprises those flood deposits that have a accumulated in the valleys in Flandrian times, and many of the tracts are still liable to flood. The alluvium normally consists of stiff clay near the surface with a thin gravel layer locally at the base. AH

Details

River Stour and tributaries

The alluvium is composed generally of brown silty clay with scattered stones; in places there is a gravel bed at its base.

River Evenlode and tributaries

The widespread alluvial deposits in these valleys are brown and blue grey silty clays with scattered pebbles. Locally these rest on quartz, flint and limestone gravels. EGP

River Cherwell

Many areas bordering the tributaries and the main river are subject to seasonal flooding. River-bank exposures show the alluvium to be generally a brown clay loam, commonly with scattered pebbles of flint and local rocks. Pebbly seams are generally more numerous towards the base of the sequence. BJW

HEAD

The deposits of Head include some that have probably resulted both from downslope mass-movement as solifluction flows under periglacial conditions and as soil-creep in milder climatic regimes. Their composition depends on the strata involved in the downslope movement. Thus an extensive accumulation of Head along the Upper Lias clay slope below the Clypeus Grit outcrop at and 4 km south of Churchill [283 240] comprises rubble derived from the breaking-up of cambered Clypeus Grit and from clay picked up from the Upper Lias. By contrast, the deposit [250 213] south of Foscot contains much boulder-clay material derived from the high ground to the south. AH

Details

Brailes Hill

The western slopes of Brailes Hill are mantled by deposits formed by a combination of solifluction and minor landslip. EGP

Broughton

Small patches of sandy head occur locally.

Great Rollright area

To the north of the village, copious springs are thrown out from the base of the escarpment of the Inferior Oolite limestones. These aid downslope movement of limestone rubble and sand, and the basal beds of the Northampton Sand and Clypeus Grit are generally obscured.

There are small benches, capped with reddish brown sandy clay on the north-facing Lias slopes. They have distinctly arcuate and steepened fronts and originated as solifluction lobes. In the head of the valley immediately north of Great Rollright, up to 0.9 m of sandy clay rests upon the Upper Lias: these deposits were formed by a combination of solifluction and alluvial deposition. Sandy loam of a similar origin floors the valley south-south-west of the Manor House, Great Rollright.

Churchill – Sarsden

Cambering of the Clypeus Grit is particularly pronounced in this area and gives rise to rubbly limestone-Head downslope of the outcrop. The deposit is heterogeneous, varying from limestone brash to brown clay with some limestone pebbles and ironstone nodules. To the south of Merriscourt Farm [290 216] solifluction lobes of clay pass down on to the Middle Lias obscuring the outcrop of the basal Upper Lias.

Figure 38
Structure contours on Jurassic formations near Cornwell based on surface mapping

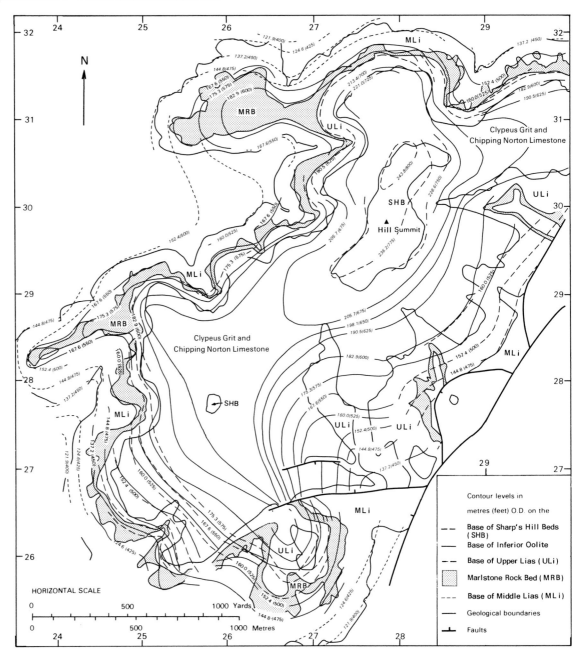

Foscot

Dull grey pebbly and sandy clay, produced largely by solifluction of boulder clay, extends along the hillside south of the hamlet.　　AH

SUPERFICIAL STRUCTURES AND LANDSLIPS

Superficial structures were widely developed concurrently with the down-cutting of the valleys. Cambering is widespread on the upper valley slopes and summits, and although valley bulging has not so far been detected within the district it may well affect the clay formations in the valley floors.

Cambering is best developed where massive well jointed and/or permeable formations such as the Marlstone Rock Bed, the Northampton Sand, and the Clypeus Grit overlie impervious soft formations.

Cambering of the Middle Jurassic is particularly pronounced in the Churchill–Sarsden area. All stages of its development can be seen from gentle valleyward dips, through the initiation of gulls and step-faults, to the complete rupturing of the beds to form limestone rubble. For example, a drainage ditch north of The Mount [279 237] showed Clypeus Grit rubble resting on bedded limestone, while farther downhill at least 0.9 m of rubble rests on rafts of Clypeus Grit which are separated by zones of Upper Lias clay up to 23 m in width. These rafts probably originated as step-faulted blocks which continued to move downhill. Structure contours of the area are given in Figure 38; they illustrate the difficulty in unravelling the effects of cambering from those caused by the dome postulated to underlie this tract (see p.9).

Superficial structures also occur, but more rarely, in the drift deposits. In the Dean Grove gravel pits in the Fourth Terrace at Chadlington, faulting is associated with incipient trough gulls and sag structures (Kellaway and others 1971, pp.9–12, fig.3, 4). These are thought to be dip-and-fault structures associated with cambering of the gravels over the Lower Lias. Comparable structures do not appear to affect drift deposits younger in age than the 'Moreton Drift'.

A landslip has been mapped on the western slopes of Brailes Hill [290 390], where there has been a combination of solifluction and minor landslipping on Lower and Middle Lias. Another, on the southern side of Tyne Hill [364 383], affects Northampton Sand resting on Upper Lias clay (Edmonds and others, 1965, p.96). Other shallow slips may have remained undetected.

A very small but active mudflow [377 296] formed on the Upper Lias south-east of the Meetings, Little Tew during the time of the survey (1957–1961).   AH

PEAT

Peaty deposits have formed near seepages in poorly-drained areas and within the alluvial tracts of some streams. The most notable occurrence is along the valley bottom southward from Swilsford Bridge [282 264], where seepage of water has occurred along the line of the Rollright Fault. Thin bands of peat and carbonaceous clay can be traced on the western bank of the stream from near Swilsford Bridge [282 264] to a point 1050 m east-south-east of Hirons Hill Farm. At the edge of the stream north-west of Cornwell Hill Farm about 0.08 m of peat was overlain by 0.30 m of bluish grey alluvial clay, peaty clay, and subsoil. The villagers of Salford are said to have dug a small quantity of peat in the field to the south-west of this point. To the north-east of Salford the deposit consists of black carbonaceous clay with thin peat layers.   AH

CALCAREOUS TUFA

Shell and plant fragments coated with calcium carbonate are common in the beds of the lime-rich streams that issue from the Middle Jurassic limestones and from some in the Lower and basal Middle Lias. During Post-glacial times, notably from c.5000 to c.3000 years BP, the climate was slightly warmer and more humid than today, and favoured the formation of tufa.

Small thin spreads of argillaceous tufa occur on the valley slopes 185 m and 272 m to the south-west of Great Rollright Manor. To the west of Hull Farm [329 296] a dome of tufa up to 3.7 m thick was exploited during the 1939–45 war. Arkell (1947a, p.247) recorded 'large numbers of snail-shells belonging to the species *Trichia hispida*, *Pomatias elegans*, *Helix hortensis* and *H. arbustorum*, with more rarely, *Helix nemoralis*, *Helicella virgatea*, and *Helicella caperata*'. He also notes that 'it rested everywhere on a layer of black peat about 0.15 m thick full of hazel-nuts. At this same time an apron of tufa from 1.52 and 2.44 m thick was worked at Cherwell Barn [371 299], 460 m south-east of Pomfret Castle. The following is a section of the north face of the pit:

	Thickness m
Soil; grey, silty calcareous loam	—
Calcareous tufa; brown-stained, massive, porous, hollow calcareous tubes (probably the casts of plant stems) abound, some vertical possibly in position of growth, others parallel to the bedding; scattered pebbles of 'race', passing into	0.53
Calcareous tufa; pale grey, loose friable; coarseness and amount of race decreasing downward; small snail shells abound throughout; bedding planes marked by traces of lignite, and by ferruginous bands	0.86

At one point the tufa can be seen resting directly on Upper Lias clay. There are two spreads of tufa on the southern slopes of the valley west of Little Tew. One [362 288], near Showell Farm, is thought to be no more than 1.5 m thick. The other [369 285], north-east of Castle Farm, was worked to a depth of at least 1.5 m during the 1939–45 war.   AH

Small aprons of tufa occur on both sides of the valleys to the north and west of Heythrop College. Most have been formed by springs thrown out at the top of the Upper Lias, but a small spread [372 259] south of Kite Wood has been produced by springs from near the base of the Middle Lias.   AH, BJW

CHAPTER 9

Economic geology

IRON ORE

The last ironstone quarries within the district closed during the 1960's. Comprehensive summaries of the history of the working of the Marlstone Rock Bed ironstone within the district have been given by Woodward (1893, pp.300–307), Wedd (*in* Lamplugh and others, 1920, pp.106–140), Whitehead and others (1952, pp.140–201), Wilson (1952) and Tonks (1961, pp.236–257). Whitehead (*in* Whitehead and others, 1952, p.171 and pl. VII) estimated the reserves of Marlstone Rock Bed iron ore in 1941 for the whole of the Banbury iron ore field. He divided the field into arbitrary areas, three of which (V, VI and VII) fall within the district. He distinguished Class A reserves ('proved' or 'reasonably proved' on geological grounds and by their proximity to well tested areas), Class B reserves ('probable' but not tested to the point at which exploitation is immediately possible, including 'proved' areas in which factors other than quality and thickness might delay development) and Class C reserves ('possible', having been tested to a slight extent or not at all, and including some 'probable' areas of small size). His statistics were based on a factor of 3355 tonnes per m-hectare, a limiting maximum of 6.1 m of overburden, and an iron content of at least 20 per cent over a workable thickness. His figures for areas V and VI have been reassessed, taking account of post-1941 workings, newly proved reserves and revised mapping.

The revised figures, in millions of tonnes, are as follows:

	Class A	Class B	Class C
Area V	31.6	61.7	20.3
Area VI	27.7	14.7	16.2

BJW

LIMESTONE AND BUILDING STONE

In the past, all the limestones of the district have been locally used for constructional purposes, the Great Oolite Limestone (especially the Taynton Stone) and the Chipping Norton Limestone having been particularly sought after. In the north-east of the district many of the villages are built largely of harder, less oxidised, blocks from the lower parts of the Marlstone Rock Bed. The Middle Jurassic limestones have also been used for lime- and cement-making and reconstituted stone blocks. Most of the localities where these limestones have been worked or are being worked are shown on the 1:10 000 sheets of the district.

BRICK AND TILE CLAYS

The clays of the Lias have been minor sources for the making of bricks, tiles, farm drain pipes and for other ceramic purposes. The Lower Lias has been dug near Twyford Wharf [483 371], north-west of Kings Sutton; at an old pit [468 305] about a mile south of Deddington; and at another pit [274 231] south-west of Churchill. Upper Lias clays were formerly dug at an old 'Brick Tile and Drain Pipe Works' [388 283] at Little Tew, and in the 'Old Clay Pit' [431 364] north of St. Mary's Church, Bloxham.

SAND AND GRAVEL

The 'Lower Estuarine Series' has been worked for building sand at several places within the district. There are two pits at Wigginton Heath, the easternmost of which [385 350] was working in 1961. In another pit near Tadmarton [400 378] these sands were dug beneath the Sharp's Hill Beds. Several pits lie south of Duns Tew, including two near Horsehay Farm, one of which [454 272] was still working at the time of survey under a progressively thicker overburden of Sharp's Hill Beds. There are also pits at Dane Hill, north-east of Duns Tew [468 293], and a recently-worked one near Steeple Aston [471 263].

Glacial Sand and Gravel, mostly comprising quartz sand with some gravel, were dug [269 223] in recent years near Rynehill Farm, Sarsden; the deposit was rapidly being exhausted at the time of survey (1961). The deposit was worked in a small pit north-east of Sarsden Lodge [272 217].

River Terrace gravels have been exploited in some places. The Fourth Terrace of the Evenlode, consisting mainly of limestone, Bunter-derived and chert pebbles, has been worked in a pit [330 212] south-south-west of Chadlington church, and an adjoining pit [330 211] was active in 1961. Farther west the Fourth Terrace has been extensively worked, particularly around Bledington village during 1939–45 for airfield construction. These gravels have the disadvantage of having little sand matrix and a pebble content which is mainly limestone.

In the extreme north-west, between Barton-on-the-Heath and Burmington, the Stour terraces have not been exploited, probably because they have a high clay content.   AH

WATER SUPPLY

The district comprises parts of hydrometric areas 39, 54 and 33, administered respectively by the Thames, Severn–Trent and Anglian Regional Water authorities which are mainly responsible for the water supply and its distribution. The boundary between hydrometric areas 39 and 54 follows the watershed between easterly- and westerly-flowing river systems and runs generally eastwards from Kitebrook House [244 313]. Most of the district lies within the catchment area of the Thames, but the remainder includes about 81.5 km² of the Severn Catchment in the north-western corner and about 6.5 km² of the Great Ouse Catchment in the east around Fritwell.

There are three groups of aquifers within the district: Firstly, the limestones of the Lower Lias, each of which forms a thin, fissured unit-aquifer confined by interbedded clays or shales, and which together form a multi-layer aquifer; secondly, the Marlstone Rock Bed, evidently in hydraulic continuity with the underlying siltstones, but confined by the overlying Upper Lias and the underlying Lower Lias clays; and finally, the Middle Jurassic limestone formations confined by the Upper Lias clay below; this system contains several individual aquifers, some of which are confined only locally. Aquifers of the same or of different systems are locally in hydraulic communication along faults (such as the Swerford and Sandford faults) or through saturated alluvium along rivers such as the Cherwell.

1 Lower Lias

Lower Lias includes thin limestones with very variable yields and quality. At Bledington a 61-m well [245 227], drilled in 1934, flowed at the surface at 0.76 l/sec with a hydraulic head of 3.66 m above surface. The water is reported to have been saline, corrosive and unfit for use. Saline water is also reported in a flowing well [257 227], 21.64 m deep at Kingham Station, with a recorded flow of 0.30 l/sec and a head of 4.27 m above surface in 1942. At Churchill, a 54.86-m well [279 238] reached 30.48 m before encountering water which rose to 27.43 m; it yielded only 0.08 l/sec on test. In the Stour Catchment, wells drilled to 25.60 m at Little Wolford [270 341] and 18.29 m at Whichford [316 345] yielded only 0.19 l/sec and 0.08 l/sec respectively, when tested. At Cherington a well [290 365] was drilled to 30.48 m without encountering water.

2 Middle Lias

Middle Lias groundwaters are predominantly confined and restricted to the Marlstone Rock Bed and locally to the underlying siltstones. The Marlstone Rock Bed is the major yielding formation, and the groundwater is contained in the regionally-developed fissure system. At Merriscourt, south of Churchill, where the Rock Bed is thin or absent, two boreholes failed to obtain water from the Middle Lias siltstones. Springs are thrown out by the underlying Lower Lias clays. Discharges are normally low, and abstraction for agricultural and domestic purposes rarely exceeds 6819 m³/yr at individual springs. At Bloxham, however, local domestic supplies of 5000 m³/yr are obtained from springs in the Marlstone Rock Bed. Three main areas of Middle Lias groundwaters have been developed. Around Tadmarton wells down to 12.8 m tap water from the Marlstone Rock Bed under confined and unconfined conditions. Yields are poor; seasonal water-level fluctuations of up to 5.5 m are recorded.

The second area lies east of the Cherwell where a few wells have been drilled into the Middle Lias and the groundwater is largely confined with a westward piezometric gradient towards the river. In the north of this area, yields for agricultural purposes up to 0.63 l/sec in the vicinity of Upper Astrop [510 375] are recorded, with drawdown values of 3 m to 13.7 m. At Fritwell and Upper Heyford, domestic supplies are obtained from the Marlstone Rock Bed. Abstractions were recorded at Upper Heyford at rates ranging between 2728 and 45006 m³/yr between 1953 and 1965, with no ap-

preciable decline in the water level.

The third, and most important, area lies in the central southern part of the district. Recharge occurs along the north-western edge of the Chipping Norton escarpment and in the headwaters of the River Glyme: groundwater is also believed to enter this system from the overlying Middle Jurassic limestones along major faults. In this area groundwater flows south-eastwards under confined conditions. Abstraction occurs from wells near Church Enstone [380 250], around Glympton [426 217], and at Steeple Barton [448 250]. At Church Enstone 6819 to 20457 m³/yr were abstracted between 1954 and 1960 for the local domestic supply, with no appreciable water-level decline. At Glympton Park, 0.7 Mm³ were abstracted during 1964 at a pumping rate of 37.9 l/sec for only 0.9 m drawdown. At Westcott Barton abstractions varying between 5455 and 26367 m³/yr are recorded for the period 1954 to 1961, but the well was closed after failing to meet local domestic requirements.

Throughout the district groundwater drawn from the Middle Lias is potable. Representative chemical analyses are given in Table 2.

3 Middle Jurassic

The distribution of springs and wells shows that groundwater is present throughout the main outcrop of the Middle Jurassic in the southern part of the district, and also in the down-faulted blocks in the north near Tadmarton [395 385] and in the Sibford–Whichford fault zone. Limestones predominate in the succession, and the groundwater is contained in fissures. The more important yielding formations are the Northampton Sand, the Clypeus Grit, the Chipping Norton Limestone and the Great Oolite Limestone. Yields increase downdip.

Springs are numerous at the base of the Inferior Oolite. Individual discharges are commonly very low, and are used only for agricultural and domestic purposes. Near Chipping Norton springs at this level have been superseded as sources of supply by piped supplies from the River Thames. Spring discharges from the same stratigraphical level have, however, been used for the supply of Duns Tew [457 285] at a rate of 68192 m³/yr, and Chipping Norton at 0.66 Mm³/yr.

Well sinkings in the Middle Jurassic have met with varying success. Woodland (1943) recorded a few wells tapping water from these rocks but many more have been drilled since. The wells range in depth up to about 60 m. Yields vary from negligible to 7.6 l/sec with no measurable drawdown.

East of the Cherwell, wells penetrating calcareous sandstones of the Northampton Sand indicate higher potential yields than from those higher in the succession. A well [525 314] at Souldern, tapping 7.32 m of Northampton Sand, yields 2.53 l/sec for 28 cm of drawdown, and at Somerton [502 285] a yield of 3.16 l/sec with no measurable drawdown is recorded from 4.27 m of saturated section. At Upper Heyford a yield of 5.05 l/sec is recorded for 3.66 m of drawdown from 4.88 m of saturated section, and at Upper Tadmarton, 0.23 l/sec with no drawdown has been obtained from 1 m of section. The most productive well [512 199] in the district, at Kirtlington Park, was tested at 7.58 l/sec and draws from 38 m of saturated section composed of Inferior Oolite and the Great Oolite Groups.

In the Great Oolite Group the available data do not allow any realistic assessment of the relative potential of the various formations, and no significant variations have been identified. Yields do, however, appear to improve with increase in thickness of the saturated section. Wells dug 18 to 21 m into the Great Oolite Limestone near Fritwell and Tackley [475 224] yield about 0.5 l/sec for domestic supplies. At Kirtlington a well tapping 35.35 m of saturated section in the Middle Jurassic yielded 2.53 l/sec for a drawdown of 15.85 m.

Groundwaters in the Middle Jurassic are almost entirely unconfined, and recharge occurs through the outcrop. Water levels in a well at Nethercott [483 228], where abstractions have varied between 6137 and 59736 m³/yr during the period 1856–1965, show no long-term decline. Other producing wells in the district show that similar conditions obtain.

Table 2 gives representative chemical analyses of waters derived from the Lias and the Middle Jurassic. Throughout the district these groundwaters have been used for domestic and agricultural purposes. The nitrate content of the water sampled from some wells in October 1970 is undesirably high; so is the fluoride content of water from the Lower Lias at Kingham Station.

JWL

Table 2 Chemical analyses of selected groundwaters in the Chipping Norton district

	Kingham Station Borehole	Glympton Park Borehole	Slade Farm Borehole, Church Enstone	Borehole near Chipping Norton	Little Tew Grounds Farm	Great Rollright	Kiddington
National Grid reference	257 227	427 218	380 250	303 261	377 261	321 325	420 229
Aquifer	Lower Lias	Middle Lias	Middle Lias	Middle Lias	Base, Middle Jurassic	Base, Middle Jurassic	Middle Jurassic
Type of sample	Pumped	Pumped	Pumped	Pumped	Spring	Spring	Spring
pH	8.35	8.3	8.1	7.9	8.0	8.2	7.9
Ca^{++} (ppm)	35	37	127	115	130	125	157
Mg^{++}	27.2	9.2	7.8	7.8	5.3	2.9	8.3
Na^+	700	36.4	9.5	11.8	6.3	5.7	12.5
K^+	8.9	3.0	1.8	2.5	0.5	0.2	30.5
Sr^{++}	?	?	0.2	0.4	0.2	0.2	0.3
HCO_3'	342	226	268	293	305	280	311
SO_4''	958	48	62	68	44	80	84
Cl'	354	16	40	23	16	19	48
NO_3'	3.5	– 0.2	42.3	13.8	55.4	24.8	105
F'	3.70	0.25	– 0.15	– 0.15	– 0.15	0.15	– 0.15

CHAPTER 10

Geophysical investigations

Although the entire district around Chipping Norton is occupied by Mesozoic rocks the regional Bouguer anomaly and magnetic maps largely reflect the nature of older rocks of the pre-Mesozoic basement. The basement in this area occurs at comparatively shallow depths of 100 m to 200 m below OD, and lies near the western edge of the London Platform. The largely undisturbed Mesozoic cover dips gently to the southeast.

PREVIOUS INVESTIGATIONS

The first systematic gravity and magnetic surveys of the district were made by the Anglo-Iranian Oil Company (Falcon and Tarrant, 1951) as part of an exploration programme covering a large part of south-central England. The gravity results, published in the form of a Bouguer anomaly map, revealed several distinct Bouguer anomalies. These results were later incorporated by the Geological Survey of Great Britain into Sheet 15 of the quarter-inch to one mile Gravity Survey Overlay Series (Geological Survey 1954) and subsequently the 1:25 000 map series (Institute of Geological Sciences 1982, 1983). The magnetic map (Falcon and Tarrant, 1951, pl.X), which was based on measurements on the ground of the vertical component of the field, revealed large magnetic highs west of Banbury. On the basis of the geophysical information Falcon and Tarrant (1951) suggested that Upper Carboniferous rocks might occur in the basement of the district.

At various times since 1962 parts of the district have been included in regional gravity surveys carried out by BGS; these results have been included in Figure 39. The district was also covered by an aeromagnetic survey flown for BGS in 1955. This survey, which formed part of the complete coverage of southern Britain (Geological Survey 1965), was made at a barometric height of 1800 feet (549 m) along east–west flight-lines 1.61 km apart with north–south tie-lines 9.65 km apart.

All the numerous boreholes put down by The Gas Council in the Chipping Norton area were logged geophysically (electrical, gamma-ray and SP logs), and comprehensive sets of detailed logs were made in the Survey's boreholes at Steeple Aston and Withycombe Farm. The geophysical results from the last two boreholes (Cornwell in Poole, 1977 and 1978), include average physical property values which are relevant to the interpretation of regional surveys and are repeated in Table 3.

GRAVITY SURVEYS

The Chipping Norton district was resurveyed by BGS at a station density of one per kilometre . The locations of the stations and the Bouguer anomaly contours based on values computed using the 1967 IGF are shown in Figure 39. A density of 2.2 Mg/m^3 was chosen as representative for the upper part of the Lias for the elevation correction and no allowance was made for the higher densities of the Jurassic limestones because of their restricted thickness.

The Bouguer anomaly map is dominated by a regular decrease of values from a maximum of $+3$ mGal near the northern edge of the district, southward to values of -15 mGal. The values decrease further beyond the southern limit of the area shown and this is due partly to an extensive regional Bouguer anomaly gradient of about 0.2 mGal per kilometre. This regional gradient must be due to a density change at a deeper crustal level than the sources of the other Bouguer anomaly features.

Superimposed on the regional gradients are several Bouguer anomaly features with steeper gradients and, in two cases, contour closures. The first of these is a circular high north-west of Banbury (the Banbury high) and the other is a more extensive Bouguer anomaly low between Bicester and Chipping Norton (the Steeple Aston low). The Banbury high lies on an east–west elongated Bouguer anomaly ridge which extends southwards as two less well defined ridges through Chipping Norton and Bicester with gradually decreasing values either side of the Steeple Aston low. Just to the south of the area shown in Figure 39 the two ridges end, and the Bouguer anomaly contours run approximately parallel, in an east–west direction.

The basement rocks generally have a significantly higher density than the overlying Mesozoic strata (Table 3), and some Bouguer anomalies would result from an appreciable change in the basement elevation. This effect is most pronounced along the western edge of the district where a steep gradient towards the west is due to the rapid thickening of Mesozoic rocks towards the basin indicated by the Winchcombe Bouguer anomaly low (Cornwell, in Williams and Whittaker, 1974, p.70). Over most of the area, however, the basement depth varies by less than 200 m (Figure 4) and the corresponding maximum Bouguer anomaly variation will be about 2.5 mGal, assuming a density contrast of 0.3 Mg/m^3.

It is apparent that most of the main Bouguer anomalies in Figure 39 must be due to changes of density within the pre-Mesozoic basement, reflecting the presence of different lithological units. Density data from the Steeple Aston and Withycombe Farm boreholes suggest that the Upper Carboniferous and at least part of the Devonian sequence have comparatively low densities compared with older Palaeozoic sediments and the igneous rocks; they would, therefore, be expected to give rise to Bouguer anomaly lows, as was predicted by Bullerwell (in Edmonds and other, 1965).

The information about the basement provided by the deeper boreholes only partly helps to explain the Bouguer anomalies. In both the Batsford Borehole (Strahan, 1913; Williams and Whittaker, 1974), immediately to the west of the district, and the Upton Borehole, Burford (Worssam,

Figure 39 Bouguer anomaly map with contours at 1-mGal (= 10-gu) intervals. Station positions are shown for the area covered by BGS surveys; for the western and southern margins contours are based on older surveys (Geological Survey, 1954)

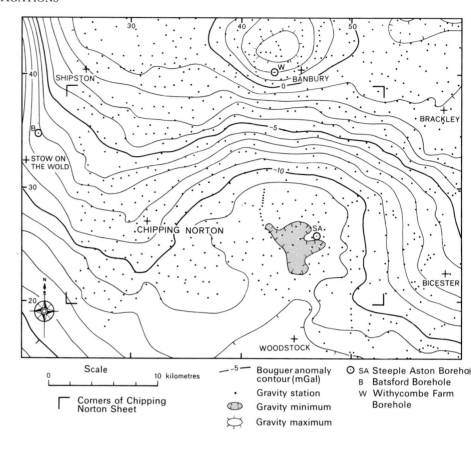

Table 3 Physical properties of rocks in the Chipping Norton area. Average values from geophysical logs from (1) the Steeple Aston and (2) the Withycombe Farm boreholes. Average values adopted for the interpretation of the Bouguer anomalies are given in column 3.

	Saturated density			mean	Sonic velocity		Resistivity	
	Mg/m³				km/s		ohm metre	
	1	2	3		1	2	1	2
Lias	2.19	2.34	2.27		1.96	2.23	4→50	
Mercia Mudstone	2.39	2.40	2.40	2.35	2.45	2.45	3→100	
Bromsgrove Sandstone	2.33	2.40	2.37		2.80	3.30	4→40	
Upper Carboniferous (Upper Coal Measures)	2.48	2.47	2.48	2.50	3.18	3.34	20	
Devonian	2.52				3.81		12	
?Silurian		2.66				4.32		18–50
Carboniferous basalt	2.81				5.55		>100	
?Ordovician basalt		2.83				5.62		>100

1963), Upper Carboniferous strata were found at approximately 200 m below OD, but the Bouguer anomaly value (– 7.2 mGal) is about 8 mGal higher at the first site. Part of this difference is due to the regional gradient, leaving about 3.5 mGal which is easily accounted for by the extra 656 m of Upper Carboniferous (base not proved) at Upton, assuming a density contrast of – 0.16 Mg/m³ against older Palaeozoic strata. Comparing the results of the Batsford Borehole with those from Withycombe Farm (Cornwell *in* Poole, 1978), however, the Bouguer anomaly value at the latter site (2.0 mGal) is about 9.2 mGal higher, despite the presence of a considerably thicker sequence of low-density Upper Carboniferous sediments. In both the Batsford and Withycombe Farm boreholes the Upper Carboniferous sediments are underlain by Lower Palaeozoic sediments. The same incon-

sistency is seen by comparing the results for Withycombe Farm with those from Steeple Aston (Cornwell *in* Poole, 1977), the former having the greater thickness of Upper Carboniferous sediments, but being at a point where the Bouguer anomaly values are about 13.8 mGal higher.

A residual anomaly map of part of the area shown in Figure 39 was, therefore, produced by applying three corrections to the observed values at the stations shown. These corrections were for the southward regional decrease of Bouguer anomalies, for the variable basement depth (based on Figure 4 and relative to a datum level of 100 m below OD), and for the thickness of low-density Upper Carboniferous. This last correction is the most uncertain of the three since thickness estimates were based on only six boreholes, three of which are situated outside the district. The residual Bouguer map produced in this way (Figure 40) shows a marked east–west high at the northern edge of the area, due to a positive correction for the Upper Carboniferous being added to the Bouguer anomaly high (at about the 0 mGal level) shown on the Bouguer anomaly map. The low around Steeple Aston is reduced somewhat both in area and amplitude, and is terminated to the west by a broad Bouguer anomaly ridge at about the zero contour level. If the corrections applied during the preparation of the residual map are valid, then these anomalies represent variations in the densities of pre-Upper Carboniferous rocks. The density data (Table 3) suggest that the highest anomaly values are due to Lower Palaeozoic sediments and igneous rocks, and that the lowest values should occur over low-density Devonian sediments such as those in the Steeple Aston Borehole.

The Bouguer anomaly ridge [c.310 260] is about 3 mGal lower than the value over the presumed Lower Palaeozoic sediments (?similar to those at depth in Withycombe Farm) to the north. This could represent the effects of an extra thickness of about 0.45 km of low-density sediments of Upper Carboniferous or, more likely, Devonian age. This estimate could be reduced if the southward regional decrease of Bouguer anomalies values was locally greater than 0.2 mGal per kilometre, but it is reasonably certain from Figure 40 that an additional thickness of Devonian rocks of at least 0.75 km would be necessary to explain the low around Steeple Aston.

The appearance of steep gradients with linear contours near the northern margin of Figure 40 suggests the presence of faults bounding this edge of the Steeple Aston basin, and it is possible that the Barford Fault Trough seen at surface is related to faults in the basement.

The explanation of the Steeple Aston low in terms of a basin of low-density Devonian sediments seems reasonable from the density data obtained (Table 3), these sediments being about 0.14 Mg/m^3 less dense than those of ?Silurian age. Such an explanation is not required, however, at the Apley Barn Borehole, 20 km farther south-west, where the combined effect of the regional anomaly field and the correction for the Upper Carboniferous is adequate to explain the Bouguer anomaly value, despite the fact that Devonian sediments were also present at depth. Five samples of Devonian rocks from the Apley Barn Borehole gave a higher density (of 2.60 Mg/m^3) than those at Steeple Aston, suggesting that the Devonian at Apley Barn is not so likely to give rise to Bouguer anomaly lows because of the absence of a marked density contrast with older rocks. If this explanation of the difference in Bouguer anomaly values between Apley Barn and Steeple Aston is valid, it implies a marked change in the physical properties of rocks of similar ages. In both boreholes the oldest sediments are Frasnian in age, but in Steeple Aston the top of this stage was encountered. The implication is therefore that there either is a rapid lateral lithological or thickness change within the Frasnian, or a change in the pre-Frasnian sequence.

An alternative explanation for the Steeple Aston

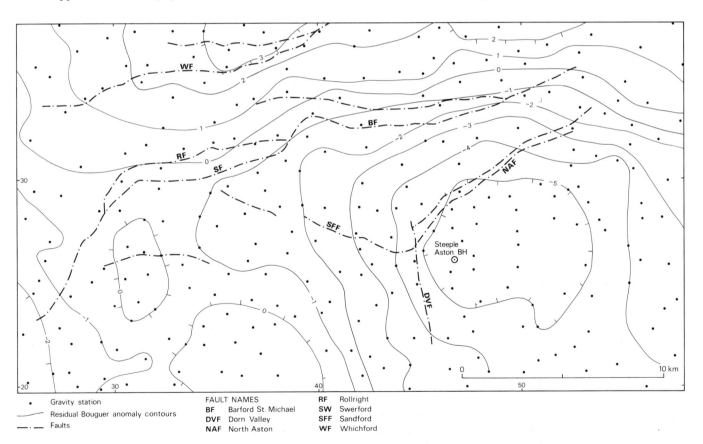

Figure 40   Residual Bouguer anomaly map of the area of the Steeple Aston low, showing station positions, contours at 1 mGal intervals, and the main faults affecting Jurassic strata

low—and one which is suggested by the circular form of the anomaly (Figure 40)—is that it is caused by a granite body intruded into the Devonian or older rocks. The absence of any metamorphic effects in the cores from the Steeple Aston Borehole and the heat flow evidence, described later, seem to argue against this possibility. In some cases, an examination of the horizontal gradient of a Bouguer anomaly field, or its derivative (Bott, 1962) can provide information useful in deciding whether the boundary of the low-density rocks slopes inwards towards the centre of the Bouguer anomaly low (as in a basin) or outwards (as in a granite). In the case of the Steeple Aston low, however, the evidence was inconclusive as the profiles showed irregular gradients. Other Bouguer anomaly lows occur in comparable areas of relatively shallow basement rocks associated with the London Platform, but no single consistent explanation has been found. The Canvey Island gravity anomaly, for example, is believed to be due to a Devonian basin (Smart and others, 1964); another, 12 km south of Reading, has been interpreted as being due to a diapiric granite (Hopkins, 1979).

Interpretation of the Bouguer anomaly low at Steeple Aston is also uncertain because of the difficulty in selecting a suitable background value. In Figure 41 the observed Bouguer anomaly profile (A) is shown together with the hypothetical profile (A^1) which makes allowance for the fact that this traverse intersects the local Bouguer anomaly high at Banbury. The regional gradient of 0.2 mGal per kilometre is indicated by B. It is obvious that regional gradient B cannot be used as a background anomaly because this would leave no low-density basement rocks at Withycombe Farm and it is known that about 490 m of Upper Carboniferous exist there. Adding 4.4 mGal to the observed Bouguer anomaly level near Withycombe Farm (as shown by curve C) would correct for this, but it is still uncertain whether such a correction is needed in the area over the Steeple Aston Borehole. Two models have, therefore, been drawn based on interpretations using the background levels shown as 1 and 2, and assuming that the anomaly is due to a single low-density body with a density contrast of -0.16 Mg/m^3. (This body would be intermediate in density between the Upper Carboniferous and the Devonian at Steeple Aston (Table 3), but the errors involved in this assumption are comparatively small.) In both models the steeper northern margin of the Devonian basin underlies the faulted Barford Trough in the Mesozoic. The maximum depth of the Devonian basin is of the order of 1.6 to 2.1 km below OD and occurs 5 km north of the Steeple Aston Borehole.

A second Bouguer anomaly profile has been drawn through Steeple Aston (BB^1 Figure 41) which passes through the boreholes at Batsford and Marsh Gibbon where the pre-Carboniferous basement has been proved. The background Bouguer anomaly value at Steeple Aston was determined by the levels 1 and 2 on profile AA^1 (Figure 41) but had to be adjusted at the two ends of the profile to produce a model compatible with the borehole evidence. Near the Batsford Borehole the background level had to be decreased rapidly westwards to allow for the small thickness of Upper Carboniferous sediments. The decrease west of the borehole is probably associated with the thickening of Mesozoic—and possibly older—rocks towards the Winchcombe low (Williams and Whittaker, 1974). In the area of the Marsh Gibbon Borehole [6481 2374] the background Bouguer anomaly level required to allow for the known depth of the pre-Devonian basement in the borehole resulted in the production of a positive Bouguer anomaly just to the east of the borehole. The implication of this is the presence of pre-Devonian basement with a density greater than 2.66 Mg/m^3; this is not unreasonable and could apply elsewhere in the area covered by the profiles. The models shown represent the simplest possible interpretation of many alternatives.

The Bouguer anomaly ridge running in an east–west direction through Banbury (Figure 39) can be explained by the presence of higher density Silurian sediments at Withycombe Farm (compared with the Devonian rocks at Steeple Aston). It is also tempting to explain the more local circular high (the Banbury high) centred north of the Withycombe Farm Borehole by the presence of dense basaltic rocks similar to those encountered at the bottom of the borehole (Table 3). Thinner cover to the basement is unlikely to be a contributory factor to the high as the available evidence suggests a thinning in the cover here (Figure 4). The form of the Banbury high is distorted to some extent by the steep gradients on its north and south sides, although on the east and west sides the anomaly gradually reduces to a background level of about -0.5 mGal. An attempt to remove the effect of these gradients by graphical methods produced a residual anomaly (Figure 42) in which the slight east–west elongation is replaced by a more circular form. The magnetic anomalies coincide with the northern and southern flanks of this anomaly, but the highest Bouguer anomaly values correspond with the low between these two magnetic features. A third related magnetic anomaly in the south-west corner of Figure 42 has no associated residual Bouguer anomaly, suggesting, together with the evidence above, that although the sources of the magnetic and Bouguer anomalies are related they are not identical. This situation could arise if the magnetic anomalies originate in shallow faulted parts of an igneous complex or if only certain components of the complex are magnetic.

Interpretations of an east–west profile through the high, according to the method of Skeels (1963) for a vertical cylindrical body, indicate depths of 7–8 km to the top and 12–13 km to the base, with density contrast in the range 0.1–0.2 Mg/m^3. However, the theoretical curve due to a model having this form shows little similarity with the observed curve, suggesting that these depth estimates are almost certainly too great (probably because a vertical-sided model is not applicable). The same lack of similarity results from a comparison of the observed profile with the curve due to vertical line elements at a depth of about 2.7 km, which could represent a vertical plug-like body. These comparisons suggest that the origin of the Bouguer anomaly high lies nearer the surface and, therefore, tend to support the suggestion the dense basaltic rocks encountered at a depth of about 1 km in the Withycombe Farm Borehole are part of a sequence with a volume sufficient to cause the feature. A circular disc with a radius of 7.5 km, a density contrast of 0.17 Mg/m^3, and an upper surface at 0.9 km below OD would need to be 0.7 km thick to cause the observed anomaly of 4.2 mGal.

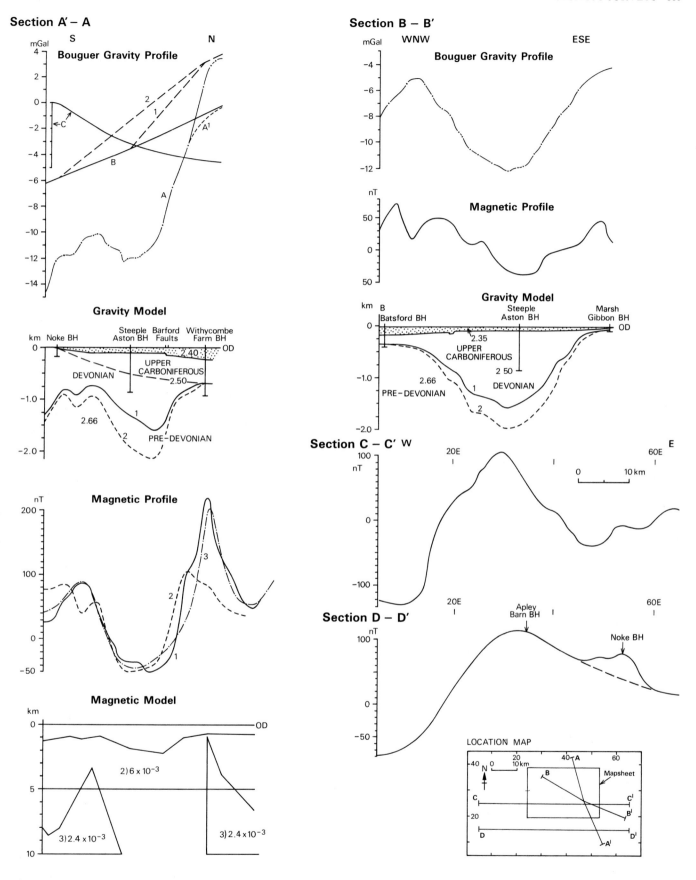

Figure 41 Bouguer anomaly and magnetic field profiles for traverses in the Chipping Norton area. Interpretations are based on two-dimensional models

Figure 42 Residual Bouguer anomaly map of the area around the Withycombe Farm Borehole (WF), showing station positions, contours at 1 mGal intervals and the area where total magnetic field values exceed + 150 nT

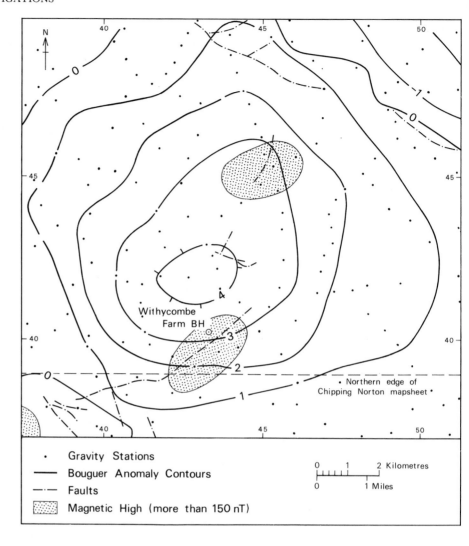

- Gravity Stations
— Bouguer Anomaly Contours
–·— Faults
░ Magnetic High (more than 150 nT)

AEROMAGNETIC SURVEYS

The Mesozoic sediments in the district are non-magnetic, and the large variations in the total field intensity on the aeromagnetic map (Figure 43) must reflect changes in the basement rocks.

The highest anomaly values in the area, reaching a level of more than + 200 nT, occur to the west of Banbury as two oval anomalies with an ENE–WSW trend (Bullerwell, *in* Edmonds and others, 1965). The anomaly values decrease to the south-east to reach the minimum values in the area (– 60 nT), near Steeple Aston; they increase again farther to the south-east, to culminate along another ENE–WSW-trending line. The broadly spaced contours in the south-western corner of the area (Figure 43) strongly suggest that the source of the magnetic anomaly trending NNW–SSE to the south of Chipping Norton is deeper than the sources of the anomalies elsewhere in the district. On a regional scale, the area shown in Figure 43 lies within a broad belt of magnetic highs extending in a north–south direction from the Thames Valley to the Birmingham area. To the west of this belt the anomaly pattern is dominated by a magnetic low over thick Mesozoic sediments in the Stratford-upon-Avon district (Cornwell *in* Williams and Whittaker, 1974).

It is likely that in a large proportion of the area shown in Figure 43 sediments of Upper Carboniferous age, 960 m thick at Apley Barn (Poole, 1969), form the basement surface. They will be essentially non-magnetic, though in the Steeple Aston Borehole (Poole, 1977) intrusions with a basaltic composition and basaltic breccias with a combined thickness of 165 m lay at the base of the preserved Upper Carboniferous sequence. The basalt has an average susceptibility of about 50×10^{-3} SI units (Cornwell *in* Poole, 1977) and strong remanent magnetisation, although the vertical components of the various samples measured have both upward and downward directions with a mean total magnetisation (induced and remanent magnetisations) of 4.1 A/m downwards. Where such a sill is horizontal and undisturbed its magnetic effect at the surface will be greatest where it is terminated by a vertical edge; here the effect 610 m above (i.e. at ground surface) reaches a maximum of 90 nT. In Figure 43 it is obvious that there is no large distinct anomaly in the area of the Steeple Aston Borehole, which is located within the zone of low magnetic values, although in Figure 41, Section AA[1], there is a small anomaly on the profile which apparently originates comparatively near to the surface. There are several irregular anomalies of less than 50 nT amplitude within 10 km of the borehole which could represent similar minor intrusions, such as the indentation of the zero nT contour 9 km east-north-east of Chipping Norton and also near Brackley (Figure 43). It is also possible that igneous bodies such as that at Steeple Aston could give rise to negative magnetic anomalies due to their strong remanent magnetisation.

Other magnetic anomalies in the district with a comparatively shallow origin occur near Bicester and west of Chipping Norton. The anomaly south of Bicester coincides with the Bouguer anomaly high through the Noke Borehole, and can be followed off the area shown in Figure 43 to the east-north-east where it resolves into two separate anomalies indicating two dyke-like bodies at the basement surface along the Noke-Islip axis. About 10 km west of Chipping Norton, an anomaly with a similar ENE–WSW trend, lying at an estimated depth of 0.9 km below OD (Bullerwell *in* Edmonds and others, 1965), seems to indicate another dyke-like magnetic body, possibly associated with a basement fault represented at the surface to the east by the Rollright–Swerford Fault system (Figure 44). This anomaly continues to the north as the north–south-trending feature south of Shipston where it appears to be due to an elongated body, almost coincident with the Vale of Moreton axis (Bullerwell *in* Edmonds and others, 1965).

The three anomalies west and north of Banbury reach the highest values in the area and were interpreted by Bullerwell (*in* Edmonds and others, 1965) as being due to an L-shaped igneous mass of rectangular outline and 3–5 km wide. The Withycombe Farm Borehole, sited on one of these anomalies, encountered no igneous material in the Upper Carboniferous, but entered basalts of ?Ordovician age with a mean susceptibility of 39×10^{-3} SI units lying at 891 m below OD beneath 194 m of ?Silurian sediments. Interpretations of a profile through this magnetic anomaly are presented in Figure 41, AA[1]. Model 1 assumes that the pre-Devonian basement rocks are uniformly magnetic; model 2 represents a more extreme interpretation with magnetic rocks extending down to a depth of 10 km below OD. Model 1 is a duplicate of the basement form derived from the gravity interpretation (and extended to a depth of 5 km below OD), and reproduces the central magnetic low and the flanking highs. It fails, however, to reproduce the sharp magnetic peak at Withycombe Farm. This was achieved in model 2 by bringing the magnetic material near the basement surface to a sharp peak, which seems rather unrealistic. There are many models capable of reproducing the form of the Withycombe Farm magnetic high, but it is obvious in all cases from a comparison with model 1 that an additional body of magnetic material is required.

Although the trough in the magnetic basement rocks represented by model 2 (Figure 41, AA[1]) appears to produce a magnetic low comparable with that observed, this interpretation is more difficult to reconcile at the Steeple Aston Borehole with the profile CC[1] (Figure 41). The source of the magnetic anomaly shown in profile CC[1] is apparently deep, judging from the smoothness and wide spacing of the contours (Figure 43), and an interpretation produced a minimum depth of least 4 km. Such a deep-seated origin would be compatible with the magnetic model 3 (Figure 41, AA[1]) extending to a depth of 10 km below OD, but not with model 2 which has a maximum depth of 2.1 km below OD to the top of the magnetic body in the vicinity of Steeple Aston.

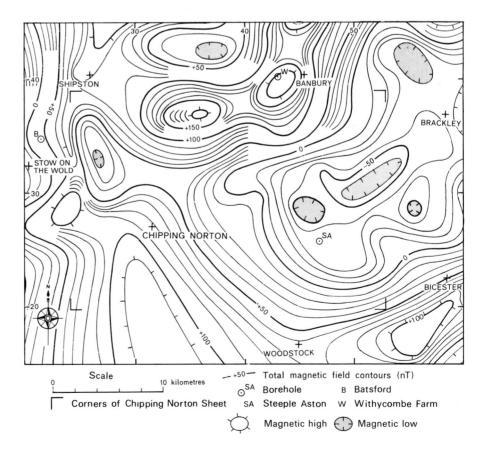

Figure 43 Aeromagnetic map with contours at 10 nT

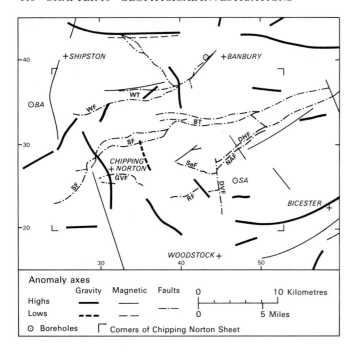

Figure 44 Locations of faults in Mesozoic rocks and axes of Bouguer and magnetic anomalies

In the case of the latter, however, there is the possibility that the basin of Devonian sediments shown in Figure 41 could be underlain by another block of non-magnetic material. Figure 41, DD[1] shows a magnetic profile parallel with—and 10 km to the south of—profile CC[1] in the vicinity of the Apley Barn Borehole, which proved the absence of magnetic rocks to a depth of at least 1.3 km below OD. The origin of the main magnetic anomaly is deeper than in profile CC[1], but the subsidiary anomaly near Noke [5386 1285] is clearly of shallower origin because of its shorter wavelength.

The detailed relationship of the magnetic material west of Banbury to the dense rocks responsible for the Bouguer anomaly high is not clear, for the former coincides with the flanks rather than the centre of the high (Figure 42). The localisation of the anomaly peaks could be due to displacement of magnetic rocks in the basement by faults or even fault-controlled intrusions, and this view is lent some support by the presence of faulting in the overlying rocks here (Figure 44).

TREND DIRECTIONS

At several localities within the Chipping Norton district the sources of the Bouguer gravity and aeromagnetic anomalies appear to be related. The apparent lack of correlation elsewhere is probably due to the fact that the sources lie at different depths in the basement. A general correlation in the trends of the gravity and magnetic anomalies (Figure 44) suggests, however, that in many cases a common structural pattern is involved and this is, in places, reflected by the fault pattern at the surface. It is not likely that displacements of the Mesozoic strata or even the basement surface are responsible for the observed geophysical anomalies but some

of the faults shown on Figure 44 could represent the effects of renewed movement along older, deeper basement structures.

The geophysical anomalies have two dominant trends—NNW–SSE and E–W—demonstrated by both magnetic and Bouguer anomalies; in a few instances these correspond broadly to similar trends in the surface faults (Figure 44).

Many of the surface faults coincide with gradients flanking the geophysical anomalies rather than with the crests of the anomalies, possibly because the gradient zones are more likely to occur over boundaries (perhaps faulted) between different basement rock types. The Barford and Swerford troughs, in particular, closely follow the Bouguer gradient thought to be due to the steeper northern margin of the ?Devonian basin beneath Steeple Aston (Figure 44). The Banbury–Whichford fault systems overlie the crest of the Banbury group of magnetic anomalies and part of the southern edge of the Banbury gravity high.

HEAT FLOW SURVEYS

Heat flow measurements for the Steeple Aston and Withycombe Farm boreholes by Cull and others (*in* Poole, 1977) and Richardson and others (*in* Poole, 1978), respectively, consisted of temperature logging (when thermal equilibrium had been recovered after drilling had ceased) and thermal conductivity measurements on samples of core from the boreholes. A good correlation between the temperature gradient profile, showing values varying between 15°C/km and 50°C/km, and the stratigraphic log is reported, although the effect of the lining pipe in the borehole is to displace the isotherms upwards.

The preferred average heat flow value at Withycombe Farm is 1.43 hfu and at Steeple Aston 1.1 hfu. This significant difference is attributed by Richardson and others (*in* Poole, 1978) to differences in the crustal contribution to the heat flow rather than to differences due to the underlying mantle. It also possibly provides indirect evidence that the Bouguer anomaly low at Steeple Aston is unlikely to be due to concealed granite, as this rock type would be expected to increase the local heat flow due to its relatively high content of radioactive elements.

RESISTIVITY SURVEYS

Numerous boreholes in the Chipping Norton district have been logged geophysically, the most detailed information being for the BGS boreholes (Bennet, *in* Poole, 1969, Cornwell, *in* Poole, 1977 and 1978). Certain horizons provide good stratigraphic correlations because of their distinct physical properties as revealed by the geophysical logging. The most useful of these marker horizons occur in the Lower Lias, where thin calcareous bands are clearly indicated on the logs, particularly on the resistivity logs, because of their strong contrasts with the predominantly argillaceous sequence (Horton and Poole, 1977).

The background resistivity values for the Liassic argillaceous sediments on the Withycombe Farm and Steeple

Aston borehole logs decrease from at least 15–20 ohm-metres at the top of the Lower Lias to minimum values of about 5 ohm-metres near the '70 marker'. A full explanation of this has not yet been found, although it may be due to a decreasing silt content in the argillaceous measures. On all the logs examined the lowest resistivity values are immediately below the Langport Member. Other features that can be correlated on the Steeple Aston and Withycombe Farm logs include the smooth zone between the '85' and '70' markers of Horton and Poole (1977) which indicates the absence of non-argillaceous material.

Resistivity measurements in The Gas Council boreholes (Figure 9) produced results characteristic of Upper Carboniferous sequences.

SEISMIC SURVEYS

Sonic velocity logs from the Steeple Aston and Withycombe Farm boreholes indicate the range of velocities to be expected in the Chipping Norton district. Interval velocities for the main rock units show a gradual increase with depth through the Lias and Triassic into the Upper Carboniferous. Apart from thin, high-velocity layers such as the Langport Member (with a velocity up to 5.0 km/s) the main velocity changes occur at the base of the Mercia Mudstone Group, at the basalts within the Coal Measures, and at the base of the Upper Carboniferous. It seems unlikely that the top of the Upper Carboniferous would be recognised in a refraction survey if it is overlain by thick Bromsgrove Sandstone, because of the lack of a distinct velocity contrast. The presence of alternating sandstones and shales in the Upper Carboniferous in both boreholes and in the Devonian at Steeple Aston gives rise to numerous velocity and density changes which would be expected to produce reflection events, unlike the general monotonous sequence of Silurian mudstones at Withycombe Farm.

The deeper structure of the Chipping Norton district, particularly that of the Carboniferous strata in the Oxfordshire Coalfield, has been investigated by private companies using seismic reflection profiling techniques; the results are held in confidence. Trial seismic investigations carried out by BGS at three sites [490 213, 463 250 and 464 430] indicate velocities of about 1.6 km/s in the near-surface part of the Lias, increasing to about 2.4 km/s at a depth of about 30 m. This last velocity is high for argillaceous measures and is possibly due to the thin calcareous horizons in the Lias. Reflection events were recorded at all three sites.   JDC

APPENDIX 1

Mesozoic faunal list

H. C. Ivimey-Cook

The following lists summarise most of the Mesozoic macrofossils collected from the district. Macrofossils belonging to the Penarth Group and the oldest beds of the Lower Jurassic were collected only from boreholes. A few of The Gas Council boreholes were partially cored and some of these cores were collected for fossils. BGS commissioned the deep Steeple Aston Borehole and had shallower boreholes drilled at Charlton, Duns Tew, Hook Norton, Ledwell and Tadmarton (see Appendix 4).

Where both an identified species and specimens only identified generally are present the letter is shown as sp.

1. Late Triassic (Penarth Group)

	Westbury Formation	Lilstock Formation	
		Cotham Member	Langport Member
Cardinia cf. *regularis* Terquem	x		
Cardinia sp.		x	
Chlamys valoniensis (Defrance)	x		
Dacryomya titei (Moore)	x		
Dimyopsis ₁*Atreta*₁ *intusstriata* (Emmrich)			x
Eotrapezium concentricum (Moore)	x	x	x
E. cf. *germari* (Dunker)	x		
'*Gervillia*' *praecursor* (Quenstedt)	x	x	x
Liostrea sp.		x	x
Lyriomyophoria postera (Quenstedt)	x		
Meleagrinella fallax (Pflucker)		x	x
Modiolus cf. *hillanoides* (Chapuis and Dewalque)	x		x
M. laevis J. Sowerby	x		
M. sp.	x	x	x
Mytilus cloacinus Tutcher	x		
Plagiostoma sp.		x	
Plicatula?		x	
Protocardia rhaetica (Merian)	x	x	x
Pteromya sp.			x
Rhaetavicula contorta (Portlock)	x		
Tutcheria cloacina (Quenstedt)	x		
acteoninid gastropods	x		
echinoid fragments			x
Ophiolepis?	x		
Euestheria minuta (Zieten)		x	
Birgeria acuminata (Agassiz)	x		
Gyrolepis alberti Agassiz	x		
Lissodus ₁*Acrodus*₁ *minimus* (Agassiz)	x		
Saurichthys sp.	x		

Occurrences identified to generic level only are shown on the same line as a species by *sp*.

2. Lower Jurassic

Summary of the main taxa of macrofossils collected from surface exposures and principal boreholes. Lower Lias strata of Hettangian age have not been proved. MRB = Marlstone Rock Bed.

	Lower Lias		Middle Lias		Upper Lias
	Sinem.	L. Pleinsb.	Upper Pleinsb.		Toarcian
			Silts & Clays	MRB	
BRACHIOPODA					
Discinisca holdeni (Tate)	x	x			
D. reflexa (J. de C. Sowerby)					x
Lingula sp.	x				x
Spiriferina sp.	x	x			
Calcirhynchia sp.	x				
Cirpa sp.	x	x			
Furcirhynchia?		x			
Gibbirhynchia amalthei (Quenstedt)			x		
G. gibbosa S. S. Buckman			x		
G. muirwoodae Ager			x		
G. northamptonensis (Davidson)			x		
G. tiltonensis Ager			x		
G. sp.		x			
Piarorhynchia juvenis (Quenstedt)	x	x			
P. rostellata (Quenstedt)	x				
Rhynchonelloidea lineata (Young and Bird)			x		
Rimirhynchia anglica (Rollier)		x			
Squamirhynchia?	x				
Tetrarhynchia cf. *subconcinna* (Davidson)				x	
T. tetrahedra (J. Sowerby)				x	
T. sp.		x	x		
Cincta cf. *numismalis* (Lamarck)	sp.	x			
Lobothyris punctata (J. Sowerby)			x	x	
L. punctata clevelandensis Ager				x	
L. sp.	x				
BIVALVIA					
Anningella faberi (Oppel)	x		x		
Antiquilima antiquata (J. Sowerby)	sp.	x			
Arcomya sp.	x				
Astarte gueuxii d'Orbigny	x	x	sp.	x	
Bakevellia laevis (J. Buckman)	sp.		x		
Camptonectes mundus Melville	x	x		x	
C. aff. *lohbergensis* (Emerson)	x				
Camptonectes sp.	x	x	x		
Cardinia attenuata (Stutchbury)	x	x			
C. sp.		x			
Chlamys textoria (Schlotheim)		x	sp.		
Ctenostreon tuberculatus (Terquem)		x			
Dacryomya gaveyi Cox	x				
D. minor (Simpson)		x			
D. ovum (J. de C. Sowerby)					x
Entolium liasianum (Nyst)		x	sp.	x	sp.
Eopecten sp.		x		x	
Gervillia sp.	x				
Goniomya hybrida (Münster)	x		sp.		
Grammatodon insons Melville	x	x	x		x
Gryphaea arcuata Lamarck	x	x			
G. cf. *gigantea* J. de C. Sowerby		x			
G. maccullochii J. de C. Sowerby		x			
G. sp.	x	x	x	x	

| | Lower Lias | | Middle Lias | | Upper Lias |
| | Sinem. | L. Pleinsb. | Upper Pleinsb. | | Toarcian |
			Silts & Clays	MRB	
Laevitrigonia troedssoni Melville		x			
Liostrea sportella (Dumortier)				x	
L. sp.		x	x	x	
Lucina sp.	x	x	x		
Mactromya arenacea (Terquem)		x			
Meleagrinella olifex (Quenstedt)	x				
M. substriata (Münster)					x
M. sp.	x				
Modiolus oxynoti (Quenstedt)	x	sp.	sp.		
Myoconcha decorata (Münster)	x	x			
M. psilonoti (Quenstedt)		x			
Nucula sp.	x				
Oxytoma inequivalvis (J. Sowerby)	x	x	x	x	
Palaeoneilo galatea (d'Orbigny)	x	x	x		
P. oviformis Troedsson	x		x		
P. sp.	x				
Palaeonucula navis (Piette)	x	x			
Parainoceramus sp.	x	x			
Parallelodon hettangiensis (Terquem)		x			
P. pullus (Tate *non* Terquem)	x				
P. sp.		x	x		
Pholadomya sp.		x			
Pinna sp.	x				
Placunopsis sp.	x	x			
Plagiostoma sp.	x				
Pleuromya costata (Young and Bird)		x	x		
Plicatula patelloides (J. A. Eudes-Deslongchamps)		x			
P. spinosa J. Sowerby			x	x	
P. sp.	x	x			
Pronoella intermedia (Moore)			x		
Protocardia truncata (J. de C. Sowerby)	sp.	sp.	x	sp.	
Propeamussium (Parvamussium) sp.			x		
Pseudolimea sp.	x	x	x		
Pseudomytiloides dubius (J. de C. Sowerby)					x
Pseudopecten acuticosta (Lamarck)		x			
P. dentatus (J. de C. Sowerby)			x	x	
P. equivalis (J. Sowerby)				x	
P. priscus (Schlotheim)	x	x			
Pteromya cf. *tatei* (Richardson and Tutcher)	x				
Rollieria bronni (Andler)	sp.	x			
Ryderia doris (d'Orbigny)	x				
Semuridia sp.	x				
Thracia?					x
Tutcheria sp.		x			

GASTROPODA

Acteonina sp.		x			
Pleurotomaria sp.		x			

AMMONOIDEA see separate table following

NAUTILOIDEA

Cenoceras sp.					x

BELEMNITIDA

Hastites spadixari (Simpson)		x			
Nannobelus spp.		x			
Passaloteuthis spp.		x	x	x	x
Pseudohastites arundineus Lang		x			

	Lower Lias		Middle Lias (Upper Pleinsb.)		Upper Lias
	Sinem.	L. Pleinsb.	Silts & Clays	MRB	Toarcian
ECHINODERMATA					
Crinoid fragments		x	x	x	
Ophiuroid fragments		x			
Eodiadema sp.	x	x			
Echinoid fragments		x	x		

AMMONOIDEA. The occurrence of the principal ammonites recovered from the district in stratigraphic order. Taxa characteristic of a subzone are shown by the initial letter of the subzone in the Zone column. (see Table 1)

	Sinemurian					L. Pliensb.			U. Pl.		Toarcian		
	s.	tu.	ob.	ox.	r.	j.	i.	d.	m.	sp.	te.	f.	b.
Crassicoeloceras aff. *crassum* (Young and Bird)													cr
Dactylioceras commune (J. Sowerby)													co
Frechiella subcarinata (Young and Bird)													x
Harpoceras cf. *soloniacense* (Lissajous)													x
Hildoceras bifrons (Bruguière)													ƒ +
H. sublevisoni Fucini													c
H. sp.													x
Peronoceras cf. *andraei* (Simpson)													ƒ
P. fibulatum (J. de C. Sowerby)													ƒ
Dactylioceras attenuatum (Simpson)												x	
D. consimile (S. S. Buckman)												ƒ	
D. vermis (Simpson)												x	
Harpoceras exaratum (Young and Bird)												e	
H. exiguum (S. S. Buckman)												ƒ	
H. falciferum (J. Sowerby)												x	x
H. sp.												x	x
Harpoceratoides strangewaysi (J. Sowerby)												x	
Hildaites sp.												x	
Lytoceras crenatum (S. S. Buckman)												x	
Nodicoeloceras sp.												x	x
Dactylioceras (Orthodactylites) semicelatum (Simpson)											s		
Tiltoniceras antiquum (Wright)											s		
Pleuroceras cf. *solare* (Phillips)										x			
P. spinatum (Bruguière)										x			
Amaltheus cf. *margaritatus* de Montfort									x				
A. cf. *stokesi* (J. Sowerby)									st				
A. subnodosus (Young and Bird)									su				
Arieticeras nitescens (Young and Bird)									x				
A. sp. nov.									x				
Aegoceras (Oistoceras) figulinum (Simpson)								ƒ					
A. (O.) aff. *sinuosiforme* (Spath)								x					
A. maculatum (Young and Bird)								m					
Androgynoceras brevilobatum (Trueman)								x					
Aegoceras (Beaniceras) dundryi Donovan							x	x					
Liparoceras cf. *cheltiense* (Murchison)							x						
L. cf. *kilsbyense* (Spath)							x						
L. sparsicosta Trueman							x						
Tragophylloceras sp.						x	x	x	x				
Uptonia sp.						j							
Platypleuroceras sp.						x							
Polymorphites sp.						x							
Apoderoceras sp.						x							
Phricodoceras taylori (J. de C. Sowerby)						t							
Gemmellaroceras tubellum (Simpson)			x	x	x								
G. anguiniforme (Simpson)				x									
Cheltonia sp.				x									

	Sinemurian					L. Pliensb.			U. Pl.		Toarcian		
	s.	tu.	ob.	ox.	r.	j.	i.	d.	m.	sp.	te.	f.	b.
Gleviceras glevense S. S. Buckman													
Leptechioceras macdonnelli (Portlock)					m								
Neomicroceras commune Donovan					m								
Paltechioceras tardecrescens (von Hauer)					m								
Paltechioceras sp.					x								
Echioceras cf. *aureolum* (Simpson)					r								
E. raricostatum Zieten					r								
Metaderoceras fulvum Trueman and Williams					x								
Eoderoceras sp.					x								
Crucilobiceras sp.					x								
'Hemimicroceras' sp.					x								
Bifericeras sp.				x	x								
Oxynoticeras oxynotum (Quenstedt)					0								
O. sp.				x	x								
Palaeoechioceras sp.					0								
Cymbites sp.					x								
Asteroceras sp.				x									
Promicroceras planicosta (J. Sowerby)													
P. sp.			x	x									
Xipheroceras sp.				x									
Caenisites sp.			x										
Microderoceras sp.			x										
Arnioceras cf. *bodleyi* (J. Buckman)	x	x	x										
A. miserabile (Quenstedt)	x	x	x										
A. semicostatum (Young and Bird)	x	x											
A. sp.	x	x	x										
Coroniceras (?Paracoroniceras) sp.	x												
Cymbites laevigatus (J. de C. Sowerby)	x	x	x										

The ammonite zones and subzones of the Lower Jurassic are listed in Table 1.p.28

3. Inferior Oolite Group

Principal invertebrate macrofossils. Key: NS/Sc = Northampton Sand/Scissum Beds; LES = 'Lower Estuarine Series': CG = Clypeus Grit.

	NS/Sc	LES	CG
ANTHOZOA			
Chomatoseris porpites (Wm. Smith)			x
Dimorpharea defranciana (Michelin)			x
D. sp.			x
Montlivaltia lens Edwards and Haime		x	
M. trochoides Edwards and Haime			x
Thamnasteria sp.			x
ANNELIDA			
Sarcinella plexus (J. de C. Sowerby)		x	sp.
BRACHIOPODA			
Lingula sp.			x
Acanthothiris sp.			x
Globirhynchia subobsoleta (Davidson)			x
Kallirhynchia acutiplicata (Brown)			x
K. sp.		x	x
Rhactorhynchia sp.			x
Rhynchonelloidea sp.		x	x
Stiphrothyris birdlipensis (Davidson)			x
S. tumida (Davidson)			x
S. sp.			x
Wattonithyris sp.			x

	NS/Sc	LES	CG
BIVALVIA			
Astarte wiltoni Morris and Lycett	x		
Barbatia pulchra (J. de C. Sowerby)			x
Camptonectes annulatus (J. de C. Sowerby)	x		
C. cf. *comatus* (Münster)			x
C. laminatus (J. Sowerby)	x		
C. (Camptochlamys) obscurus (J. Sowerby)	x		
C. (C.) rosimon (d'Orbigny)	x		
C. sp.	x		x
Ceratomya sp.			x
Chlamys viminea (J. de C. Sowerby)			x
C (Radulopecten) aff. *vagans* (J. de C. Sowerby)			x
C. (R.) sp.			x
'Corbula' sp.	x		x
Ctenostreon rugosum (Wm. Smith)	x		
Cucullaea minchinhamptonensis Cox and Arkell	sp.		x
Cuspidaria cf. *ibbetsoni* (Morris)	x		
Eopecten?	x		
Entolium corneolum (Young and Bird)	x		x
Eryphlopsis minima (Phillips)			x
Gervillella monotis (J. A. Eudes-Deslongchamps)	x		
Grammatodon sp.	x		x
Gresslya abducta (Phillips)	sp.		x
Homomya?	x		
Inoperna plicatus (J. Sowerby)	x		
Isocyprina cf. *sharpi* Cox			x
Isognomon isognomonoides (Stahl)	x	sp.	
Limatula gibbosa (J. Sowerby)			x
Liostrea cf. *hebridica* (Forbes)	sp.		x
L. (Praeexogyra) acuminata (J. Sowerby)			x
Lithophaga sp. and burrows	x		x
Lopha?	x		
Lucina sp.	x		
Mactromya?	x		
Meleagrinella lycetti (Rollier)	x		x
Modiolus imbricatus (J. Sowerby)			x
M. cf. *substriata* Zieten	x		
Musculus sp.	x		x
Myophorella cf. *formosa* (Lycett)	x		
M. signata (Agassiz)	sp.		x
Nanogyra?	x		
Neocrassina elegans (J. Sowerby)	x		
Opis sp.			x
Oxytoma inequivalvis (J. Sowerby)	x		x
Pachymya (Arcomya) crassiuscula (Morris and Lycett)	x		x
Pholadomya deltoidea (J. Sowerby)			x
P. ovulum L. Agassiz			x
Pinna sp.	x		
Placunopsis sp.	x		
Plagiostoma sp.	x		x
Pleuromya subelongata (d'Orbigny)	sp.		x
P. uniformis (J. Sowerby)			x
Plicatula sp.	x		x
Propeamussium (Parvamussium) laeviradiatum (Waagen)	x		
Protocardia lycetti (Rollier)	x		x
P. cf. *buckmani* (Morris and Lycett)	x		
Pseudolimea duplicata (J. de C. Sowerby)			x
P. interstincta (Phillips)	x		
Quenstedtia sp.	x		
Tancredia brevis (Morris and Lycett)			x
T. planata Morris and Lycett	x		
Trigonastarte sp.	x		
Trigonia sculpta cheltensis Lycett	sp.		x
Vaugonia sp.			x
Vaugonia (Orthotrigonia) gemmata (Lycett)			x

	NS/Sc	LES	CG
GASTROPODA			
Aptyxiella subconica (Hudleston)	x		
Cossmannea (Eunerinea) cf. *eudesii* (Morris and Lycett)	sp.		x
Cylindrobullina antiqua (Lycett)			x
Procerithium (Rhabdocolpus) vetustus-majus Hudleston			x
Pseudomelania sp.			x
AMMONOIDEA			
Bredyia cf. *subinsignis* (Oppel)	x		
Leioceras sp.	x		
Parkinsonia parkinsoni (J. Sowerby)			x
P. schloenbachi Schlippe			x
BELEMNITIDA			
belemnite fragments	x		
NAUTILOIDEA			
Cenoceras aff. *inornatum* (d'Orbigny)	x		
ECHINODERMATA			
crinoid fragments	x		
Clypeus ploti Salter			x
Holectypus hemisphaericus (Lamarck)			x
Pygurus michelini Cotteau			x
echinoid fragments	x		x

4. Great Oolite Group

Principal invertebrate macrofossils. Key: CNL = Chipping Norton Limestone; SHB = Sharp's Hill Beds; TS = Taynton Stone; HMB = Hampen Marly Beds; WL = White Limestone; FM = Forest Marble; LCb = Lower Cornbrash.

	CNL	SHB	TS	HMB	WL	FM	LCb
PORIFERA							
Peronidella sp.	x						
ANTHOZOA							
Chomatoseris porpites (Wm. Smith)				sp.	x		
Cyathophora sp.					x		
Isastraea limitata (Lamouroux)					x		
Montlivaltia smithi Edwards and Haime					x		
Thamnasteria lyelli (Edwards and Haime)		x			sp.		
ANNELIDA							
Sarcinella plexus (J. de C. Sowerby)						x	
BRACHIOPODA							
Burmirhynchia spp. (incl. Buckman's species *B. dromio,* *gibba, ornithea, patula, polystema, tumida* and *vagans*).		x		x			
Kallirhynchia spp. (incl. Buckman's species *K. decora,* *deliciosa, expansa, lauta, obtusa* and *superba*).	x	x	x	x	x		
Rhactorhynchia obsoleta (Davidson)	x				sp.		
Avonothyris?			x				
Cererithyris intermedia (J. Sowerby)							x
Dictyothyris sp.							x
Epithyris bathonica S. S. Buckman				x	x		
E. oxonica v. *transversa* Arkell				x			
E. oxonica Arkell		x	x	x	x	x	
Obovothyris magnobovata S. S. Buckman							x
O. obovata (J. Sowerby)							x
Ornithella aff. *rugosa* Douglas and Arkell							x
Stiphrothyris sp.					x		
Wattonithyris?			x				

	CNL	SHB	TS	HMB	WL	FM	LCb
BIVALVIA							
Anisocardia caudata (Lycett)				x	x		
A. islipensis (Lycett)				x	x		
A. cf. *longicaudata* Cox					x		
A. truncata (Morris)		x		x	x		
A. (Antiquicyprina) loweana (Morris and Lycett)			x	x	x	x	
Astarte (Coelastarte) oolitharum Cossmann	sp.				x		
A. squamula d'Archiac			x				
Bakevellia waltoni (Lycett)	sp.	x	x	x	x	x	
Barbatia prattii (Morris and Lycett)					x		
Camptonectes annulatus (J. de C. Sowerby)	sp.	sp.	x	x	x		
C. laminatus (J. Sowerby)			x		x		
C. rigidus (J. Sowerby)			x	x	x		
Camptonectes (Camptochlamys) rosimon (d'Orbigny)	x						
Catinula matisconensis (Lissajous)	x	x		sp.	sp.		sp.
Ceratomya concentrica (J. de C. Sowerby)		sp.	x	x	x		
Ceratomyopsis undulata (Morris and Lycett)					x		sp.
Chlamys (Radulopecten) hemicostata Morris and Lycett	sp	x	x	x	sp		x
C. (R.) vagans (J. de C. Sowerby)				x			
Coelopis cf. *pulchella* (Lycett)			x				
'Corbula' buckmani Lycett		x					
'Corbula' hulliana Morris				x	x	x	
Costigervillia crassicosta (Morris and Lycett)					x	sp.	
Cucullaea sp.	x	x	x		x		
Cuspidaria bathonica Cox and Arkell		x		sp.	x		
C. aff. *ibbetsoni* (Morris)		x			x		
Eocallista antiopa (Thevenin)		?		x	x		
Eomiodon angulatus (Morris and Lycett)		x	x	sp.	x		
E. fimbriatus (Lycett)					x		
E. nortonensis (Cox)		x					
Falcimytilus sublaevis (J. de C. Sowerby)		x	x		x		
Fimbria lajoyei (d'Archiac)				x	x		
Gervillella monotis (J. A. Eudes Deslongchamps)		sp.	x				
G. ovata (J. de C. Sowerby)		x	x	x	x		
Gresslya sp.				x	?		
Homomya gibbosa (J. Sowerby)				sp.	x		x
Inoperna plicatus (J. Sowerby)		x	x	x	x		
Isocyprina depressiuscula (Morris and Lycett)		x		x	sp.		
Isognomon isognomonoides (Stahl)	?	x		sp.	x		
I. oxoniensis (Paris)		x					
I. (Mytiloperna) murchisonii (Forbes)		x			sp.		
I. patchamensis Cox		x					
Limatula gibbosa (J. Sowerby)					x		?
Limopsis minima (J. de C. Sowerby)		x			sp.		
Liostrea (Praeexogyra) acuminata (J. Sowerby)		x					
L. hebridica (Forbes)	x	x	x	x	x	x	
L. hebridica elongata (Dutertre)		x	x	x	x		
L. subrugulosa (Morris and Lycett)					x		
L. undosa (Phillips)				x			
Lithophaga fabella (J. A. Eudes-Deslongchamps)	sp.				x		
Lopha costata (J. de C. Sowerby)				x			
L. gregarea (J. Sowerby)	x		x				
'Lucina' bellona d'Orbigny		?	x		x	sp.	sp.
Mactromya impressa (Morris and Lycett)		sp.			x		
M. varicosa (J. Sowerby)		x		x			
Meleagrinella echinata (Wm. Smith)							x
Modiolus cf. *anatinus* Wm. Smith					x		
Modiolus imbricatus (J. Sowerby)	sp.	x	x	x	x	x	
M. cf. *lonsdalei* (Morris and Lycett)				x	x		x
Myoconcha cf. *actaeon* Morris and Lycett					x		
Myophorella signata (L. Agassiz)	x			sp.	sp.		
Nanogyra crassa (Wm. Smith)	x				x		
Neocrassina sp.		x		x			
Osteomya sp.					x		
Pachymya (Arcomya) unioniformis (Morris and Lycett)					x		

	CNL	SHB	TS	HMB	WL	FM	LCb
Parallelodon bynei Cox and Arkell				x	x		
P. hirsonensis (d'Archiac)			x	x	x		
Pholadomya (Bucardiomya) deltoidea (J. Sowerby)					x		
P. (B.) lirata (J. Sowerby)		x	x	x	x		
P. (B.) socialis Morris and Lycett				x			
Pinna sp.					x		
Placunopsis socialis Morris and Lycett	x	x	x	x	x	x	
Plagiostoma cardiiformis J. Sowerby	x	sp.	sp.	x			
P. subcardiiformis (Greppin)	x			x	x		
Pleuromya subelongata (d'Orbigny)	sp.	sp.	sp.	x	x		
P. uniformis (J. Sowerby)				x	x		x
Plicatula sp.	x			x	x		
Praeconia rhomboidalis (Phillips)					x		
Pronoella lycetti (Cossmann)					x		
Protocardia buckmani (Morris and Lycett)		x	?				
P. citrinoidea (Phillips)							x
P. lingulata (Lycett)					x		
P. lycetti (Rollier)				x	x		
P. stricklandi (Morris and Lycett)		x		x	x		
Pseudolimea duplicata (J. de C. Sowerby)						sp.	x
Pseudotrapezium aff. *cordiforme* (Deshayes)					x		sp.
Pteroperna costatula (J. A. Eudes-Deslongchamps)		?		x	x		
Quenstedtia sp.					x		
Sphaeriola oolithica (Rollier)				x	x		
Tancredia brevis Morris and Lycett		sp.		x			
T. extensa Lycett	x		x		x		
T. gibbosa Lycett				x			
T. similis Lycett				x			
T. subcurtansata Lycett	x						
T. truncata Lycett	x						
Thracia curtansata Morris and Lycett		sp.			x		
Trigonia pullus J. de C. Sowerby	sp.	x	x	x	x		
Vaugonia flecta (Morris and Lycett)					x		
V. impressa (Broderip)					x		
V. moretoni (Morris and Lycett)	x		x	x	x		
V. producta (Lycett)	?						

GASTROPODA

	CNL	SHB	TS	HMB	WL	FM	LCb
Ampullospira sharpei (Morris and Lycett)				sp.	x		
A. stricklandi (Morris and Lycett)					x		
Aphanoptyxis ardleyensis Arkell					x		
A. bladonensis Arkell					x		
A. eulimoides (Lycett)		sp.	sp.		x		
Ataphrus heliciformis (Morris and Lycett)		x	x				
A. labadyei (d'Archiac)		x					
Bactroptyxis bacillus (d'Orbigny)					x		
Bathonella langtonensis (Hudleston)		x					
Chartroniella bunburii (Morris and Lycett)					x		
Cossmannea (Eunerinea) eudesii (Morris and Lycett)		x	x	x	x		
'Cylindrites' sp.	x				x		
Endiaplocus cf. *roissyi* (d'Archiac)					x		
Fibula phasianoides (Morris and Lycett)		sp.			x		
Globularia formosa (Morris and Lycett)				x	x		
G. morrisi Cox and Arkell					x		
Katosira sp.		x			x		
Naricopsina sp.				x	x		
Neridomus anglica Cox and Arkell				sp.	x		
N. cooksonii (J. A. Eudes-Deslongchamps)					x		
N. costulata (Deshayes)					x		
Nerinella sp.		x	?		x		
Pleurotomaria sp.					x		
Procerithium (Xystrella) tancredi (Cox and Arkell)			x				
Promathildia (Teretrina) sp.					x		
Pseudomelania communis (Morris and Lycett)				sp.	x		
Ptychomphalus?		x					

	CNL	SHB	TS	HMB	WL	FM	LCb
NAUTILOIDEA							
Procymatoceras sp.		x					
AMMONOIDEA							
Oppelia (Oxycerites) limosa (S. S. Buckman)	x						
ECHINODERMATA							
Acrosalenia hemicidaroides Wright		x		x			x
A. pustulata Forbes					x		
Clypeus mülleri Wright		sp.		x	x		
C. cf. *rimosus* L. Agassiz			x		x		
Nucleolites clunicularis (Wm. Smith)							x
Nucleolites griesbachii (Wright)		x	sp.	x			
Pseudodiadema sp.			x				
cidarid radioles			x				

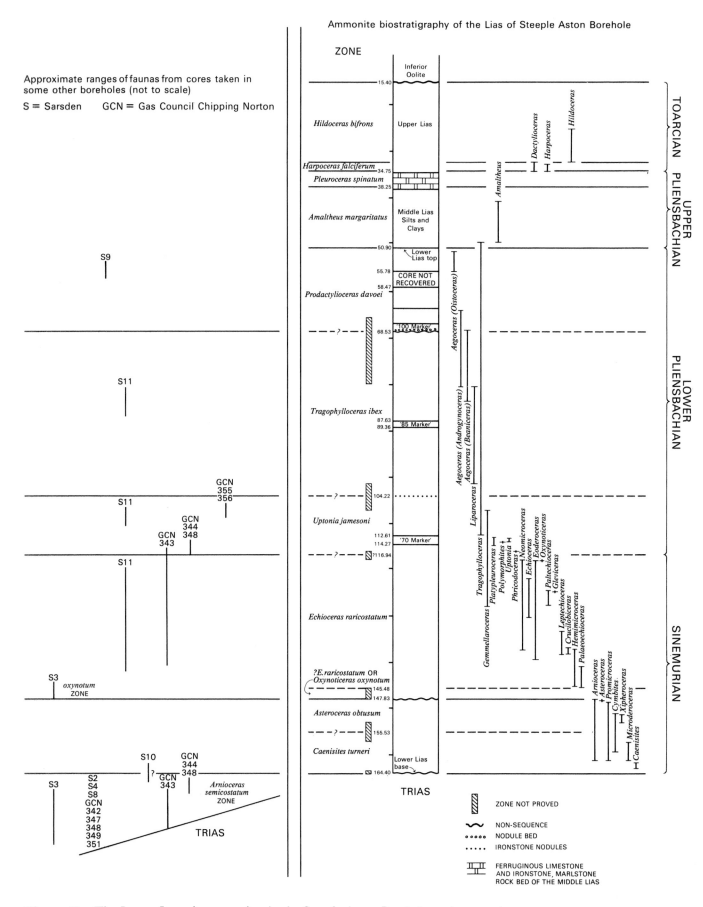

Figure 45   The Lower Jurassic ammonites in the Steeple Aston Borehole and ammonite zones proved in some boreholes

APPENDIX 2

Triassic palynology

G. Warrington

Palynological work on the Triassic rocks of the Chipping Norton district involved the examination of samples from eleven boreholes within the district (Figure 46); the results from one of these, Steeple Aston, have been documented elsewhere (Warrington, 1977). The results obtained from a further thirteen boreholes in adjoining districts (Figure 46) have also been taken into consideration.

Sherwood Sandstone Group

The few samples from the Bromsgrove Sandstone Formation in the district were devoid of indigenous palynomorphs; material from a possible representative of this unit in the Sarsden No. 10 Borehole yielded reworked Carboniferous miospores (Table 4). Miospores assigned a middle Triassic age have been recovered from the Bromsgrove Sandstone Formation in the Withycombe Farm Borehole (Warrington, 1978), about 1 km to the north of the present district, and also in the Stowell Park and Knight's Lane boreholes (Table 5; and Warrington, 1970, *in* Williams and Whittaker, 1974); the formation in the Chipping Norton district is presumably of

similar age. Middle Triassic miospores occur as reworked components in late Triassic assemblages from the Cotham Member of the Penarth Group (see below).

Mercia Mudstone Group

Except in the Steeple Aston Borehole (Warrington, 1977), this unit has proved devoid of palynomorphs in the district (Table 4). Sporadic indeterminate bisaccate miospores of late Triassic aspect were recovered from beds below the Blue Anchor Formation in the Steeple Aston borehole. The Blue Anchor Formation in that borehole yielded sporadic specimens of the miospores *Classopollis torosus*, *Ovalipollis pseudoalatus*, *?Rhaetipollis germanicus* and *Ricciisporites tuberculatus*, and the dinoflagellate cyst *Rhaetogonyaulax rhaetica*. Though these mainly late Triassic taxa are known from the Blue Anchor Formation elsewhere in England, they are more typical of the Penarth Group, and the Steeple Aston specimens may be derived from that Group (Warrington, 1977); there may not, therefore, be any direct evidence for the age of the Mercia

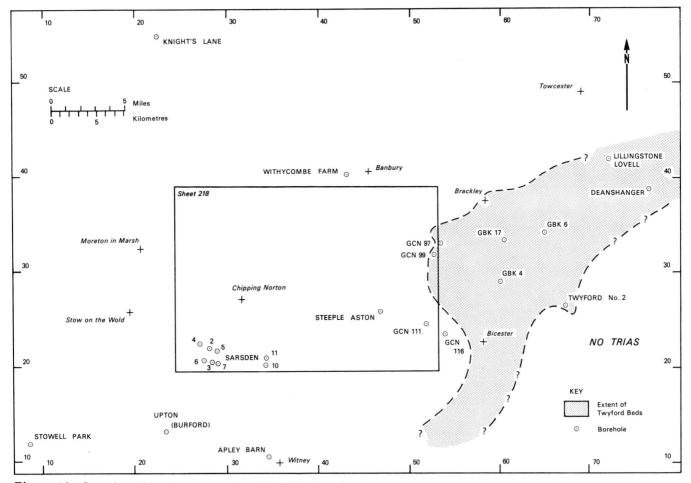

Figure 46 Location of boreholes examined for Triassic palynomorphs

Mudstone Group in the Chipping Norton district.

In the adjoining Stratford-upon-Avon district, the Mercia Mudstone Group is inferred to include deposits of late Triassic (Carnian) age (Warrington, p.21 *in* Williams and Whittaker, 1974). This is the nearest point to the Chipping Norton district at which an age has been assigned to any part of this succession with justification and confidence. Samples from the Apley Barn (Witney) Borehole proved barren, and those from the Upton (Burford) Borehole (Table 5) yielded specimens which are of no stratigraphic value.

Within the district the Mercia Mudstone succession is probably most complete in the north-west; towards the south-east the younger beds are believed to be progressively overstepped and cut out at the sub-Penarth Group unconformity (p.13). This contention

is supported by the evidence, from the presence of reworked middle Triassic miospores in late Triassic assemblages from the Penarth Group, of erosion of the Mercia Mudstone and Sherwood Sandstone groups during late Triassic times. Thus, it may be inferred that only the older part of the Mercia Mudstone Group is present in the Steeple Aston borehole and that successively younger deposits appear progressively north-westwards from that site.

Penarth Group

Palynomorph assemblages comprising miospores and organic-walled microplankton associated, in some instances, with tectinous test linings of foraminifera (Figure 47) have been recovered from the Penarth Group in the Steeple Aston borehole (Warrington,

Table 4
Boreholes examined for Triassic palynomorphs in the Chipping Norton district

Borehole	National Grid reference	Lithostratigraphic unit sampled	Samples Total	Productive
Steeple Aston	SP 4687 2586	Penarth Group		
		Langport Member	2	2
		Cotham Member	4	4(?RC)
		Westbury Formation	3	3
		Mercia Mudstone Group (including Blue Anchor Formation)	4	4
Sarsden No.2	SP 2768 2220	Mercia Mudstone Group		
		Blue Anchor Formation	3	0
		Sherwood Sandstone Group		
		Bromsgrove Sandstone Formation	1	0
Sarsden No.3	SP 2807 2074	Penarth Group		
		Cotham Member	2	2
		Sherwood Sandstone Group		
		Bromsgrove Sandstone Formation	1	0
Sarsden No.4	SP 2695 2258	Penarth Group		
		Langport Member	1	1
		Cotham Member	2	2(RT + ?RC)
		Westbury Formation	3	3
		Mercia Mudstone Group		
		Blue Anchor Formation	1	0
Sarsden No.5	SP 2873 2194	?Mercia Mudstone Group	1	0
Sarsden No.6	SP 2736 2095	Penarth Group		
		Cotham Member	3	3
		Westbury Formation	2	2
		Mercia Mudstone Group		
		Blue Anchor Formation	1	0
Sarsden No.7	SP 2858 2065	?Mercia Mudstone Group	2	0
Sarsden No.10	SP 3420 2040	Mercia Mudstone Group		
		Blue Anchor Formation	1	0
		?Sherwood Sandstone Group	1	1(RC)
Sarsden No.11	SP 3417 2110	?Mercia Mudstone Group	3	0
GCN 99	SP 5262 3197	Twyford Beds	1	0
GCN 111	SP 5182 2455	Penarth Group		
		Cotham Member	5	5(RT + ?RC/P)

(RT)   Reworked Triassic miospores present
(RC)   Reworked Carboniferous miospores present
(RC/P) Reworked Carboniferous miospores and Palaeozoic acritarchs present

Table 5 Boreholes examined for Triassic palynomorphs in adjoining districts

Geological Survey district; borehole	National Grid reference	Lithostratigraphic unit sampled	Samples Total	Productive
Stratford-upon-Avon (Sheet 200)				
Knight's Lane	SP 2242 5497	Mercia Mudstone Group	14	0
		Sherwood Sandstone Group		
		Bromsgrove Sandstone Formation	15	1
Banbury (Sheet 201)				
Withycombe Farm	SP 4319 4017	Penarth Group		
		Langport Member	5	5
		Cotham Member	14	13
		Westbury Formation	6	6
		Mercia Mudstone Group		
		(including Blue Anchor Formation)	7	2
		Sherwood Sandstone Group		
		Bromsgrove Sandstone Formation	2	2
Towcester (Sheet 202)				
Lillingstone Lovell (Towcester No.2)	SP 7197 4197	Twyford Beds	3	3(RC)
Deanshanger (Towcester No.10)	SP 7652 3880	Twyford Beds	9	0
Buckingham (Sheet 219)				
GCN 97	SP 5330 3320	Twyford Beds	1	0
GCN 116	SP 5380 2350	Penarth Group		
		Langport Member	1	1
GBK 4	SP 6007 2909	Twyford Beds	1	0
GBK 6	SP 6520 3413	Twyford Beds	2	0
GBK 17	SP 6059 3330	Twyford Beds	2	0
Twyford No.2	SP 6760 2650	Twyford Beds	9	2
Cirencester (Sheet 235)				
Upton (Burford)	SP 2315 1313	Mercia Mudstone Group (including Blue Anchor Formation)	5	2
		Sherwood Sandstone Group		
		Bromsgrove Sandstone Formation	1	1(RC)
Stowell Park	SP 084 118	Sherwood Sandstone Group		
		Bromsgrove Sandstone Formation	1	1
Witney (Sheet 236)				
Apley Barn (Witney)	SP 3438 1066	Mercia Mudstone Group (including Blue Anchor Formation)	4	0

(RC) Reworked Carboniferous miospores present

1977) and in the GCN 111 and Sarsden No. 3, No. 4 and No. 6 boreholes (Table 4). These assemblages are of late Triassic (Rhaetian) age and are comparable in composition and stratigraphic distribution of taxa with those documented from the same unit elsewhere in Britain, for example, in the Withycombe Farm Borehole (Warrington, 1978) and the Upton (Burford) Borehole (Orbell, 1973).

Assemblages from the Westbury Formation are characterised by associations of the miospores *Classopollis torosus*, *Ovalipollis pseudoalatus*, *Rhaetipollis germanicus* and *Ricciisporites tuberculatus* with the dinoflagellate cyst *Rhaetogonyaulax rhaetica*. The presence of *R. rhaetica* with other organic-walled microplankton (acritarchs and Tasmanaceae) and remains of foraminifera supports the customary interpretation of this formation as marine in origin.

Assemblages of similar character persist into the overlying Cotham Member but are commonly more diverse in composition (Figure 47). In the higher part of this member, taxa dominant in Westbury Formation and lower Cotham Member assemblages decline in abundance (see Warrington, 1977, fig. 23). The Cotham Member is commonly regarded as having continental affinities, but

the presence of dinoflagellate cysts, acritarchs and remains of foraminifera in assemblages from that unit is evidence for its having formed in an environment connected to a marine source. A peak of relative abundance of *Rhaetogonyaulax rhaetica* occurs in the lower part of the member at Steeple Aston (Warrington, 1977, fig. 23); in the Upton Borehole (Orbell, 1973, fig. 4) it is partly within the Westbury Formation but largely within the Cotham Member; at Withycombe Farm (Warrington, 1978, fig. 10c) specimens occur abundantly in both units.

The similar associations of organic-walled microplankton and the remains of foraminifera in assemblages from both the Cotham Member and the more obviously marine Westbury Formation, make it evident that considerable environmental affinity exists between these facies. Indications of non-marine depositional environments (e.g. *Euestheria*) in the Cotham Member are usually regarded as indigenous to that facies. The possibility that such remains were transported from a non-marine environment into one dominated by marine influences, or that they reflect only minor incursions of a non-marine environment into one of predominantly marine character, should be considered.

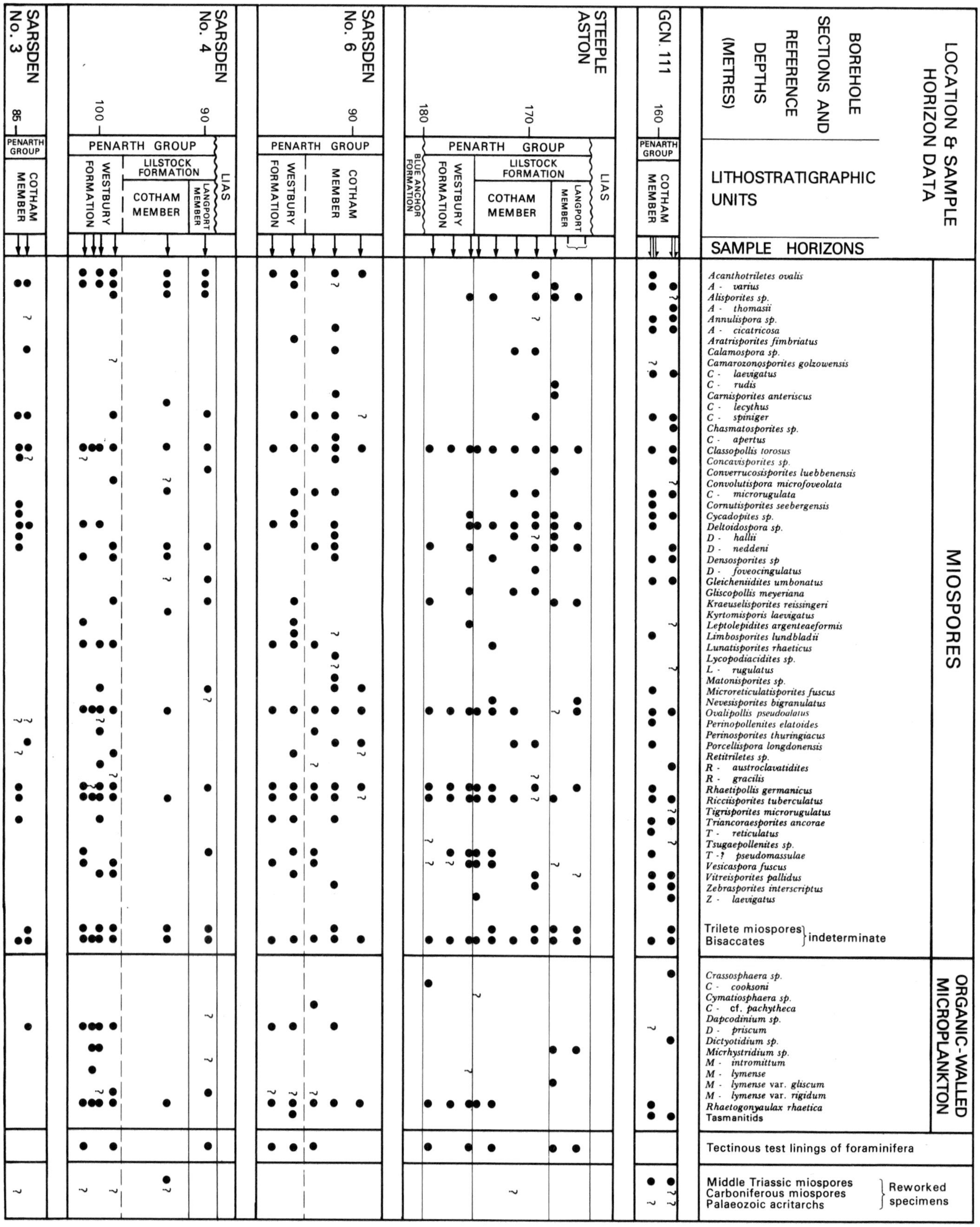

Figure 47   Distribution of Triassic palynomorphs

Assemblages from the Langport Member are less diverse than those from lower beds in the Penarth Group. In the Steeple Aston borehole (Warrington, 1977, fig. 23) they are dominated by miospores, principally *Classopollis torosus* and *Kraeuselisporites reissingeri*, and the sparse organic-walled microplankton associations present largely comprise acanthomorph acritarchs. Reworked middle Triassic miospore associations including *Alisporites grauvogeli*, *A. toralis, Angustisulcites gorpii, A. klausii, Protodiploxypinus potoniei, Tsugaepollenites oriens, Tubantiapollenites schulzii, Verrucosisporites thuringiacus* and *Voltziaceaesporites heteromorpha* have been observed in assemblages from the Cotham Member in the GCN 111 and Sarsden No. 4 boreholes (Table 4); they indicate erosion of the Triassic sequence, locally at least, to the level of the Bromsgrove Sandstone Formation, during the late Triassic. From this it may be conjectured that the Mercia Mudstone Group and possibly the Sherwood Sandstone Group originally extended farther south-eastwards on to the London Platform than is now the case, and that only the older beds of the Mercia Mudstone succession remain in the south-eastern part of the Chipping Norton district (see above and p.13).

The Twyford Beds are present only in a small area in the east (Figures 12, 46) where they were examined in The Gas Council GCN 99 borehole (Table 4) but proved devoid of palynomorphs. The Twyford Beds were sampled more extensively from boreholes farther east, in the Buckingham and Towcester districts (Figure 46 and Table 5). A sparse assemblage of reworked Carboniferous miospores associated with some possibly indigenous miospores and an acritarch was recovered from the Lillingstone Lovell Borehole; no stratigraphic conclusions can be based upon this material. Two sparse assemblages were recovered from the Twyford Beds in the Twyford No. 2 Borehole. One, comprising the miospores *Alisporites* cf. *thomasii, Classopollis torosus, Kraeuselisporites reissingeri, Leptolepidites argenteaeformis, Retitriletes sp.* and *Tsugaepollenites sp.*, in association with organic-walled microplankton (*Cymatiosphaera* cf. *pachytheca* and *Tasmanites suevicus*) and tectinous test linings of foraminifera, was recovered from a depth of 129.24 m, near the top of the formation. The second, comprising the miospores *Acanthotriletes ovalis, Calamospora sp., Chasmatosporites apertus, Classopollis torosus, Gliscopollis meyeriana, Retitriletes clavatoides* and *Tsugaepollenites sp.*, in association with the polygonomorph acritarch *Veryhachium*, was obtained from 138.99 m, near the base of the unit.

The presence of these palynomorphs indicates that the Twyford Beds are no older than the Langport Member of the Penarth Group and may be a correlative of that member, though the possibility that they equate, at least partly, with the basal (pre-Hettangian) beds of the Lias, or even with beds of early Jurassic age, is not precluded. That the Twyford Beds formed in a marine depositional environment is indicated by the presence of organic-walled microplankton and the remains of foraminifera in the palynomorph assemblages.

Author citations for cited palynomorph taxa:

Acanthotriletes ovalis Nilsson 1958
A. varius Nilsson 1958
Alisporites grauvogeli Klaus 1964
A. thomasii (Couper) Nilsson 1958
A toralis (Leschik) Clarke 1965
Angustisulcites gorpii Visscher 1966
A. klausii Freudenthal 1964
Annulispora cicatricosa (Rogalska) Morbey 1975

Aratrisporites fimbriatus (Klaus) Mädler emend. Morbey 1975
Camarozonosporites golzowensis Schulz 1967
C. laevigatus Schulz 1967
C. rudis (Leschik) Klaus 1960
Carnisporites anteriscus Morbey 1975
C. lecythus Morbey 1975
C. spiniger (Leschik) Morbey 1975
Chasmatosporites apertus (Rogalska) Nilsson 1958
Classopollis torosus (Reissinger) Balme 1957
Converrucosisporites luebbenensis Schulz 1967
Convolutispora microfoveolata Schulz 1967
C. microrugulata Schulz 1967
Cornutisporites seebergensis Schulz 1962
Crassosphaera cooksoni Kriván-Hutter 1963
Cymatiosphaera cf. *pachytheca* Eisenack 1957
Dapcodinium priscum Evitt 1961
Deltoidospora hallii Miner 1935
D. neddeni (Potonié) Orbell 1973
Densosporites foveocingulatus Schulz 1967
Gleicheniidites umbonatus (Bolkhovitina) Schulz 1967
Gliscopollis meyeriana (Klaus) Venkatachala 1966
Kraeuselisporites reissingeri (Harris) Morbey 1975
Kyrtomisporis laevigatus Mädler 1964
Leptolepidites argenteaeformis (Bolkhovitina) Morbey 1975
Limbosporites lundbladii Nilsson 1958
Lunatisporites rhaeticus (Schulz) Warrington 1974
Lycopodiacidites rugulatus (Couper) Schulz 1967
Micrhystridium intromittum Wall 1965
M. lymense Wall 1965
M. lymense var. *gliscum* Wall 1965
M. lymense var. *rigidum* Wall 1965
Microreticulatisporites fuscus (Nilsson) Morbey 1975
Nevesisporites bigranulatus (Levet-Carette) Morbey 1975
Ovalipollis pseudoalatus (Thiergart) Schuurman 1976
Perinopollenites elatoides Couper 1958
Perinosporites thuringiacus Schulz 1962
Porcellispora longdonensis (Clarke) Scheuring emend. Morbey 1975
Protodiploxypinus potoniei (Mädler) Scheuring 1970
Retitriletes austroclavatidites (Cookson) Döring, Krutzsch, Mai and Schulz 1963
R. clavatoides (Couper) Döring, Krutzsch, Mai and Schulz 1963
R. gracilis (Nilsson) Döring, Krutzsch, Mai and Schulz 1963
Rhaetipollis germanicus Schulz 1967
Rhaetogonyaulax rhaetica (Sarjeant) Loeblich and Loeblich emend. Harland, Morbey and Sarjeant 1975
Ricciisporites tuberculatus Lundblad 1954
Tasmanites suevicus (Eisenack) Wall 1965
Tigrisporites microrugulatus Schulz 1967
Triancoraesporites ancorae (Reinhardt) Schulz 1967
T. reticulatus Schulz 1962
Tsugaepollenites oriens Klaus 1964
T.? pseudomassulae (Mädler) Morbey 1975
Tubantiapollenites schulzii Visscher 1966
Verrucosisporites thuringiacus Mädler 1964
Vesicaspora fuscus (Pautsch) Morbey 1975
Vitreisporites pallidus (Reissinger) Nilsson 1958
Voltziaceaesporites heteromorpha Klaus 1964
Zebrasporites interscriptus (Thiergart) Klaus 1960
Z. laevigatus (Schulz) Schulz 1967

APPENDIX 3

Petrography of the Marlstone Rock Bed

J. R. Hawkes

The following petrographical descriptions are largely based on specimens from surface exposures. In accordance with the terminology introduced by Taylor (1949, p.5), the Marlstone Rock Bed ironstone of the Chipping Norton district is broadly a calcitic, sideritic, chamositic, chamosite-oolite, that commonly grades into calcitic, sideritic, chamositic, chamosite-oolite limestone where fossil debris is abundant (Plate 13). The shelly limestone material (E29687, 29692, 29697, 29708, 29745, 29747) forms bands and scattered lenses (the 'jacks' of quarrymen), ranging from 0.05 to 0.6 m thick, in dominantly siderite-bearing, chamosite-oolite rock (E23617, 29703, 29706, 29725).

The base of the formation is generally conglomeratic, consisting of rounded fragments of shelly limestone, chamosite-mudstone and collophane, abundant shell debris, scattered pockets of chamosite and sideritised chamosite-ooliths, scattered rhombohedral siderite crystals, irregular patches of chamosite-mudstone, and some detrital quartz (E19962, 19964). Rolled chamosite-mudstone fragments, some containing scattered chamosite ooliths and calcite shell debris, also occur in shelly lenses at higher levels (E29695, 29732, 29739).

Along the western margin of the ironstone field between Lower Brailes [315 390] and Kingham Hill School [268 263] and in the south at Steeple Aston [476 261], chamositic material tends to be relatively scarce. The rocks here are composed chiefly of calcite (occurring as shell debris, ooliths, sparry crystals and, in some instances, as micrite), with subordinate siderite and, typically, 5 to 10 per cent detrital quartz (E19624–5, 19768–9, 19886a, 19890). A similar calcite- and siderite-rich, chamosite-poor specimen (E29735), with 10 to 20 per cent detrital quartz and some muscovite and feldspar, was recovered from the Deddington area where local thinning occurs (Figure 20). Although the specimen is from the basal 15 cm of the formation, it resembles the western and southern marginal facies rather than the basal conglomerate. To the east the ironstone field passes beneath younger Jurassic beds; consequently, the marginal facies is not exposed.

In describing most specimens it is necessary to employ the additional prefix limonitic, since much of the chamosite and siderite in the Marlstone Rock Bed has been oxidised. Some of the oxidation seems to have been penecontemporaneous (pre-burial), in that the nucleii of chamosite-ooliths commonly consist of single limonitised chamosite crystals (E29707–8, 29725, 29737, 29739, 29742). A few ooliths show alternating concentric zones of chamosite and limonitised chamosite (E29698). Several other features suggest penecontemporaneous oxidation; for example, the presence of limonitised chamosite-ooliths and flakes in fresh chamosite mud (E23617, 29743), the appearance of limonitised chamosite-mud fragments (false ooliths) in fresh chamosite-oolite (E29711), or the juxtaposition of large rolled chamosite and limonitised mud fragments in the basal conglomerate and in shelly bands at higher levels. In some instances, limonitised chamosite-ooliths occur in calcitic matrices that also contain unoxidised siderite (E29737). Further oxidation probably occurred at the close of Middle Lias times when the top of the Rock Bed suffered erosion (Edmonds and others, 1965, p.63).

Most of the limonite, however, results from recent weathering. Movement of groundwater in the zone of oxidation has caused an effective redistribution of much of the iron contained in the original chamosite and siderite, at the same time partially leaching calcite from the rock. Thus the most heavily limonitised material is found to contain a higher proportion of iron, silica and aluminium, but less lime than fresher chamosite-siderite rock (Whitehead and others, pp.167–168). In extreme cases, specimens consist of scattered calcite shell debris in a dark brown, or locally red, limonitic matrix (E29715–7). Such material provides the highest grade ore.

Mineralogy and textural features

Chamosite According to Edmonds (*in* Edmonds and others, 1965, pp.71–73), the green, iron aluminium silicate (chamosite) present in the Banbury sector ironstone field is the kaolinite type, and occurs in both monoclinic and hexagonal forms (Youell, 1958). Mr R. J. Merriman reports that a chamosite sample (E29725) from the southern part of the field also shows a kaolinite structure (X4810). As in the north, the chamosite appears as scattered micaceous crystals (typically 0.1–0.2 mm across), and in a very finely-divided state as mudstone and as a component of ooliths. Spherulitic developments of the mineral occur, but are rare (E29739, 29742).

Plate 13 Photomicrographs of thin sections from the Marlstone Rock Bed

Fig.1. Shelly limestone, containing limonitised chamosite ooliths, false ooliths and flakes, and also rolled pellets of partly limonitised chamosite oolite-bearing chamosite mud. E 29697, Sydenham area, Borehole No.13, depth 7′11″ (approx. 2.4 m). Plane polarised light, × 31. Average grain size: 0.27 mm.

Fig.2. Chamosite mud, ooliths (partly limonitised) and flakes set in a sparry calcite matrix. Granular siderite is common in areas of chamosite mud. E 29707, Sydenham area, Borehole No.17, depth 16′10″ (approx. 5.2 m). Plane polarised light, × 125. Average grain size: 0.30 mm.

Fig.3. Rolled chamosite flakes (some with damaged overgrowths of chamosite oolite), chamosite ooliths and false ooliths set in a sparry calcite matrix containing scattered idomorphic rhombs of siderite. Some of the calcite material is fossil debris with chamosite infilling of pores. Much of the chamosite in the ooliths and false ooliths has been replaced by granular siderite. E 29711, Sydenham area, Borehole No.21, depth 17′6″ (approx 5.3 m). Plane polarised light, × 125. Average grain size: 0.25 mm.

Fig.4. Quartz fragments (clear, moderately high relief), scattered chamosite flakes (some partially limonitised) and false ooliths (one replaced by granular siderite), and clacitic fossil debris set in a calcite matrix. E 29746, Iron Down Hill, Borehole No.25, depth 11′2″ (approx 5.36 m), × 125. Average grain size: 0.14 mm.

Fig.5. Marginal facies. Scattered quartz fragments, granular sideritised calcite ooliths and fossil debris, subidiomorphic crystals of limonitised siderite and limonitised flakes of chamosite set in a calcite matrix. E 19768, Small Quarry, 548, 64 m WNW of Long Leys Barn, Lower Brailes. Crossed nicols, × 125. Average grain size: 0.25 mm.

Fig.6. Recrystallised calcite ooliths, originally developed on quartz fragments, set in a matrix of limonitised siderite. E 29704, Sydenham area, Borehole No.17, depth 6′5″ (approx. 2.0 m). Crossed nicols, × 125.

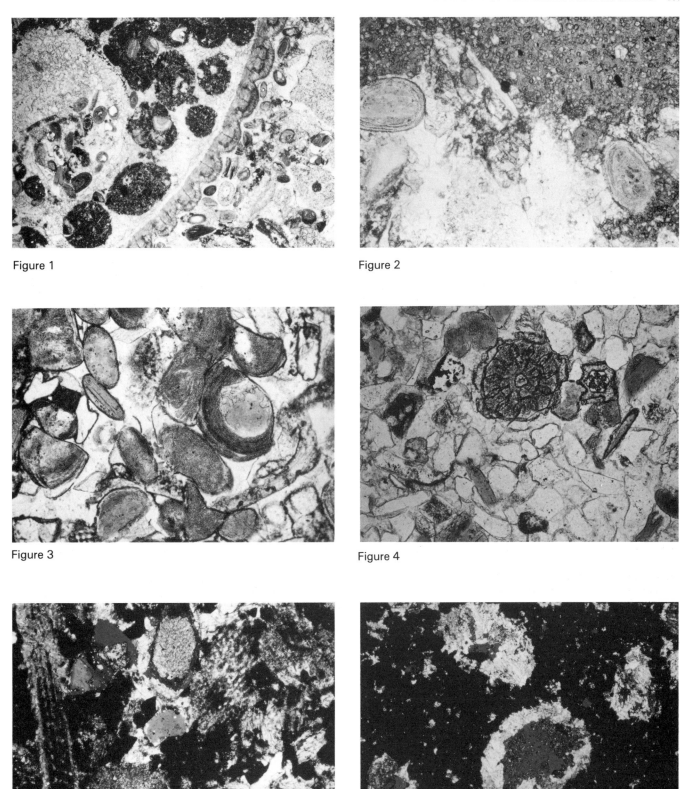

Figure 1

Figure 2

Figure 3

Figure 4

Figure 5

Figure 6

Plate 13   Photomicrographs of thin sections from the Marlstone Rock Bed. For details, see opposite

Micaceous chamosite crystals tend to have rounded outlines indicative of rolling, and some are broken. They commonly show signs of oxidation to limonite. A few crystals are present in the calcite or chamosite-mudstone matrices of specimens (E29711), but the majority are contained in oolith-rich portions. Many are thinly coated with finely divided chamosite (E23621, 29706-8, 29739, 29742); a few with granular siderite (E23617, 29711).

The finely-divided chamosite mudstone occurs as irregular patches, chiefly in the calcitic parts of specimens (E29706, 29731, 29737). It is also present as partial fillings in shells (E29727) and in the pore canals of echinoderm fragments (E29707, 29710-11, 29726, 29739). Rolled fragments of mudstone (false ooliths), ranging from 0.2-4.0 mm across, are common among concentrations of ooliths (E29711, 29718, 29725-6).

In the ooliths, the finely divided chamosite component consists of small flakes arranged with their basal cleavage planes tangential to the concentric structure of the bodies. In some cases these flakes constitute the whole oolith (E29726, 29729), but in most instances they form the outer zones around nuclei consisting of false-ooliths (E29726, 29729, 29739) or rounded micaceous chamosite crystals (E29703, 29739). The ooliths are mostly ovoid, typically measuring 0.1 to 0.2 mm along their longest axis. Some are flattened due to compaction; others are broken, suggesting damage during transport. Their abundance in specimens varies between the extremes of a few scattered individuals in a chamosite-mudstone or calcite matrix (E29708, 29729), to concentrations in which the individuals are so closely packed (but not necessarily deformed) that relatively little matrix is visible between them (E29706, 29725).

Siderite   Edmonds (*in* Edmonds and others, 1965, pp.68-69) states that values for the refractive index (ω) of most unoxidised siderite samples from the Banbury area range between 1.785 and 1.807. Comparing these values with those of spectrographically analysed material, he concluded that the siderite is a mixed carbonate with an approximate percentage composition $FeCO_3$ 83 per cent, $CaCO_3$ 9 per cent, $MgCO_3$ 8 per cent and $MnCO_3$ 0.65 per cent.

The siderite occurs in finely divided granular form, and as scattered idiomorphic crystals (typically 0.1 to 0.25 mm across) that commonly show rhombohedral outlines. The granular material locally replaces calcite in some parts of fossil fragments (E29727, 29730), but it is chiefly a replacement of the finely divided chamosite comprising ooliths (E29697, 29707, 29711, 29749), fossil fillings (E29745) and matrix mudstone (E29707, 29726, 29730, 29735, 29742). In a few examples micaceous chamosite crystals are partly replaced by granular siderite (E29736). The scattered, larger idiomorphic siderite crystals appear mainly among the recrystallised fossil debris of the matrix, there apparently replacing calcite (E29697, 29736, 29742, 29747). Similar crystals in the oolitic parts of specimens probably result from the recrystallisation of fine granular siderite (E29697, 29711, 29731).

The fine granular siderite commonly shows partial alteration to limonite, yet in certain specimens idiomorphic crystals in the matrix are fresh (E29726). Selective limonitisation seems an improbable explanation for this feature. It is more likely that the development of the granular carbonate and its subsequent oxidation occurred before final accumulation and burial of the host fossil and chamositic material, while the idiomorphic siderite of the matrix (like that associated with oolitic parts of specimens) formed during later diagenetic processes.

Limonite   Analytical and X-ray work (Taylor, 1949, pp.2-3; Dunham *in* Whitehead and others, 1952, p.23) indicates that the limonite of Jurassic ironstones consists of crystalline iron oxide (goëthite), kaolinite and, possibly, amorphous iron oxide. The limonite of the Marlstone Rock Bed is brown, orange-brown and red-brown in colour, and results from the oxidation and hydration of chamosite and siderite. Although there are numerous examples in which individual crystals, ooliths and mudstone patches of chamosite or siderite are pseudomorphed by the oxide, the location of much of the limonite suggests extensive redistribution of iron. Some specimens consist only of scattered calcite shell fragments in a limonitic matrix (E29715-7).

Calcite   From a study of refractive index values, Edmonds (*in* Edmonds and others, 1965, p.74) concluded that the calcite of the Marlstone Rock Bed is generally pure ($\omega < 1.659$). He suggested that anomalous higher values might be due to the presence of small amounts of dolomite and calcium manganese carbonate.

Except in the case of finely-divided calcite which coats occasional ooliths or false ooliths (E29697, 29739), there is no evidence to suggest penecontemporaneous precipitation of the carbonate. The calcite appears to be derived almost entirely from fossil debris. The debris has suffered diagenetic recrystallisation, and individual crystals typically range from 0.002 mm to about 1.5 mm in size (E29720, 29727, 29735, 29739). Some fragments, notably crinoid ossicles and echinoid plates, consist of single crystals 2-3 mm across.

Numerous chamosite flakes contain calcite along cleavage fractures (E29697, 29707, 29711, 29723). Calcite also appears in concentric shrinkage cracks in many chamosite and sideritised chamosite ooliths (E29707, 29723), and in the central parts of broken ooliths (E29707, 29723, 29731, 29739). Some of this carbonate may represent fossil material which acted as nucleii for chamosite ooliths (E29707, 29737), but most was probably introduced during the early stages of diagenesis. The calcite in a few of the ooliths has been replaced by idiomorphic siderite (E29697, 29737).

Clay minerals   Clay constituents have been observed in only one specimen (E29732). This material (probably kaolinite) occurs in a limonitised ironstone pebble which also contains detrital quartz and muscovite. However, Taylor (1949, p.2) stated that kaolinite, fine-grained quartz and goëthite are commonly associated with chamosite. Bannister (*in* Taylor) suggested that these minerals result from the alteration of chamosite. Therefore, it is likely that considerable amounts of kaolinite (and finely divided quartz) are present in the limonitic parts of the Rock Bed, although they are not readily seen in thin sections.

Other constituents   The most common accessory mineral is pyrite. It occurs as finely-divided crystal aggregates associated with fossil fragments, or as a replacement of the chamosite comprising ooliths and patches of mudstone (E29697, 29727, 29742). Locally the pyrite is oxidised to limonite (E29736).

Detrital minerals include quartz, feldspar and muscovite. Edmonds (*in* Edmonds and others, 1965, p.74) notes that magnetite is rare in the northern part of the ironstone field. Quartz is present as angular or subangular fragments 0.03 mm to 0.15 mm in diameter (averaging 0.06-0.07 mm) and, along with minor quantities of feldspar and muscovite, is confined chiefly to the basal bed and to the western and southern marginal facies of the Rock Bed (E19825, 19886A, 29735). Rounded fragments of collophane appear in the basal conglomerate.   JRH

APPENDIX 4

BGS boreholes

A. Horton

The formational abstract of boreholes drilled by BGS in the district is given below. Detailed lithological descriptive logs and specimens are available for inspection by arrangement at BGS Keyworth.

The records of all the boreholes drilled by The Gas Council and descriptions of core lengths and specimens from them, and of water wells and boreholes are also available.

Hook Norton (Belleisle Farm) Borehole [3565 3588]

Surface level 147.16 m above OD.
Drilled by Foraky Ltd., 1965. Core examined by A. Horton.

Formational abstract	Thickness	Depth
JURASSIC	m	m
Forest Marble	6.15 +	6.15
White Limestone	10.56	16.71
Hampen Marly Beds	12.55	29.26
Taynton Stone	4.14	33.40
Sharp's Hill Beds	4.09	37.49
Chipping Norton Limestone	1.80	39.29
Clypeus Grit	0.46	39.75
Northampton Sand	11.20	50.95
Upper Lias	seen to 3.61	54.56

Charlton (Camp Farm) Borehole [52905 34870]

Surface level 145.85 m above OD
Drilled by Foraky Ltd., in 1965. Core examined by A. Horton.

Formational abstract	Thickness	Depth
JURASSIC	m	m
Hampen Marly Beds (?'Upper Estuarine Series')	1.83 +	1.83 +
Taynton Stone (?'Upper Estuarine Limestone')	c.5.46	7.29
'Lower Estuarine Series'	c.2.69	9.98
Northampton Sand	c.5.62	15.60
Upper Lias	seen to 5.43 +	21.03

A second borehole was drilled adjacent to the one above but poor core recovery again prevented precise location of the geological boundaries.

Duns Tew (Blue Barn) Borehole [4632 2773]

Surface level 154.84 m above OD.
Drilled by Foraky Ltd., in 1965. Core examined by A. Horton.

Formational abstract	Thickness	Depth
JURASSIC	m	m
Taynton Stone	5.28 +	5.28
Sharp's Hill Beds	3.46	8.74
'Lower Estuarine Series' (base from geophysical logs)	6.35	15.09
Northampton Sand	4.27	19.36
Upper Lias Cephalopod Limestones Member to 40.08 m		

Fish Beds Member to 41.45 m	22.09	41.45
Marlstone Rock Bed	1.68	43.13
Middle Lias Silts and Clays	seen to 3.10	46.43

Ledwell (Manor Farm) Borehole [40932 28209]

Surface level 181.36 m above OD.
Drilled by Foraky Ltd., in 1965. Core examined by A. Horton.

Formational abstract	Thickness	Depth
JURASSIC	m	m
?Taynton Stone	c.4.01 +	4.01
Sharp's Hill Beds	4.68	8.69
Chipping Norton Limestone	5.89	14.58
Clypeus Grit	c.2.29	16.87
Upper Lias	seen to 9.22	26.09

Tadmarton (Camp Farm) Borehole [40678 37830]

Surface level 128.32 m above OD.
Drilled by Foraky Ltd., in 1964. Cores examined by A. Horton.

Formational abstract	Thickness	Depth
JURASSIC	m	m
Cornbrash	1.52 +	1.52
Forest Marble	10.29	11.81
White Limestone	7.98	19.79
Hampen Marly Beds	8.45	28.24
Taynton Stone	5.81	34.05
Sharp's Hill Beds, faulted near base	2.37	36.42
'Lower Estuarine Series' (base from geophysical log)	3.64	40.06
Northampton Sand faulted against Lias	6.27	46.33
Upper Lias	seen to 5.79	52.12

Steeple Aston Borehole [4687 2586]

Surface level 130.7 m above OD.
Drilled by Foraky Ltd., in 1970 – 1. Core examined by E. G. Poole.

Formational abstract	Thickness	Depth
JURASSIC	m	m
Sharp's Hill Beds (including		
Stonesfield Slate	0.91	0.91
'Upper Estuarine Series'	0.53	1.44
Sharp's Hill Beds	1.00	2.44
Core loss (including Chipping Norton Limestone and 'Lower Estuarine Series')	12.34	14.78
Northampton Sand	0.62	15.40
Upper Lias Cephalopod Limestone Member 1.235 m at 34.62 m Transition Bed 0.135 m at base	19.35	34.75
Marlstone Rock Bed	3.50	38.25
Middle Lias Silts and Clays	12.65	50.90
Lower Lias	113.50	164.40

TRIASSIC
Penarth Group

Langport Member	3.60	168.00
Cotham Member	7.16	175.16
Westbury Formation	4.67	179.83
Mercia Mudstone Group	31.98	211.81
Sherwood Sandstone Group	17.17	228.98

CARBONIFEROUS
Upper Coal Measures

Burford Coal Formation	93.46	322.44
Crawley Formation	102.22	424.66
Witney Coal Formation	42.74	467.40
Arenaceous Coal Formation	143.27	610.67

IGNEOUS

Basalt; agglomerate and dolerite	165.25	775.92

DEVONIAN

Holt Farm Group	162.97	938.89
Hopcroft Holt Group	28.01	966.90

IGNEOUS (basalt)	seen to 8.23	975.13

Detailed borehole log published: POOLE, E. G. 1977. Stratigraphy of the Steeple Aston Borehole. *Bull. Geol. Surv. G.B.*, No.57.

APPENDIX 5

Formation levels proved in British Gas Council and British Petroleum boreholes in the Chipping Norton district and its environs

Nearly all the boreholes were drilled by open-hole methods. The geological classification of the sequences proved has been based on examination of rock-bit samples and geophysical logs. Gamma logs were recorded for nearly all the boreholes whilst electrical logs were recorded only in the most important boreholes. Specimens of these cores and those taken in the BGS boreholes (Appendix 3) can be inspected by arrangement at Keyworth. The Formation levels are recorded in metres above and below Ordnance Datum.

Borehole number	National Grid reference	Surface level m AOD	Top Inferior Oolite	Top Upper Lias	Top Middle Lias	Top Lower Lias	100 Marker	85 Marker	70 Marker	Top White Lias	Top Cotham Beds or Twyford Beds[1]	Top Keuper Marl	Top Keuper Sandstone	Top Palaeozoic Floor	Availability of core samples[3]
GBK															
1	59590.36820	110.0		+103.9	+82.6	+72.2	+54.3	+34.4	+9.5						
2	59170.38470	120.4		+112.8	+79.5	+65.5	+49.1	+29.3	+4.3	-50.6[2]					
3	61620.39180	111.9		+106.7	+72.8	+57.3	+42.7	+22.9	-1.5	-53.0	-55.5[1]	-62.2			
4	60070.29090	97.5	+75.0	+65.5	+46.9	+39.6	+21.6	+4.6	-21.3	-46.0	-48.8[1]	-51.8			LT
5	62640.35300	112.2	+94.2	+90.2	+71.9	+61.0	+46.3	+27.4			-33.8[1]				
6	65200.34130	89.0	+70.7	+66.1	+46.9	+34.7	+19.5	+0.9	-24.1		-53.0[1]	-59.1			T
7	57450.29550	112.8	+81.1	+74.4	+51.5	+44.2	+25.9	+7.3	-18.0		-49.4[1]	-54.9			
8	61820.41270	139.9	+117.0	+108.2	+78.6	+63.7	+47.2	+27.7	+3.4						
9	54720.28270	110.0	+87.5	+79.9	+58.5	+51.5	+32.6	+14.0	-10.7		-48.8[2]				
10	56250.31360	124.7	+109.1	+100.0	+73.8	+65.5	+47.5	+28.4	+4.0		-35.4[1]				
11	58000.36590	107.3		+98.8	+84.7	+65.8	+42.7	+14.6		-35.1[2]					
12	53030.29100	125.9	+106.7	+100.3	+77.4	+67.4	+50.6	+31.4	+7.0		-32.3[1]	-33.8			
13	59140.40130	133.5		+119.5	+85.3	+70.1	+55.2	+35.0	+10.7	-49.4	-51.5[1]	-56.7[2]			
14	52690.34170	136.5		+133.8	+99.4	+88.1	+70.1	+49.1	+23.8		-37.8[1]	-40.2			
15	57850.34100	133.2	+116.7	+109.4	+82.9	+69.8	+59.1	+38.1	+14.6	-30.5[2]					
16	56140.35550	142.6		+121.0	+87.8	+76.8	+59.1	+39.0	+14.0	-40.2	-41.5				
17	60590.33300	122.8	+103.9	+97.5	+71.6	+61.9	+45.1	+26.2	+1.2		-36.3[1]	-38.7	-85.9		T
18	56230.36390	124.1		+120.4	+84.7	+73.2	+55.8	+35.0	+10.1	-40.8	-42.1				
GCN															
1	48010.25080	71.3					+59.7	+35.7	+10.1	-38.4	-40.8	-50.0	-81.7	-95.1	
2	38225.16250	78.3				+74.7	+38.4	+17.4	+4.0	-48.5	-50.3	-63.1	-111.3	-122.8	
4	42600.31590	108.8						+105.5	+77.7	+11.0	+6.4	-11.9	-68.0	-86.6	
5	47750.30520	82.6						+61.3	+32.9	-26.2	-30.8	-40.5	-85.0	-110.3	
6	43875.25680	109.1		+102.1	+81.7	+64.9	+43.3	+21.3	+0.9						
8	44150.30265	91.4							+58.5	-4.9	-7.9	-27.4	-78.0		
9	22290.21400	134.7						+115.5	+89.3	+7.0	+5.2	-5.2			
10	23015.18760	157.0				+136.3	+114.9	+85.7	+59.7	-17.4	-19.8				
11	28560.23590	125.3						+93.3	+65.5	-10.7	-13.4				
12	23390.23460	118.3						+116.1	+86.6	-1.8	-4.9				
13	22950.23760	115.2							+86.9	-7.0	-9.1				
14	23290.21800	118.0						+116.7	+87.8	+4.3	+2.7	-7.9			
15	23125.20820	134.7						+106.3	+79.3	-1.8	-3.3				
16	27900.21375	118.0						+99.4	+73.8	+6.7	+4.9				
18	32370.22365	108.5					+93.9	+66.5	+39.3	-24.7	-27.7				
19	33915.22310	108.8			+105.8	+89.0	+61.9	+36.6	+25.6	-29.3					
20	25880.23300	108.2						+96.0	+63.4	-20.7	-23.8				
21	30375.24265	152.1			+149.1	+137.5	+113.4	+94.5	+68.6	-3.7	-6.1				

Formation levels m ± OD

Borehole number	National Grid reference	Surface level m AOD	Top Inferior Oolite	Top Upper Lias	Top Middle Lias	Top Lower Lias	100 Marker	85 Marker	70 Marker	Top White Lias	Top Cotham Beds or Twyford Beds[1]	Top Keuper Marl	Top Keuper Sandstone	Top Palaeozoic Floor	Availability of core samples[3]
GCN															
22	31530.22550	137.8		+134.4	+130.5	+120.4	+93.0	+66.5	+41.1	-26.8	-29.9				
23	25715.24130	118.6						+112.2	+79.9	-7.3	-10.4				
24	32575.21800	99.4						+74.7	+46.0	-18.0	-20.1				
25	28555.23055	134.4								-14.9					
26	25740.25015	119.5						+108.2	+81.1	-11.6	-14.6				
27	35150.21260	98.5					+89.0	+61.9	+36.3	-21.6	-23.5				
28	31420.20265	93.0						+81.7	+56.7	-6.7	-7.6				
29	21950.24820	130.8							+100.3	-2.7	-5.2				
30	27230.18135	100.9						+89.6	+62.5	OD	-1.2				
31	23590.24300	119.5							+88.7	-4.9	-7.3				
32	28750.20590	116.1						+112.5	+86.9	+24.1	+22.3				
33	34725.21440	110.0			+106.3	+96.3	+82.6	+58.8	+34.4	-24.4	-26.2				
34	27450.23525	123.1				+121.0		+95.7	+68.6	-7.6	-11.6				
35	25610.19410	115.5						+107.3	+81.4	+15.9	+13.7				
36	27330.23260	121.0						+95.1	+67.7	-9.1	+12.8				
37	23710.19775	146.6					+130.5	+100.6	+75.6	+17.1	+15.2				
38	38675.32300	116.7				+103.0	F	F	+56.7	+7.3	+3.3	-13.1			
39	35135.19410	91.1					+84.4	+56.4	+33.5	-20.7	-22.3	-36.3			
40	27280.23055	117.7						+98.5	+69.5	-8.8	-11.6				
41	27095.22035	109.4							+103.3	+32.9	+31.1				
42	37510.31375	129.5				+112.5	+85.3	+58.8	+28.3						
43	27540.19540	103.0							+85.7	+20.1	+18.3				
44	32630.19665	112.8					+96.0	+73.1	+49.4	-7.3	-8.5				
45	41595.32755	109.4				+106.3	+83.8	+54.6	+26.2	-50.3	-53.9				
46	28415.17705	100.9						+92.1	+59.4	+0.6	-0.9	-13.4	-93.6	-108.5	
47	26025.21665	105.2							+84.1	+12.2	+9.7				
48	26220.23030	118.3						+98.5	+72.5	+2.1	+0.6				
49	36870.26940	150.9				+142.6	F	+93.9	+68.0	+4.6	+1.5				
50	25445.22535	104.9							+95.1	+21.6	+19.5				
51	29470.20500	164.0		+156.7	+144.5	+129.2	+122.5	+101.2	+78.0	+17.4	+16.1				
52	26825.23265	123.1						+100.6	+72.5	-7.3	-9.7				
53	31570.24510	186.8	+184.4	+177.7	+161.2	+149.0	+125.3	+97.2	+71.6	+2.7	OD				
54	27080.22685	125.0							+107.6	+37.8	+36.0				
55	27925.20590	107.3							+92.6	+27.4	+26.2				
56	26400.19585	121.9						+101.8	+77.4	+11.6	+9.4				
57	32600.23160	138.4								-25.3					
58	29905.21300	193.9								+15.9					
59	29890.17480	113.7						+71.3	+49.1	-6.1	-7.6				
60	30185.22060	202.4	+183.8	+173.7	+155.8	+138.7	+118.3	+92.1	+67.7						
61	33115.20645	87.8						+71.3	+50.3	-11.0	-12.5				
62	26475.18525	103.3							+68.9	+5.2	+3.6	-8.8	-100.9	-112.2	
63	30590.22815	191.4	+168.2	+159.4	+139.3	+126.2	+100.0	+73.5	+47.6						
64	25800.21010	107.0							+86.3	+16.8	+15.2				
65	29820.19740	106.7						+103.0	+72.9	+13.4	+11.3				
66	27240.21670	120.7						+107.0	+81.7	+13.7	+12.2				
67	28465.19690	130.5				+123.7	+114.6	+99.1	+76.8	+18.6	+16.1				
68	44640.32120	118.6						+95.1	+68.8	+3.1	-0.6				
69	48340.33150	94.2						+76.5	+49.1	-14.3	-17.7	-25.0			
70	49995.32510	82.6						+65.2	+37.5	-21.9	-24.7	-26.8			
71	48820.31805	94.8					+83.2	+61.9	+35.7	-22.9	-27.1	-30.2			
72	46430.33730	93.3					+79.9	+57.0	+26.8	-42.2	-48.1	-65.2			
73	43720.37450	97.5					+86.9	+59.4	+29.3	-55.2	-60.1	-78.6			
74	43185.28310	130.8			+126.5	+112.5	+93.0	+69.8	+44.5	-15.5	-18.3	-35.0			
75	45970.37125	92.3					+81.4	+54.6	+24.1	-53.3	-57.6	-74.4			
76	50950.31160	97.2	+85.9	+66.8				+45.4	+19.5	-35.1	-36.9	F			
77	42120.30010	103.3						+100.6	+71.0	+4.6	+0.9	-17.4			
78	48340.37240	87.5					+85.3	+58.2	+28.0	-46.9	-51.5	-64.3			
79	49680.34165	85.0				+75.9	+61.3	+38.7	+11.0	-56.4	-61.3	-68.3			
80	43105.30915	99.4						+93.9	+65.8	-0.6	-51.8	-24.4			
81	49960.37330	103.3				+91.7	+72.9	+55.5	+27.1	-43.0	-48.2	-54.6			
82	50990.33155	107.9			+100.3	+86.6	+66.1	+45.7	+20.4	-40.2	-42.1	-45.1			
83	49610.39230	89.9						+69.5	+41.1	-34.7	-39.0	-50.0			
84	45930.29380	97.5					+89.2	+63.7	+37.5	-21.9	-25.6	-43.9			
85	49625.33270	89.0				+85.0	+64.3	+42.7	+35.6	-27.7	-31.7	-36.6			

Formation levels m ± OD (spanning the columns Top Inferior Oolite through Top Palaeozoic Floor)

Borehole number	National Grid reference	Surface level m AOD	Top Inferior Oolite	Top Upper Lias	Top Middle Lias	Top Lower Lias	100 Marker	85 Marker	70 Marker	Top White Lias	Top Cotham Beds or Twyford Beds[1]	Top Keuper Marl	Top Keuper Sandstone	Top Palaeozoic Floor	Availability of core samples[3]
GCN															
86	48020.39540	89.3						+75.9	+46.6	-32.3	-35.7				
87	47870.33665	83.2			+70.4	+56.4	+35.7	+13.1	-12.2	-69.5	-74.1	-85.6	-137.8		T
88	50070.31470	88.7			+77.1	+63.7	+39.3	F	-31.1	-34.1					
89	49045.38395	89.0					+85.9	+59.4	+29.9	-46.0	-50.9	-62.5	-125.9		T
90	51820.39995	99.4					+91.1	+68.0	+38.4	-33.8	-36.6				
91	54715.39240	134.1		+125.6	+94.5	+79.3	+61.0	+40.5	+11.6	-50.3	-53.3				
92	37870.32865	121.3				+103.9	+81.7	+55.1	+24.4	-59.1	-61.0				
93	48210.43485	101.8						+101.8	+68.6	+20.1	-23.5				
94	40835.31735	131.7						+111.6	+82.3	+14.6	+10.7				
95	49515.41660	119.5					+105.8	+77.4	+48.8	-31.4	-34.1				
96	52260.35420	103.9			+93.0	+77.7	+59.4	+37.5	+11.0	-55.5	-57.3	-60.7	-115.5		
97	53300.33200	114.9			+85.7	+74.1	+61.0	+42.7	+15.2	-38.7	-40.2	-42.7			
98	56815.38050	110.6			+94.5	+81.4	+61.9	+41.4	+14.3	-40.2	-42.7	-46.9			
99	52620.31970				+71.6	+62.5	+43.0	+21.3	-4.3		-59.1[1]	-61.9			T
100	46470.27380	143.6			+131.4	+111.9	+99.1	+77.1	+58.2	+29.9	-24.7	-28.0			
101	45280.42800	93.6						+79.6	+47.6	-45.4	-49.7				
102	43010.33820	106.7				+96.3	+73.5	+49.7	+19.2	-59.1					
103	48800.47570	103.6						+70.7	+42.1	-51.8	-55.8	-70.4			
104	32000.34740	132.6						+127.4	+94.2	-13.4	-18.0	-33.8			
105	51840.47880	109.7				+101.8		+53.9	+24.7	-66.1	-69.5				
106	49960.35660	86.3				+83.8	+64.9	+42.1	+14.0	-56.4	-61.3				
107	46800.47325	102.1						+93.0	+61.0	-37.8	-41.8				
108	39710.40480	115.2						+74.1	+40.8	-57.6	-61.9	-78.0			
109	51470.43880	149.1			+137.5	+116.7	F	+89.0	+59.4	-22.0	-25.9				
110	37610.43860	161.2				+146.6		+106.7	+75.3	-31.1	-34.8				
111	51825.24550	106.1	+82.0	+78.3	+60.4	+52.5	+31.4	+14.3	-11.0	-49.7	-52.4	-55.5	-79.6	-95.4	T
112	34450.46820	99.7							-11.9	+8.5	-7.3				
113	50000.24450	116.1	+90.5	+84.7	+66.7	+57.6	+36.6	+18.0	-6.7	-48.8	-50.9	-56.7	78.9		
114	35530.34500	168.9			+165.8	+141.4	+118.3	+93.6	+62.2	-34.1	-37.5				
115	43030.47240	108.5						+105.5	+69.5	-32.6	-36.0				
116	53800.23500	87.2	+60.4	+54.2	+38.7	+31.7	+11.9	-4.0	-23.2	-52.4	-54.9	-57.3	-72.2	-85.3	TC
117	37720.35080	192.6		+187.5	+135.9	+111.9	+89.9	+65.8	+34.8						
118	39120.33900	146.3			+142.9	+118.0	+97.5	+72.8	+42.1	-45.1	-49.4				
119	47180.33340	79.5				+66.8	+42.4	+22.9	-1.8	-47.2	-49.7				
120	46800.21360	118.6	+62.2	+57.9	+48.5	+35.4	+15.9	-4.0	-27.7	-70.1	-73.2	-84.7			
121	28860.33300	109.1							+100.6	-8.8	-12.8	-26.8			
122	33970.34440	181.1			+181.1	+157.0	+134.7	+110.6	+78.6	-23.2	-28.0				
123	32250.31900	228.3		+217.9	+169.2	+146.0	+122.5	+95.7	+64.0						
124	28980.31760	125.6						+118.9	+84.4	-21.3	-25.0	-39.0			
125	45140.22075	110.3	+83.2	+79.2	+70.1	+57.3	+34.4	+15.4	-8.8	-55.5	-58.5				
126	32380.30175	167.3	+120.1	+110.3	+57.3	+38.1									
127	31690.35550	132.0				+130.2	+103.3	+79.9	+54.0	+21.6					
128	30660.32980	131.7						+116.4	+83.2	-21.0					
129	35170.32775	157.9				+134.7	+109.7	+84.7	+53.0	-42.7	-47.8				
130	30310.31330	188.4			+153.6	F	+121.6	+96.0	+64.0						
131	31780.33620	143.6					+140.8	+116.4	+83.8	-20.1	-24.7				
132	31350.34130	186.2				+173.4	+148.4	+123.4	+91.4	-14.6	-18.9				
133	31040.34580	131.4							+98.4	-9.8	-14.0				
134	31660.34500	139.3						+127.4	+93.9	-11.9	-16.8				
135	24050.30820	131.7						+126.2	+96.3	-20.4	-24.7				
136	33150.34660	186.5				+165.2	+140.5	+115.8	+83.8	-19.8	-24.7				
137	36960.33850	145.1				+119.5	+96.3	+72.8	+48.2	-43.0	-47.8				
138	25580.33420	113.4						+108.2	+78.9	-36.0	-39.6				
139	30070.34580	180.7								-14.3					
140	27680.33150	100.6								+17.4	+12.8	-0.6			
141	31750.35060	115.5				+97.8	F	F	+82.6	-9.8	-14.3	-29.9			
142	30020.35440	161.9		+159.4	+132.3	+108.2	+86.3	+61.9							
143	25920.32400	104.2						+104.2	+70.4	-39.6	-43.6				
144	26450.33130	94.8							+83.8	-34.4	-38.4				
145	33800.35920	162.1		+154.8	+96.9	+71.9	+49.4	+25.0							
146	35900.35070	184.7		F	+137.2	+113.7	+89.3	F	+52.4						
147	26160.31880	133.2						+110.9	+82.6	-34.8	-38.7				
148	29250.32450	113.7						+89.6		-17.7	-21.9				

Formation levels m ± OD

Borehole number	National Grid reference	Surface level m AOD	Top Inferior Oolite	Top Upper Lias	Top Middle Lias	Top Lower Lias	100 Marker	85 Marker	70 Marker	Top White Lias	Top Cotham Beds or Twyford Beds[1]	Top Keuper Marl	Top Keuper Sandstone	Top Palaeozoic Floor	Availability of core samples[3]
GCN															
149	22800.32210	128.6				+104.2					−20.1	−22.9	−35.0		
150	53560.31050	135.9	+122.5	+116.4	+92.7	+82.3	+65.2	+45.7	+21.3		−24.7[1]	−25.9			
151	49390.29160	77.4				+74.4		+40.5	+13.4		−40.2	−40.8	−45.7		
152	47030.28920	131.4			+115.2	+101.5	+79.2	+57.9	+33.2		−25.3	−30.2	−43.3		
153	46810.30010	86.6						+61.6	+33.8		−26.5	−30.8	−45.7		
154	51450.30450	100.6			+99.1	+87.8	+68.0	+47.2	+22.0		−30.8[1]	−32.3			
155	46820.29720	100.0				+96.9	+79.6	+57.0	+31.1		−27.1	−31.4			
156	46890.29150	123.1	+105.8	+96.9	+75.0	+61.0	+42.7	+22.0	+2.7		−26.8	−31.7			
157	44880.25650	122.8		+119.8	+101.5	+87.5	+65.8	+44.5	+19.2		−34.8	−37.8			
158	46830.29420	117.7	+106.7	+98.8	F	+76.8	+57.9	+37.2	+12.5	−44.8	−49.1	F	−89.6	−104.6	
159	45950.25170	121.3		+112.2	+95.1	+81.7	+59.7	+39.6	+14.9		−36.3	−39.3			
160	62770.28450	90.8	+54.2	+48.2	+32.9	+25.6	+7.9	−8.5	−34.8		−48.8[1]			−51.8(?)	
161	48220.27870	82.3						+57.3	+29.3		−24.1	−27.7	−34.1		
162	46020.22230	117.3	+80.8	+77.1	+67.4	+54.9	+32.0	+13.7	−10.7		−55.5	−58.5			
163	45160.18450	96.3	+57.0	+52.1	+43.9	+32.3	+5.8	−11.6	−35.0	−71.6	−75.0	−86.0	−108.5	−125.3	
164	29180.33770	123.4				+100.6					−9.8	−13.4			
165	26980.33220	94.8				+78.6					−33.5	−37.2			
166	32930.35145	146.3		F	+117.4	+84.1					−21.0	−24.7	−40.8		
167	31155.34958	114.6	+114.0	+107.9	+75.6	+53.6	+28.0	+16.7	F	−10.1	−14.3	−28.6			
168	49680.19225	97.8	+42.4	+38.1	+31.4	+21.6	−5.2	−21.3	−44.8	−78.0	−81.1	−89.0	−98.2	−109.4	TC
169	27818.34330	117.0			+94.2	+60.4					−52.7	−57.0			
170	27810.33630	107.3			+100.6	+77.1					−36.9	−39.9			
171	30350.34890	174.3	+173.1	+162.8	+122.5	+99.4	+73.8	+60.1	+28.0						
172	27820.33320	98.1									−9.5	−13.4			
173	29800.33900	201.2	+179.8	+153.6	+128.6	+96.0					−11.9	−16.2			
174	28180.33220	100.3									+1.2	−3.1			
175	27200.32930	98.8									−7.0	−10.7			
176	27670.32360	115.8				+100.6					−9.5	−13.4			
177	27930.33010	102.1									+8.5	+4.6			
178	27050.32450	104.5									−9.1	−12.8			
179	27560.33150	100.0									+13.7	+12.5			
180	29560.32770	118.0				+89.9					−15.8	−20.4			
181	27455.33020	100.0									+22.6	+18.3	+5.2		
182	27200.33630	96.6				+84.4					−32.6	−36.3			
183	30060.32800	128.0			+117.6	+85.3					−19.2	−23.5			
184	25150.33160	114.0				+85.6					−33.8	−37.5	−50.2		
185	28250.33450	111.9				+103.0					−2.4	−5.8			
186	25800.32900	118.3			+109.7	+79.2					−34.4	−38.4			
187	27450.33160	100.6									+14.9	+11.0			
188	27535.33045	100.6									+15.2	+11.0			
189	27130.33410	93.6				+87.5					−29.5	−33.5			
190	26680.33740	118.0			+101.5	+75.0									
191	28520.33910	160.6	+141.7	+138.1	+96.6	+70.7	+41.8	+13.4	−20.4						
192	27310.33190	104.2				+91.1					−3.7	OD			
193	27180.33190	104.9				+82.9					−24.4	−28.4			
194	28170.33460	111.9				+98.2					−15.8	−19.8			
195	36360.35000	189.9		+188.7	+138.1	+114.9	+106.4	+81.4	+48.8						
196	36080.32880	150.9				+127.4	+104.2	+79.2	+48.5		−42.4	−46.9			
197	36270.34600	156.4				+134.7	+111.0	+86.3	+54.6		−43.3				
198	37410.33870	152.7			+145.4	+119.2	+96.6	+72.2	+41.4						
199	37210.33510	142.6			+140.8	+112.2	+90.2	+66.4	+36.6		−45.1	−49.1			
200	36430.34250	149.3				+126.8	+104.2	+79.6	+48.2		−49.4	−53.6			
201	36770.33820	145.4				+119.5	+96.9	+72.2	+41.4		−50.3	−54.9			
202	35740.34790	174.7			+173.1	+148.4	+124.7	+99.7	+68.0		−31.1	−35.0			
203	35520.35000	177.4		+170.1	+140.8	+117.6	+93.9	+67.1	+38.1		−25.6	−29.9			
204	35040.33950	172.8			+167.6	+143.6	+120.4	+95.7	+65.2		−33.2	−37.8			
205	36320.33640	152.7				+128.3	+106.1	+81.4	+50.3		−42.7				
206	35550.33980	164.9				+141.1	+118.0	+93.6	+61.6		−37.5	−41.8			
207	27250.22850	115.5				+87.8					F	F	+17.4		
208	27060.22460	122.8				+105.8					+36.0	+34.1			
209	26850.20700	106.3				+88.1					+20.1	+18.0			
210	26500.22640	114.3			+111.6	+85.0					+8.2	+6.1			
211	28590.22716	135.9				+132.9	+112.2	+87.2	+61.6		−14.9	−18.0			

Formation levels m ± OD

Borehole number	National Grid reference	Surface level m AOD	Top Inferior Oolite	Top Upper Lias	Top Middle Lias	Top Lower Lias	100 Marker	85 Marker	70 Marker	Top White Lias	Top Cotham Beds or Twyford Beds[1]	Top Keuper Marl	Top Keuper Sandstone	Top Palaeozoic Floor	Availability of core samples[3]
GCN															
212	28750.22100	134.1						+116.7	+91.4	+22.6	+20.7				
213	28910.21000	132.3					+124.4	+99.1	+75.6	+11.3	+10.1				
214	28500.21220	120.1						+105.5	+75.0	+10.1	+8.8				
215	28790.21550	142.6				+135.6	+122.5	+98.8	+74.7	+8.2	+7.0				
216	29080.22170	158.2			+148.4	+141.7		+108.8	+86.9	+18.6	+16.8				
217	27950.22060	116.4							+99.4	+30.2	+28.4				
218	27550.20960	117.7							+92.4	+28.4	+27.1				
219	29760.21800	205.4		+180.1	+167.6	+152.1	+128.9	+103.0	+78.0	+12.5	+10.7				
220	29700.20960	178.3	+169.2	+163.1	+146.9	+133.5	+116.4	+93.0	+69.2	+6.1	+4.9				
221	32470.21520	98.8					+97.8	+74.4	+46.0	-16.8	-18.9				
222	29270.22530	162.1		+153.0	+137.8	+128.6	+108.2	+82.3	+55.5	-17.7	-20.1				
223	27610.19780	107.9							+86.6	+22.2	+21.0				
224	26620.22260	119.2						+115.5	+88.4	+14.3	+12.2	+0.3			
225	25930.22050	103.9							+84.7	+11.6	+8.8	-3.1			
226	27350.21400	121.6						+105.2	+78.9	+11.6	+10.4				
227	29080.21780	165.2	+129.2	+157.0	+149.4	+149.4	+143.3	+108.8	+80.6	+21.3	+20.1				
228A	26990.22580	124.7							+106.7						
B	26870.22630	122.8							+105.2						
C	26730.22610	117.7							+99.7						
D	26750.22400	119.2							+100.3						
E	26620.22600	116.1							+91.4						
F	26670.22300	119.5						+114.9	+91.7						
G	26480.22210	118.6						+113.4							
229A	28170.22220	117.7							+99.0						
B	28120.22370	121.6							+98.8						
C	28000.22470	119.5							+98.8						
230A	28100.20710	111.6							+92.4						
B	28220.20880	124.7						+108.2							
C	28380.20740	127.4						+111.0							
D	28170.20500	115.5							+86.9						
E	28140.20790	118.6						+92.0							
F	28530.20630	121.0						+115.8	+88.4						
231A	26110.22270	107.0							+86.6						
B	26190.22480	115.8						+112.2	+86.0						
232A	25330.22680	105.8							+100.3						
B	25250.22860	106.7							+100.3						
C	25230.23000	106.3							+92.4						
D	25220.22930	106.7							+100.6						
E	25630.22520	105.2							+95.7						
F	25730.22420	106.1							+92.4						
G	25790.22270	105.5							+90.2						
233A	25650.21770	103.3							+87.8						
B	25770.21510	102.7							+86.3						
234	26150.23090	114.9						+92.7							
235	25270.19920	123.1						+112.8	+86.3	+19.5	+17.1				
236	27280.21530	122.2						+105.5	+80.2						
237A	24500.22250	118.6							+93.0						
B	24600.22100	113.7							+93.0						
C	24720.21950	108.8							+92.7						
238A	27460.21020	118.0							+91.4						
B	27360.20940	114.0							+95.7						
C	27260.20850	107.9							+95.4						
D	27150.20790	105.8							+95.4						
E	27340.21140	119.5						+110.0							
F	27030.20900	106.7							+87.5						
G	27150.20980	111.9							+94.5						
H	27240.21060	115.5						+108.2							
J	27380.21080	118.9							+89.3						
239	29900.19070	95.4						+89.6							
240A	27360.20670	107.9							+96.9						
B	27750.20720	113.4							+93.6						
241A	30820.19200	102.7						+96.0							
B	31780.19830	98.1						+83.2							

Borehole number	National Grid reference	Surface level m AOD	Top Inferior Oolite	Top Upper Lias	Top Middle Lias	Top Lower Lias	100 Marker	85 Marker	70 Marker	Top White Lias	Top Cotham Beds or Twyford Beds[1]	Top Keuper Marl	Top Keuper Sandstone	Top Palaeozoic Floor	Availability of core samples[3]
			|			Formation levels m ± OD									|
GCN															
C	31600.20100	90.8							+ 67.4						
D	31490.19990	90.5							+ 68.0						
242	29100.21400	149.1						+ 95.4							
243	29220.21130	149.1				+ 130.7	+ 119.5	+ 95.1	+ 71.6						
244	29310.20900	152.4		+ 149.4	+ 140.8	+ 127.7	+ 116.4	+ 94.2	+ 70.1						
245	29350.20660	154.5		+ 148.7	+ 141.7	+ 132.6	+ 118.3	+ 98.2	+ 77.4						
246	29210.20310	138.1				+ 131.7	+ 122.8	+ 99.7	+ 78.0						
247	28620.20070	117.7						+ 101.2	+ 80.2						
248	28060.20100	111.6						+ 106.4	+ 86.6						
249	28650.20760	120.7						+ 118.0	+ 88.7						
250	30830.20790	132.3		+ 129.2	+ 123.7	+ 117.6	+ 104.2	+ 83.5							
251	30610.20040	105.2						+ 88.1	+ 68.3			+ 8.2	+ 7.0		
252	30520.20320	125.3		+ 122.8	+ 118.9	+ 114.6	+ 103.6	+ 84.1							
253	30580.20520	131.4			+ 126.8	+ 121.0	+ 104.8	+ 82.3	+ 60.4						
254	30450.19790	93.6							+ 72.2						
255	30380.19600	92.7							+ 69.8						
256	30080.19190	95.4						+ 89.9	+ 67.4			+ 7.0	+ 5.8		
257	30320.19410	93.0							+ 67.4						
258	30230.19230	93.0							+ 67.4						
259	30200.18850	93.9							+ 64.0						
260	30500.19040	93.3							+ 63.4						
261	31540.19750	94.8						+ 78.9	+ 59.1						
262	31020.19440	93.9						+ 88.4	+ 61.9			+ 0.9	OD		
263	31260.19540	93.6						+ 78.3	+ 57.9						
264	31730.20350	89.9							+ 52.1						
265	31210.20140	94.8						+ 84.1	+ 64.3						
266	31460.21420	139.9		+ 135.5	+ 123.8	+ 113.7	+ 98.2	+ 77.7							
267	31000.19960	98.1						+ 86.9	+ 67.4						
268	30740.19910	97.2						+ 91.1	+ 67.7						
269	30800.18040	128.6	+ 117.4	+ 114.0	+ 107.3	+ 103.3	+ 87.8	+ 66.7							
270	31510.18560	128.0	+ 114.9	+ 112.5	+ 107.9	+ 103.3	+ 88.7	+ 66.4	+ 44.8						
271	27710.20590	107.9							+ 93.6						
272	31710.21820	137.8		+ 132.3	+ 123.8	+ 114.6	+ 97.2	+ 72.8	+ 47.2						
273	27420.20210	104.5							+ 90.5						
274	27520.20390	106.3							+ 91.4						
275	27620.20490	106.7							+ 92.4						
276	28410.20350	109.7							+ 87.2						
278	28010.20280	106.1							+ 89.9						
279	27820.20260	104.5							+ 89.3						
280	27250.20720	104.5							+ 96.0						
281	27180.20620	103.6							+ 93.6						
282	27080.20550	102.7							+ 91.4						
283	26960.20410	99.7							+ 86.6						
284	32890.21480	100.3						+ 73.8	+ 46.3						
285	32850.21660	104.9						+ 70.1	+ 40.8						
286	32770.20290	98.8						+ 70.4	+ 50.0						
287	33120.21710	115.2						+ 71.6	+ 39.9						
288	33100.21380	107.6						+ 80.5	+ 55.8						
289	34100.19770	117.7		+ 106.7	+ 100.0	+ 96.6	+ 78.6	+ 59.1	+ 34.8						
290	33470.21450	100.3						+ 68.6	+ 43.0						
291	33500.21850	114.0						+ 66.8	+ 36.9						
292	34040.20520	88.4						+ 78.6	+ 55.5						
293	34170.21160	105.2					+ 97.5	+ 72.8	+ 48.2						
294	34110.20850	97.5					+ 95.4	+ 69.2	+ 43.0						
295	34050.21790	111.9			+ 107.3	+ 100.0	+ 87.8	+ 64.0	+ 38.7						
296	35310.20630	115.5		+ 111.2	+ 102.1	+ 89.6	+ 78.0	+ 58.2	+ 37.8						
297	35430.20360	113.7						+ 62.8	+ 42.4						
298	35420.19870	86.9						+ 57.3	+ 37.5						
299	35040.20010	86.3						+ 77.1	+ 49.4						
300	34840.20170	88.7						+ 71.6	+ 50.3						
301	33020.21100	101.5						+ 74.4	+ 50.3						
302	33860.21010	90.2						+ 71.3	+ 46.0						
303	33480.21110	90.5						+ 71.3	+ 46.6						

Borehole number	National Grid reference	Surface level m AOD	Top Inferior Oolite	Top Upper Lias	Top Middle Lias	Top Lower Lias	100 Marker	85 Marker	70 Marker	Top White Lias	Top Cotham Beds or Twyford Beds[1]	Top Keuper Marl	Top Keuper Sandstone	Top Palaeozoic Floor	Availability of core samples[3]
GCN															
303	33480.21110	90.5						+71.3	+46.6						
304	33380.20900	87.8						+63.7	+45.4						
305	33630.20960	86.9						+70.4	+43.6						
306	33760.20720	87.2						+69.2	+42.1						
307	33740.20490	89.9						+83.2	+55.5						
308	33840.20160	96.0						+71.0	+51.2						
309	36130.20200	118.0							+37.5	-11.3	-12.5				
310	34060.20800	94.5						+69.5	+43.6						
311	34070.20650	91.4						+69.8	+43.6						
312	34140.20300	85.9						+82.3	+57.3						
313	34460.20190	85.7							+52.7						
314	34490.20320	88.4						+74.7	+48.5						
315	34590.20430	91.7						+71.0	+48.8						
316	34550.20590	95.7						+70.1	+43.6						
317	34810.20700	103.3						+67.0	+40.8						
318	33950.21380	104.9						+68.9	+44.5						
319	34130.21470	109.4					+89.6	+64.0	+39.6						
320	34010.21190	106.1						+74.0	+48.8						
321	34160.20980	100.3						+70.1	+44.8						
322	34330.20810	90.5						+69.5	+43.3						
323	34130.21330	103.9					+93.0	+67.7	+42.7						
324	33860.21140	96.0						+70.7	+47.2						
325	34410.21140	94.2						+71.9	+46.3						
326	34290.21040	98.1						+72.8	+46.6						
327	33510.20590	94.2						+68.6	+42.7						
328	33280.20450	97.8						+76.8	+54.9						
329	32920.20480	89.6						+76.2	+54.2						
330	33500.20470	94.2						+80.2	+55.8						
331	33610.20300	99.7						+74.1	+52.1						
332	33330.20240	110.0						+70.7	+49.4						
333	33430.20310	103.9						+75.0	+52.4						
334	32740.20980	92.1						+87.5	+59.7	-0.6	-3.1				
335	35070.20950	108.8					+94.8	+69.8	+46.9						
336	32560.19790	107.0						+73.5	+49.7						
337	36110.21880	127.7			+117.0	+106.1	+79.2	+55.5	+31.7	-22.2					
338	33040.21010	97.8						+75.3	+51.2						
339	33390.19990	125.9						+70.1	+48.2						
340	34515.22770	135.3		+132.6	+121.3	+119.9	+89.9	+64.9	+39.3	-23.8	-27.1				
341	33070.20010	125.0						+69.5	+49.4						
342	28310.20630	122.8							+89.6	+25.3					LT
343	28200.20410	111.3							+89.0	+23.8	+22.6				LT
344	27990.20380	107.9							+89.9	+24.4	+23.2				LT
345	28250.20280	107.6							+89.0	+22.6					LT
346	28195.20005	115.2						+111.2	+84.1	+19.8	+18.6				LT
347	28080.20270	107.3							+88.7	+22.9	+21.6				LT
348	29170.20400	138.7					+122.2	+100.9	+79.9	+19.2					LT
349	27580.20680	112.5							+96.6	+29.0					LT
350	27520.20640	110.9							+94.2	+28.7					LT
351	27640.20870	117.3							+93.9						LT
352	27700.20820	117.0							+93.9						L
353	27570.20840	114.6							+94.5						L
354	27530.20800	111.9							+95.1						L
355	27490.20775	110.3							+95.1						L
356	27450.20745	109.4							+95.7						L
357	27410.20720	108.2							+95.7	+30.2			+15.5		LT
358	27410.20640	108.5							+96.3						
359	27440.20610	109.1							+94.5						
360	28480.20480	111.3							+87.8	+22.6					LT
GS															
1	17415.24415	150.3					+146.9	+119.8	+83.8						
2	20027.24524	138.7						+138.7	+108.2	-0.6	-3.1	-13.4			
3	22604.24158	121.6							+89.6	-7.6		-21.0			
4	25030.22164	106.7							+94.2	+19.5	+16.8				

Borehole number	National Grid reference	Surface level m AOD	Formation levels m ± OD												Availability of core
			Top Inferior Oolite	Top Upper Lias	Top Middle Lias	Top Lower Lias	100 Marker	85 Marker	70 Marker Lias	Top White Beds or Twyford Beds[1]	Top Cotham Marl	Top Keuper Sandstone	Top Keuper Floor	Top Palaeozoic samples[3]	
GS															
5	26880.24568	113.4							+89.0	+5.2	+3.4				
6	22291.26747	121.6						+101.8	+71.3						
7	29160.26695	132.0						+123.1	+92.4	+9.8	+7.3				
8A	21500.19975	186.5			+171.3	+151.8	+129.8	+100.6	+72.8						
10	26300.20455	107.9							+89.6	+18.6	+16.8				
11	19313.21194	157.0						+131.7	+102.1	+5.5	+2.7				
12	32680.21300	94.2						+88.1	+57.9	-5.2	-7.3	-20.7	-91.4	-104.8	
13	24450.18850	123.4						+109.4	+82.0	+14.3	+12.5	+0.9			
14	29095.18340	95.4						+91.7	+63.7	+3.7	+2.4				
15	23230.17230	140.8					+105.2	+73.8	+48.5	-22.2	-24.7				
16	19280.17800	128.3					+126.8	+94.5	+64.6						
17	37710.24765	127.7				+119.5	+95.1	+69.2	+43.6	-16.5	-19.2	-33.8			
18	31470.27990	172.2				+164.9	+139.3	+112.2	+85.0						
20	33570.27975	195.7			+176.2	+164.0	+140.8	+115.5	+88.7	+18.0					
21	33815.29900	192.9			+183.2	+171.9	+147.8	+121.6	+93.3	+17.1	+13.4				
22	21800.21990	129.2						+118.3	+87.2	-0.9					
23	25790.16990	122.8					+111.6	+80.5	+57.6	-2.7	-4.0	-15.8			
24	28440.22465	122.8							+96.6	+26.2	+24.4	+11.9			
25	27910.26050	121.0						+116.1	+85.6	-0.6	-4.0	-16.1			
26	24290.20775	119.8						+108.8	+81.7	+11.0					
27	23955.23075	112.8						+111.2	+79.6	-5.2	-7.9	-20.7			
28	30385.29515	151.5			+102.1	+89.3	+62.2	+35.4	+1.8						
29	35750.24800	150.3				+135.3	+110.0	+85.0	+59.4	-2.1	-5.2				
30	22540.22675	125.3						+110.0	+81.1	-10.7					
31	24380.22390	119.5						+119.5	+93.6	+16.1					
SARSDEN															
2	27689.22203	113.1							+100.3	+30.5	+29.5	+16.5	-69.8	-89.6	LTC
3	28005.20755	108.5							+92.4	+26.5	+25.0	+13.7	-70.1	-87.2	LT
4	26950.22580	123.7							+102.4	+34.8	+32.3	+19.8	-67.4	-84.4	LT
5	28735.21940	139.9						+115.2	+93.0	+25.9	+23.8	+11.3	-73.2	-90.8	T
6	27365.20955	115.5							+95.4	+30.8	+28.7	+15.9	-69.8	-86.9	T
7	28580.20650	118.3						+114.6	+87.8	+24.1	+22.9	+10.4	-71.3	-88.7	LTC
8	29700.20970	178.9	+169.8	+164.6	+147.8	+135.9	+118.0	+93.3	+69.5	+5.5	+4.3	-5.2	-87.5	-106.1	LT
9	29660.17390	127.1	+123.4	+116.7	+112.8	+105.5		+69.2	+48.8	-8.2	-9.5	-22.3	-96.0	-115.2	LT
10	34140.20430	86.3						+80.5	+57.3	-6.4	-7.6	-22.3	-83.2	-101.2	LT
11	34175.21100	102.7					+81.1	+63.4	c +40.9	-2.1	-4.3	-18.0	-80.8	-101.2	LTC
STOW															
Well 1	19250.23460	153.0						+140.2	+107.9	+0.9	-1.8	-11.6	-165.5	-194.5	
Well 2	20197.20742	249.6		+235.0	+224.3	+175.9	+153.6	+124.0	+96.0	+8.5	+6.7	+4.0	-140.8	-176.2	
Well 3	25085.21650	113.7						+112.8	+85.0	+12.8	+10.7	-1.2	-108.5	-129.5	TC
Well 4	29325.23515	168.9		+153.0	+140.2	+130.2	+112.8	+87.2	+61.0	-12.8	-16.2	-28.6	-116.1	-135.9	
WHICHFORD															
1	32650.34920	140.2						+119.8	+87.2	-18.3	-23.2	-39.3	-130.8	-152.7	TC
2	35280.34750	177.1				+157.3	+132.9	+108.2	+75.9	-22.2	-27.1	-43.6	-127.4	-150.0	C
3	37030.34950	194.8		+182.9	+136.6	+109.4	+87.5	+64.0	+37.2	-47.9	-52.1	-68.0	-149.7	-171.9	TC
MARSH GIBBON															
	6481.2374	75.3		+35.4	+30.8	+21.7	?	?	?					-46.1	LTP
NOKE	5386.1285	95.9	?	Absent	Absent	+52.6	?	?	?	-14.5[1]				-20.9	
TWYFORD															
1	6802.2569	88.7	?	+13.2	?	?	+4.3	-12.4	-37.6	-44.1[1]				-50.2	LTP
2	6760.2650	84.5	+29.0	Absent	?	?	+5.9	-9.3	-34.5	-44.4[1]				-55.2	LTP
3	6859.2659	84.6	?	Absent	? +20.5	?	+1.5	-16.1	-41.6					-49.7	LP
4	6697.2561	c89.9	?	Absent	?	?	+1.5	-16.4	-40.7					-50.9	LTP

1 Datum on top surface of Twyford beds is prefixed[1]
2 Datum based on driller's estimate—no geophysical logs or core
3 Availability of core samples is indicated thus: Lias—L, Trias—T, Carboniferous—C and Palaeozoic—P

APPENDIX 6
List of Geological Survey photographs

Copies of these photographs are deposited for public reference in the Library of the British Geological Survey, Keyworth, Nottinghamshire NG12 5GG. Prints are available on application. The photographs belong to Series A.

TOPOGRAPHY

Marlstone Rock Bed plateau and other features

8392 View of face in Marlstone Rock Bed, Redlands Quarry [360 347]

8393 Marlstone Rock Bed capping Bury's Hill; viewed SSE from about 0.4 km NNE of the church, Wigginton.

9876 View to SSW from Stourton [298 365], showing Lower, Middle and Upper Lias.

9877 View from Sutton-under-Brailes looking N. to Middle Lias scarp at Cherington Hill [289 379].

9878 Mine Hill near Stourton [300 365]; Lower Lias in foreground, with Middle and Upper Lias and Northampton Sand.

9879 View to SSE from a point north of Chastleton [244 299], showing Middle Lias scarp.

9880 Middle Lias scarp of Peasewill Wood, NE of Adlestrop [232 263].

9881 Middle Lias scarp at Barton Hill, NE of Little Compton [255 303].

9882 View to the NE from a point [253 253] about 1.6 km NNW of the church, Kingham; showing the Middle Lias topography in the Kingham Hill School area.

9883 A view to the NNE from a point [385 327] 770 m south-west of Wigginton church; showing down-faulted Middle Lias. Valley of River Swere in foreground.

9884 View eastward from a point S of Swalcliffe [384 370], showing steep-sided channel.

9885 Iron Down, a Marlstone Rock Bed plateau, seen from a locality [424 321] about 0.8 km SW of St Michael's Church, Barford St Michael.

9886 View from Hempton Plateau [448 315], on Marlstone Rock Bed, towards the south.

9887 View from Hempton Plateau [443 316], on Marlstone Rock Bed, towards the east.

9888 Panorama from Hill Barn [312 316], NW of Great Rollright, looking to NNE.

9889 View from a point [466 334] N of Deddington looking S, showing Marlstone Rock Bed capped by Upper Lias.

Inferior Oolite Group and Great Oolite Group features

9894 View from crossroads [349 348] 1.6 km NNW of the church, Hook Norton; showing bench of Marlstone Rock Bed with overlying Upper Lias capped by Chipping Norton Limestone.

9895 View from a point [431 285], 730 m S 10°E of the church, Over Worton, looking S to Worton Wood; Chipping Norton Limestone on Upper Lias.

9896 Looking SE from a point [393 361] about 1.6 km SW of Lower Tadmarton: Northampton Sand on Upper Lias in background.

9897 From a point [290 342] about 2.4 km WSW of the church, Whichford; view SE to Long Compton Woods across fault to Middle Lias hills.

9898 Long Compton [283 331], view northwards to Harrow Hill; shows Lias and Middle Jurassic strata.

9899–9900 View to the NE (9899) and NW (9900) respectively, from a point [360 305] about 1.2 km WSW of Swerford church, across axis of syncline.

9901 View to the west along Stour valley from quarry [313 363] about 1.6 km north of Whichford.

9902 From Mitford Bridge [263 371], S of Burmington. View south along the 2nd Terrace of the River Stour.

9903 Roadside [271 332], 1.6 km NE of Barton-on-the-Heath; view to the NNE across 2nd Terrace of Nethercote Brook.

9904 Long Compton [283 331], looking south across 2nd Terrace.

9905–6 From St Nicholas Church, Idbury [237 202], views north and east of the Evenlode valley.

9907 The Evenlode valley seen from near Lyneham Barrow [295 205], about a mile east of Lyneham.

9908 From the Mount, Churchill [279 237], looking W across the River Evenlode. Kingham village built on 3rd and 4th Terraces.

9909–10 King's Men Stone Circle, Rollright Stones [296 308], Little Rollright.

9911 William Smith Memorial [283 243] at Churchill (Plate 1 in this volume).

LIAS

4598–9; 8392; 9817–8 Marlstone Rock Bed, showing small-scale step-faulting; Redlands Quarry, near Hook Norton.

8394 Marlstone Rock Bed, showing small-scale step-faulting; Sydenham Quarry, East Adderbury.

8395, 9814 Marlstone Rock Bed, Bloxham Quarry, 0.8 km W by N of Bloxham.

9815–6 Marlstone Rock Bed in old Quarry NW of Court Farm, Great Tew.

INFERIOR OOLITE GROUP

9819–20 Clypeus Grit and Chipping Norton Limestone above Upper Lias, Hook Norton railway cutting.

9821 Northampton Sand (Scissum Beds), Old Grange Farm Quarry, Sibford Ferris.

9822 Overturned Scissum Beds in valley bulge near Temple Mills, SW of Sibford Ferris.

9823 'Lower Estuarine Series' Sand pit on Wigginton Heath.

9824 'Lower Estuarine Series' Sand pit [455 272], south of Duns Tew.

9844 'Lower Estuarine Series' in quarry [436 269] near Downhill Farm, Westcot Barton.

GREAT OOLITE GROUP

(a) Chipping Norton Limestone

9825   Roadside section at crossroads [305 312] Great
Rollright; showing Chipping Norton Limestone.

9826   Oyster lumachelle within Chipping Norton Limestone
section [348 280] 440 m N 53°W of St Nicholas'
Church, Heythrop.

9827–8; 9839   Cambered Chipping Norton Limestone, Cross
Hands Quarry [272 293], 3.2 km NW of Chipping
Norton.

9829   Hook Norton railway cutting, north end of cutting.

9830–2   Boulter's Barn Quarry [292 253], NNE of Churchill.

9833   The Warren, NW of Heythrop.

9834   Quarry [341 291], east side of Over Norton Common.

9835, 9839   Oakham Quarry [279 306], 460 m E 20°N of
Oakham Farm, near Little Compton.

9836   Fulwell Quarry [375 230], 320 m SW of Fulwell.

9837   Quarry [385 250], 550 m S of the Square, Church
Enstone.

9840–1   Roadside section [314 302] of west side of A34, 1.6 km
SW of Great Rollright.

9890   View north-eastward from a locality [333 334], about
2.1 km W of Hook Norton Church.

9891   From the same locality as 9890 looking E; small ridge on
right of the Marlstone Rock Bed feature is capped by
Chipping Norton Limestone.

9892   To the SE from same locality as 9890; Northampton Sand
caps the distant ridge.

9893   From Atchill [331 368] looking NE; Marlstone Rock Bed
plateau in foreground with Upper Lias and Northampton
Sand in background.

9842   'Sand' pit [394 286] at Great Tew.

9843   Hook Norton railway cutting [358 316], south end of
cutting.

(b) Sharp's Hill Beds

9845   Radford [411 237]; Sharp's Hill Beds on Chipping
Norton Limestone.

9846   Old Quarry at Moorlake Spring [410 231], Kiddington.
Sharp's Hill Beds on Chipping Norton Limestone.

9847   Glympton Park Quarry [427 217], Glympton. Sharp's Hill
Beds on Chipping Norton Limestone.

9848   Jolly's Ricks Cross-roads Quarry [381 240], Neat
Enstone.

9849   Sand pit [399 378], Tadmarton; basal 'Great Oolite'
Group.

9850   Sharp's Hill beds on 'Lower Estuarine Series' white sands
in a sand pit [455 272] south of Great Tew.

9851   Sharp's Hill Quarry [338 358], 2.8 km NE of the church,
Whichford.

(c) Great Oolite Limestone

9852   Quarry [297 210] near Lyneham.

9853   Section [314 250] SE of Walterbush Farm, Chipping
Norton; basal Great Oolite Limestone on Chipping
Norton Limestone.

9854   Section at the 'Camp' [300 213], Barter's Hill, east of
Lyneham.

9855   Quarry [424 194] at Wootton.

9858–9   Old limestone quarry in garden [437 184], 440 m S
20°W of the church, Wootton.

9860–1   Whiteway Quarry [421 246] about 1.6 km SW of
Westcott Barton church.

9862–4, 9867   Quarry section [377 362] near Stour Well,
Swalcliffe, thin Forest Marble on Great Oolite Limestone.

9865   The Fritwell railway cutting [526 280], S of Fritwell.

9866   Old section [323 303], 1.23 km at S 20°W from the
church, Great Rollright.

9868–9   Temple Mills Quarry [360 347], 1.6 km north of Hook
Norton church: flaggy Forest Marble on Great Oolite
Limestone.

9870   Quarry [373 363], 457 m NNE of Beacon Farm, Swalcliffe
Common.

3170–4, 6571, 6577   Views in the extensive Kirtlington Cement
Pit [487 198] at Kirtlington, showing Great Oolite
Limestone (White Limestone) with Forest Marble and
Cornbrash above.

9871   Lower Cornbrash in old quarry at Gibraltar Farm [348
363], about 1.6 km SSW of Sibford Ferris.

DRIFT DEPOSITS

9872–3   Water-logged pit in Glacial Sand and Gravel [270 224],
south of Rynehill Farm, about 1.6 km SW of Churchill.

9874   Gravel pit [249 223] at Bledington; showing a clay-filled
pipe in the 4th Terrace gravel.

9875   Cherwell Barn Pit [370 299], 1.2 km SW of Swerford; a
quarry face of white calcareous tufa.

REFERENCES

ARKELL, W. J. 1931. The Upper Great Oolite, Bradford Beds and Forest Marble of South Oxfordshire and the succession of Gastropod faunas in the Great Oolite. *Q. J. Geol. Soc. London*, Vol. 87, 563–629.

— 1933. *The Jurassic System in Great Britain.* 681 pp. (Oxford: University Press.).

— 1939. A map of the Corallian Beds between Marcham and Faringdon, Berkshire. *Proc. Geol. Assoc.* Vol. 50, 487–509.

— 1941. Map of the Corallian Beds around Highworth, Wiltshire. *Proc. Geol. Assoc.,* Vol. 52, 79–109.

— 1947a. *The geology of Oxford.* 276 pp. (Oxford: University Press.).

— 1947b. The geology of the Evenlode Gorge, Oxfordshire. *Proc. Geol. Assoc.,* Vol. 58, 87–114.

— 1951–1958. A monograph of English Bathonian ammonites. *Palaeontogr. Soc. G.B. (Monogr.)* 1–264.

— RICHARDSON, L. and PRINGLE, J. 1933. The Lower Oolites exposed in the Ardley-Fritwell railway cuttings, between Bicester and Banbury, Oxford. *Proc. Geol. Assoc.,* Vol. 44, 340–354.

AUDLEY-CHARLES, M. G. 1970a. Stratigraphical correlation of the Triassic rocks of the British Isles. *Q. J. Geol. Soc. London,* Vol. 126, 19–47.

— 1970b. Triassic palaeogeography of the British Isles, *Q. J. Geol. Soc. London,* Vol. 126, 49–89.

AVELINE, W. T. and TRENCH, R. 1860. Geology of part of Northamptonshire. *Mem. Geol. Surv. G.B.,* (Old Series Sheet 53 SE). 19 pp.

BATE, R. H., 1965. Freshwater ostracods from the Bathonian of Oxfordshire. *Palaeontology,* Vol. 8, 749–759.

BEESLEY, T. 1873. A sketch of the geology of the neighbourhood of Banbury. *Proc. Warwicks. Nat. Field Club,* 1872, 11–34. *See also* DE RANCE, C. E., 1872. *Geol. Mag.,* Vol. 9, 246–264.

— 1877. On the geology of the eastern portion of the Banbury and Cheltenham Direct Railway. *Proc. Geol. Assoc.,* Vol. 5, 165–185.

BISHOP, W. W. 1958. The Pleistocene geology and geomorphology of Three Gaps in the Midland Jurassic Escarpment. *Phil. Trans. R. Soc., (B),* Vol. 241, 255–306.

BOTT, M. H. P. 1962. A simple criterion for interpreting negative gravity anomalies. *Geophysics,* Vol. 27, 376–381.

BRIGGS, D. J. and GILBERTSON, D. D. 1974. Recent studies of Pleistocene deposits in the Evenlode Valley and adjacent areas of the Cotswolds. *Sound (J. Plymouth Polytechnic Geol. Soc.),* Vol. 3, 7–22.

BRODIE, P.B. 1845. *A history of the fossil insects in the Secondary Rocks of England.* 130 pp. London.

BULMAN, O. M. B. and RUSHTON, A. W. A. 1973. Tremadoc faunas from boreholes in Central England. *Bull. Geol. Surv. G.B.,* No. 43, 1–40.

BUCKMAN, S. S. 1887–1907. A Monograph of the ammonites of the 'Inferior Oolite Series.' *Palaeontogr. Soc. G.B. (Monogr.)* 1–456, i–cclxii.

— 1901. Bajocian and contiguous deposits in the North Cotteswolds; the Main Hill Mass. *Q. J. Geol. Soc. London,* Vol. 57, 126–155.

— 1918. The Brachiopods of the Namyau Beds. Northern Shan States, Burma. *Mem. Geol. Surv. India, (Pal. Indica), New Series,* Vol. III, Mem.2, pp.299.

CAYEUX, L. 1922. Les minerais de fer oolithique de France, II. Minerais de fer secondaires. (Paris.).

COPE, J. C. W., GETTY, T. A. HOWARTH, M. K., MORTON, M. and TORRENS, H. S. 1980. A correlation of Jurassic rocks in the British Isles. Part 1: Introduction and Lower Jurassic. *Spec. Rep. Geol. Soc. London.* No. 14, 73pp.

DAVIES, A. M. and PRINGLE, J. 1913. On two deep borings at Calvert Station (North Buckinghamshire) and on the Palaeozoic floor north of the Thames. *Q. J. Geol. Soc. London,* Vol. 69, 308–340.

DEAN, W. T., DONOVAN, D. T. and HOWARTH, M. K. 1961. The Liassic ammonite zones and subzones of the north-west European province. *Bull. Br. Mus. (Nat. Hist.), Geol. London,* No. 4, 435–505.

DIX, E. 1934. The sequence of Upper Carboniferous Floras, with special reference to South Wales. *Trans. R. Soc. Edinburgh,* Vol. 57, 789–838.

DONOVAN, D. T., HORTON, A. and IVIMEY-COOK, H. C. 1979. The transgression of the Lower Lias over the northern flank of the London platform. *J. Geol. Soc. London,* Vol. 136, 165–173.

DOUGLAS, J. A. and ARKELL, W. J. 1932. The stratigraphic distribution of the Cornbrash: II, The North-Eastern Area. *Q. J. Geol. Soc. London.*

DUNHAM, K. C. and POOLE, E. G. 1974. The Oxfordshire Coalfield. *Q. J. Geol. Soc. London,* Vol. 130, 387–391.

DUNHAM, R. J. 1962. Classification of carbonate rocks according to depositional texture. 108–120 in *Classification of carbonate rocks. Memoir 1.* HAM, W. E. (editor) (Tulsa: American Association of Petroleum Geologists.)

EDMONDS, E. A., POOLE, E. G. and WILSON, V. 1965. Geology of the country around Banbury and Edge Hill. *Mem. Geol. Surv. G. B.* 137 pp.

FALCON, N. L. and KENT, P. E. 1960. Geological results of petroleum exploration in Britain 1945–1957. *Mem. Geol. Soc. London,* No. 2. 56pp.

— and TARRANT, L. H. 1951. The gravitational and magnetic exploration of parts of the Mesozoic-covered areas of South–Central England. *Q. J. Geol. Soc. London,* Vol. 106, 141–170.

Geological Survey. 1954. Gravity survey overlay map. Sheet 15. Scale 1:253 440.

Geological Survey. 1965. Aeromagnetic map of Great Britain. Sheet 2. Scale 1:625 000.

GREEN, G. W. and MELVILLE, R. V. 1956. The stratigraphy of the Stowell Park Borehole (1941–51). *Bull. Geol. Surv. G.B.,* No. 11, 1–66.

HALLAM, A. 1958. The concept of Jurassic axes of uplift. *Sci. Prog. London.* No. 46, 441–488.

HAUBOLD, H. and SARJEANT, W. A. S. 1973. Tetrapodenfährten aus den Keele und Enville Groups (Permo Karbon: Stephan und Autun) von Shropshire und south Staffordshire, Grossbritannien [Tetrapod footprints in the Keele and Enville Groups (Permocarboniferous: Stephanian and Autunian) of Shropshire and south Staffordshire, England]. *Z. Geol. Wiss., Berlin,* Vol. 1, 893–933.

HEUNE, F. VON. 1908. Nene und verkante Pelycasaurier—Reste aus Europe. *Centralb. Für Min. Geol. Pal. Jahrb.*, 431–434.

HOPKINS, D. T. 1979. A 3-D interpretation of a circular gravity feature south of Reading. *Abstr. Geophys. J.R. Astr. Soc.*, Vol. 57, 275.

HORTON, A. 1977. The age of the Middle Jurassic 'white sands' of Oxfordshire. *Proc. Geol. Assoc.*, Vol. 88, 147–162.

— and HAINS, B. A. 1972. Development of porcellanous rocks and the reddening of the Coal Measures in the South Derbyshire, Leicestershire and Warwickshire coalfields. *Bull. Geol. Surv. G.B.*, No. 42, 51–77.

— IVIMEY-COOK, H. C., HARRISON, R. K. and YOUNG, B. R. 1980. Phosphatic öoids in the Upper Lias (Lower Jurassic) of central England. *J. Geol. Soc. London*, Vol. 137, 731–740.

— and POOLE, E. G. 1977. The lithostratigraphy of three geophysical marker horizons in the Lower Lias of Oxfordshire. *Bull. Geol. Surv. G.B.*, No. 62, 13–23.

— SHEPHERD-THORN, E. R. and THURRELL, R. G. 1974. The geology of the new town of Milton Keynes (Explanation of 1:25 000 Special Geological Sheet SP 83 with parts of SP 73, 74, 84, 93 and 97). *Rep. Inst. Geol. Sci.* No. 74/16. 102 pp.

HOWARTH, M. K. 1973. The stratigraphy and ammonite fauna of the Upper Liassic Grey Shales of the Yorkshire coast. *Bull. Br. Mus. (Nat. Hist.), Geol. London*, No. 24, 235–277.

— 1978. The stratigraphy and ammonite fauna of the Upper Lias of Northamptonshire. *Bull. Br. Mus. (Nat. Hist.), Geol. London*, No. 29, 235–288.

— 1980. The Toarcian age of the upper part of the Marlstone Rock Bed of England. *Palaeontology*, Vol. 23, 637–656.

HUDLESTON, W. H. 1878. Excursion to Chipping Norton. *Proc. Geol. Assoc.*, Vol. 5, 378–389.

HULL, E. 1855. On the physical geography and Pleistocene phaenomena of the Cotteswold Hills. *Q. J. Geol. Soc. London*, Vol. 11, 477–496.

— 1857. The geology of the country around Cheltenham. *Mem. Geol. Surv. G.B.* 104pp.

— 1859. The geology of the country around Woodstock, Oxfordshire. *Mem. Geol. Surv. G.B.*, 30pp.

INSTITUTE OF GEOLOGICAL SCIENCES. 1980a. Aeromagnetic Anomaly Map, Chiltern Sheet 51°N 02°W 1:250 000. Provisional Edition. (London: IGS.)

— 1980b. Aeromagnetic Anomaly Map, East Midlands Sheet 52°N 02°W 1:250 000. Provisional Edition. (London: IGS.)

— 1982. Bouguer Anomaly Map, East Midlands Sheet 52°N 02°W 1:250 000. (London: IGS.)

— 1983. Bouguer Anomaly Map, Chilterns Sheet 51°N 02°W 1:250 000. (London: IGS.)

IVIMEY-COOK, H. C., GAUNT, G. D., GREEN, G. W., HORTON, A., WARRINGTON, G. and WHITTAKER, A. 1980. The Triassic–Jurassic boundary in Great Britain. *Geol. Mag.*, Vol. 117, 617–618.

JUDD, J. W. 1875. The geology of Rutland and parts of Lincoln, Leicester, Huntingdon and Cambridge. *Mem. Geol. Surv. G.B.* 320pp.

KELLAWAY, G. A., HORTON, A. and POOLE, E. G. 1971. The development of some Pleistocene structures in the Cotswolds and Upper Thames Basin. *Bull. Geol. Surv. G.B.*, No. 37, 1–28.

KENT, P. E. 1937. The Lower Lias of south Nottinghamshire. *Proc. Geol. Assoc.*, Vol. 48, 163–174.

— 1949. A structure contour map of the surface of the buried pre-Permian rocks of England and Wales. *Proc. Geol. Assoc.*, Vol. 60, 87–104.

— 1970. Problems of the Rhaetic in the East Midlands. *Mercian Geologist*, Vol. 3, 361–373.

KLEIN, G. DE V. 1965. Dynamic significance of primary structures in the Middle Jurassic Great Oolite Series, southern England. 173–191 *in* Primary sedimentary structures and their hydrodynamic interpretation. MIDDLETON, G. V. (editor). *Soc. Econ. Paleontol. Mineral Spec. Publ.* No. 12.

KRYNINE, P. D. 1949. The origin of the Red Beds. *Trans. N.Y. Acad. Sci.*, Vol. 2, 60–68.

LAMPLUGH, G. W., WEDD, C. B. and PRINGLE, J. 1920. Special reports on the mineral resources of Great Britain, Vol. 12: Iron ores; bedded ores of the Lias, Oolites and later formations in England. *Mem. Geol. Surv. G.B.* 240pp.

McKERROW, W. S., JOHNSON, R. T. and JAKOBSON, M. E. 1969. Palaeoecological studies in the Great Oolite at Kirtlington, Oxfordshire. *Palaeontology*, Vol. 12, 56–83.

— and KENNEDY, W. J. 1973. The Oxford District. *Geol. Assoc. London*, Guide No. 3., 46pp.

ODLING, M. 1913. The Bathonian rocks of the Oxford District. *Q. J. Geol. Soc. London*, Vol. 69, 484–513.

ORBELL, G. 1973. Palynology of the British Rhaeto-Liassic. *Bull. Geol. Surv. G.B.*, Vol. 44, 1–44.

PALMER, T. E. 1979. The Hampen Marly and White Limestone formations: Florida-type carbonate lagoons in the Jurassic of central England. *Palaeontology*, Vol. 22, 189–228.

— and JENKYNS, H. C. 1975. A carbonate island barrier from the Great Oolite (Middle Jurassic) of central England. *Sedimentology*, Vol. 22, 125–135.

PHILLIPS, J. 1860. Notice of some sections of the strata near Oxford. No. 1. The Great Oolite in the valley of the Cherwell. No. 2. Sections south of Oxford. *Q. J. Geol. Soc. London*, Vol. 16, 115–119, 307–311.

POOLE, E. G. 1969. The stratigraphy of the Geological Survey Apley Barn Borehole, Witney, Oxfordshire. *Bull. Geol. Surv. G.B.* Vol. 29, 1–104.

— 1971. The Oxfordshire Coalfield. *Nature, London*, Vol. 232, 394–395.

— 1975. Correlation of the Upper Coal Measures of Central England and adjoining areas and their relationship to the Stephanian of the Continent. *Bull. Soc. Belge Géologie*, Vol. 84, pp.57–66.

— 1977. Stratigraphy of the Steeple Aston Borehole, Oxfordshire. *Bull. Geol. Surv. G.B.*, No. 57, 85pp.

— 1978. Stratigraphy of the Withycombe Farm Borehole, near Banbury, Oxfordshire. *Bull. Geol. Surv. G.B.*, No. 68, 63pp.

— 1979. The Triassic–Jurassic boundary in Great Britain. *Geol. Mag.*, Vol. 116, 303–311.

RICHARDSON, J. B. 1967. Some British Lower Devonian spore assemblages and their stratigraphic significance. *Rev. Palaeobot. Palynol.*, Vol. 1, 111–129.

RICHARDSON, L. 1907. The Inferior Oolite and contiguous deposits of the district between the Rissingtons and Burford. *Q. J. Geol. Soc. London*, Vol. 63, 437–444.

— 1911. The Inferior Oolite and contiguous deposits of the Chipping Norton district. *Proc. Cotteswold Nat. Field Club.*, Vol. 17, 195–231.

— 1922. Certain Jurassic (Aalenian–Vesulian) strata of the

Banbury district, Oxfordshire. *Proc. Cotteswold Nat. Field Club*, Vol. 21. 109–132.

— 1923.   Certain Jurassic (Aalenian–Vesulian) strata of southern Northamptonshire. *Proc. Geol. Assoc.*, Vol. 34, 97–113.

— 1925.   Certain Jurassic (Aalenian–Vesulian) strata of southern Northamptonshire. *Proc. Cotteswold Nat. Field Club*, Vol. 22, 137–152.

— 1929.   The Country around Moreton in Marsh. *Mem. Geol. Surv. G.B.*, 162pp.

— and FLEET, W. F. 1926.   On sandstone with breccias below the Trias at Stratford-on-Avon, and elsewhere in south Warwickshire. *Proc. Geol. Assoc.*, Vol. 37, 283–305.

SANDFORD, K. S. 1924.   The river-gravels of the Oxford district. *Q. J. Geol. Soc. London*, Vol. 80, 113–179.

SELLWOOD, B. W. and JENKYNS, H. C. 1975.   Basins and swells and the evolution of an epeiric sea (Pliensbachian–Bajocian of Great Britain). *J. Geol. Soc. London*, Vol. 131, 378–388.

— and McKERROW, W. S. 1974.   Depositional environments in the lower part of the Great Oolite of Oxfordshire and North Gloucestershire. *Proc. Geol. Assoc.*, Vol. 85, 190–220.

SHOTTON, F. W. 1953.   Pleistocene deposits of the area between Coventry, Rugby, and Leamington and their bearing on the topographic development of the Midlands. *Phil. Trans. Roy. Soc. (B)*, Vol. 237, 209–260.

— 1973.   A mammalian fauna from the Stretton Sand at Stretton-on-Fosse, south Warwickshire. *Geol. Mag.*, Vol. 109, 473–476.

— GOUDIE, A. S., BRIGGS, D. J. and OSMASTON, H. A. 1980. Cromerian interglacial deposits at Sugworth, near Oxford, England and their relation to the Plateau Drift of the Cotswolds and the terrace sequence of the Upper and Middle Thames. *Phil. Trans. R. Soc.*, (B), Vol. 289, 55–86.

SKEELS, D. C. 1963.   An approximate solution of the problem of maximum depth in gravity interpretation. *Geophysics*, Vol. 28, 724–735.

SMART, J. G. O., SABINE, P. A. and BULLERWELL, W. 1964. The Geological Survey exploratory borehole at Canvey Island, Essex. *Bull. Geol. Surv. G.B.*, No. 21, 1–36.

SMITH, N. J. P., JACKSON, D. I. ARMSTRONG, E. J., MULHOLLAND, P., JONES, S., AULD, H. A., BULAT, J., SWALLOW, J. L., QUINN, M. F., OATES, N. K. and BENNETT, J. R. P. 1985.   Map 1: Pre-Permian Geology of the United Kingdom (south). *British Geological Survey*, Keyworth. 1:1 000 000.

STRAHAN, A. 1913.   Batsford (or Lower Lemington) Boring, near Moreton-in-Marsh. *Summ. Prog. Geol. Surv. G.B. for 1912*, 90–91.

STRONG, G. E. 1972.   Petrography of Upper Triassic (Rhaetian?) marginal sediments from the Bicester area, Oxfordshire. Open File Report, Petrology Unit, No. 37. 29pp.

SUMBLER, M. C. 1984.   The stratigraphy of the Bathonian White Limestone and Forest Marble Formations of Oxfordshire. *Proc. Geol. Assoc.*, Vol. 95, 51–64.

TAYLOR, J. H. 1949.   Petrology of the Northampton Sand Ironstone Formation. *Mem. Geol. Surv. G.B.* 111pp.

— 1963.   Geology of the country around Kettering, Corby and Oundle. *Mem. Geol. Surv. G.B.*, Sheet 171. 149pp.

THOMPSON, B. 1910.   Northamptonshire (including contiguous parts of Rutland and Warwickshire; Geology in the field. *Geol. Assoc. London, Jub. Vol.*, 450–487.

— 1924.   The Inferior Oolite sequence in Northamptonshire and parts of Oxfordshire. *Proc. Geol. Assoc.*, Vol. 35, 67–76.

TOMLINSON, M. E. 1929.   The drifts of the Stour–Evenlode Watershed and their extension into the valleys of the Warwickshire Stour and Upper Evenlode. *Proc. Birmingham Nat. Hist. Soc.*, Vol. 15, 157–196.

— 1935.   The superficial deposits of the country north of Stratford on Avon. *Q. J. Geol. Soc. London*, Vol. 91, 423–462.

TONKS, E. S. 1961.   *The Ironstone Railways and Tramways of the Midlands.*   316pp. (London: Locomotive Publishing Co. Ltd.)

TORRENS, H. S. 1968.   The Great Oolite Series. 227–263. *in* SYLVESTER-BRADLEY, P. C. and FORD, T. D. (editors). *The geology of the East Midlands* 400pp. (Leicester: University Press.)

— 1980.   Bathonian correlation chart. B12, Oxford area. *In* a correlation of Jurassic rocks in the British Isles. Part 2: Middle and Upper Jurassic. COPE, J. C. W., and others. *Spec. Rep. Geol. Soc. London*, No. 15, 109pp.

TROTTER, F. M. 1953.   Reddened beds of Carboniferous age in north-west England and their origin. *Proc. Yorks. Geol. Soc.*, Vol. 29, 1–20.

— 1954.   Reddened beds in the Coal Measures of south Lancashire. *Bull. Geol. Surv. G.B.*, No. 5, 61–80.

WALFORD, A. E. 1878. On some Middle and Upper Lias beds, in the neighbourhood of Banbury. *Proc. Warwick. Nat. Archaeol. Fld Club.*, suppl for 1878, 1–23.

— 1883.   on the relation of the so-called 'Northampton Sand' of North Oxon to the Clypeus-Grit. *Q. J. Geol. Soc. London*, Vol. 39, 224–245.

— 1899.   *The Lias Ironstones of North Oxfordshire (around Banbury).* 36pp. (Banbury and London: printed privately.)

— 1906.   *On some new Oolitic strata in north Oxfordshire.*   32pp. (Buckingham: printed privately.)

WARRINGTON, G. 1970.   The stratigraphy and palaeontology of the 'Keuper' Series in the central Midlands of England. *Q. J. Geol. Soc. London*, Vol. 126, 183–223.

— 1977.   Appendix 3: Palynology of the White Lias, Cotham and Westbury beds and the Keuper Marl of the Steeple Aston Borehole. 40–43 *in* Stratigraphy of the Steeple Aston Borehole, Oxfordshire. POOLE, E. G. *Bull. Geol. Surv. G.B.*, Vol. 57, 85pp.

— 1978.   Appendix 1: Palynology of the Keuper, Westbury and Cotham Beds and the White Lias of the Withycombe Farm Borehole. 22–28 *in* Stratigraphy of the Withycombe Farm Borehole, near Banbury, Oxfordshire. POOLE, E. G. *Bull. Geol. Surv. G.B.*, Vol. 68, 63pp.

WARRINGTON, G., AUDLEY-CHARLES, M., ELLIOTT, R. E., EVANS, W. B., IVIMEY-COOK, H. C., KENT, P. E., ROBINSON, P. L, SHOTTON, F. W. and TAYLOR, F. M. 1980.   A correlation of Triassic rocks in the British Isles. *Spec. Rep. Geol. Soc. London*. No. 13, 78pp.

WHITEHEAD, T. H., ANDERSON, W., WILSON, V. and WRAY, D. A. 1952.   The Mesozoic Ironstones of England. The Liassic Ironstones. *Mem. Geol. Surv. G.B.*, 1–211.

— and ARKELL, W. J. 1946.   (Report of a) Field meeting at Hook Norton and Sibford, Oxfordshire. *Proc. Geol. Assoc.*, Vol. 57, 16–18.

WILLIAMS, B. J. and WHITTAKER, A. 1974.   The geology of the country around Stratford-upon-Avon and Evesham. *Mem. Geol. Surv. G.B.* 125pp.

WILLS, L. J. 1956.   *Concealed coalfields.*   208pp. (London: Blackie & Son.)

— 1970. The Triassic succession in the central Midlands and its regional setting. *Q. J. Geol. Soc. London*, Vol. 126, 225–285.

— 1973. A palaeogeological map of the Palaeozoic floor below the Permian and Mesozoic formations in England and Wales. *Mem. Geol. Soc. London*, No. 7.

— 1978. A palaeogeological map of the Lower Palaeozoic floor below the cover of Upper Devonian, Carboniferous and later formations, with inferred and speculative reconstruction of Lower Palaeozoic and Cambrian outcrops in adjacent areas. B. E. LEAKE (editor) *Mem. Geol. Soc. London*, No. 8. 36pp.

WILSON, V. 1952. The Jurassic Ironstone fields of the East Midlands of England. *Symposium sur les Gisements de Fer du Monde*, Tome 2, 441–450. 19e Congres Geologique International, Algiers.

WOODLAND, A. W. 1943. Water Supply from Underground Sources of the Oxford-Northampton District (Quarter-inch Geological Sheet 15, Eastern Half), Part V. Well Catalogue for New Series Sheets 218 (Eastern Half), 219 and 220. *Wartime Pamphlet Geol. Surv. G.B.* No. 4, pt.5. 2nd edition.

WORSSAM, B. C. 1963. The stratigraphy of the Geological Survey Upton Borehole, Oxfordshire. *Bull. Geol. Surv. G.B.*, No. 20, 107–162.

WOODWARD, H. B. 1893. The Jurassic rocks of Britain, Vol. 3. The Lias of England and Wales (Yorkshire excepted). *Mem. Geol. Surv. U.K.* 399pp.

— 1894. The Jurassic rocks of Britain. Vol. 4. The Lower Oolitic rocks of England (Yorkshire excepted). *Mem. Geol. Surv. U.K.* 628pp.

YOUELL, R. F. 1958. A clay minerological study of the Ironstone at Eastern Neston, Northamptonshire. *Clay Miner. Bull.*, Vol. 3, No. 19, 264–269.

FOSSIL INDEX

Some workers quoted in the text have used outdated or unrevised taxonomic combinations and the specimens are not available. In these cases the 'species' are indexed without a taxonomic author, e.g. '*Ammonites Murchisonae*'.

GENERAL INDEX

BRITISH GEOLOGICAL SURVEY

Keyworth, Nottingham NG12 5GG

Murchison House, West Mains Road,
Edinburgh EH9 3LA

The full range of Survey publications is available through the Sales Desks at Keyworth and Murchison House. Selected items are stocked by the Geological Museum Bookshop, Exhibition Road, London SW7 2DE; all other items may be obtained through the BGS London Information Office in the Geological Museum. All the books are listed in HMSO's Sectional List 45. Maps are listed in the BGS Map Catalogue and Ordnance Survey's Trade Catalogue. They can be bought from Ordnance Survey Agents as well as from BGS.

The British Geological Survey carries out the geological survey of Great Britain and Northern Ireland (the latter as an agency service for the government of Northern Ireland), and of the surrounding continental shelf, as well as its basic research projects. It also undertakes programmes of British technical aid in geology in developing countries as arranged by the Overseas Development Administration.

The British Geological Survey is a component body of the Natural Environment Research Council.

Maps and diagrams in this book use topography based on Ordnance Survey mapping

HER MAJESTY'S STATIONERY OFFICE

HMSO publications are available from:

HMSO Publications Centre
(Mail and telephone orders)
PO Box 276, London SW8 5DT
Telephone orders (01) 622 3316
General enquiries (01) 211 5656
Queueing system in operation for both numbers

HMSO Bookshops
49 High Holborn, London WC1V 6HB
   (01) 211 5656 (Counter service only)
258 Broad Street, Birmingham B1 2HE
   (021) 643 3740
Southey House, 33 Wine Street, Bristol BS1 2BQ
   (0272) 264306
9 Princess Street, Manchester M60 8AS
   (061) 834 7201
80 Chichester Street, Belfast BT1 4JY
   (0232) 238451
71–73 Lothian Road, Edinburgh EH3 9AZ
   (031) 228 4181

HMSO's Accredited Agents
(see Yellow Pages)

And through good booksellers